# Modern China
# and Japan

## A Brief History

# Modern China and Japan

## A Brief History

### Conrad Schirokauer
The City College of The City University of New York

**HARCOURT BRACE JOVANOVICH, PUBLISHERS**
San Diego   New York   Chicago   Atlanta   Washington, D.C.
London   Sydney   Toronto

About the cover: Photo © Thomas Hopker 1981, from Woodfin Camp & Associates.

Calligraphy by Dr. Léon L. Y. Chang, Distinguished Visiting Professor at the Center of Asian Studies, St. John's University; Member, Board of Directors, Chinese National Museums.

Maps by J. P. Tremblay

Timelines by Rino Dussi

For Lore and our sons, David and Oliver

# *Preface*

This book is based on my earlier book, *A Brief History of Chinese and Japanese Civilizations*, in which I give an account of traditional as well as modern China and Japan. The present book is intended for those who prefer to begin the study of East Asia with the modern period. Underlying both books is the conviction that the study of Chinese and Japanese history can illuminate the human condition and enrich our lives, as well as help us to understand the world in which we live. That China, the most populated nation on earth, and Japan, a major global economic power, are important parts of that world hardly needs stressing today. Likewise, it is readily apparent that China and Japan have undergone profound changes during the past two centuries and that today they share many values and institutions with other contemporary countries. Yet the People's Republic of China is hardly a "typical" socialist state, any more than Japan is a typical capitalist society. Like other countries, they are products of their past as well as their present. It follows that the study of their past can illuminate their present and even help to elucidate their future as it unfolds.

The aim of this book is to present an account that is informative and coherent enough to enable students to continue on their own, and brief enough to encourage them to do so and to enable instructors to assign collateral readings. The book is intended as a general introduction reflecting the state of scholarship in Chinese and Japanese history, not as a vehicle for expanding the frontiers of that scholarship or advancing new hypotheses—and it certainly is not intended as the last word on the subject. It attempts to supply the basis for further study and exploration. To enable readers to gain a sense of what is available and help them find their way through the literature, an appendix of suggested readings is included.

All those, named and unnamed, to whom I was indebted in writing the earlier volume have also, by that very fact, contributed to making this a better book. I wish to thank them once more. In addition, I have incurred some new obligations. For a careful reading and helpful comments on the last chapter, I wish to thank Professor Maurice Meisner and Lee M. Sands. Professor Robert Somers again read the entire manuscript and gave particularly helpful advice concerning the first chapter. As before, it has been a pleasure working with the people at Harcourt Brace Jovanovich, especially Paula Lewis and Eleanor Lahn, who edited and copy-edited this book. Thanks are also due to the team of George, Ken, and Oliver for their labors on the index.

CONRAD  SCHIROKAUER

# Note on Names and Romanization

In Chinese and Japanese, surnames precede given names, and that has been the order followed in this book, except for modern Chinese and Japanese scholars who, writing for a Western audience, have adopted the Western name sequence. Furthermore, members of Japanese political and cultural dynasties, as well as certain other individuals, are commonly known by their given names (for example, Tokugawa Ieyasu) or their appellations (for example, Hokusai), and that practice that has been followed here.

All Japanese terms have been rendered in accordance with the standard Hepburn system, except that macrons have been omitted for Tokyo. Chinese geographical terms have been rendered according to customary usage.

In transcribing Chinese words it has long been customary to employ the Wade-Giles system, and that practice has been followed here, except that in the last chapter *Hanyu* Pinyin is introduced. Pinyin is the system adopted by the People's Republic of China. After the establishment of diplomatic relations between the United States and China, in 1979, many American publications switched to Pinyin, but Wade-Giles remains indispensable for the serious student. Conversion tables for both Wade-Giles to Pinyin and Pinyin to Wade-Giles have been supplied, in the hope that they will assist the reader in coping with the two systems. There are also a few Southern names (Sun Yat-sen, Chiang Kai-shek) and the name of one overseas scholar (Chu-tsing Li) that conform to neither Wade-Giles nor Pinyin.

The following is intended only as a basic, nontechnical guide to the sounds of Chinese and Japanese as Romanized. It is not an introduction to the phonetics of the languages but does indicate roughly how the various letters should be pronounced.

## Vowels

In both Chinese and Japanese, vowels are pronounced as in Italian, German, or Spanish.

> *a* as in c*a*r
> *e* as in sp*e*nd
> *i* as in m*e*
> *o* as in b*o*ld (but in Chinese, sometimes as in s*o*ft, and after
>       *k*, *k'*, or *h* like the *u* in b*u*t)
> *u* as in r*u*de (but hardly pronounced after *tz*, *tz'*, or *ss* in
>       Chinese or after *s* in Japanese)
> *ü* as the German *ü* or the French *u*

## Vowel Combinations

*Chinese*   Diphthongs are always run together. Thus *ai* = *I* (the personal pronoun); *ao* = *ow* as in b*ow*; *ei* = *a* as in m*ay*; *ou* = *o* as in l*ow*.

*Japanese*   *Ai* and *ei* are diphthongs pronounced as in Chinese. Other vowels occurring together are pronounced individually. Long vowels (indicated by a macron) are pronounced like short vowels but the sound is held longer.

## Consonants

In Japanese, consonants approximate their English equivalents. In Chinese, however, aspirated consonants are distinguished from their unaspirated counterparts by the use of an apostrophe.

| Wade-Giles | Rough English Equivalent | Wade-Giles | Rough English Equivalent |
|---|---|---|---|
| ch | j | ch' | ch |
| k | g | k' | k |
| p | b | p' | p |
| t | d | t' | t |
| ts, tz | dz | ts', tz' | ts |

The consonant *j* is pronounced something like *r*; *ih* is pronounced something like *ir* as in s*ir*.

### *Hanyu Pinyin / Wade-Giles Conversion Table*

| Pinyin | Wade-Giles | Pinyin | Wade-Giles | Pinyin | Wade-Giles | Pinyin | Wade-Giles |
|---|---|---|---|---|---|---|---|
| a | a | bin | pin | che | ch'e | cui | ts'ui |
| ai | ai | bing | ping | chen | ch'en | cun | ts'un |
| an | an | bo | po | cheng | ch'eng | cuo | ts'o |
| ang | ang | bu | pu | chi | ch'ih | | |
| ao | ao | | | chong | ch'ung | da | ta |
| | | ca | ts'a | chou | ch'ou | dai | tai |
| ba | pa | cai | ts'ai | chu | ch'u | dan | tan |
| bai | pai | can | ts'an | chuai | ch'uai | dang | tang |
| ban | pan | cang | ts'ang | chuan | ch'uan | dao | tao |
| bang | pang | cao | ts'ao | chuang | ch'uang | de | te |
| bao | pao | ce | ts'e | chui | ch'ui | dei | tei |
| bei | pei | cen | ts'en | chun | ch'un | deng | teng |
| ben | pen | ceng | ts'eng | chuo | ch'o | di | ti |
| beng | peng | cha | ch'a | ci | tz'u | dian | tien |
| bi | pi | chai | ch'ai | cong | ts'ung | diao | tiao |
| bian | pien | chan | ch'an | cou | ts'ou | die | tieh |
| biao | piao | chang | ch'ang | cu | ts'u | ding | ting |
| bie | pieh | chao | ch'ao | cuan | ts'uan | diu | tiu |

From Endymion Wilkinson, *The History of Imperial China: A Research Guide*, Harvard East Asian Monographs, No. 49 (Cambridge, Mass.: Harvard University Press, 1973).

| Pinyin | Wade-Giles | Pinyin | Wade-Giles | Pinyin | Wade-Giles | Pinyin | Wade-Giles |
|--------|-----------|--------|-----------|--------|-----------|--------|-----------|
| dong | tung | hao | hao | la | la | nang | nang |
| dou | tou | he | he, ho | lai | lai | nao | nao |
| du | tu | hei | hei | lan | lan | ne | ne |
| duan | tuan | hen | hen | lang | lang | nei | nei |
| dui | tui | heng | heng | lao | lao | nen | nen |
| dun | tun | hong | hung | le | le | neng | neng |
| duo | to | hou | hou | lei | lei | ni | ni |
|  |  | hu | hu | leng | leng | nian | nien |
| e | e, o | hua | hua | li | li | niang | niang |
| ei | ei | huai | huai | lia | lia | niao | niao |
| en | en | huan | huan | lian | lien | nie | nieh |
| eng | eng | huang | huang | liang | liang | nin | nin |
| er | erh | hui | hui | liao | liao | ning | ning |
|  |  | hun | hun | lie | lieh | niu | niu |
| fa | fa | huo | huo | lin | lin | nong | nung |
| fan | fan |  |  | ling | ling | nou | nou |
| fang | fang | ji | chi | liu | liu | nu | nu |
| fei | fei | jia | chia | long | lung | nuan | nuan |
| fen | fen | jian | chien | lou | lou | nuo | no |
| feng | feng | jiang | chiang | lu | lu | nü | nü |
| fo | fo | jiao | chiao | luan | luan | në | nüeh |
| fou | fou | jie | chieh | lun | lun |  |  |
| fu | fu | jin | chin | luo | lo | o | o |
|  |  | jing | ching | lü | lü | ou | ou |
|  |  | jiong | chiung | lüe | lüeh |  |  |
| ga | ka | jiu | chiu |  |  | pa | p'a |
| gai | kai | ju | chü |  |  | pai | p'ai |
| gan | kan | juan | chüan | ma | ma | pan | p'an |
| gang | kang | jue | chüeh | mai | mai | pang | p'ang |
| gao | kao | jun | chün | man | man | pao | p'ao |
| ge | ke, ko |  |  | mang | mang | pei | p'ei |
| gei | kei | ka | k'a | mao | mao | pen | p'en |
| gen | ken | kai | k'ai | mei | mei | peng | p'eng |
| geng | keng | kan | k'an | men | men | pi | p'i |
| gong | kung | kang | k'ang | meng | meng | pian | p'ien |
| gou | kou | kao | k'ao | mi | mi | piao | p'iao |
| gu | ku | ke | k'e, k'o | mian | mien | pie | p'ieh |
| gua | kua | ken | k'en | miao | miao | pin | p'in |
| guai | kuai | keng | k'eng | mie | mieh | ping | p'ing |
| guan | kuan | kong | k'ung | min | min | po | p'o |
| guang | kuang | kou | k'ou | ming | ming | pou | p'ou |
| gui | kuei | ku | k'u | miu | miu | pu | p'u |
| gun | kun | kua | k'ua | mo | mo |  |  |
| guo | kuo | kuai | k'uai | mou | mou | qi | ch'i |
|  |  | kuan | k'uan | mu | mu | qia | ch'ia |
| ha | ha | kuang | k'uang |  |  | qian | ch'ien |
| hai | hai | kui | k'uei | na | na | qiang | ch'iang |
| han | han | kun | k'un | nai | nai | qiao | ch'iao |
| hang | hang | kuo | k'uo | nan | nan |  |  |

| Pinyin | Wade-Giles | Pinyin | Wade-Giles | Pinyin | Wade-Giles | Pinyin | Wade-Giles |
|--------|-----------|--------|-----------|--------|-----------|--------|-----------|
| qie | ch'ieh | shei | shei | tun | t'un | yue | yüeh |
| qin | ch'in | shen | shen | tuo | t'o | yun | yün |
| qing | ch'ing | sheng | sheng | | | | |
| qiong | ch'iung | shi | shih | wa | wa | za | tsa |
| qiu | ch'iu | shou | shou | wai | wai | zai | tsai |
| qu | ch'ü | shu | shu | wan | wan | zan | tsan |
| quan | ch'üan | shua | shua | wang | wang | zang | tsang |
| que | ch'üeh | shuai | shuai | wei | wei | zao | tsao |
| qun | ch'ün | shuan | shuan | wen | wen | ze | tse |
| | | shuang | shuang | weng | weng | zei | tsei |
| | | shui | shui | wo | wo | zen | tsen |
| ran | jan | shun | shun | wu | wu | zeng | tseng |
| rang | jang | shuo | shuo | | | zha | cha |
| rao | jao | si | szu | xi | hsi | zhai | chai |
| re | je | song | sung | xia | hsia | zhan | chan |
| ren | jen | sou | sou | xian | hsien | zhang | chang |
| reng | jeng | su | su | xiang | hsiang | zhao | chao |
| ri | jih | suan | suan | xiao | hsiao | zhe | che |
| rong | jung | sui | sui | xie | hsieh | zhei | chei |
| rou | jou | sun | sun | xin | hsin | zhen | chen |
| ru | ju | suo | so | xing | hsing | zheng | cheng |
| ruan | juan | | | xiong | hsiung | zhi | chih |
| rui | jui | | | xiu | hsiu | zhong | chung |
| run | jun | | | xu | hsü | zhou | chou |
| ruo | jo | ta | t'a | xuan | hsüan | zhu | chu |
| | | tai | t'ai | xue | hsüeh | zhua | chua |
| | | tan | t'an | xun | hsün | zhuai | chuai |
| sa | sa | tang | t'ang | | | zhuan | chuan |
| sai | sai | tao | t'ao | ya | ya | zhuang | chuang |
| san | san | te | t'e | yan | yen | zhui | chui |
| sang | sang | teng | t'eng | yang | yang | zhun | chun |
| sao | sao | ti | t'i | yao | yao | zhuo | cho |
| se | se | tian | t'ien | ye | yeh | zi | tzu |
| sen | sen | tiao | t'iao | yi | i | zong | tsung |
| seng | seng | tie | t'ieh | yin | yin | zou | tsou |
| sha | sha | ting | t'ing | ying | ying | zu | tsu |
| shai | shai | tong | t'ung | yong | yung | zuan | tsuan |
| shan | shan | tou | t'ou | you | yu | zui | tsui |
| shang | shang | tu | t'u | yu | yü | zun | tsun |
| shao | shao | tuan | t'uan | yuan | yüan | zuo | tso |
| she | she | tui | t'ui | | | | |

# Wade-Giles / Pinyin Table

Each entry in the Wade-Giles column represents the initial letter or letter pair of a syllable or word. Unless otherwise indicated, conversion is accomplished simply by changing that initial letter. Where other changes are necessary or the conversion is irregular, the entire word or syllable is listed.

| Wade-Giles | Pinyin | Wade-Giles | Pinyin | Wade-Giles | Pinyin | Wade-Giles | Pinyin |
|---|---|---|---|---|---|---|---|
| a | a | ch'en | chen | i | yi | p'ien | pian |
| | | ch'eng | cheng | | | | |
| cha | zha | ch'i | qi | j | r | s | s |
| chai | zhai | ch'ia | qia | jih | ri | shih | shi |
| chan | zhan | ch'iang | qiang | jo | ruo | so | suo |
| chang | zhang | ch'iao | qiao | jung | rong | sung | song |
| chao | zhao | ch'ieh | qie | | | szu | si |
| che | zhe | ch'ien | qian | k | g | | |
| chen | zhen | ch'i | chi | ko | ge | t | d |
| cheng | zheng | ch'in | qin | kuei | gui | tieh | dieh |
| chi | ji | ch'ing | qing | kung | gong | tien | dian |
| chia | jia | ch'iu | qiu | | | to | duo |
| chiao | jiao | ch'iung | qiong | k' | k | tung | dong |
| chieh | jie | ch'o | chuo | k'o | ke | | |
| chien | jian | ch'ou | chou | k'ung | kong | t' | t |
| chih | zhi | ch'u | chu | | | t'ieh | tie |
| chin | jin | ch'ü | qu | l | l | t'ien | tian |
| ching | jing | ch'uai | chuai | lieh | lie | t'o | tuo |
| chiu | jiu | ch'uan | chuan | lien | lian | t'ung | tong |
| chiung | jiong | ch'üan | quan | lo | luo | | |
| cho | zhuo | ch'uang | chuang | lüeh | lüe | ts, tz | z |
| chou | zhou | ch'üeh | que | lung | long | tso | zuo |
| chu | zhu | ch'ui | chui | | | tsung | zong |
| chü | ju | ch'un | chun | m | m | tzu | zi |
| chua | zhua | ch'ün | qun | mieh | mie | | |
| chuai | zhuai | ch'ung | chong | mien | mian | ts', tz' | c |
| chuan | zhuan | | | | | ts'o | cuo |
| chüan | juan | f | f | n | n | ts'ung | cong |
| chuang | zhuang | | | nieh | nie | tz'u | ci |
| chüeh | jue | h | h | nien | nian | | |
| chui | zhui | ho | he | no | nuo | w | w |
| chun | zhun | hung | hong | nüeh | ne | | |
| chün | jun | | | | | y | y |
| chung | zhong | hs | x | o | o | yeh | ye |
| | | hsieh | xie | | | yen | yan |
| ch'a | cha | hsien | xian | p | b | yu | you |
| ch'ai | chai | hsiung | xiong | pieh | bie | yü | yu |
| ch'an | chan | hsü | xu | pien | bian | yüan | yuan |
| ch'ang | chang | hsüan | xuan | | | yüeh | yue |
| ch'ao | chao | hsüeh | xue | p' | p | yün | yun |
| ch'e | che | hsün | xun | p'ieh | pie | yung | yong |

# Contents

## 3 East Asia and Modern Europe: First Encounters 61

## PART TWO China and Japan in the Modern World

## 4 The Intrusion of the West: China 81

## 5 The Intrusion of the West: Japan 105

## 6 *The Emergence of Modern Japan: 1874–1894    127*

## 7 *Self-Strengthening in China: 1874–1894    147*

PART THREE    East Asia since the Second World War

### 11 *The Aftermath of the Second World War in East Asia*    245

### 12 *Contemporary Japan: 1952–Present*    267

### 13 *The New China*    289

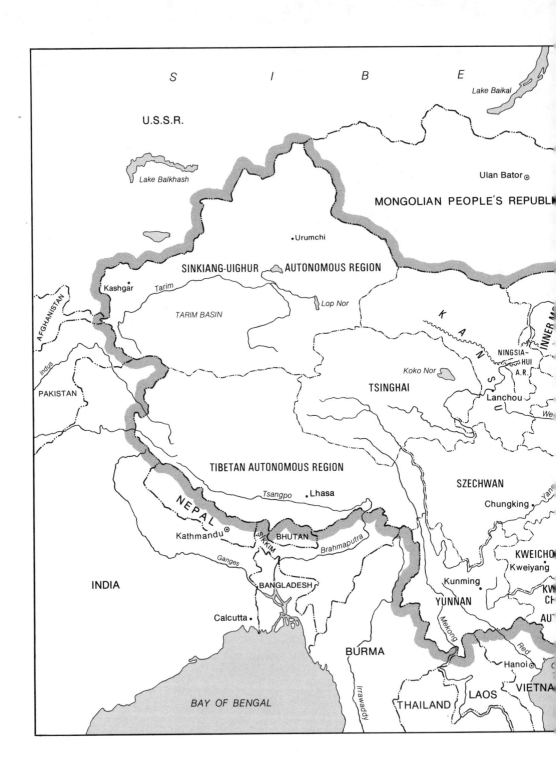

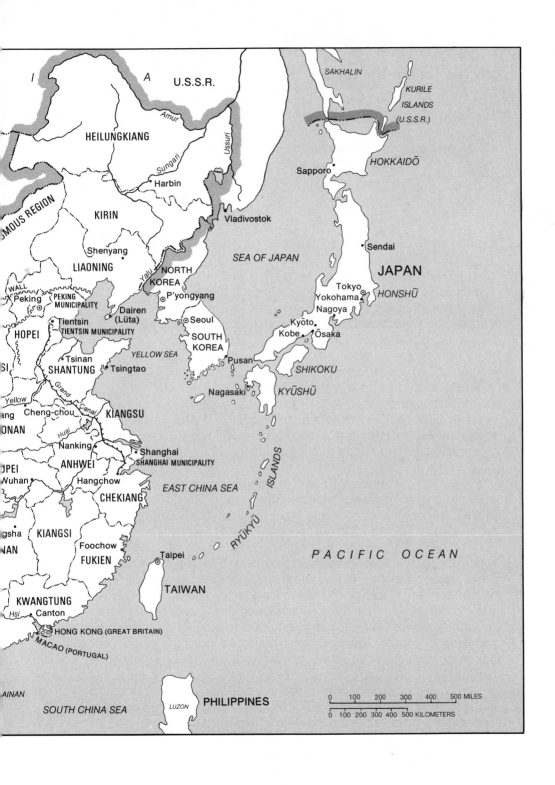

# Modern China
# and Japan

## A Brief History

Hall of Annual Prayers (*Ch'i-nien-tien*). Ch'ing Dynasty
(rebuilt late nineteenth century). Peking.

# PART ONE
# China and Japan in Early Modern Times

滿人治下之中國

ca.
1600                1644                                                                                          1911

| Late Ming 1590–1644 | C H ' I N G   D Y N A S T Y | Late Ch'ing |
|---|---|---|
| | K'ang-hsi (1662–1722)     Ch'ien-lung (1736–95) | Opium War (1839–42) |

# 1 *China under the Manchus*

China, from any standpoint, must be considered one of the world's great civilizations, impressive in its accomplishments as well as in its duration and extent. Like other civilizations it experienced periods of profound crisis, but, unlike many, it emerged from such times to flourish with renewed vigor. The history of traditional Chinese social and political institutions continues to fascinate scholars while China's artistic and literary masterpieces and its contributions to the world of ideas continue to instruct and delight.

3

## Basic Geography

In China, as elsewhere, the physical environment provided the opportunities and challenges out of which civilization was wrought, and civilization, in turn, over many centuries shaped and altered the environment. Geography not only provided the setting for history but itself became part of history as new lands were opened to agriculture, marshes were drained, canals were built, mountains were terraced, and dikes were constructed to contain rivers. In this sense, Chinese history consists of the interaction of man and nature, each leaving a deep imprint on the other. Yet the basic configuration of the land remained constant. The essential features of climate and landscape did not change.

Since Chinese civilization was based on intensive farming, it spread over the centuries into those areas suitable for agriculture. At the same time, nomadic peoples were able to sustain a different kind of life in the vast areas of Inner Asia and the region beyond the Great Wall, which comprise roughly half of China's land area today. However, today, as earlier, the majority of China's people continue to live in the region within the wall frequently termed China proper.

In the north of China proper the outstanding geographical feature is the Yellow River, which flows from the highlands of the west through the alluvial lowlands of the Great Plain and empties into the sea near the Shantung Peninsula. In its slow progress to the sea, the Yellow River carries an enormous quantity of loess, a fine-grained, yellowish brown silt, which gives the river its color and name. Loess also accounts for the river's reputation as "China's sorrow," because the steady silting process raises its bed so high that dikes are necessary to confine the river to its channel. Since in many places the riverbed rises higher than the surrounding countryside, a break in the dikes can have devastating effects, and it may take several years of flood and famine before the river digs itself a new channel. Such a catastrophe occurred during the period 1851–1855 when the course of the river shifted. By the end of the devastation, the mouth of the river had moved from south of the Shantung Peninsula to its present location north of the peninsula.

The North is a region with a temperate climate, cold winters and warm summers, but rainfall is scarce. This is particularly true in the arid west, although even in the moister areas the annual rainfall is extremely variable. Although the area is subject to drought, the soil (loess) is fertile, retains moisture, and is easy to work. The North is suitable for growing millet, kaoliang (a kind of sorghum), and, in the moister parts, wheat and beans.

Very different conditions prevail south of a line that runs roughly along the 33rd parallel, following the Tsinling Mountains and the Huai River. Here rain is abundant, the climate subtropical, but minerals and nutrients have largely been drained out of the soil. The dominant river is the Yangtze, which is about 3200 miles long, roughly 500 miles longer than the Yellow River. Once the necessary technology was developed and the land laboriously drained, a process that took many centuries, this region proved ideal for rice culture. Wet-

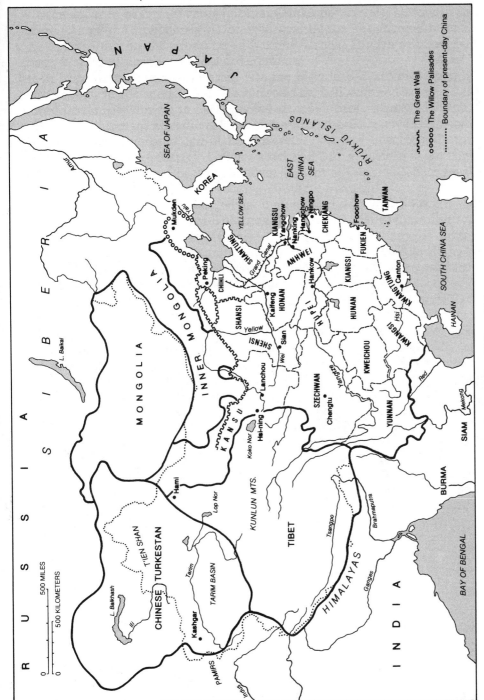

Figure 1-1  Ch'ing China

rice cultivation requires and supports a large labor force. Consequently the rice-growing areas are heavily populated and of paramount importance to the Chinese economy.

The anthropologist G. William Skinner has shown that Central and South China form six macroregions, economically integrated areas defined in terms of river drainage basins, that correspond only in part to political subdivisions.[1] The Middle Yangtze River (Hupeh, Hunan, Kiangsi provinces) and the Lower Yangtze River (Kiangsu, Chekiang provinces) are major centers of rice cultivation, with the lower Yangtze having a rich cultural history as well. The Upper Yangtze is centered on the Red Basin of Szechwan Province, a fertile zone whose red soil and mild climate support a large population that is separated from the rest of China by mountains. In periods when China lacked a strong central government, Szechwan was often autonomous. Two other regions of the South, the Southeast Coast (Southern Chekiang and Fukien provinces) and Lingnan (Kwangtung and Kwangsi provinces) share in the agriculture of the South but also have maritime traditions. Many overseas Chinese emigrated from this part of the country. Finally there is the region formed by the two provinces of Kweichow and Yunnan, a mountainous area without navigable rivers. Here can still be found some of China's aboriginal people and its most spectacular scenery.

Like other long-settled agricultural peoples, the Chinese developed a deep attachment to and identification with their land. Indeed, they tended to see themselves not as alienated beings struggling against the forces of nature but as organic parts of the natural landscape. An example is provided by one of China's rare creation myths, the legend of P'an-ku, first mentioned in a text of the third century A.D. According to this myth, a cosmic egg gave birth to P'an-ku, who grew continually for 18,000 years and separated heaven and earth. When he died, his eyes became the sun and moon; his blood, the rivers and oceans; his hair, the grasses and trees. Humans and animals derived from his body lice. The importance of nature is also reflected in classical Chinese landscape paintings, where mountains tower over minute human figures.

Such widely shared attitudes, however, should not obscure the diversity of China's people and their local customs, institutions, and even languages. China possessed the natural resources, the size, and the geographical diversity to develop and sustain a civilization varied in place as well as in time. Therefore, the study of the history of China and the exploration of its geography may proceed hand in hand.

## The Ch'ing Dynasty

A major theme in Chinese history is the interaction between the Chinese and their neighbors, whose way of life made them formidable horsemen and warriors. The Chinese, with their superior material resources, generally had the upper hand when they were united under vigorous leadership, even though they could never fully control their highly mobile neighbors. In its heyday, the Ming (1368–1644), China's last native dynasty, succeeded in keeping the Mongols divided and weak by a combination of military and diplomatic means. It secured the Manchurian frontier in the northeast—partly by patronizing tribal leaders and partly by building the Willow Palisades, consisting of lines of willows and a deep trench fortified by military checkpoints. It was the Ming misfortune that Nurhachi (1559–1626), a Manchu leader they originally supported, became the founder of the state that eventually supplanted their own.

Trouble with the Manchus was only one of a number of problems besetting the late Ming. The traditional Chinese analysis of dynastic decline is that internal decay precedes foreign disasters, and the Ming fits the case nicely. During its last half century the dynasty clearly suffered from the ossification of its institutions, which failed to adapt to changing conditions and generally lacked the vitality to renew and revitalize a decaying political apparatus. In the face of a deepening fiscal crisis, vital public works were neglected, grain stored for emergency use was sold off, soldiers went unpaid for months, and even the postal system was shut down. Meanwhile, local elites were left free to exploit the poor and powerless. Desperate men formed outlaw gangs that gradually coalesced into a full-fledged rebel organization. Finally the dynasty was overthrown by a rebellion headed by Li Tzu-ch'eng (ca. 1605–45), a former postal attendant.

Li Tzu-ch'eng was, however, unable to consolidate his triumph. The key to the military situation was in the hands of the Ming general Wu San-kuei (1612–78), whose army controlled Shanhaikuan, the strategic pass between the mountains and the sea that formed the eastern terminus of the Great Wall and controlled access from Manchuria into China. When Wu decided to throw in his lot with the Manchus rather than the Chinese rebels, Li Tzu-ch'eng's fate was sealed. The Manchus, who in 1636 had adopted the name "Ch'ing" (pure) for their dynasty, entered Peking, the capital, in June 1644. The Ch'ing ruler then buried the deceased Ming emperor and empress with full honors and announced that he had come to punish the rebels.

The process of dynastic consolidation was slow, but the Ch'ing became only the second foreign dynasty to rule over all of China, and they did so for longer and with more success than their predecessors, the Mongol Yüan dynasty (1279–1368). By honoring the last Ming emperor they claimed to be the legitimate successors of the old dynasty. Furthermore, they retained many Ming institutions. This they did not only to satisfy the expectations of their Chinese subjects but also in the conviction that they were building their state on the most secure, time-tested foundations.

# Chinese Society

The transition from Ming to Ch'ing appears to have had little effect on the basic structure of Chinese society on the local level. Local society operated according to its own rhythms, its patterns influenced and affected by government to be sure, but not fundamentally shaped by it. Particularly important was the landed hereditary local elite, or gentry, as it is commonly called. The continuity of gentry prominence in local affairs from the Ming onward contributed greatly to the stability of Chinese society. In a recent study of a district in Anhwei Province, Hilary J. Beattie found that some members of the local gentry traced their ancestry back to the early Ming, that the gentry lineages were formally organized in the sixteenth century, and that they were able to survive the rebellions and upheavals of the late years of the Ming dynasty as well as the establishment of the Ch'ing dynasty.[2] These gentry lineages even survived the great nineteenth-century Taiping Rebellion. They were able to accomplish this by maintaining solid economic roots in local land ownership and by investing their income in education. Education strengthened their local status in addition to providing the requisites for competing in the civil service examinations. Members of the gentry who succeeded in becoming officials used their political influence and their economic assets to benefit the lineage, but the gentry were able to sustain themselves even during periods lean in examination success. This suggests that local social and economic status was the primary source of their power and that there was greater continuity in the family background of the local elite than there was among those capable and fortunate enough to gain access to a career in the imperial bureaucracy.

Among the means to secure lineage cohesion were the periodic compilations of genealogies. These not only fostered a sense of historical continuity but also identified the individuals belonging to the lineage. Prominent lineages maintained ancestral halls and graveyards and conducted ceremonial sacrifices to their ancestors. Not infrequently, the income from lineage land was used for these purposes. Lineage solidarity was also maintained by general guides for the conduct of the members and by formal lineage rules. Penalties for infraction of these rules could include expulsion from the lineage. The contrast in status between the local elite and the government underlings who served the district magistrate as clerks, messengers, and so on is revealed by the stipulation found in many lineage rules that any member sinking to such employment be promptly expelled. Gentry lineages also strengthened each other through a network of marriage relationships, for in China, as throughout East Asia, marriages were arranged between families, not left to individual choice.

The gentry were enormously influential in all local matters in part because government did not reach far down into society. At the local level, government was represented by the district magistrate, who was assisted by only a very small number of subordinate officials, his private staff, and notoriously venal underlings always looking for bribes. Yet, in theory, the magistrate was responsible for the taxes, security, and general well-being of about 200,000 people. Furthermore, the magistrate lacked roots in the locality, for it was Ch'ing practice to rotate magistrates frequently and never to assign a man to his home province. The magistrate consequently tended to be influenced by the local gentry, who were his social peers and who traditionally looked after such matters as the construction and upkeep of roads and bridges. The gentry, for their part, served as intermediaries between the locality and the state.

# The State

The Ch'ing dynasty essentially continued the Ming political system but designed certain policies to assure Manchu predominance. Since Manchus constituted only about 2 percent of the population of their empire, they required the support not only of the Mongols but also the cooperation of the Chinese elite and the tacit assent of the Chinese populace. This they obtained by retaining traditional forms and theories of government and working within established patterns and structures.

The emperor was, of course, a Manchu, and his power was absolute in theory, even if in practice he was restricted by considerations of custom and his need not to alienate the bureaucracy or to provoke the people into rebellion. During the early Ch'ing, the emperor was assisted by the Grand Secretariat, a six-man board composed of three Manchu and three Chinese officials. However, under K'ang-hsi (r. 1662–1722), the Grand Secretariat lost influence and was superseded by the Grand Council under Yung-cheng (r.1723–35), although it continued as an honorary body.

Administration during the Ch'ing dynasty was supervised by six ministries responsible for personnel administration, revenue, rites and rituals, war, justice, and public works. China proper was divided into eighteen provinces that were further subdivided into circuits, prefectures, and districts. Inner Asian affairs were handled by the Court of Colonial Affairs, a Manchu innovation. To keep the bureaucracy in line there was an independent Censorate whose officials reported on the conduct of the civil service and also had the right and duty to criticize the emperor himself. In another important Ch'ing innovation, the main responsibility for military security was placed in the hands of hereditary armies known as "banners." There were twenty-four of these: eight Manchu, eight Mongol, and eight Chinese banner organizations garrisoned in strategic locations throughout the empire.

One of the most important and remarkable institutions inherited by the Ch'ing dynasty was a system of civil service recruitment through an elaborate series of public examinations. The Ch'ing held their first examinations in 1646, in an early attempt to draw on the talents of Chinese scholars and reassure the Chinese elite. With the exception of a small minority of men whose family background included criminals, brothel keepers, or other undesirables, the examinations were open to all. Consequently, there was a considerable infusion of new blood into officialdom, which was no hereditary aristocracy. There were documented cases of men from truly humble backgrounds winning the coveted highest degree, the *chin-shih* (presented scholar), although the system favored families with scholarly traditions and the means to pursue them. Great pains were taken to avoid dishonesty, since the credibility of the government was at stake. Under the Ch'ing, as in earlier dynasties, the examinations called for a thorough command of the Confucian classics and literature. The idea that government should be by the best was an idea that was itself profoundly Confucian.

## Confucianism

By the time of the Ch'ing, Confucianism had evolved into a varied and complex body of thought which, while still based on the teachings of Confucius (ca. 551–ca. 479 B.C.), went far beyond them in comprehensiveness and sophistication. Functioning simultaneously as ideology, philosophy, and creed, Confucianism addressed itself to man's social, intellectual, and spiritual needs, with each aspect reinforcing the others.

At the heart of the Confucian political as well as moral theory was the concept of *jen*, frequently translated as "benevolence" or "humanity" but also signifying the ground for all other virtues, the condition of being fully human in dealing with others. A father should manifest *jen* toward his family, and a child in turn must be filial, giving parents whole-hearted obedience and genuine devotion. The relationship between father and son formed one of the classic Five Relationships of Confucianism. The four others—between ruler and minister, husband and wife, older brother and younger brother, and between friends—also emphasize the importance of reciprocal obligations between people of superior and inferior status. They illustrate the existence of these values at the family level, at the community level (friendship), and at the state level (ruler and minister). While the Confucians felt that the values expressed in the Five Relationships applied to all people, their concept of society was essentially hierarchical.

The Confucians' hierarchical concept was not an egalitarian view of state and society. Yet Mencius (371–289 B.C.?), whose views were accepted as orthodox after the Sung dynasty (960–1279), stressed government's responsibility for the people's welfare. Refining the ancient concept that government is based on divine and moral sanctions, Mencius insisted that a dynasty rules by virtue of a Mandate of Heaven, which will be revoked if a ruler fails to conduct himself as a ruler should. Heaven, in making its judgment, follows the voice of the people. Mencius quoted a now lost part of *The Classic of History*: "Heaven sees with the eyes of its people. Heaven hears with the ears of its people."[3] This right of rebellion became a permanent part of Chinese political thought, used by reformers to intimidate and influence recalcitrant rulers as well as by those who actually took up arms against the government. "Removing the mandate" (*ke-ming* in Chinese or *kakumei* in Japanese) became the modern word for revolution.

During the Sung, Confucian thinkers fashioned a new metaphysics, partly in response to the challenge presented by Buddhism, which attracted them with its lofty speculations but offended them with its rejection of society and the world. The result of this challenge was a new philosophy known in the West as

Neo-Confucianism. It found its classical formulation in the works of Chu Hsi (1130–1200), whose ideas were accepted as orthodox in Korea and Japan as well as China. One powerful component of Chu Hsi's subtle and comprehensive philosophy was his vision of the world as structured by a network of principles (*li*), with moral principles having the same existential validity as the principles found in nature. The counterpart of *li* is *ch'i*, the force and substance that constitutes the body and the energy of things. According to Chu Hsi, people too are a combination of *li* and *ch'i*. The *li* assures the fundamental goodness of all people, but the *ch'i* accounts for human imperfections.

The primary goal for Neo-Confucians was not theoretical knowledge but self-perfection and the perfection of society. A major disagreement within Neo-Confucian thought was between Chu Hsi's followers, who believed in "the investigation of things"—meaning primarily the study of conduct and the classics—and the more inner directed approach of the followers of Wang Yang-ming (1472–1529), who stressed inner illumination and the identity of knowledge and action. "Knowledge in its genuine and earnest aspect is action, and action in its intelligent and discriminating aspect is knowledge."[4]

There were differences within Neo-Confucianism as different individuals emphasized various aspects or interpretations; it supplied a set of values not only for men of action and scholars but also for those inclined toward contemplation and meditation. However, the ultimate goal for self-perfection in Neo-Confucianism remained social. Neo-Confucians rejected the Buddhist quest for personal release from the wheel of birth and rebirth, and they also rejected the Taoist search for identification with an ineffable *Tao* ("Way"), which transcends social morality. There was much that was new in Neo-Confucianism, but it remained a profoundly civic faith.

Among those who shared this faith, there continued to be ample room for disagreement and for new developments. The turbulent years of the mid-seventeenth century, which resulted in the change of dynasties from Ming to Ch'ing, was an especially fruitful period in the history of Neo-Confucianism. While some of the period's most original thinkers had little impact on later Ch'ing intellectual life, this was not true of Ku Yen-wu (1613–82), whose writings and teachings made a deep impression on Ch'ing scholarship. Objecting to the speculations of Sung and Ming Neo-Confucians, Ku insisted on what he considered real and practical learning, solidly based on scholarship in the original classical sources. Ku himself wrote important studies on historical geography and inscriptions, but he is especially famous for his work on historical phonetics. His essays, collected under the title *Records of Daily Knowledge* (*Jih-chih lu*), discuss government, the examination system, and economics as well as the classics and history, showing a range and critical spirit representative of the best seventeenth-century thought. His influence, however, stems from his role as virtual founder of Ch'ing philological scholarship and what was termed "Han Learning," referring to the scholarship of the Han dynasty as contrasted to the philosophical speculations of the Sung. Textual scholarship was a field in which Ch'ing scholars subsequently made great contributions. It was a field encouraged and patronized by K'ang-hsi and other Ch'ing emperors.

## The Reign of K'ang-hsi

Emperor K'ang-hsi was the greatest of the Ch'ing emperors and indeed one of China's grandest and most illustrious rulers. In Figure 1-2, he is portrayed resplendent in his dragon robe and vermilion (scarlet) hat. The nineteenth-century artist has given him an expression of concern appropriate to the ruler of a vast empire, but never having seen him, has perhaps not fully conveyed his strength of character.

K'ang-hsi was on the throne for sixty years, from 1662 to 1722, and actually ruled from 1668 on. One of his first tasks as emperor was the consolidation of the still young Ch'ing dynasty. A costly war known as the War of the Three Feudatories (1673–81), undertaken by the emperor at the age of fifteen, ended in the destruction of states in Kwangtung, Fukien, and Yunnan/Kweichow that were then incorporated into the empire. The most prolonged resistance to the new dynasty was along the southeast coast; Taiwan did not come under Ch'ing control until 1683. The island then was placed under the administration of Fukien Province. K'ang-hsi's campaigns were fought largely by Chinese (not Manchu) troops and generals.

After the incorporation of Taiwan, K'ang-hsi turned his attention to China's borders in the north and west. In the Amur River region, his army destroyed a Russian Cossack base. This military success was followed by a diplomatic success: the Treaty of Nerchinsk, signed with Russia in 1689, which settled frontier problems between the two great empires and regularized relations between them. The treaty also removed the threat of a possible alliance between the Russians and a confederation of Western Mongols. Against the latter, K'ang-hsi personally led his troops in 1696–97 and won a great victory. Around the middle of the seventeenth century, Western Mongols had intervened in the politico-religious struggles taking place in Tibet and had remained as conquerors. Under K'ang-hsi, the Ch'ing too became deeply involved. In 1720 Ch'ing armies entered Tibet and installed a pro-Chinese Dalai Lama (the spiritual and secular ruler of Tibet). This was to be the first but not the last Ch'ing intervention in Tibet.

K'ang-hsi's martial exploits were, in part, a reflection of a conscious sense of identification with his Manchu forebears and his desire to preserve the traditional Manchu way of life, which he saw as essential to maintaining Manchu supremacy. Another expression of this feeling was the organization of great hunting expeditions, in which he took considerable delight. To help preserve Manchu distinctiveness, one of the first acts of K'ang-hsi's reign was the closing of Manchuria to Chinese immigration. During the Ch'ing, Manchus were not allowed to marry Chinese, and Manchu women were not allowed to bind their feet. K'ang-hsi was very much the Manchu, but he was not anti-Chinese. Like previous non-Chinese invaders, however, he felt impelled to take steps to avoid being submerged in the larger Chinese population and more sophisticated Chinese culture.

Under K'ang-hsi a strict balance was maintained between Manchus and Chi-

Figure 1-2 Portrait of K'ang-hsi, by an unidentified nineteenth-century court painter. Colors on silk, 158 cm. × 76 cm. Metropolitan Museum of Art, New York (Rogers Fund, 1942).

nese in the top metropolitan administrative posts, and in the provinces, generally, a Chinese governor was counterbalanced by a governor-general, usually placed over two provinces, who was a Manchu, a Mongol, or a Chinese bannerman. The hereditary banner forces lived apart from the general population in their own communities and were commanded by a general responsible directly to Peking. Another group used by the emperor for confidential tasks were his Chinese bondservants, who managed the imperial household. Like eunuchs, they were dependent on imperial favor, but unlike eunuchs, they did not offend Chinese feelings. Bondservants were used by K'ang-hsi to submit secret memorials (reports) on conditions in the provinces and also managed the emperor's personal treasury and the monopolies, including the maritime customs.

K'ang-hsi was a very vigorous man. He rose well before dawn each day to go through a great stack of memorials before receiving officials, beginning at 5 A.M. (later changed to 7 A.M. to accommodate officials not living near the palace). His tours of personal inspection in the South are famous. To show his benevolence, he reduced taxes and forced Manchu aristocrats to desist from

山川渾厚
草木華滋
甲辰春倣巨然筆為
惕翁老先生壽　王翬

Figure 1-3   Wang Hui,
*Landscape in the Style of
Chü-jan.* Hanging scroll,
ink on paper, dated 1664,
131 cm × 65.5 cm.
Collection of Mr. and
Mrs. Earl Morse.

seizing Chinese lands. He was also a man of wide intellectual interests, including Western learning. He won the affection of many of the Chinese literati by holding a special honorific examination in 1679 to attract scholars who had remained loyal to the Ming, and sponsored the compilation of the official Ming history, a great phrase dictionary, a giant encyclopedia, and an exhaustive dictionary of Chinese characters. The philosophy of Chu Hsi received his special support.

K'ang-hsi was also a patron of the arts. Among the visual arts, calligraphy and painting were particularly valued in China as "high arts" befitting a Confucian gentleman. The seventeenth century produced highly individualistic and creative spirits whose work is much appreciated today, but it was artists working in a more orthodox style who won favor at K'ang-hsi's court. One of these was Wang Hui (1632–1717), whose landscape done in the style of the Sung master Chü-jan, shown in Figure 1-3, is typical in that he uses a past master as his point of departure to create a painting very much his own. The overall composition may not be new, but as Wen Fong has pointed out, his originality lies in the vitality of his brushwork, which infuses his painting with kinetic energy.[5]

In 1691 Wang Hui received an imperial commission to supervise the painting of a series of scrolls commemorating K'ang-hsi's southern tour. Shown even more favor by the emperor was Wang Yüan-ch'i (1642–1715), who became K'ang-hsi's chief artistic adviser in 1700. His fascination with form and structure and his concentration on surface space have been compared with Cézanne. Both "seem to have occupied a comparable position in their respective painting traditions; each in his way representing the rejection of a traditional, rationalized spatial organization in favor of a formal construction in abstract space."[6] They differ in that the art of Wang Yüan-ch'i, like that of Wang Hui, was at heart calligraphic. Another difference was that the Chinese artist had the good fortune to be understood and appreciated by the political and artistic establishment of his day.

Detail Figure 1-3   Wang Hui, *Landscape in the Style of Chü-jan.*

## Yung-cheng

K'ang-hsi's reign was of a length unprecedented in China's history, and he was altogether one of the most successful Chinese emperors, but he was unable to provide for a smooth succession. After his death, the throne was seized in a military coup by K'ang-hsi's fourth son, who became Emperor Yung-cheng (r. 1723–35). After he became emperor, Yung-cheng censored the record of his accession to the throne and also suppressed other writings he deemed inimical to his regime, particularly those with an anti-Manchu bias. He was a tough and hard-working ruler bent on effective government at minimum expense. Like his father, Yung-cheng used military force to preserve the dynasty's position in Outer Mongolia, and when Tibet was torn by civil war during 1717–28, he intervened militarily, leaving a Ch'ing resident backed by a military garrison to pursue the dynasty's interests. His reign was despotic, efficient, vigorous, and brief. By the simple device of sealing the name of the heir-apparent in a box kept in the throne room, Yung-cheng was able to assure that on his death there would be no struggle over the succession. Thus he prepared the way for what was to be the Ch'ing's most splendid reign.

## Ch'ien-lung

During Ch'ien-lung's reign (1736–95), the Ch'ing achieved its greatest prosperity, and geographic expansion into Central Asia reached its greatest extent. (See map, p. 5.) This was made possible not only by Chinese strength but also by the disunity and declining strength of the Inner Asian peoples. The declining vitality of these peoples has been subject to various interpretations. As summarized by Morris Rossabi, the most plausible explanations include the diminishing importance of the international caravan trade in an age of developing maritime commerce, a trend toward the development of sedentary societies marked by urbanization, and Russian expansion that reduced the area to which tribes could flee in retreat, thereby reducing their mobility.[7]

Under Ch'ien-lung, Chinese Turkestan was incorporated into the Ch'ing dynasty's rule and renamed Sinkiang, while to the West, Ili was conquered and garrisoned. The Ch'ing also dominated Outer Mongolia after inflicting a final defeat on the Western Mongols. Its policy there was to preserve Mongol institutions, but it allowed Chinese merchants to enter and exploit the people, thus reinforcing the anti-Chinese animosities of the animal-herding Mongols. It is no accident that when the Ch'ing fell in the twentieth century, the Mongols promptly declared their independence. Throughout this period there were continued Mongol interventions in Tibet and a reciprocal spread of Tibetan Lamaism in Mongolia. Ch'ien-lung again sent armies into Tibet and firmly established the Dalai Lama as ruler, with a Ch'ing resident and garrison to preserve Chinese suzerainty. Other than that, no attempt was made to integrate Tibet into the empire after the manner of Sinkiang. Further afield, military campaigns against the Annamese, Burmese, Nepalese, and Gurkhas forced these peoples to submit and send tribute.

This expansion involved millions of square miles and brought into the empire non-Chinese peoples (such as Uighurs, Kazakhs, Kirghiz, and Mongols) who were at least potentially hostile. It was also a very expensive enterprise. The dynasty enjoyed unprecedented prosperity and managed in the mid-1780s to accumulate a healthy financial reserve, but its resources were not inexhaustible. Yet the emperor delighted in the glory and wealth. He built a sumptuous summer residence, partly of Western design, and undertook grand tours of the empire, including six tours of the South. In his policy toward the literati, he combined K'ang-hsi's generous patronage of scholarship with Yung-cheng's suspiciousness of anti-Manchu writings. The greatest project sponsored by him was the *Complete Library of the Four Treasuries* (*Ssu-k'u ch'üan-shu*) of 36,000 volumes. It preserved many books, but it was also intended as a means of ferreting out and suppressing those deemed offensive.

## Decorative Arts

The splendor and opulence of the age was reflected in its ceramics and decorative arts. In this respect also the Ch'ien-lung period built on the achievements of the two preceding reigns. Under K'ang-hsi, the royal kilns produced great numbers of bowls, vases, plates, and vessels, many of them manufactured especially for the growing foreign market. Among the most admired are oxblood vases, although more common were pieces whose basic color was green (*famille verte*). The plate shown in Figure 1-4 is painted to show a scene with six ladies sitting on a terrace. Along with their artistic qualities, such decorated ceramics provide much information about dress, architecture, and upper-class life and leisure.

Figure 1-4  Dish painting in *famille verte* enamels. K'ang-hsi period, diam. 61 cm.

In the Yung-cheng period a pinkish rose color (*famille rose*) became the favorite. Fine copies of Sung ware were produced during the Ch'ien-lung period, but there was no general return to the refined and elegant taste of the earlier period. Among the most exquisite and finely crafted products of the Ch'ien-lung kilns were porcelains produced at the imperial kilns. Fine examples of the colorful ceramics in many shapes abound in museum collections.

Bright colors were an important feature of interior decoration. The use of colored tiles as well as paint helped to produce a vibrant effect. Enamelware (especially cloisonné, ware in which the enameled areas are separated by thin strips of metal), intricately carved lacquers and ivories, ornate embroideries, highly decorated furniture all testify to the era's taste for fine craftsmanship and rich detail. The entire style of this era evoked the enthusiasm of European visitors and helped to encourage the eighteenth-century European craze for "chinoiserie" and the manufacture, both in China and in Europe, of highly commercial Sino-European products for the Western market. At their best, Chinese art objects of the eighteenth century are impressive in their high craftsmanship. Yet, to borrow a term used by early eighteenth-century Chinese scholars in their discussions of painting, the art was rather "overripe."

During the last years of the Ch'ien-lung era there were definite indications that the dynasty had passed its peak and that there was trouble ahead. Before discussing these, however, it is well to consider some of the other aspects of the century when the Ch'ing was strong and seemed well.

## Culture of the Literati in the Eighteenth Century

Scholarship continued to flourish in eighteenth-century China. At the beginning of the dynasty, Ku Yen-wu, as already noted, wrote extensively on both statecraft and philology. Today he is famous for his statecraft writings, but his immediate successors were more interested in his philosophical scholarship. As a result, Ch'ing scholars made important, even iconoclastic, discoveries concerning the questionable historicity of parts of such venerated classics as *The Classic of Change, The Classic of History,* and the *Records of Rites.* However, the concentration on philology easily led to the view that textual studies alone were truly "solid" (in the sense that they avoided abstract speculation) and "practical" (in the sense that this seemed the best way to uncover the meaning of the classics). The resulting narrowing of intellectual interest is exemplified by the contrast between Yen Yüan (1635–1704) and his chief disciple, Li Kung (1659–1733). Although Yen Yüan was born too late to be a Ming loyalist, he shared the concerns of the generation that lived through the Ming-Ch'ing transition. Accordingly, Yen condemned quiet sitting and book learning as standing in the way of true self-cultivation capable of "changing the world," and he studied military science and medicine. But Li Kung expounded his teachings in the form of commentaries on the classics.

A major scholar and theorist was Tai Chen (1723–77), who made important contributions to linguistics, astronomy, mathematics, and geography as well as philosophy. Like most of the creative seventeenth-century thinkers, he rejected the metaphysical existence of *li*, which he considered simply the pattern of things. Similarly, he disputed Chu Hsi's dualistic theory of human nature, insisting that this went against the teachings of Mencius, that human nature is one whole and all good, and that moral perfection consists in the fulfillment of one's natural inclinations.

Tai Chen shared his age's faith in philology, but this was not true of his contemporary Chang Hsüeh-ch'eng (1738–1801), who strongly disliked philological studies and sought for meaning in the study and writing of history. Chang is perhaps most famous for his thesis that "the six classics are all history," by which he meant that they were not "empty" theoretical discussions but that they document antiquity and illustrate the Tao. A scholar must not stop at the facts but get at the meaning. Chang once compared a work of history to a living organism: Its facts are like bones, the writing is like the skin, and its meaning corresponds to the organism's vital spirit.

Along with history and philosophy, another subject of perennial concern to Chinese scholars was the function and evaluation of literature. The poet Yüan Mei (1716–97) held that the purpose of poetry is to express emotion, that it must give pleasure, and rejected the didactic view, held, among others, by Chang Hsüeh-ch'eng, that it must convey moral instruction. Yüan's poetry and prose reflect the life of a talented, refined eighteenth-century hedonist, unconventional within the bounds of good taste, and marginally aware of the exotic West. One of his prize possessions was a large Western mirror much admired by his female pupils. Among Yüan's less conventional works are a cookbook and a collection of ghost stories. His interest in the latter was shared by his friend, the painter Lo P'ing (1735–99), the youngest, and last, of the so-called "Eight Eccentrics of Yangchow," a man who claimed actually to have seen the apparitions he painted.

In the eighteenth century, painters of various schools were at work: professionals working in the meticulous and mannered "northern" style, eclectics drawing on diverse traditions and models, and individualists striving, sometimes excessively, for originality. An interesting and prolific artist was the Manchu painter Kao Ch'i-p'ei (1672–1734). Even in the Sung and earlier, artists had experimented with unconventional materials instead of using a brush, but none had gone as far as Kao who painted with the balls of his fingers, the side of his hand, and a long fingernail split like a pen for drawing lines. Some six hundred years separate Kao's *Young Crane under a Wu-t'ung Tree* (see Figure 1-5) and the classic moment of the genre, the Sung emperor Hui-tsung's carefully studied, realistic yet idealistic bird paintings (see Figure 1-6). In that time not only the means but the purpose of art, and the artist's self-conception, had changed.

Ch'ing painters and scholars generally perceived themselves as latecomers in a long and revered tradition. As such they faced a dilemma similar to that of painters, poets, and composers of our own time who no longer feel they can

Figure 1-5   Kao Ch'i-p'ei, *Young Crane under a Wu-t'ung Tree.* Hanging scroll, ink on paper, 95 cm × 44 cm.

contribute to the traditional lines of development in their arts, that is, be another Rembrandt, Beethoven, and so forth. The classical masters had said what needed to be said, and the creative opportunities available to those who would imitate or compete with them were limited. Moreover, what had been valid for one age could not serve another. But if the time for classical achievements was past, future directions were by no means clear.

It was characteristic of the age—and here the analogy to our own times is also instructive—that old canons of art were rejected. Thus some artists cultivated the notion that the epitome of art was non-art, that is, the deliberate cultivation of innocent awkwardness. Similarly, it was now quite acceptable for an eccentric to display his eccentricity by selling his paintings. Both Kao and Lo did so without jeopardizing their "amateur" status. The favorite place for such men was Yangchow, where wealthy salt merchants derived prestige as well as pleasure from supporting a world of painting, poetry, and calligraphy. Including, but extending beyond, the circle of such sophisticates was the audience for popular drama and vernacular literature. The latter in particular reached new heights.

## Ch'ing Fiction

Many of the dynasty's best writers and thinkers were men who had failed in the examination route to success, an experience which perhaps helped them to view society with a measure of critical and even satiric detachment. The ex-

Figure 1-6　Sung Hui-tsung, *Five-Colored Parakeet.* Hanging scroll, colors on silk, 53 cm high. Museum of Fine Arts, Boston.

aminations themselves were a favorite target. P'u Sung-ling (1640–1715), a short story writer, wrote this account of the seven transformations of a candidate in the provincial examination:

> When he first enters the examination compound and walks along, panting under his heavy load of luggage, he is just like a beggar. Next, while undergoing the personal body search and being scolded by the clerks and shouted at by the soldiers, he is just like a prisoner. When he finally enters his cell and, along with the other candidates, stretches his neck to peer out, he is just like the larva of a bee. When the examination is finished at last and he leaves, his mind in a haze and his legs tottering, he is just like a sick bird that has been released from a cage. While he is wondering when the results will be announced and waiting to learn whether he passed or failed, so nervous that he is startled even by the rustling of the trees and the grass and is unable to sit or stand still, his restlessness is like that of a monkey on a leash. When at last the results are announced and he has definitely failed, he loses his vitality like one dead, rolls over on his side, and lies without moving, like a poisoned fly. Then, when he pulls himself together and stands up, he is provoked by every sight and sound, gradually flings away everything within his reach, and complains of the illiteracy of the examiners. When he calms down at last, he finds everything in the room broken. At this time he is like a pigeon smashing its own precious eggs. These are the seven transformations of a candidate.[8]

This examination was held in a labyrinthine compound, with the candidates housed in individual cells where they had to spend the night. It was an eerie place sealed off from the rest of the world, for during an examination session the great gates could not be opened for any reason whatsoever. (If a man died during the examination, his body was wrapped in straw matting and thrown over the wall.) Thus it was a perfect setting for numerous tales of ghosts, usually the spirits of jilted maidens come to wreak their vengeance on the men who had done them wrong.

One of the two outstanding novels of the Ch'ing was *The Scholars (Ju-lin wai-shih)*, by Wu Ching-tzu (1701–54). It is primarily a satire on the examination system but also catches in its net an assortment of other human follies, and presents vignettes of the pompous and the ignorant, the unworldly scholar and those who cheat him, the intricacies of social and political life, and so on. Although it is episodic in organization and somewhat uneven in quality, it incorporates certain technical advances in the art of storytelling, notably in the way it allows its characters to reveal their personalities gradually rather than labeling them at the very start. It is a fine work of literature as well as a treasure house for the social historian.

China's most beloved and greatest novel is *The Dream of the Red Chamber (Hung-lou meng)*, also translated as *The Story of the Stone.* Like *The Scholars* it offers priceless insights into Ch'ing society, this time from the vantage point of a large, eminent family in decline. With rich detail embedded in its narrative fabric, it reveals much about how such a family was organized and functioned, the relationship between the generations and the sexes, the life of women, the status of servants, and so on, and it does this with fine psychological characterization based on the personal experience of its author, Ts'ao Hsüeh-ch'in (1715?–63). Ts'ao's Buddhist-Taoist view of life gives the novel philosophical depth; C. T. Hsia has written that "it embodies the supreme tragic expression in Chinese literature,"[9] and that for its main protagonist, "the ultimate tragic conflict lies in a tug of war between the opposing claims of compassion and detachment."[10]

Despite its excellence, *The Dream of the Red Chamber* did not gain respectability in scholarly circles; it was not until modern times that novels were appreciated as a serious literary genre on a level with poetry, essays, and history. As a literary genre, novels were considered frivolous and low class by the elite, who nevertheless read them in secret. Today, the novel is regarded as the Ch'ing period's greatest literary achievement and remains one of its most valuable mirrors, reflecting a society that was prosperous but whose continued well-being was far from assured.

## Economic Prosperity

The eighteenth century was a period of great prosperity in China. Economic development had been retarded by the destruction and dislocation that accompanied the collapse of the Ming, but once peace and order were restored by the Ch'ing, the economy more than recovered.

The central economic fact of this period was an increase in agricultural production. This was partly the result of the maximum geographical spread of known products and farming techniques: superior strains of rice, improved irrigation methods, and better fertilizers, such as soybean cakes. However, production was also increased through the introduction of new crops originally native to America: corn, the sweet potato, and the peanut. The sweet potato and the peanut were of special importance because they did not require the same quality soil or climatic conditions as other Chinese agricultural products and thus could be grown on land not previously cultivated. One beneficial result of increased output was tax reduction: with agricultural production up, tax rates could be lowered without reducing revenues. Emperor Yung-cheng's reform of the tax system particularly benefited poor peasant farmers. The century saw an increase in Chinese life expectancy and an all-around improvement in the standard of living. These, in turn, undoubtedly made further contributions to agricultural production and to economic development generally.

Agriculture provided a foundation for the development of trade and manufacturing. Of the latter, the pottery kilns have already been mentioned. Another industry that now flourished was the cotton trade. Silk and hemp, brewing, paper making, mining and metal working deserve mention as areas of strong activity, as do the increased production of tea and sugar. Stimulated by an increase in internal trade there was a growth of market towns and the flourishing of merchant guilds, which operated on an interprovincial and interregional basis. The salt merchants of Yangchow, dealing in a government mo-

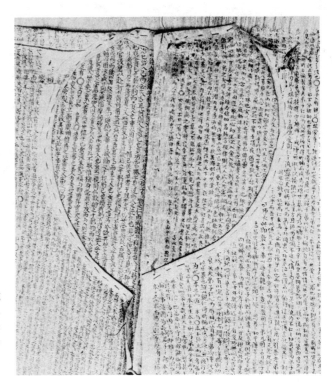

Figure 1-7  Cheating shirt. Fujii Museum (Fujii Saiseikai Yurinkan), Kyōto.

nopoly, were especially prosperous. Although the total value of internal trade far outweighed that of foreign commerce, the latter, too, contributed to Chinese well-being. Throughout the century the balance of overseas trade was in China's favor, and there was a strong inflow of gold and silver.

A major result of agricultural growth, peace, and prosperity was an increase in the size of China's population. By the end of the eighteenth century more people lived in China than in Europe; the Chinese population was in the neighborhood of 300 million, about double what it had been two centuries earlier. An increased population made increased demands on the economy. Growth in production could not keep up with expanding population. Thus, by the end of the eighteenth century, population growth was putting new strains on the economy, the state, and society. It may be worth noting that this phenomenon was not unique to China. The improvement in the living standards of Chinese peasants in this period was mirrored in other parts of the world (for example, France and Japan), and the stresses resulting from population growth helped to undermine the traditional order in China as elsewhere. The challenge of population growth did not go unnoticed. The Chinese scholar Hung Liang-chi (1746–1809) first wrote about the dangers inherent in this process in 1793.

The new population pressures resulted in population shifts: the "filling up" of previously marginal areas in China, and the emigration of Chinese people into Southeast Asia, where they subsequently became important minorities in a number of states. Population pressures also helped contribute to the increasing difficulty even superbly educated men had in winning an official appointment, for there was no increase in the number of positions in the civil service to keep pace with the growing numbers of candidates. Even in the Sung there were cases of men who spent a lifetime taking examinations—when the emperor asked his age, one such man replied, "fifty years ago twenty-three." Now the aged *chin-shih* became a stock figure in literature. The government even relaxed standards for men over seventy so that, past retirement age, they could at least enjoy the psychological satisfaction of receiving a degree. In an effort to weed out candidates, new examinations were introduced. Thus in 1788 the re-examination of provincial and metropolitan graduates was introduced. That brought the total minimum number of examinations required for the *chin-shih* to eight, not counting a final placement examination. By this time the criteria for judging papers had become exceedingly formalistic. Candidates spent years practicing eight-legged essays, and bookshops did a thriving business selling model answers. In the meantime, the old battle of wits between examiners and cheaters remained a draw. (See the "cheating shirt," Figure 1-7.) The unsatisfactory state of the examination system, and the tendency of the government to tinker and elaborate rather than reform and innovate, suggests a dangerous hardening of the institutional arteries during the last twenty years of Ch'ien-lung's reign.

## Internal Decay

As the expense of military campaigns far beyond the bounds of China proper mounted, the resources of even the prosperous Ch'ien-lung regime were strained to the utmost, while administrative laxity and corruption were rendering the government less efficient and more expensive. The worst offender was a Manchu favorite of Emperor Ch'ien-lung, a man named Ho-shen (1750–99), who rode high for twenty-three years. Assured of imperial support, he built up a network of corruption and amassed a huge fortune. Although bitterly detested he could not be removed, for he never lost Ch'ien-lung's confidence and affection. An attack on Ho-shen implied an attack on the aging emperor's own judgment and, furthermore, suggested the presence of the disease of factionalism. Perhaps Ch'ien-lung was especially sensitive to any signs of factionalism since his father, Emperor Yung-cheng, had written a very strong critique on this subject. Like his political authority, the moral and intellectual authority of the emperor were now beyond question. Emperor Ch'ien-lung abdicated after his sixtieth year of rule in order not to rule longer than his illustrious grandfather, but he continued to dominate the government until his death in 1799. Only then was Ho-shen removed and, in lieu of execution, allowed to take his own life.

As always, the burden of extravagance and corruption was borne by the common people. As a result many of them joined in the White Lotus Rebellion, which broke out in 1796 and was not completely suppressed until 1804. At its height it affected Szechwan, Hupeh, Honan, Kansu, and Shensi. The rebellion drew its following by promising the coming of Maitreya (the Buddha of the future), a restoration of the Ming, and the rescue of the people from all suffering. It gained momentum as it attracted the destitute and displaced and proved the power of its cause. It was also assisted by the ineffectiveness of the dynasty's response: government generals used the occasion to line their own pockets and bannermen proved their total incompetence. Not until after Ho-shen's fall did the government make real headway. A new, very capable commander was appointed, disaffected areas were slowly taken from the rebels, and militia bands organized by the local elite, whose members had the most to lose from radical social change, proved effective in putting down insurgency.

Ho-shen and the rebellion were both destroyed in the end, but corruption in government and misery in the countryside remained to plague the dynasty in the nineteenth century. Yet on the local level Chinese society remained resilient. The problems faced by the government and the people were not without precedent and seemed capable of solution within the boundaries of existing values and institutions. On the international level, the perennial problem of invasion from Inner Asia had been laid to rest, but a new, very different and threatening foreign problem was about to emerge. Entering the new century, China was stable but not particularly vigorous; and perhaps this very stability was a liability when China was drawn into the unstable world of modern global history.

## NOTES

1. G. William Skinner, ed., *The City in Late Imperial China* (Stanford: Stanford University Press, 1977), pp. 212–16 and *passim*.

2. Hilary J. Beattie, *Land and Lineage in China: A Study of T'ung-ch'eng County, Anhwei, in the Ming and Ch'ing Dynasties* (New York: Cambridge University Press, 1979).

3. *Mencius*, V, pt. A, chap. 5, translated by D. C. Lau, *Mencius* (Baltimore: Penguin Books, 1970), p. 144.

4. Wing-tsit Chan, trans., *Instructions for Practical Living and Other Neo-Confucian Writings* (New York: Columbia University Press, 1963), p. 159.

5. Wen Fong, quoted in Roderick Whitfield, *In Pursuit of Antiquity: Chinese Paintings of the Ming and Ch'ing Dynasties from the Collection of Mr. and Mrs. Earl Morse* (Princeton: The Art Museum, Princeton University, 1969), p. 41.

6. *Ibid.*, p. 183.

7. Morris Rossabi, *China and Inner Asia—From 1368 to the Present Day* (New York: Pica Press, 1975), pp. 139–40. Rossabi does not think Buddhism was a major factor, although it may have contributed to the decline. *Ibid.,* pp. 140–41.

8. Quoted in Ichisada Miyazaki, *China's Examination Hell,* trans. Conrad Schirokauer (Tokyo and New York: John Weatherhill, 1976), pp. 57–58.

9. C. T. Hsia, *The Classic Chinese Novel* (New York: Columbia University Press, 1968), p. 246.

10. *Ibid.* p. 264.

徳川時代之日本

| 1600 | 1651 | 1700 | 1800 | 1868 |

TOKUGAWA SHOGUNATE

Consolidation

(1688–1704)
Genroku

Late Tokugawa

Perry Expedition → 1853

# $2$ Tokugawa Japan

A major theme in the history of Japan is the interplay between native and imported elements in culture and government. Before modern times, the main source of foreign influence in Japan was China. Yet, no matter how extensive and profound the impact of foreign models and ideas, Japan has always retained its own traditions and developed in its own distinctive way.

## Geography and Culture

Geography helps to explain both Japan's receptivity to influences from the Asian continent and its ability not to be overwhelmed by them. Although it is considerably smaller than China, Japan is not an unusually small state—its 142,707-square-mile area is substantially larger than that of the British Isles

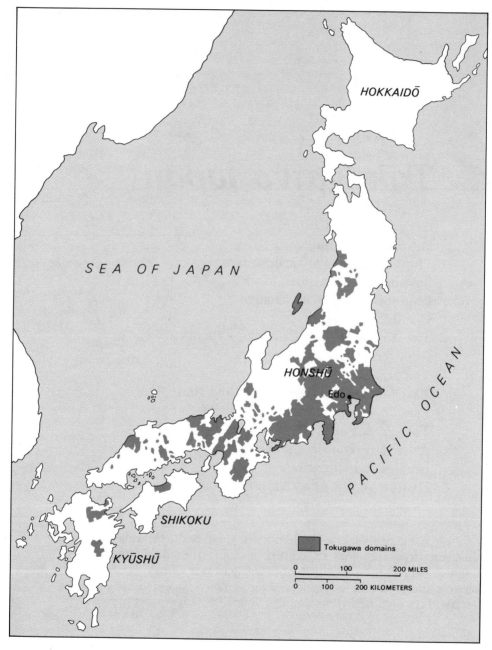

Figure 2-1  **Japan ca. 1664.**

(99,909 square miles). Approximately four-fifths of this land is too mountainous to permit cultivation. But Japan's climate is warm and wet enough to permit rice cultivation, and through intense cultivation, the Japanese developed a highly efficient agricultural production that contributed to their population growth. The small proportion of arable land thus was able to support relatively large populations.

Honshū, the largest of Japan's four major islands, is divided by mountain ranges but also contains three plains that have served as population centers. The largest, measuring 3.2 million acres, is the Kantō Plain where Tokyo is located. Another plain of 450,000 acres is at the head of Ise Bay with Nagoya as its largest city, and the third, with 310,000 acres, is at the head of Ōsaka Bay where Kyoto, Ōsaka, and Kobe are located. To the west, the island of Shikoku helps to form the scenic Inland Sea. Of Japan's other two large islands, Hokkaidō in the north remained largely undeveloped until the nineteenth century, but Kyūshū, the southernmost island, played an important role in Japan's history from the beginning, for it was the gateway to the Asian continent. At its closest point, Kyūshū is about 120 miles from the mainland, across the Korean Strait. Although conquerors from the mainland may have played an important part in Japan's prehistory, no mainland power ever succeeded in conquering or dominating Japan in historical times. The Japanese could adapt foreign ideas, institutions, and techniques to their own needs without military or political interference from abroad.

Language was an important factor in preserving the integrity of Japanese culture, for the Japanese language (like Korean) is not related to Chinese. It belongs to an entirely different family of languages. These are languages (called *agglutinative*) in which words are often formed by a process of adding words and word elements ("gluing together"). Chinese is totally uninflected, but Japanese verbs and adjectives are highly inflected, with differences in tense, mood, level of formality, and so forth expressed by adding to the stem one element after another. The function of nouns in a sentence is indicated through the use of postpositions. These are similar to English prepositions except that they follow rather than precede nouns, and no noun can appear without one. These postpositions and various particles delineate the sentence structures, which, in contrast to the compact mode of classical Chinese, tend to be long and rambling. Thus, even when Japanese men of letters immersed themselves in Chinese learning, they continued to speak (and think) in the language they shared with the great majority of their compatriots. In premodern times there were always Japanese scholars who wrote in Chinese, but Japan's finest literature was written in the native language. To accomplish this the Japanese at first used a difficult system of writing that utilized Chinese characters, sometimes for their meaning but at other times to represent the sounds of Japanese words. Then, during the Heian Period (794–1185), they developed a *kana* syllabary. This was a system of phonetic symbols originally derived from Chinese characters. (See Figure 2-2.) Each symbol represented a syllable. Within this system there was no longer any need to employ Chinese characters to repre-

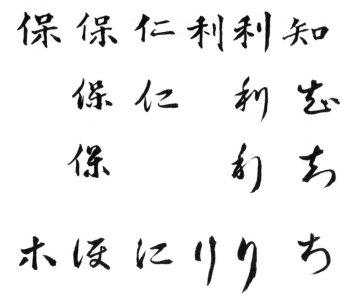

Figure 2-2  Development of *kana* syllabary. The top row contains Chinese characters and the bottom row shows the *kana* into which they eventually developed. Reading from right to left, the *kana* are pronounced *chi, ri, ri, ni, ho, ho.* All except the third and the last rows are in *hiragana*, the most commonly used form; the third and last rows illustrate *katakana*, the form used primarily for foreign terms and for emphasis. (Taken from G. B. Sansom, *Japan: A Short Cultural History* [Stanford: Stanford University Press, 1978], p. 238; calligraphy by Dr. Léon L. Y. Chang.)

sent Japanese sounds, but they were retained nevertheless, since Japanese has numerous homonyms. In the modern language, the Chinese characters, used to write nouns and the stems of verbs and adjectives, float in a sea of *kana*, representing particles, endings, and certain other common words. Foreign words, however, are today written in an alternate *kana* system.

Another cultural element unique to Japan was the native religion called Shinto, "the way of the gods" or *kami* (spirits) who were believed to inhabit the Japanese countryside. *Kami*, it was believed, could be found in a special stone, a stream, an old tree, a mountain, or any other object, or even a skill felt to be imbued with a special quality. Stories about the *kami* were numerous but unsystematized. The absence of theoretical elaboration or doctrinal demands did not detract from the belief in the *kami*, who, strongly rooted as they were in nature, were intrinsic to the spiritual life of the communities that looked after them. The most revered of all the *kami* was the Sun Goddess, whose shrine at Ise is still rebuilt every twenty years, preserving essential features of very early Japanese architecture. The Sun Goddess is an important figure in Japan's oldest myths and was considered the progenitor of the imperial line.

# Political Background

By virtue of his divine descent from the Sun Goddess, the Japanese emperor continued to serve as the source of political legitimacy for centuries after real political power had shifted away from the court and into the hands of warrior families. These families were bound in ties of vassalage culminating in a hereditary leader who was recognized as shogun (originally a military title) by the emperor. Theoretically the shogun was the emperor's delegate, but in practice his power was based on the military strength of his family and its vassals. The shoguns administered their affairs through their *bakufu*, a term that originally designated a military field-headquarters but was used for the shogun's government ever since the first shogunate was established. Local power was left in the hands of the vassals. Not only self-interest but a warrior ethic (*bushidō*) emphasizing loyalty and readiness to offer up his life bound the vassal to his lord.

This system of government was first developed by the Kamakura shogunate (1185–1333) and continued under the Ashikaga (1336–1573). That shogunate, however, ended in a century of warfare (1467–1573) with the shogun, like the emperor, reduced to a mere symbol while feudal lords (*daimyo*) fought each other, trying to preserve and, if possible, enlarge their own territories. Eventually, military and political success went to those houses best able to mobilize the resources of their domains and turn them into small states. Thus the breakdown of central unity was accompanied by the formation of more highly integrated local political entities. The daimyo's castle-towns often served as the centers of the daimyo states. Warriors (*samurai*) tended to be concentrated there and, instead of living directly on the land, such warriors received stipends. The peasant villages were then left to manage their own affairs as long as they provided the payments required for the warriors. Naturally, given the overall fragmented state of Japan, there were many local variations and regional differences in the system.

The unification of Japan after such a long period of instability and strife was a cumulative process accomplished under a succession of three leaders. Oda Nobunaga (1534–82) began from a strategic base in central Honshū, Japan's main island, and by a combination of political ruthlessness, cunning, and military skill dominated about one-third of Japan by the time of his death. Toyotomi Hideyoshi (1536–98) was born a peasant but adopted an aristocratic name and rose to become one of Nobunaga's foremost generals, defeating other contenders for the succession. He continued to increase his power much in the manner of Nobunaga. When he was unable to destroy the strongest daimyo, Tokugawa Ieyasu (1542–1616), Hideyoshi used diplomacy, marrying his sister to Ieyasu and assigning him very substantial holdings in the Kantō Plain of eastern Japan. He also relocated his own vassals to assure maximum security. A man of overweening ambition, Hideyoshi had visions of subduing China as well as Japan and twice sent armies to Korea in abortive attempts to begin that process. When Hideyoshi died, the Japanese forces immediately returned home.

At home, Hideyoshi's pacification measures did not stop at the daimyo level, and some of those measures had long-lasting effects. One of his most important acts was the great "sword hunt" of 1588, in which all peasants who had not already done so were ordered to surrender their weapons, the metal being used in building a great statue of Buddha. Depriving peasants of their weapons did more than discourage them from rioting or rebelling—although it did that too. A major, and intentional, consequence of the measure was to draw a sharp line between peasants and warriors. This created an unbridgeable gulf between the tiller of the soil and the bearer of arms, where hitherto there had been low-ranking samurai who had also worked the land.

By this time Hideyoshi's land survey was well underway, although it was not completed for all Japan until 1598. In this great survey, the value of cultivated land was assessed in terms of productivity, not extent; productivity was measured in *koku* of rice, a *koku* being equal to 4.96 bushels (approximately enough rice to feed an adult for a year). The resulting listings were used to assess the taxes due from each village. The holdings of the daimyo were also calculated in terms of the assessed value rather than acreage. From this time on, a daimyo, by definition, held land assessed at a minimum of 10,000 *koku*. Large daimyo held much more than that. Some of the greatest had several hundred thousand *koku*, and there were a few with over one million. Hideyoshi personally held two million *koku*, not including the lands of his major, most trustworthy vassals. Tokugawa Ieyasu held 2,557,000. Like the confiscation of weapons, the land survey, which listed the names of the peasant proprietors, effectively separated farmers and fighters.

An edict of 1591 carried the process still further. The first of its three articles prohibited fighting men from becoming peasants or townsmen, and the second forbade peasants to leave their fields and become merchants or artisans. It also prohibited artisans from becoming farmers. The third article of the edict prohibited anyone from employing a samurai who had left his master without permission. If discovered, the offending samurai was to be returned to his master for disposition. If this was not done and the culprit was knowingly allowed to go free, then the edict declared that "three persons shall be beheaded in place of the one, and their heads sent to the offender's original master. If this threefold substitution is not effected, then there is no alternative but to punish the new master."[1] In this way, Hideyoshi, who had himself risen from the peasantry to the greatest heights, did his best to make sure that henceforth everyone would remain within his hereditary social status. The policy of seeking social stability by freezing class lines was continued by Hideyoshi's successors.

Hideyoshi had hoped that these successors would be his own descendants, but his desire to found a dynasty, like his dream of foreign conquest, came to naught. Before he died, he made his most powerful vassals solemnly swear allegiance to his five-year old son. But this proved futile, and in the ensuing struggle for power Ieyasu emerged the victor. The decisive battle was fought in 1600 at Sekigahara in central Honshū.

# The Tokugawa Political System

Although Tokugawa Ieyasu did not assume the title of shogun until 1603, it is customary and convenient to date the beginning of the Tokugawa period from the battle of Sekigahara in 1600. The Tokugawa thus antedates the Ch'ing by forty-four years; interestingly, its end also antedates the end of the Ch'ing by forty-four years.

The essential structure of the Tokugawa political system was devised by Ieyasu and completed by his two immediate successors, Hidetada (shogun, 1616–23) and Iemitsu (shogun, 1623–51), so that by the middle of the seventeenth century, the system was in full operation. Iemitsu concluded the process of closing the country to all but the Dutch and Chinese at Nagasaki, although the basic policy of seclusion had been set by the founder (see Chapter 3). The main problem facing the Tokugawa, however, came from home, not from abroad.

Ieyasu rose to supremacy as the leader of a group of daimyo, each of whom was backed by his own vassals and supported by his independent power base. The daimyo were by no means all deeply committed to the Tokugawa. Hideyoshi's recent failure to establish a dynasty demonstrated, if any demonstration was needed, the folly of relying solely on the loyalty of such men, especially when passing on the succession to a minor. Ieyasu himself assured the smooth transfer of power to his son by resigning from the office of shogun, in 1605, after holding it for only two years. But he continued in actual control until his death, working to ensure the continuity of Tokugawa rule.

All the daimyo were the shogun's vassals, bound to him by solemn oath, and when a daimyo's heir succeeded to his domain, the new daimyo had to sign his pledge of vassalage to the shogun in blood. Still, some vassals were more reliable than others, and the Tokugawa classified them into three groups. Least trusted and potentially the most dangerous were the "outside," or allied, daimyo (*tozama*), who were too powerful to be considered Tokugawa subordinates. Virtually all of these, like Ieyasu, had been vassals of Hideyoshi. Some had supported Ieyasu at the battle of Sekigahara, but others came over to the Tokugawa only after the outcome of that battle left them no other choice. More trustworthy were the "house daimyo" (*fudai*), most of whom had been Tokugawa family vassals raised to daimyo status by the Tokugawa and thus, unlike the outside daimyo, they were indebted to the *bakufu* (shogun's government) for their status and domains. The third group, the "collateral daimyo" (*shimpan*), were daimyo belonging to Tokugawa branch families. The Tokugawa also held its own lands, which supported its direct retainers. Some of these held fiefs of less than the 10,000 *koku* required for daimyo status, but many of them received stipends directly from the *bakufu*.

When Ieyasu was transferred to the Kantō region by Hideyoshi, he chose as his headquarters the centrally located village of Edo (modern Tokyo), then consisting of about one hundred houses but destined to become one of the world's great cities. The shogunate also maintained castles at Ōsaka and Shizuoka (then called Sumpu) as well as the Nijo Castle in Kyōto, residence of a *bakufu* deputy responsible for governing the capital city and serving concurrently as the shogun's representative at the Imperial court.

To secure itself militarily, the Tokugawa placed its house daimyo in strategic areas. It dominated the Kantō, central Japan, and Kyōto-Ōsaka regions, while the outside daimyo had their territories in the outer areas. A number of policies were initiated to keep the daimyo from acquiring too much strength. They were restricted to one castle each and had to secure *bakufu* permission before they could repair this castle. They were allowed to maintain only a fixed number of men at arms, and, in line with the seclusion policy, were forbidden to build large ships. To keep the daimyo from forming political alliances which might threaten the *bakufu,* they were required to obtain *bakufu* assent for their marriage plans.

During the first half of the seventeenth century the shogunate enacted a vigorous policy of increasing its own strength at the expense of the daimyo. In this period there were 281 cases in which daimyo were transferred from one fief to another, shuffles that strengthened some and weakened others. Another 213 domains were confiscated outright. This happened sometimes as a disciplinary measure, as when a lord proved incompetent or the domain was torn by a succession dispute. More often confiscation resulted from failure to produce an heir. Deathbed adoptions of an heir were not recognized. By such means the Tokugawa more than tripled the size of its holdings, until its own domain was calculated as worth 6.8 million *koku* of rice. The distribution of their holdings also favored the Tokugawa economically, as it did militarily, since they were in possession of many of Japan's mines and most of the important cities such as Ōsaka, Kyōto, and Nagasaki. In the mid-Tokugawa period collateral daimyo held land worth 2.6 million *koku;* house daimyo, 6.7 million; and outside daimyo, 9.8 million. It is indicative of the decline of their economic and political power that religious institutions held only around 600,000 *koku,* and the emperor and the court nobility could draw on land worth only 187,000 *koku.*

To ensure that the daimyo obeyed *bakufu* orders, the shogunate sent out its own inspectors. It also devised a highly effective system of strengthening itself politically (while at the same time draining the daimyo financially) by requiring them to spend alternate years in residence in Edo, where the *bakufu* could keep them under surveillance. When they did go back home to their domains, they had to leave their wives and children behind as hostages. This system of alternate attendance (*sankin kōtai*) forced the daimyo to spend large sums traveling back and forth with their retinues. The maintenance of suitably elaborate residences in Edo was a further strain on daimyo resources. The daimyo were also called upon to support public projects such as waterworks or the repair of the shogun's castle at Edo, but such exactions were not as burdensome as the constant expense of alternate attendance. The residence requirement had the additional effect of turning Edo into a capital not only of the *bakufu* but of all Japan.

In theory the shogun was the emperor's deputy as well as the feudal overlord of all the daimyo. Thus he had political legitimacy as well as standing at the apex of the military hierarchy. This dual role made him, in effect, responsible for the conduct of foreign affairs. The early *bakufu* also asserted its financial predominance when it reserved for itself the right to issue paper currency. Its regulations extended even to the dress of the daimyo. The final provision of a code issued in 1635 declared, "all matters are to be carried out in accordance with the laws of Edo."[2] The *bakufu's* own domain comprised about a fourth of Japan.

## Bakufu-Han Relations

Despite this tendency of the shogunate to establish its preeminence as the central power, the daimyo remained largely free to manage affairs in their own domains or *han*. The *bakufu* usually interfered only when the daimyo proved themselves incapable of managing their *han*, or when problems involving more than one *han* arose. The daimyo themselves were naturally concerned to develop the strength of their own domains while keeping *bakufu* interference to a minimum. Even while tightening the administration of their *han*, their self-interest lay in preserving the decentralized aspect of the larger political system, thereby retaining their own feudal autonomy. Tokugawa government is sometimes described as a "centralized feudalism." Using this terminology, we may say that it was to the daimyo's advantage to keep the system feudal. Their ability to accomplish this is suggested by another expression used by scholars, "*baku-han*," signifying a system composed of the *bakufu* and the *han*. Both formulations allude to the mixed composition of the Tokugawa system.

Under the fourth shogun, Ietsuna (shogun, 1651–80), the daimyo regained much of the ground they had lost under his three predecessors. *Bakufu* policy was reversed. There was a drastic decline in the number of daimyo transferred and *han* confiscated. Deathbed adoptions were recognized as legitimate. The shogunate even began permitting *han* to issue their own paper money, a policy that led to the proliferation of local currencies. Anxious to protect their own money, some *han* in the eighteenth century prohibited the use of outside currencies—including the *bakufu's* money!

The vigorous but eccentric fifth shogun, Tsunayoshi (shogun, 1680–1709) presided over a reassertion of *bakufu* power, which earned him the enmity of the daimyo and lasting ignominy. A scant five years after his death, Tsunayoshi was satirized in a puppet play by Chikamatsu. He was an easy target, for he carried to an extreme his Buddhist devotion to the preservation of animal life and especially his solicitude for dogs. His exaggerated concern for these animals was often expressed at the expense of human well-being and sometimes at the cost of human life; this earned him the epithet "dog shogun." Despite the shogun's personality quirks, his period saw a great flowering of culture as well as a significant return to the policies of the early Tokugawa. However, this resurgence of centralizing activity did not lead to a permanent shift in the power balance nor did it initiate a long-term trend toward greater *bakufu* control. If it had, the shogun's historical image would have been rather different.

Until the end of the Tokugawa, the pendulum continued to swing between the *bakufu* and the *han*. The history and dynamics of this process have been analyzed by Harold Bolitho, who has shown that periods of *bakufu* assertiveness tended to occur under vigorous shoguns working in conjuction with trusted advisors drawn from among the shogunate's low-ranking retainers. Unencumbered by fief or vassals, totally dependent on the shogun, they became his men, free from potential conflicts of interest. Under such regimes, the high-ranking Senior Councilors, always selected from among the house daimyo (*fudai*), were treated with an outward show of respect, but in actual practice they were bypassed and disregarded. Little love was lost between the *fudai* and the new men.

When the shogun was a minor or an incompetent, control over the *bakufu* reverted back to the Senior Councilors, descendants of the Tokugawa's most favored and highly trusted vassals. The service of these vassals had formed the core of Ieyasu's strength, and accordingly he relied on their descendants for continued loyal service to his house. While these men were conscious of their heritage of special obligations toward the shogunate, they also had to consider their particular responsibilities and opportunities as daimyo. The tensions between shogunate and *han*, characteristic of the system, were mirrored in their own persons as they faced the demands of *bakufu* and *han*, demands often in conflict with each other. The usual pattern was for them to act more as daimyo than as *bakufu* officials. It was they who were responsible for the relaxation of *bakufu* policies. Such Senior Councilors did not work to strengthen the shogunate at the expense of the *han* nor were they prepared to sacrifice *han* privileges for the sake of the larger body politic. There were even cases of *han* held by incumbent Senior Councilors prohibiting the export of grain badly needed to combat famine elsewhere in Japan. Thus there were periodic shifts in the balance of power between the *bakufu* and the *han*, but the issue was never resolved completely in favor of one or the other.

The more than 250 *han* varied widely in size, local conditions, and prosperity, nor were all the lands held by a daimyo necessarily contiguous. Some domains were more easily organized than others. In general, the daimyo tended to centralize the administration of their *han* even while guarding their independence vis-à-vis Edo. Operating on a smaller scale than the *bakufu*, the *han* governments were generally more successful in controlling their lord's retainers. Accordingly, the trend for samurai to be divorced from the land and concentrated in the *han* capitals, already visible in the sixteenth century, continued strong under the Tokugawa. By the last decade of the seventeenth century over 80 percent of the daimyo were paying stipends to their samurai. Looking at the system in terms of the samurai rather than their lords, it is significant that by the end of the eighteenth century 90 percent of the samurai were entirely dependent on their stipends. Only 10 percent still retained local roots in the country districts.

Assigned to various administrative, financial, and military duties, the samurai staffed the increasingly bureaucratized administrative machinery of the domains and the *bakufu*. Many of them were now occupied more with government than with military affairs, and numerous samurai followed the urgings of the Tokugawa that, in times of peace, samurai should devote themselves to study. In this respect as in others, Ieyasu had shown the way when he showed special favor to the Confucian scholar Hayashi Razan (1583–1657), whose family continued to supply the heads of the *bakufu's* Confucian Academy. Confucianism meshed with Ieyasu's anti-Buddhist proclivities. Furthermore, in Japan as in China it proved entirely compatible with bureaucratic government. Intellectually as well as professionally, the samurai of 1800 was quite different from his ancestor of two centuries earlier. In other ways also, Japan experienced great changes during this period.

## Economic and Social Change

Economic growth was made possible by peace. Moreover, it was stimulated by a rise in demand created by the need to support the roughly 7 percent of the population that enjoyed samurai status and to meet the growing expenses of the daimyo.

Agricultural productivity increased substantially. During the Tokugawa, cultivated acreage doubled. Other factors contributing to the increase in output were improvements in technology, the practice of multiple cropping, better seed strains, and improved fertilizers. Useful knowledge was disseminated through agricultural handbooks and manuals. The development of a market network was accompanied by regional specialization in cash crops such as cotton, mulberry trees for the rearing of silk worms, indigo, tobacco, sugar cane, and so forth, but grain continued to be grown in all parts of Japan. Population rose from about 18 million at the beginning of the Tokugawa to around 30 million by the middle of the period. From then until the end of the Tokugawa there were fluctuations in population but no additional long-term increase, as hunger and disease took their toll. Historians report three major Tokugawa famines, 1732–33, 1783–87, and 1833–36, and many lesser ones. As an agricultural land, Japan remained at the mercy of the elements; too much rain or too little, a cold wave, typhoons, or locusts brought widespread starvation. In desperate times people resorted to infanticide.

With the samurai now largely removed from the land, the villages were left virtually autonomous units. They were responsible for the payment of taxes to the *han* government or, in the case of those held directly by the Tokugawa, to the *bakufu*. Within the village, neither the benefits of agricultural growth nor the burdens of taxation were shared equally: there were wide gradations in wealth and power in the countryside. Since tax reassessments were infrequent, wealthy peasants who were able to open new lands and otherwise increase their yields found their incomes rising and were able to accumulate funds with which to acquire still more land.

An increased use of money brought with it a decline in the traditional village social-economic order. Under this order the economic functions and relations of a household were determined by its standing within the extended family to which it belonged. The main house of the extended family had claims on the services of the lesser households as well as some obligations to look after the poorer members. Furthermore, the heads of the main houses formed the traditional village leadership. During the Tokugawa, wealthy villagers turned more and more to hired labor or tenant farmers to work their land. They also put their money to work in rural commerce and industry, and engaged in money-lending, vegetable oil processing, soya sauce production, and sake brewing. Since these wealthy villagers did not necessarily belong to the old main-house families, there were considerable tensions in the village.

These tensions were accentuated by economic disparities. In contrast to those who profited from the commercialization of agriculture were the poorer villagers and the landless, who shared little, if at all, in the prosperity of the countryside. They, in particular, suffered the dislocations caused by economic and social change as contractural relationships replaced those based on family. Most often they endured in silence, but there were also times when they gave vent to their resentment in uprisings. Peasant unrest was on the increase in the late Tokugawa. An indication of this change is the contrast between early Tokugawa rural uprisings, which were often led by village headmen, and those of the late period, which were frequently directed in the first place against those same wealthy and powerful village leaders. However, neither the uprisings nor the changes in agricultural technology seriously threatened the basic stability of the village. Violence was a form of protest, not a means toward revolution. Changes in agriculture increased yield but did not alter the basic pattern of rice farming with its need for intensive labor and community cooperation.

The official Confucian theory recognized only four social classes—the samurai elite, farmers, artisans, merchants—and thus failed to reflect the more complex social stratification of the countryside. Nor did moral admonitions and sumptuary laws directed at wealthy peasants (laws defining who could own what) change matters. Still less acceptable in Confucian eyes was the growing wealth of the merchant class, theoretically considered economic parasites and relegated to the bottom of society. The authorities found that they could control the merchants politically and keep them in their place socially, but they were too dependent on their services to do them permanent harm, as a class, economically. In addition to Edo, where a little over half of the population consisted of townspeople (chōnin), Ōsaka developed as a prosperous commercial and shipping center while Kyōto also continued as a major city. Han capitals, like Edo, originally founded as political and military centers, also became focuses for marketing systems and centers of trade. Privileged merchants, usually operating under license, supplied the link between the cities and the rural hinterlands, and between the local centers and the capital.

Merchants also handled the warehousing of rice and other commodities and were licensed to operate the han monopolies. Brokers converted rice into cash or credit for the sellers. Important merchants acted as financial and forwarding agents for the daimyo, handling shipments to Ōsaka for exchange or to Edo for the daimyo's consumption. They supplied banking services, dealing in the manifold *han* currencies, transferring funds, and repeatedly issuing loans to the political authorities and to hard-pressed samurai. The position of individual commercial establishments could be precarious, and in extreme cases a wealthy merchant with heavy loans out to the powerful might suffer confiscation so that the loans could go unpaid, as happened to a great Ōsaka merchant in 1705. However, these were exceptions, and government measures to force creditors to settle for less than full repayment or for the cancellation of loans simply had the effect of raising the cost of new loans, since the authorities never found a way to eliminate the need for such borrowing. The *bakufu*, daimyo, and samurai depended on the merchants as fiscal agents, and the merchants prospered; so much so, indeed, that in the second half of the eighteenth century there were over two hundred mercantile establishments valued at over 200,000 gold *ryo*, a monetary unit worth roughly a *koku* of rice. Such merchants were fully the economic equals of daimyo. Some of modern Japan's great commercial and financial empires go back to the early Tokugawa, most notably the largest of them all, the house of Mitsui founded in 1620.

As in the villages, there were also great differences in status and wealth among the town dwellers, and for every great merchant there were many more humble shopkeepers and artisans producing and repairing the various utensils required for everyday life. At the very bottom of society were people who did not belong even theoretically in the four Confucian classes. Bearing the designation *"hinin"* (non-people) were beggars, traveling performers, prostitutes, scavengers, and so forth. These were outcasts by occupation. Still worse off were pariahs* whose position beyond the pale of ordinary society was hereditary. Their origins are unknown but go back into much earlier Japanese history. Some were people engaged in butchering and tanning, tasks considered unclean. Others were simple artisans working in straw and reed (for example, making baskets, straw sandals, mats, and the like) or rural families who farmed. Considered defiling, they were discriminated against in law and kept in enforced segregation. The number of people falling into these categories is estimated at around 380,000 for the closing years of the Tokugawa.

## Classes and Values

As part of his efforts to create an enduring order Ieyasu followed Hideyoshi's example in drawing a clear line between samurai and commoner, using all the weight of the law and official ideology. On the surface at least, there was no conflict with the four classes of Confucian theory, for the character read *shih*

---

* Formerly they were known as the *eta*, but this term has become pejorative, and at present the term *burakumin* is commonly used.

in Chinese and designating the scholar (at the top of the social hierarchy) was in Japanese pronounced *samurai*. There were, to be sure, exceptions here and there to the rigid maintenance of hereditary class identity. It did happen that destitute *rōnin*, masterless samurai, dropped out of their own class, and that through marriage or adoption an alliance was sometimes formed between the family of an affluent commoner and that of an impoverished samurai, but such cases of social mobility remained uncommon. Members of the warrior class proudly cherished their status while most urbanites contented themselves with the pursuit of wealth and its attendant pleasures.

The most visible sign of the samurai's privilege was his sole right to wear swords, symbols of the samurai even after they had ceased to be his major tools. In an era of peace, when his duties were largely civil, the samurai was sent to school to attain a certain minimal mastery of Chinese learning and, more importantly, to absorb the Confucian ethic of dutiful obedience to superiors and conscientious concern for those below him on the social scale. He was also expected to acquire a degree of proficiency in at least one of the martial arts, although during the long years of peace these became "a matter of formal gymnastics and disciplined choreography"[3] rather than practical military techniques. Ideally the samurai was supposed to combine the virtues of the Confucian scholar and those of the old time *bushi* (warrior), to serve as both the moral leader and the defender of society, totally devoted to his moral duty (*giri*) even at the expense of his life.

This combination of Confucian and warrior values is apparent in the writings of Yamaga Sokō (1622–95). A student of the Confucian scholar Hayashi Razan and a devotee of the martial arts, he is considered a founding father of modern *bushidō*, a more systematized and Confucianized version of the old code of the warrior. One of his followers became the leader of the famed forty-seven *rōnin* who persevered in seeking vengeance for the wrong done their dead lord. In 1703 their carefully nurtured plans were rewarded with success as they stormed into the Kyōto mansion of the offending daimyo and killed him. They immediately achieved the status of heroes and have remained popular exemplars of the ideal of loyalty. Theirs was an act of warrior courage and devotion, but it was also illegal. For a time the shogunate debated what should be done. Then the shogun (Tsunayoshi) decided to uphold the substance of the civil law while preserving the warrior's honor: they were ordered to commit ritual suicide. Playwrights lost no time in adapting their story for the puppet theater and kabuki stage. It has remained a Japanese favorite; in the twentieth century both the cinema and the television versions were enormously popular.

The puppet theater and kabuki belonged to the world of the town dweller and not to that of the samurai proper, for whom the aristocratic Nō drama was considered more suitable. Nevertheless, the popularity of *Chūshingura* (Treasury of Royal Retainers), to give the drama of the forty-seven *rōnin* its proper title, shows that commoners could appreciate this aspect of samurai culture. And there was a good deal more on which samurai and commoners, urban and rural, could agree. The official morality was presented through periodic lectures, and was spread by the many schools which came into existence during the Tokugawa period. (By 1800, 40 to 50 percent of all Japanese males were literate to some degree.) As in China, the official Confucian values gave support to the hierarchical order within the family as well as in society at large, although the overriding emphasis on filial piety was somewhat relaxed among urban commoners.

Hierarchical principles of organization operated throughout the society as did a tendency to rank people in grades. Like samurai, even the inhabitants of the demimonde of the pleasure quarters in the great cities were carefully ranked. The great merchant establishments resembled feudal fiefs not only in their wealth but also in their expectation of lifelong loyal service from their employees, who in turn, were entitled to be treated with due paternalistic solicitude. This relationship survives in Japanese industry to this day.

Merchant and samurai held many values in common, but there were also major differences in their mores and norms. It was a mark of samurai pride to regard considerations of financial benefit as beneath contempt. Fukuzawa Yukichi (1853–1901) in his famous autobiography tells how his father took his children out of school when, much to his horror, their teacher began to instruct them in arithmetic; a subject fit only for merchants and their offspring. Merchants perceived the distinction in much the same way:

> A samurai's child is reared by samurai parents and becomes a samurai himself because they teach him the warrior's code. A merchant's child is reared by merchant parents and becomes a merchant because they teach him the way of commerce. A samurai seeks a fair name in disregard for profit, but a merchant, with no thought to his reputation, gathers profit and amasses a fortune. This is the way of life proper to each.[4]

The speaker is a rich merchant in a puppet play whose son has married the daughter of a samurai. They are addressed to his son's father-in-law, who now regrets having married his daughter outside her class.

The merchant's occupation was legitimized by the strain in Buddhism that considered all occupations as legitimate forms of devotion and, especially, by "Heart Learning" (Shingaku), a religion founded by a Kyōto merchant and philosopher, Ishida Baigan (1685–1744). Heart Learning combined elements of Shinto, Confucianism, and Buddhism to create an ethic for the artisan and merchant, reinforcing a traditional morality that stressed honesty, frugality, and devotion to one's trade. Long years of training and supervision in the system of craft and business apprenticeships helped to perpetuate values as well as skills. Meanwhile, a different ethos developed in the urban pleasure quarters officially designated by the *bakufu* as the sole areas where courtesans were permitted to ply their trade. Here a new theater and new arts flourished. However, the older aristocratic traditions also remained very much alive. Thus the distinctive character of the classes of Tokugawa Japan as well as their influence on each other is evidenced by developments in the arts.

## The Aesthetic Culture of the Aristocracy

The upper classes of the Tokugawa period inherited and perpetuated much of the Ashikaga cultural tradition. Such arts as the tea ceremony and flower arranging were continued without major change. Government officials still patronized schools of Sino-Japanese painting in the Kano line and the native style of painting in the Tosa tradition, both founded in the fifteenth century. The Nō theater continued to receive enthusiastic support; indeed, the shogun Tsunayoshi was so enamored of the art that he himself performed in Nō plays. Although new plays were written for the Nō stage, there were few fresh departures or new themes.

The variety of Tokugawa architectural style reminds us, however, that aristocratic taste was by no means uniform, that the simple aesthetics of the tea ceremony could coexist with a love for the ornate that would have delighted the men and women of Hideyoshi's time. The detached imperial villa at Katsura, outside Kyōto, is an exquisite example of studied simplicity in the use of natural materials. It is famed, not only for its architectural excellence, but equally for the subtle composition of its garden and tea houses. In striking contrast to the calculated restraint shown at Katsura is the profuse display at Nikkō, the mausoleum where Ieyasu's remains are interred. In chaotic flamboyance, its brightly painted and gilded decorations luxuriate in endless variety, free of any restraining notions of functional or aesthetic logic. A similar indulgence in decoration at the expense of form marks the final phase of the Gothic style in Europe, but the structures at Nikkō are ultimately saved from empty vulgarity by their setting in a magnificent forest, creating as Alexander Soper says, "a serene depth of shadow into which their tumult sinks without an echo."[5]

In Kyōto the aristocratic aesthetic tradition, going back to court circles in the Heian period, was given new life in a final surge of vitality. The movement was led by Hon'ami Koetsu (1558–1637), descendant of a family of professional sword repairers and sword connoisseurs, and was tinged with elements of artistic defiance, for Koetsu and his group rejected the values of the new military class, especially their continued patronage of Chinese styles in art and philosophy.

Koetsu's movement was practical, not merely intellectual. On a site north of Kyōto, granted him by Ieyasu in recognition of his prominence as a member of that city's Nichiren Buddhist community, Koetsu established an artistic and religious colony of fifty-five houses. Here a new group of artists and craftsmen sought to carry on the artistic traditions of Heian Japan. Their success is indicated by the fact that Koetsu became the arbiter of taste for his generation in the old imperial capital.

Koetsu had, of course, been trained in his family's traditional art: sword repair and connoisseurship, but his talents were far-ranging. His tea bowls are considered among the very finest achievements in Raku Ware; he made new departures in lacquer inlay work and was equally accomplished in the medium

Figure 2-3 *Thousand Cranes.* Section of hand-scroll. Painting by
Tawaraya Sōtatsu, calligraphy by Hon'ami Koetsu. Gold and silver underpainting
on paper, 341 cm × 1460 cm.

of cast metal vessels. He excelled in painting and, above all, in calligraphy. Frequently he worked in collaboration with other artists. An example is the hand-
scroll *Thousand Cranes* painted by Tawaraya Sōtatsu (d. 1643?) with Koetsu
contributing the bold and free calligraphy. The result is a decorative elegance
that does honor to the old tradition. (See Figure 2-3.)

   Sōtatsu was a younger contemporary of Koetsu and apparently related to him
by marriage. Tawaraya was the name of Sōtatsu's fan and painting atelier (that
is, workshop) in Kyōto. Although influenced by Koetsu, Sōtatsu did not actually move out of town to the former's arts village. Both men were con-
sciously influenced by the Heian tradition, which, among other things, originated the art of painting on fans. Also characteristically native in inspiration is
the softness of Sōtatsu's "boneless" technique, which avoids the strong ink
lines found in the work of the Kano painters. This style, as well as a gift for
composition, he carried over to his work on large screens. Hiroshi Mizuo[6] has
pointed out the influence of fan-painting techniques on such masterpieces as
Sōtatsu's pair of screens *The God of Wind* and *The God of Thunder.* (See Fig-

Figure 2-4 Tawaraya Sōtatsu, *God of Thunder.* One of a pair of twofold screens. Color on foil, 153.7 cm × 171 cm.

gure 2-4.) Each god swirls down from the far corner of his screen and the two screens form a single composition, with the pivot in the empty center pulling the gods in and preventing them from spinning right off the painted surface. In this and in his *bugaku* (court dance) screen pair, Sōtatsu reveals his greatness as a master of dynamic movement.

A third great pair of screens, *Waves at Matsushima*, shows Sōtatsu as a daring stylist. It is this quality of decorative stylization that is most character-istic of the third great artist in this tradition, Ogata Kōrin (1658–1716), who studied and copied Sōtatsu's works. It is from the last syllable of his name, Kō*rin*, that there was derived the term "Rimpa" ("Rin school") designating the entire school of artists. A perennial favorite is Korin's pair of iris screens. Elise Grilli compares this pair to Mozart's variations on a musical theme; the painter, like the composer, "first stating his motif, then adding variations, shifts, repetitions, pauses, leaps, intervals, changes of tempo, accents, chords, rise and fall, inversions, and more repetitions with subtle variations . . . and also with changes of mood from major to minor."[7] The theme derives from a poem in *The Tales of Ise* (ninth century), yet it is not the literary reference but Kōrin's color orchestration and his superb eye for the decorative that link him most clearly to the native Japanese tradition. (See Figure 2-5.)

# Genroku Urban Culture

Equally Japanese but drawing its nourishment from different roots was the urban culture of Edo, which reached a high point during the Genroku Era.

Technically this era name applies to a period of only sixteen years, 1688–1704, but more broadly it designates the cultural life of the last quarter of the seventeenth century and the first quarter of the eighteenth. It was a remarkable period during which some of Japan's most creative artists were at work. These include the foremost playwright, Chikamatsu (1653–1724); the most gifted traditional short story writer, Saikaku (1642–93); Moronobu (1618–94), generally credited with developing the Japanese print; and Bashō (1644–94), the Tokugawa period's finest poet, master of the haiku.

Most large cities of the world have "pleasure districts," which are more or less tolerated by the political authorities, that is, sections of town devoted to bohemian life, erotic activities, entertainment, and gambling. The cities of Tokugawa Japan were no exception. But rarely, if ever, have such quarters produced a first-rate aesthetic as they did in seventeenth-century Yoshiwara, the home of Edo's "floating world." Here, and in similar quarters in the other large towns, the Japanese tradition of aesthetic discrimination once more led to keen appreciation of stylistic excellence in dress and coiffure, in gesture and perfume, and in life itself. The worldly flair of the man-about-town was greatly admired; the spirit and elegant chic of the great courtesans who presided over this world were particularly appreciated. There was nothing but disdain for the country boor, for the gaudy or gauche.

## The Japanese Print

The life and values of this "floating world" left their imprint on Japanese culture: on fiction, and the stage, and particularly on the visual arts. A unique achievement is the *ukiyo-e,* "pictures of the floating world," perhaps the last major accomplishment of the native tradition of Japanese art.

Figure 2-5   Ogata Kōrin, *Irises.* One of a pair of sixfold screens. Color on gold foil over paper, 151.2 cm × 360.7 cm.

Figure 2-6  Okumura Masanobu,
*Girl in Transparent Dress Tying Her
Obi.* Woodcut print.

Among the precursors of the *ukiyo-e* were genre paintings such as early seventeenth-century screens depicting kabuki performances in the dry river bed in Kyōto or spring excursions to picnic under blossoming cherry trees, and *ukiyo-e* painting remained an important art even after the full development of the color woodcut. The immediate antecedents of the prints were illustrations for books such as the *Yoshiwara Pillow* (1660), a combination sex manual and "courtesan critique," combining two of the perpetually popular themes of the prints. The production of erotica, much of it unpublishable even today, and of portraits of courtesans remained two of the mainstays of the *ukiyo-e* artist.

The fullest expression of *ukiyo-e* was the Japanese print. Portraits of courtesans, theater scenes, nature subjects, or scenes from urban life were carved in wood blocks. These were then inked and printed on paper. First efforts were highly experimental. Hishikawa Moronobu, sometimes considered the founder of the Japanese print, consolidated these early efforts. His work represents the establishment of the genre.

At the beginning the prints were in black and white, but then color was added, first by hand, then by developing techniques of multicolor printing. The early prints were limited first to basic red and green, but by the middle of the eighteenth century three- or four-color prints were produced. A versatile master who contributed importantly to the development of the print was Okumura Masanobu (1686–1764). Figure 2-6 shows an eighteenth-century beauty dressed in a characteristically sumptuous kimono. In the center of the stamp at the bottom is a gourd, colored red. The text to the right of the gourd reads, "The genuine brush of the Japanese painter Okumura Masanobu. Tori-shio Street Picture Wholesale Shop." To the left, the text resumes, "Sale of red pictures and illustrated books. The red gourd seal is enclosed. Okumura."[8] The lower part of the kimono is in bright red (*beni*) while the upper part is yellowish, with the obi (sash) decorated with a brown design painted in lacquer.

Masanobu was a many-sided master whose virtuosity extended to a variety of styles and who himself influenced other artists such as the creator of the hand-colored print illustrated in Figure 2-7. This print depicts the interior of a house in Yoshiwara and features a game of backgammon. The composition experiments with the receding perspective of European painting. The print also shows such standard features of Japanese interior architecture as rooms sepa-

Figure 2-7  *Game of Backgammon in the Yoshiwara.* Attributed to Torii Kiyotada (fl. ca. 1720–50). Hand-colored woodcut print.

rated by sliding partitions, the *tatami* floor, and that sense of spaciousness created by the virtual absence of furniture.

Masanobu was a publisher as well as an artist, but usually these functions were separate, carried out by different people. Indeed, numerous people had a hand in the creation of a print. The publisher was very important. He not only distributed and sold the block prints but also commissioned them from the artist with more or less explicit instructions on subject and style, with an eye on what would sell. The artist drew the picture and designed the print, but then turned it over to the engraver and the printer. The craftsmanship of these men did much to determine the quality of the finished product. However, the artist's contribution remained central. The essential vision was his.

## The Popular Theater: Kabuki and Bunraku

A favorite pastime of the Genroku man-about-town, and an unceasing source of inspiration for the print-artist, was the popular kabuki theater, whose celebrated actors enjoyed as much acclaim and attracted as avid a group of admirers as did the most elegant of Yoshiwara courtesans. A similarly enthusiastic audience was drawn to *bunraku,* the puppet theater.

Important in the evolution of kabuki were the dances and skits presented in Kyōto during the early years of the seventeenth century by a troupe of female performers led by a priestess named Okuni. But this women's kabuki lasted only until 1629, when it was banned by the authorities. This action was not prompted by the *bakufu's* disapproval of the offstage behavior of the actress-courtesans, but by its desire to put an end to the periodic outbursts of violence that erupted as rivals competed for the favors of these ladies. Then, for two decades, young men's kabuki flourished, until it too ran into similar difficulties and was prohibited in 1652, after which date all actors were mature men. Even then kabuki continued to be under government restrictions, tolerated as a form of plebeian amusement, licensed and controlled, since, like other indecorous pleasures, it could not be suppressed.

Kabuki theater was wildly popular during the Tokugawa period, pleasing its audience with its spectacular scenery, gorgeous costumes, and expressions of violent passion. It was very much an actor's art, dominated by dynasties of actors who felt quite free to take liberties with the texts of the plays. The virtuoso performances of the great actors were greeted by shouts of approval from the audience. The raised walkway on which the actors made their way to the stage through the audience also provided a link between performers and spectators. Particularly esteemed was the artistry of the men who played the female roles. These masters devoted their lives to achieving stylizations of posture, gesture, and voice, conveying the quintessence of femininity, always operating in that "slender margin between the real and unreal,"[9] which Chikamatsu defined as the true province of art. In this sense, the *bakufu's* prohibition against female performers enriched kabuki artistically.

Chikamatsu wrote for the kabuki stage but actually preferred the puppet theater (*bunraku*), in which large wooden puppets manipulated by three-man teams acted out a story told by a group of chanters, accompanied by the three-stringed *samisen*. This theater achieved such popularity that live actors even imitated the movements of the puppets. Even after kabuki carried the day in Edo, *bunraku* continued to flourish in Ōsaka. The puppets, like the masks employed in Nō, assured that the action on stage would not be a mere mirror of ordinary life but would have a more stylized and symbolic aspect. For the playwright, *bunraku* held an added attraction in that the puppets, unlike their flesh and blood counterparts, did not meddle with his text. There are also scenes of violence and fantastic stage business which, impossible for live actors, pose no problems for figures that do not bleed and are not bound by the usual limits of human physiology. Spectacular elements helped to attract a wide audience and were used frequently by Chikamatsu in his plays on historical subjects, such as *The Battle of Coxinga*, his most famous work in this genre.

Chikamatsu also wrote more subtle domestic plays set in his own contemporary world. These center on conflicts between moral obligations (*giri*) and human emotions (*ninjō*), the irreconcilable tensions between duty and feeling. One, for example, tells of the tragic love of a small shopkeeper and a lovely courtesan whom he cannot ransom from her house for lack of funds. A frequent solution is the lovers' flight to death, a trip which provides the poetic high point of the play. Often the ladies exhibit greater strength of character than the men, but both are turned into romantic heroes through the purity and intensity of their emotions. Art imitates life, but life also imitates art: the plays produced such a rash of love suicides that the government finally banned all plays with the words "love suicide" in the title.

## Popular Prose Literature

In prose the life and mentality of the townspeople were best expressed in the writing of Saikaku, Chikamatsu's senior by eleven years. Both writers chronicled as well as molded the urban culture of the Genroku period.

The life of Saikaku's typical urbanite was centered on love and money. Although he also wrote about samurai, his best work deals with recognizable city types: the miser and money grubber, the playboy who squanders his patrimony, the young beauty mismatched to an elderly husband, the fan maker, and men and women in love with love. His erotic works, exuberant and witty, mixing humor and sex, were in keeping with the times and are of a robust directness far removed from the subtle delicacy of Heian sensibility even when, as in his later works, he recounted the darker aspects of his subject matter. In his writing, too, can be seen the conflict between duty and feeling that animated the plays of Chikamatsu. Saikaku was not only the finest of prose writers but also a prolific composer of *haikai* (light verse), a poetic genre widely popular among the townspeople.

## Tokugawa Poetry: The Haiku

A haiku is a poem with seventeen syllables arranged in three lines 5/7/5. Its antecedents are very old, for this is the form of the opening lines of the old thirty-one syllable *tanka*. It was also the usual form for the opening lines of the *renga* (linked verse). From the Ashikaga on, linked verse remained highly popular, and in the sixteenth and seventeenth centuries this was especially true of *haikai*, or light verse, enlivened by infusions of everyday speech and of humor. That some of the resulting verse departed considerably from the refined taste of the aristocracy is shown by a famous pair of links in a sixteenth-century anthology:

> Bitter, bitter it was
> And yet somehow funny.

> Even when
> My father lay dying
> I went on farting.[10]

Vulgar as it is, the second verse does contrast sharply with the first, as required in this poetic form. The popularity of *haikai* is attested by the appearance of several seventeenth-century anthologies, one of which contained verses by over 650 contributors.

The haiku came into its own thanks to the work of Matsuo Bashō, an almost exact contemporary of Saikaku. Bashō was born a samurai but gave up his rank to live the life of a commoner, earning his living as a master poet. His own pupils came from all strata of society from wealthy samurai to beggars. His finest poetry was written in the last decade of his life and shows the influence of Zen, which he began studying in 1681, but few of his haiku are overtly religious.

Not every seventeen-syllable poem is a true haiku, for the real measure of a haiku lies not in its formal structure or surface meaning but in its resonance, not in what it says but in what is left unsaid. It invites, indeed demands, that the reader himself become an artist, entering into its spirit and exploring (even creating) its manifold shades of meaning. As Harold G. Henderson observes, "really great haiku suggest so much that more words would lessen their meaning."[11] This may be true of great poetry generally, but it is especially true of what must be the shortest poetic form in any major poetic tradition.

The essence of haiku is that rather than describe a scene or feeling, it presents the reader with a series of images, which when connected in the imagination, yield a wealth of associations, visions, and emotions. Consider, for example, Bashō's best known haiku:

> An old pond
> Frog jumps in
> Sound of water.

Characteristically it presents a scene from nature composed of two elements. The first ("an old pond") supplies the setting. But more than that, it implies a

Figure 2-8
Yokoi Kinkoku,
*Portrait of Bashō.*
Ink and color on paper.

condition—the stillness of water, shaded perhaps by overhanging boughs—
that contrasts with the subsequent action ("frog jumps in"), and results in a
delightful visual image, which also has aural resonance, that is, splashing
water. The inner spring of the poem is the juxtaposition of two contrasting
elements, a juxtaposition that sets off waves in the reader's mind.

Some of Bashō's finest poems were composed on his travels and are contained in his *The Narrow Road of Oku.* One such haiku reads:

> At Yoshino
> I'll show you cherry blossoms—
> Cypress umbrella.[12]

He wrote the poem on his umbrella, and there is a gentle whimsy in Bashō's
idea of sharing the beauty of the cherry blossoms with his umbrella. The word
translated "umbrella" can also mean "hat." Figure 2-8 shows Bashō, with his
traveling hat, ready to begin his trip.

The painting itself is an example of the genre known as *haiga* in which a
*hai*ku and a painting (*ga*) were integrated. It is by Yokoi Kinkoku (1761–1832)
and exemplifies "literati painting" (*bunjinga;* Chinese, *wen-jen-hua*) in the
general manner of Yosa Buson (1716–83), the most eminent artist in this mode.
These artists looked to China for basic inspiration, although they did not limit
themselves to Chinese subjects in their art. Like their Chinese models, Buson
and other *bunjin* wrote poetry as well as painting pictures, but they represent
only one of several trends during the post-Genroku period.

# Art and Literature after the Genroku Period

After the Genroku period artists continued to work in the Genroku genres, but the classic age of the popular theater, the print, and haiku was past. Notable among the *ukiyo-e* artists of this time was the strikingly original Tōshūsai Sharaku (dates unknown), famous for the prints of actors that he turned out during a ten-month outburst of creativity in 1794–95. His prints, theatrical, psychologically penetrating, and bitterly satirical, ran counter to the tastes of his time. More appreciated in his own day was Suzuki Harunobu (1724–70), who excelled in the subtle use of color and in the freshness of his young beauties. Controversial and uneven was the prolific Kitagawa Utamaro (1754–1806), who achieved great popularity with his prints of the ladies of the "floating world." Reproduced in Figure 2-9 is one of a series on the physiognomies of women, this one illustrating the "wanton" type.

With the end of the eighteenth century, there was a falling off in the artistic quality of the figure prints, but the *ukiyo-e* tradition retained enough vigor to achieve excellence in another form—the landscape print. A master of this art was the "old man mad with painting," Katsushika Hokusai (1760–1849), an eclectic genius. He is represented here by one of his depictions of the scenery

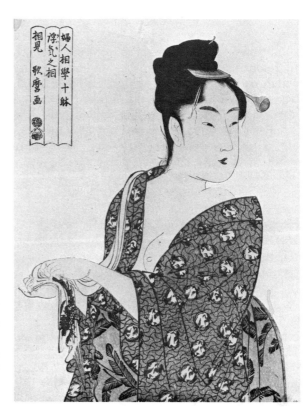

Figure 2-9
Kitagawa Utamaro,
*Beauty Wringing Out a Towel.*
Woodcut print,
37.8 cm × 25.1 cm.

Figure 2-10   Katsushika Hokusai, *The Station Hodogaya on the Tōkaidō.*
Woodcut print, 25.9 × 38.8 cm.

along the Tōkaidō, the great road leading to Edo traveled by the daimyo and
their retinues. (See Figure 2-10.) Less versatile but at his best producing works
imbued with a delicate lyricism was Andō Hiroshige (1797–1858), who was
still alive when Commodore Perry arrived in Japan (1853).

In the course of two centuries the Japanese artists and craftsmen achieved a
level of artistic and technical excellence unrivaled anywhere in the world.
They developed styles appropriate to their medium, creating an art of colors
and planes and of crisp lines, with only a hint of the old calligraphic tradition.
It was an art of great immediate appeal, not only to the Tokugawa townspeople
and country folk looking for a souvenir of their trip to the great city, but also to
European artists who, later in the nineteenth century, found they had much to
learn from this art.

Prose and poetry continued to be produced and enjoyed by a wide audience,
although they did not again reach the quality attained by Saikaku or Bashō.
Perhaps the best loved of the later haiku poets was Kobayashi Issa (1763–
1827). He achieved a wide identification with nature and showed sympathy for
even the humblest of animals and insects.

> Lean frog,
>    don't give up the fight!
> Issa is here![13]

## Intellectual Currents

During the Tokugawa period, Buddhism, out of favor politically, showed little intellectual or religious creativity. But secular theorizing flourished as never before, as Japanese scholars assimilated and developed the various strands of what in the West is known as Neo-Confucianism, and explored alternate ways of thought. As a result, the Tokugawa achievement in philosophy and the originality and complexity of the period's intellectual history are unmatched by any previous period of Japanese history.

In Japan, as in China, the appeal of Neo-Confucianism was varied and profound. In it, many found religious fulfillment, intellectual stimulation, and moral inspiration. Sung Neo-Confucianism enjoyed the support of the *bakufu* from the time of Hayashi Razan and Ieyasu down to the end of the Tokugawa era. Important as this was, the effectiveness of official patronage was limited, since in Japan, unlike China, there was no civil service examination system to enforce orthodoxy, and Japan's political divisions provided diverse sources of patronage for scholars. When the shogunate, in its most restrictive period, officially prohibited heterodox doctrines in 1790, it had little permanent effect on Japanese intellectual life.

Among the outstanding exponents of Sung Confucianism after Razan was Yamazaki Ansai (1618–82), a stern and forceful teacher who stressed "devotion within, righteousness without" and was so dedicated to Chu Hsi that he said he would follow the master even into error. Some Tokugawa Confucians were extreme Sinophiles, but Ansai did not let his veneration for the Chinese philosophers interfere with his love for Japan. When asked the supremely hypothetical question: what should be done were Confucius and Mencius to lead a Chinese invasion of Japan, he answered that he would capture the two sages and put them at the service of his own land. Deeply interested in Shinto, Ansai attempted to fuse Confucian ethics with Shinto religion. Other major orthodox thinkers include the moralist Kaibara Ekken (1630–1714) and Muro Kyūsō (1658–1734). Most Confucians justified the shogunate by incorporating it into the hierarchy of loyalty, but Kyūsō argued that the Tokugawa ruled by virtue of a heavenly mandate. He found it necessary to defend Sung philosophy against increasingly vigorous challenges from other schools, the Japanese counterparts of the varieties of Confucianism that developed on the continent after the Sung.

The man considered the founder of the Wang Yang-ming school in Japan was Nakae Tōju (1608–48). Like the Chinese philosopher, he stressed the inner light of man and insisted on the importance of action. It was his lofty and unselfish character especially that attracted the admiration of contemporaries and of later activist intellectuals. His best known disciple, Kumazawa Banzan (1619–91) ran into political difficulties, not because of his unorthodox philosophic ideas, but for unconventional policy recommendations, including a relaxation of the daimyo's attendance requirements in Edo to save expenses. He was traditionally Confucian in his concern for the well-being of the peasantry and in his lack of sympathy for the merchant class, as reflected in his advocacy of a return to a barter economy using rice in place of money.

In Japan, as in China, Chu Hsi's philosophy was repudiated by those who denied the authority of the Sung scholars and insisted on going back to the classical sources. This was the stance of Yamaga Sokō, whose connection with *bushidō* was noted earlier in this chapter. Others who argued that the Sung thinkers had distorted the authentic Confucian message differed on the contents of that message. A great teacher and moralist known for his humanism and his emphasis on *jen* (loving benevolence) was Itō Jinsai (1627–1705), who drew inspiration from the *Analects:*

> The *Analects* is like the boundless universe which men live in without comprehending its full magnitude. Enduring and immutable throughout the ages; in every part of the world it serves as an infallible guide. Is it not, indeed, great![14]

Philosophically Itō rejected the Neo-Confucian distinction between *li* and *ch'i,* two concepts by then as much at home in Japan as in China.

Another attack on the Sung philosophy of principle (*li*) was made by Ogyū Sorai (1666–1728), who insisted on going back not just to the *Analects* but to the earlier Six Classics, according to him the genuine repositories of true doctrine. A complex, many-sided thinker, in his political thought he represented the tough-minded pole of Confucianism with its emphasis on rites and institutions. Like some of the seventeenth-century Chinese critics of Sung philosophy, Ogyū Sorai was interested in practical as well as theoretical subjects. A prolific writer, he dealt with many topics: philosophy and politics; literature, linguistics, and music; military science; and economics.

## Historiography and "National Learning"

A perennial field of Confucian scholarship was the study of history, but in the Tokugawa period it was not only Confucian scholars who were interested in the Japanese past.

Hayashi Razan, himself, began work on a history of Japan which was completed by his son and accepted as the official history of the shogunate. Among those who made major contributions to scholarship was the statesman and scholar Arai Hakuseki (1657–1725), noted for his careful attention to the evidence and a willingness to reexamine traditional beliefs.

A different emphasis appeared in *The Great History of Japan* (*Dainihonshi*), which was begun in the seventeenth century under the sponsorship of the Lord of Mito, Tokugawa Mitsukuni (1628–1700), but not completed until the twentieth century. Mitsukuni, a grandson of Ieyasu, enlisted the services of a Chinese emigree Ming loyalist, Chu Shun-shui (1600–1682). The resulting history was highly moralistic and loyalist in tone, exalting the Japanese imperial house. Since, in theory, the shogun himself derived his authority from this source, there was nothing inherently anti*bakufu* in Mito historiography. That its focus on the emperor rather than on the shogun was potentially subversive, however, was shown later when it provided an emperor-centered source for nationalistic sentiments, and eventually it supplied ammunition for the anti-*bakufu* arguments of the movement to "restore the emperor," which culminated in the Meiji Restoration of 1868.

Interest in Japan's past often went hand in hand with a new appreciation of the Shinto tradition, attracting Confucians such as Yamazaki Ansai and stimulating non-Confucian scholars of the "National Learning" variety. This school began with the study of old Japanese literature, such as the *Man'yōshū*, and its greatest exponent made the study of the *Kojiki* his life's work. This was Motoori Norinaga (1730–1801) who believed that the *Kojiki* mirrored the age of the *kami*, whom he accepted as both real and irrational. According to Motoori, it is arrogant not to recognize the limitations of the human intellect and wrong to attempt to understand the *kami* rationally. Indeed the irrationality of the old legends was a sign of their truth, for "who would fabricate such shallow sounding, incredible things?"[15] For Motoori, the *kami* are the starting point: "People try to explain matters in the age of *kami* by referring to human affairs whereas I have understood human affairs by referring to the matters in the age of *kami*."[16] Supreme among the *kami* was the Sun Goddess. In Motoori, absolute faith in the *kami* did not conflict with fine empirical scholarship, and his belief in nonrational understanding enabled him to appreciate the old Heian aesthetic, and to value especially the feminine sensibility of that age. Motoori left a dual heritage, academic philology and ideological nativism. Among those who drew on the latter aspect of Motoori's thought the most influential was Hirata Atsutane (1776–1843), an ultranationalist whose narrow Japanism proved attractive to many in the nineteenth and twentieth centuries.

While some scholars emphasized the native tradition, a small number of their compatriots were fascinated by what they could learn about the West by way of the limited contact Japan maintained with the Dutch at Nagasaki. These masters of "Dutch Learning" are considered in the next chapter, but we should note here that implicit in their intellectual orientation was dissatisfaction with the Tokugawa seclusion policy, which stood in the way of their learning more about Western civilization and prevented them from traveling overseas. Meanwhile, by stressing the royal line, Mito Confucians and National Learning scholars also helped to weaken the *bakufu* ideologically. Even orthodox Confucianism did not really require a shogun or a *bakufu*.

Thus by 1800 there were fissures in the Tokugawa's intellectual, as well as political and economic, foundations, but it was a new challenge from abroad that eventually destroyed them.

# Notes

1. David John Lu, *Sources of Japanese History* (New York: McGraw-Hill, 1974), 1:189. Trans. from Ōkubo Toshiaki et al., eds., *Shiryo ni yoru Nihon no Ayumi* (Japanese History Through Documents), *Kinseihen* (Early Modern Period) (Tokyo: Yoshikawa Kobunkan, 1955), pp. 40–41.

2. Harold Bolitho, *Treasures Among Men: The Fudai Daimyo in Tokugawa Japan* (New Haven: Yale University Press, 1974), p. 17.

3. Ronald P. Dore, *Education in Tokugawa Japan* (Berkeley and Los Angeles: University of California Press, 1965), p. 151.

4. Donald Keene, *Four Major Plays of Chikamatsu* (New York: Columbia University Press, 1961), p. 151.

5. Robert Treat Paine and Alexander Soper, *The Art and Architecture of Japan* (Baltimore: Penguin Books, 1955), p. 274.

6. See Hiroshi Mizuo, *Edo Painting: Sotatsu and Korin*, trans. John M. Shields (New York and Tokyo: Weatherhill/Heibonsha, 1974), pp. 40–41.

7. Elise Grilli, *The Art of the Japanese Screen* (Tokyo and New York: John Weatherhill, 1970), pp. 111–12.

8. Willy Boller, *Masterpieces of the Japanese Color Woodcut; Collection W. Boller*, Photo. by R. Spreng (Boston: Boston Book and Art Shop, [1950?]), p. 20.

9. Attributed to Chikamatsu by his friend Hozumi Ikan. Hozumi's account of Chikamatsu's views has been translated by Donald Keene as "Chikamatsu on the Art of the Puppet Stage," in Donald Keene, ed., *Anthology of Japanese Literature* (New York: Grove Press, 1955), p. 389.

10. Ryusaku Tsunoda, Wm. Theodore de Bary, and Donald Keene, comps., *Sources of Japanese Tradition* (New York: Columbia University Press, 1958), p. 454.

11. Harold G. Henderson, *An Introduction to Haiku* (New York: Doubleday, 1958), p. 8.

12. Calvin French, *The Poet-Painters: Buson and His Followers*, exhibition catalog (Ann Arbor: University of Michigan Museum of Art, 1974), p. 132.

13. Henderson, *An Introduction to Haiku*, p. 133.

14. Tsunoda et al., *Sources of Japanese Tradition*, p. 419.

15. *Ibid.*, p. 524.

16. Shigeru Matsumoto, *Motoori Norinaga, 1730–1801* (Cambridge: Harvard University Press, 1970), p. 81.

東亞與現代歐洲
初次之接觸

# 3 East Asia and Modern Europe: First Encounters

**The Portuguese in East Asia**
**The Jesuits in Japan**
**The Closing of Japan**
**Dutch Learning**
**The Jesuits in China**
**The Rites Controversy**
**The Decline of Christianity in China**
**The Canton System**

The early contacts between post-Renaissance Europe and East Asia had nothing like the impact of those that were to follow in the nineteenth century, but they form part of the essential historical background of modern times. Moreover, study of the earlier period allows us to compare Chinese and Japanese responses to very similar foreign stimuli. Perhaps most significant is the fact that the ultimate failure of the early missionaries and merchants left East Asia comparatively isolated from developments in Europe just when, for the first time in the history of the globe, what was happening in Europe would inexorably affect all humanity.

When maritime Europeans first reached East Asia in the sixteenth century, they encountered very different situations in China and in Japan. In the early fifteenth century the Ming had sent out maritime expeditions that ranged as far as Arabia and the east coast of Africa, but it subsequently abandoned maritime activity so completely that Chinese waters became the domain of pirates and smugglers. Meanwhile the dynasty's foreign relations were conducted in terms of the traditional tributary system administered by the Ministry of

**61**

Rites. The Ming, like their predecessors and like the Ch'ing, were confident that China was the center of the world, culturally as well as geographically, and that the emperor, "the Son of Heaven," was responsible for all humanity. In actual practice, there had been times when Chinese dynasties had to deal on an equal basis with rival states. However, the theory of Chinese superiority and centrality was too strong to be discarded, founded as it was on China's historical experience. The less civilized peoples, then, had the privilege of coming to Peking to pay obeisance to the emperor. On these occasions they presented tribute and, as befitted "the Son of Heaven," the emperor gave them handsome presents in return. Such tribute missions were attractive to peoples such as the Koreans and the Japanese because they provided occasions for profitable trade, but the Chinese court placed restrictions on the number of missions it would accept.

The situation, both intellectually and politically, was very different in Japan. With their long and fruitful history of borrowing from abroad, the Japanese were less apt to dismiss the foreign as barbarous. The process of Japanese unification was just getting under way and indeed Europe helped to accelerate, although it did not determine, the process. Within ten years after the Portuguese introduced firearms to Japan in 1543, the daimyo of Western Japan were using imported and domestic muskets in their armies. Oda Nonunaga employed the new weapons effectively and won a crucial battle in 1575 through the superior firepower of his three thousand musketeers. It is no wonder that initially the Japanese were more open to the Europeans than were the Chinese.

## The Portuguese in East Asia

The pioneers of European expansion in East Asia, as elsewhere at this time, were the Portuguese, who reached India in 1498, China in 1514, and Japan in 1543. Having wrested control of the seas from their Arab rivals, they established their Asian headquarters at Goa (1510), a small island off the coast of West India. They then went on to capture Malacca (1511), a vital center for the lucrative spice trade, located on the straits which separate the Malay Peninsula from Sumatra. It was the desire to break the Arab spice monopoly that supplied the economic motive for this initial European expansion. Spices were highly valuable relative to their bulk and weight. Easily transported and fetching a high price, they formed an attractive cargo. And there was an assured market for them in Europe, where they added flavor to an otherwise dull diet and made meat palatable in an age when animals were slaughtered in the fall for want of sufficient fodder to sustain them through the winter. They were also used in medicine and in religious ceremonies.

Prospects for trade were hampered, however, by the fact that Europe, needing pepper and other spices from Asia, had no European commodities of equal importance to offer in return. Initially, therefore, Portuguese adventurers in East Asia supported themselves by a mixture of trade and piracy—like their

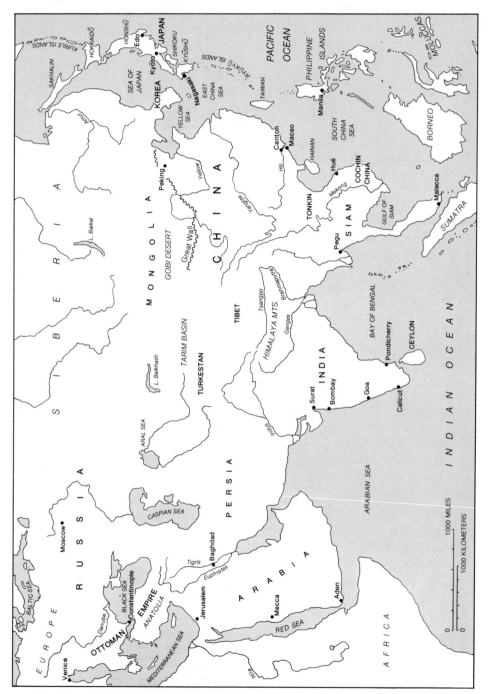

Figure 3-1   **Eastern Europe and Asia in the Sixteenth and Seventeenth Centuries**

Japanese predecessors in these waters. They were able to do this successfully because they had superior ships and weapons, and were better seamen. Eventually, however, they became the primary carriers of goods in the East Asian trade, taking goods from one Asian country to another—Southeast Asian wares to China, Chinese silk to Japan, and Japanese silver to China. Their profits from this trade were used to purchase spices and other products for European markets. (See map, Figure 3-1.) But before this trade could prosper, they had to secure entry to China and Japan. This posed problems quite different from those they had encountered in seizing a small island off the coast of politically divided India or in driving the Arabs from Malacca.

In China they got off to a very bad start. Not waiting for official permission to trade, they engaged in illegal commerce and even built a fort on Lintin Island, located at the mouth of the river that connects Canton to the sea. Their unruly behavior did not endear them to the Ming authorities, and served to confirm the opinion that these "ocean devils" were a new kind of barbarian. The outrageous behavior of the Portuguese traders was further embellished by the Chinese imagination. When the Portuguese bought kidnapped Chinese children as slaves, the Chinese concluded that their purpose was to eat them. They long continued in the firm belief that they were dealing with barbarous child eaters. Not just a popular rumor held by the ignorant, this belief found its way into the official history of the Ming dynasty.

The first Portuguese envoy to China not only failed to obtain commercial concessions; he ended his life in a Cantonese prison. It was a most inauspicious beginning. But the Portuguese would not leave, and their superiority on the seas made it impossible for the Chinese to drive them out. A *modus vivendi* was reached in 1557 when the Portuguese were permitted to establish themselves in Macao in exchange for an annual payment. There the Portuguese administered their own affairs, but the territory remained under Chinese jurisdiction until Macao was ceded to Portugal in 1887. Today Macao and nearby Hong Kong still remain under European control, vestiges of European overseas empire.

## The Jesuits in Japan

Trade and booty were not the only objectives of the Europeans who ventured into Asian waters. Missionary work was also important: mid-sixteenth-century Goa boasted some eighty churches and convents. From the beginning, the missionary impulse provided a strong incentive as well as religious sanction for European expansion; and it was the missionary rather than the trader who served as prime intermediary between the civilizations of East Asia and the West from the sixteenth to the twentieth centuries.

Among the early missionaries, the great pioneers and the most impressive leaders were members of the Society of Jesus (Jesuits). Founded in 1540, this tightly organized and rigorously disciplined religious order formed the vanguard of the Catholic Counter-Reformation. They were the "cavalry of the church," prepared to do battle with Protestant heretics in Europe or the heathen in the world beyond. Along with its stress on martial discipline and intensive religious training, the Society was noted for its insistence on intellectual vigor and depth of learning. The latter included secular as well as sacred studies, and the ideal Jesuit was as learned as he was disciplined and devout.

In 1549, less than ten years after the founding of the Jesuit order, St. Francis Xavier (1506–52), one of the original members of the Society, landed in Kyūshū. This was just six years after the Japanese had encountered their first Europeans, some shipwrecked Portuguese who landed on the island of Tanegashima. Xavier was well received and was soon able to establish cordial relations with important men in Kyūshū. First impressions on both sides were favorable. Xavier and his successors liked the Japanese; he himself referred to them as "the best [people] who have yet been discovered."[1] Likewise, the Japanese were impressed by the strong character and dignified bearing of the European priests. The Jesuit combination of martial pride, stern self-discipline, and religious piety fitted well with the ethos of sixteenth-century Japan. Nor did the Christian religion seem altogether strange. On the contrary, initially Christianity, brought to Japan from Goa, seemed just another type of Buddhism. It was similar in some of its ceremonies to those found in Buddhism, and it was difficult for the early priests to convey the subtleties of theology, to explain the difference between God and the cosmic Buddha, for example, or to distinguish Paradise from the Pure Land. At last, the Jesuit fathers concluded that the devil, in all of his malicious cleverness, had deliberately fashioned Buddhism to resemble the true faith so as to confound and confuse the people.

The initial meeting of the Jesuits and the Japanese was facilitated by the similarities in their feudal backgrounds. In Japan, Xavier and other Europeans found a society that resembled their own far more than did any other outside Europe. "The people," wrote Alessandro Valignano (1539–1606), "are all white, courteous and highly civilized, so much so that they surpass all the other known races of the world."[2] Only the Chinese were to receive similar praise— and, indeed, to be regarded as "white." Donald Lach has summarized the qualities the Jesuits found to admire in the Japanese: "their courtesy, propriety, dignity, endurance, frugality, equanimity, industriousness, sagaciousness, cleanliness, simplicity, discipline, and rationality."[3] On the negative side, aside from their paganism, the Jesuits were appalled at the prevalence of sodomy among the military aristocracy and the monks. They criticized the Japanese propensity to suicide and also found fault with the "disloyalty of vassal to master, their dissimulation, ambiguity, and lack of openness in their dealings, their bellicose nature, their inhuman treatment of enemies and unwanted children, their failure to respect the rule of law, and finally their unwillingness to give up the system of concubinage."[4] Nevertheless, the similarities between Japanese culture and their own gave the Jesuits high hopes for the success of their mission.

In their everyday behavior the Jesuits tried to win acceptance by adapting themselves to local manners and customs, as long as these did not run counter to their own creed. "Thus," Valignano observed, "we who come hither from

Europe find ourselves as veritable children who have to learn to eat, sit, converse, dress, act politely, and so on."[5] They learned how to squat Japanese style, learned to employ the Japanese language with its various levels of politeness, and mastered the art of tea—the Jesuit dwelling was usually equipped with a tea room so that their guests could be properly entertained. C. R. Boxer has pointed out that the Christian monks came from a land with rather different standards of personal cleanliness: "Physical dirt and religious poverty tended to be closely associated in Catholic Europe where lice were regarded as the inseparable companions of monks and soldiers."[6] But in Japan the devoted monks even learned to wash, a major concession to Japanese sensibilities. Still there were limits: Valignano could not bring himself to endorse the Japanese custom of taking a hot bath every day. That would really be going too far!

Careful attention to the niceties of etiquette was required of the Jesuit fathers in their strategy of working from the top down. It was their hope to transform Japan into a Christian land by first converting the rulers and then allowing the faith to seep down to the populace at large. The purpose of their labors was not to Europeanize Japan or China, but to save souls. They realized that the enthusiastic support of the ruling authority would be an invaluable asset, while without at least the ruler's tacit approval they could do nothing.

This approach met with considerable success in Kyūshū, where they converted important local daimyo, who ordered their people to adopt the foreign faith. Although there were numerous cases of genuine conversion, some daimyo simply saw the light of commerce, adopting a Christian stance in the hope of attracting the Portuguese trade to their ports. On at least one occasion it happened that the great Portuguese ship did not appear; they promptly turned their backs on the new faith. The Jesuits themselves became involved in this trade and also in politics. For seven years they even held the overlordship of Nagasaki, granted to them by a Christian daimyo.

Xavier and the monks who came after him realized that real progress for their mission depended on the will not only of local Kyūshū daimyo but of the central government. Xavier's initial trip to Kyōto came at an unpropitious time —the city was in disorder. But Nobunaga soon became a friend of the Jesuits. Attracted by their character and interested in hearing about foreign lands, perhaps he was also happy to talk with someone not part of the hierarchical order which he himself headed. This personal predilection also coincided nicely with reasons of state. It was consistent with his hostility toward the Buddhist orders and with his desire to keep the trading ships coming in. Hideyoshi was similarly well disposed toward the foreign religion. He liked dressing up in Portuguese clothes, complete with rosary, and he once said that the only thing which kept him from converting was the Christian insistence on monogamy.

The political and economic success of the Jesuits helped the spread of Christianity, but power, or the semblance of power, always entails risks. There was the danger that the ruler might perceive the activities of the monks not as assets bolstering his own position but as liabilities, actual or potential threats to his authority. A portent of future disaster came in 1578 when Hideyoshi is-

Figure 3-2 Namban screen. Section of a sixfold screen, 164 cm × 365.6 cm, Kano Mitsonobu school, ca. 1610. Namban Bunkakan, Ōsaka.

sued an order expelling the monks. Eager to encourage trade and not really feeling seriously threatened, Hideyoshi did not enforce the decree, but it foreshadowed the persecutions which were to begin in earnest thirty-six years later, in 1614.

There was a surge of popularity for things Western, for instance, "Southern Barbarian Screens," showing the giant black ships of the foreigners. The barbarians themselves were depicted as exceedingly tall and rather ungainly, with sharp, long noses and red hair, wearing the ballooning pantaloons that formed the standard fashion in the Portuguese empire. (See Figure 3-2.) Other scenes, based on paintings from Europe, depicted various barbarian topics: the battle of Lepanto, an Italian court, European cities, maps of the world, not to mention religious subjects. While some artists painted European subjects in Japanese style, others experimented with Western perspective and techniques of shading to produce three-dimensional effects. Nor were Western motifs limited to painting. Western symbols were widely used in decoration, a cross on a bowl, a few words of Latin on a saddle, and so forth. In a letter written in 1594 a missionary described the foreign fad. Writing of non-Christian daimyo he stated:

They wear rosaries of driftwood on their breasts, hang a crucifix from their shoulder or waist, and sometimes even a handkerchief. Some, who are especially kindly disposed, have memorized the Our Father and the Hail Mary, and recite them as they walk in the streets. This is not done in ridicule of the Christians, but simply to show off their familiarity with the latest fashion, or because they think it good and effective in bringing success in daily life. This has led them to spend no small sums in ordering oval earrings bearing the likeness of Our Lord and the Holy Mother.[7]

This was a passing fashion, but some new products entered Japan to stay, and new words were added to the language, for instance *tabako* (tobacco), *pan* (bread), and *karuta* (playing cards). Another Portuguese contribution was tempura, the popular Japanese dish prepared by deep fat frying vegetables and seafood dipped in batter. The Japanese word is derived from *temporas* (meatless Friday).

## The Closing of Japan

Despite the order of 1578, Western influences continued to enter Japan: religious, commercial, cultural. The situation was complicated, however, by the arrival of other Europeans. The first Spaniards arrived from the Philippines, headquarters of the Spanish in Asia, in 1587; and the first Franciscans came from Manila in 1592. By the early 1600s, representatives of the Protestant Dutch and English had also arrived. Although the prospects for trade were attractive, the proliferation of foreigners was disturbing. The various nations competed with each other for Japanese trade. The Dutch and English sought to encourage Japanese suspicions of their Catholic rivals. Moreover, the Japanese were not unaware that the Spanish role in the Philippines was that of colonial master, and that the Spaniards might harbor imperial ambitions with regard to Japan as well. Finally, the Japanese became increasingly concerned that growing Catholic influence might prove subversive of internal stability. The Jesuits had been unable to avoid a degree of involvement in Japanese politics; now the Franciscans, working among the poor, seemed to threaten the traditional social order.

The Jesuits had sought to carry out their missionary activities within the framework of Japanese society and social values. They associated primarily with the upper classes, with a view to working their way down. The Franciscans were suspicious of the Jesuit approach. They were much less well informed concerning conditions in Japan and also much less discreet in their work. Instead of associating with the samurai, the Franciscans worked among the poor and forgotten, the sick and miserable, those at the very bottom of society. The Jesuits did not disguise their contempt for the ignorance and poverty of the Franciscans, the "crazy friars" (*frailes idiotas*) as they called them, and these sentiments were heartily reciprocated by the friars, who scoffed at Jesuit pretensions.

Rivalry between the Portuguese and the Spanish, between Goa and Manila, compounded the instability of the situation. On one hand, Manila presented the possibility of a new source of profitable trade; on the other, the colonization of the Philippines demonstrated the imperialistic ambitions of the Europeans and the connection between Christian evangelism and colonialism. It was an omen of things to come when Hideyoshi, in 1597, crucified six Franciscan missionaries and eighteen of their Japanese converts after the pilot of a Spanish ship driven ashore in Japan reportedly boasted about the power and ambitions of his king. Ieyasu was at first friendly to the Christians, but he too turned against them. In 1606 Christianity was declared illegal, and in 1614 he undertook a serious campaign to expel the missionaries.

By 1614 there were over 300,000 converts in Japan. The destruction of Christianity was long and painful. Tortures, such as hanging a man upside down with his head in a pit filled with excrement, were used to induce people to renounce their faith. Before it was all over, there were more than 3000 recognized martyrs, of whom less than 70 were Europeans. Others died without achieving martyrdom. In 1637–38 there was a rebellion in Shimabara, near Nagasaki, against a daimyo who combined merciless taxation with cruel suppression of Christianity. Fought under banners on which Christian slogans were written in Portuguese, and led by some masterless samurai, it was a Christian version of the rural uprisings characteristic of the century of warfare before Nobunaga. In its suppression, some 37,000 Christians lost their lives.

Persuasion as well as violence was employed in the campaign against Christianity. Opponents of Christian dogma argued that the idea of a personal creator was absurd and asked why, if God was both omnipotent and good, he should have tempted Adam and Eve and devised eternal punishment in Hell for non-Christians even though they led exemplary lives. According to Christian teaching, even the sage emperors Yao and Shun would end in hell. The First Commandment was attacked as leading to disobedience of parents and lord; a loyal retainer should accompany his lord even into hell.

Such arguments suggest that the Japanese saw Christianity as potentially subversive, not only of the political order, but of the basic social structure, for it challenged accepted values and beliefs and demanded a radical reappraisal of long-revered traditions. Its association with European expansionism posed a threat from abroad, and, as exemplified by the Shimabara Rebellion, it also harbored the seeds of radical disruption at home. Thus the motivation for the government's suppression of Christianity was secular not religious. The shogunate was not worried over the state of its subjects' souls, but it was determined to wipe out a dangerous doctrine. An indication that the government's concerns were secular is provided by the oath of apostasy demanded of all former Christians. In it the recanters had to swear that if they had the slightest thought of renouncing their apostasy, "then let us be punished by God the Father, God the Son, and God the Holy Ghost, St. Mary, and all the Angels and Saints."[8] Thus they had to take a Christian oath that they no longer believed in Christianity! The persecutions succeeded in destroying all but a small underground group of secret Christians, who passed from generation to generation a faith increasingly infused with native elements. Meanwhile every Japanese family was registered with a Buddhist temple, and once a year the family head had to swear that there were no Christians in his household. Incidentally, the resulting demographic data, the most complete for any premodern society, constitutes an invaluable resource for modern scholars.

Not only Christianity but all foreign influences were potentially subversive, including trade that would tend to the advantage of the Kyūshū daimyo rather than the Tokugawa. With this in mind, the Tokugawa *bakufu* gradually closed the country off from the rest of the world. The Spaniards were expelled in 1624, one year after the voluntary withdrawal of the English. In 1630 Japanese were forbidden to go overseas or to return from there or to build ships capable of traveling long distances. The Portuguese were expelled after the Shimabara Rebellion on the grounds of complicity in that uprising. When they sent an embassy in 1640, its members were executed. The only Europeans left were the Dutch (see Figure 3-3), and in 1641 they were moved to the tiny artificial island of Deshima in Nagasaki harbor. There they were isolated and virtually confined, as in a prison. The annual Dutch vessel to Deshima and some limited commerce with China was all that remained to link Japan to the outside world.

## Dutch Learning

Once a year the Dutch were granted an audience with the shogun, thereby providing the Japanese an opportunity to satisfy their curiosity about the exotic:

Figure 3-3    *A Dutch Dinner Party.* Nagasaki color print, 22 cm × 33 cm.

He [the shogun, mistaken for the emperor by the Dutch chronicler] order'd us to take off our Cappa, or Cloak, being our Garment of Ceremony, then to stand upright, that he might have a full view of us; again to walk, to stand still, to compliment each other, to dance, to jump, to play the drunkard, to speak broken Japanese, to read Dutch, to paint, to sing, to put our cloaks on and off. Meanwhile we obey'd the Emperor's commands in the best manner we could. I join'd to my dance a lovesong in High German. In this manner, and with innumerable such other apish tricks, we must suffer ourselves to contribute to the Emperor's and Court's diversion.[9]

This is from a report of the embassy of 1691 or 1692. The "Red-haired Barbarians," as the Dutch were commonly known, continued to be objects of wild rumor. But they also drew the attention of serious scholars after the *bakufu*, in 1720, permitted the importation of books on all subjects except Christianity. One result was the influence of Western art which we have already noted in the discussion of the *ukiyo-e*, and in the eighteenth century, there were also Japanese painters who produced reputable Western-style works in oil.

Most remarkable were the achievements of a small group of truly dedicated scholars who wrestled with the difficulties of the Dutch language and laboriously made the first translations, compiled the early dictionaries, and wrote the first treatises on Western subjects, initially concerning geography, astronomy, medicine, and other sciences. Thus Shiba Kōkan (1738–1818), the first in Japan to produce copper engravings, was fascinated by the realistic aspect of Western art, by its ability to portray objects as they appear to the eye. The practical, scientific value of Western studies had already been recognized by Arai Hakuseki, and to Shiba, too, this is what was of value in the Western tradition. For spiritual nourishment the Japanese continued to turn to their own heritage, thus foreshadowing the nineteenth-century formula "Eastern ethics—Western science." Thanks to *bakufu* policy, they knew little about Western political, philosophical, or religious thought.

By the end of the eighteenth century, there were also scholars of Dutch Learning who turned to matters political, military, and economic at considerable personal risk. Hayashi Shihei (1738–93) was arrested for defying a *bakufu* prohibition by publishing a book dealing with political issues: he advocated defense preparations against the threat he saw impending from abroad. Takano Chōei (1804–50) and Watanabe Kanzan (1795–1841) were persecuted for disagreeing with the *bakufu's* seclusion policy and ended as suicides. Honda Toshiaki (1744–1821), who wanted to turn Japan into the England of the East, complete with mercantile empire, escaped persecution by not publishing his ideas. Nevertheless, these scholars produced a legacy on which their successors would build when exclusion proved untenable.

# The Jesuits in China

The beginnings of the Jesuit missions in China and Japan were closely linked. Xavier himself hoped to begin the work in China. He realized this was not only a great project in itself but also a major step in the Christianization of Japan, providing an answer to the question he was constantly asked there: "If yours is the true faith why have not the Chinese, from whom comes all wisdom, heard of it?"[10] But Xavier died before he could reach his goal. Three further Jesuit attempts to enter China also failed. Then Valignano established a special training center in Macao so that missionaries could study the Chinese language and culture in preparation for work in China. As in Japan, it was Jesuit policy in China to concentrate on gaining the support and, if possible, conversion of the upper classes. To this end, they once more went as far as possible to accommodate themselves to native sensibilities and ways of doing things.

Again, as in Japan, the strong character and attractive personalities of the first missionaries were of great importance in gaining them entree. The outstanding pioneer was Matteo Ricci (1551–1610). A student of law, mathematics, and science, he also knew a good deal about cartography and something of practical mechanics. Once in the East, he was also able to master the Chinese language and the classics. Ricci's ability to make maps and build clocks aroused the interest of the Chinese scholars, while his command of Chinese classical learning impressed them. Slowly Ricci made his way in Chinese officialdom. At last in 1601, after eighteen strenuous years, Ricci was received in an imperial audience and won permission for himself and his colleagues to reside in the capital. (By this time they had discarded the Buddhist robes worn by Jesuits in Japan and had adopted Confucian dress as more acceptable to the Chinese.) In Peking he was able to win over and convert a number of prominent men. By the time Ricci died in Peking in 1610, the mission was well established in the capital and accepted by the government. Ricci's body was laid to rest in a plot donated by the emperor.

During the period when the Japanese were persecuting Christians with increasing ferocity, the Jesuits in China labored fruitfully, building on the foundations laid by Ricci. They were particularly successful in demonstrating the superior accuracy of European astronomical predictions. Thereby they succeeded in displacing their Muslim and Chinese competitors and established themselves in the Bureau of Astronomy. This was an important and prestigious office, reflecting the importance of the heavenly bodies in Chinese thought. Jesuit gains in this area were solidified by the work of Adam Schall von Bell (1591–1666), a German Jesuit who was a trained astronomer and served as chief astronomer in Peking. Schall von Bell also assisted in casting cannon for the Ming, although the weaponry did not save the dynasty.

The Jesuits made some notable converts among the literati, particularly during the troubled years of the declining Ming. Most notable was Hsü Kuang-ch'i (Paul Hsü, 1562–1633), who translated Euclid's *Elements* and other works on mathematics, hydraulics, astronomy, and geography, thereby becoming the first Chinese translator of European books. With the help of such men, Western science and geography were made available to China, but European influence remained limited. There was a social and intellectual crisis in China during the early seventeenth century, but this stimulated fresh currents within the Chinese tradition rather than inducing men to explore foreign ideas.

Thus, when Li Chih, one of the most forceful and independent Late Ming think-ers, met Ricci, he was impressed with the Jesuit's personality but saw no merit in his proselytizing mission.

The triumph of the Manchus did not seriously disrupt Jesuit activity. Schall von Bell was retained by the new dynasty as their astronomer, and he was fol-lowed by the Belgian Jesuit, Ferdinant Verbiest (1633–88), the last of the trio of great and learned missionary fathers. Verbiest, like Schall von Bell, cast can-non and in other ways won the favor of the great Manchu emperor, K'ang-hsi (r. 1662–1722). A good account of Jesuit activities at court comes from the em-peror's own brush:

> With Verbiest I had examined each stage of the forging of cannons, and made him build a water fountain that operated in conjunction with an organ, and erect a wind-mill in the court; with the new group . . . I worked on clocks and mechanics. Pereira taught me to play the tune *"P'u-yen-chou"* on the harpsichord and the struc-ture of the eight-note-scale, Pedrini taught my sons musical theory, and Gheradini painted portraits at the Court. I also learned to calculate the weight and volume of spheres, cubes, and cones . . .[11]

The Emperor accepted the Jesuits' science with alacrity and took their quinine for the sake of his health. He also discussed religion with them, but here they were less successful: "I had asked Verbiest why God had not forgiven his son without making him die, but though he had tried hard to answer I had not un-derstood him."[12] Nevertheless, the middle years of his reign were the high-point of early Christianity in China, after which it declined. By 1700 there were no more than 300,000 Christians in China, roughly the same number as in much smaller Japan a century earlier.

In both cases the missionaries were there on sufferance, dependent on the good will of the authorities. And in China, as they had earlier in Japan, divi-sions between the Europeans themselves strongly contributed to their un-doing.

## The Rites Controversy

The controversy that brought an end to the missionary activity in China cen-tered on the Jesuit policy of accommodation, which was opposed by the rival orders, particularly and vigorously by the Dominicans. It revolved around the question of the proper attitude a Christian should adopt toward Confucianism, its doctrines and practices. This kind of dispute had not arisen in Japan, where Catholic fathers of all orders agreed in their condemnation of Buddhism and Shinto and in their absolute refusal to allow their converts to have anything to do with such heathen religions.

In China, however, the basic strategy used by Ricci and followed by his suc-cessors was to accept the teachings of Confucius, "the prince of philosophers." They argued that they had come, not to destroy Confucius, but to make his teachings complete, capping his doctrines with the truths of revealed religion. Like Chinese thinkers intent on using Confucius in new ways, the Jesuits also discarded and condemned previous interpretations and commentaries on the classics. They attacked Neo-Confucianism and developed new theories of their own. In their enthusiasm for the classics, the Jesuits turned Confucius into a religious teacher. Some members of the order went as far as to trace the origin of the Chinese people to the eldest son of Noah. The most extreme even claimed to find Christian prophecies in the *I Ching.* Meanwhile, the Dominicans held that the ancient Chinese were atheists and argued against the Jesuit portrayal of Confucius as a deist. The resulting literature greatly influenced Western understanding of Chinese philosophy. At its best it was a serious effort by Europeans to understand Chinese thought in what they believed to be universally valid terms.

The status of Confucius and the acceptability of the classics were major issues for missionaries operating in a society dominated by the Confucian examination system. Even more troublesome, however, was the related problem posed by Confucian observances. Were the ceremonies in veneration of Confucius, held in the temples of Confucius throughout the land, acts of religious devotion and therefore anathema to a Christian? Or were they social and political in character, secular expressions of respect for China's greatest teacher? Even more important, what about the rites performed by every family in front of the tablets representing its ancestors? Was this a worship of the departed spirits and thus the most iniquitous idolatry? Or did these acts of commemoration to one's forebears merely convey a deep sense of filial piety? Were the two kinds of ceremonials civic and moral in nature, or were they religious, and therefore sacrilegious? Consistent with their stand on Confucianism, the Jesuits claimed the ceremonies were nonreligious and therefore permissible. The Dominicans disagreed.

The issue was fiercely debated, for much was at stake. Theology aside, it is easy to see the practical reasons for the Jesuit standpoint. To exclude Christians from performing the ceremonies for Confucius would be to exclude them from participation in Chinese political life. Worse still, to prohibit the ritual veneration of ancestors would not only deprive Chinese Christians of their sense of family but would make them appear as unfilial, immoral monsters in the eyes of their non-Christian fellows. If Christianity rejected the classics and advocated this kind of nonconformist behavior, it would be turned into a religion subversive of the Chinese state and society. Persecuted and condemned, Christianity would be unable to reach many souls, who would thus be deprived of their chance for salvation.

But the Dominicans could muster strong counterarguments. Why should a church that condemned Protestant Christianity condone Confucian Christianity? The issue was not the acceptability of Christianity to the Chinese but whether the salvation of souls would be fatally jeopardized by tolerating false Confucian doctrines. In their eyes, nothing could be allowed to interfere with the Christian's sacred duty to maintain the purity of the faith.

Figure 3-4 Anonymous, *Portrait of Hsiang Fei.* Mid-eighteenth century. Palace Museum, Peking.

## The Decline of Christianity in China

The question, "when does Christianity cease to be Christianity" was to reappear in the nineteenth century and is not all that different from the question, "when does Marxism cease to be Marxism," which agitates some thinkers today. Such questions are never easy to resolve and perhaps only true believers need grapple with them. Be that as it may, in the papacy, the church had a source of authority that could rule on what was acceptable and what was not. The process of reaching a decision was complicated and involved. What is important here is that the outcome went against the Jesuits. In 1704 the pope favored the Dominicans, and in 1742 a decree was issued that settled all points against the Jesuits. This remained the position of the Catholic Church until 1938. Grand and powerful emperors like K'ang-hsi, however, saw no reason to abide by the judgment of Rome as to what was fitting for their realm. They naturally favored the Jesuit point of view. In the end, the pope would send only those missionaries the emperor of China would not accept.

Some missionaries remained in China after the break, including the Jesuit Guiseppe Castiglione, who served as court painter for half a century, 1715–66. Among other things, he designed a miniature Versailles for the Summer Palace, destroyed in the nineteenth century. Michael Sullivan has described his fusion of artistic traditions as a "synthetic style in which with taste and skill and the utmost discretion, Western perspective and shading, with even an occasional hint of chiaroscuro, were blended to give an added touch of realism to painting otherwise entirely Chinese in manner."[13] Figure 3-4 shows a painting in the European manner done at the Chinese court. It is an anonymous portrait of an imperial concubine playing at being a European peasant girl. Just as Louis XV of France sometimes amused himself by having his courtiers and their ladies assume Chinese dress, the Ch'ing emperor Ch'ien-lung enjoyed exotic Western costume on occasion.

Regardless of the Rites Controversy, the Christians also had opponents in China itself, motivated by the usual combination of self-interest and conviction. There was no Chinese counterpart to Nagasaki: instead, Canton and the surrounding area, the part of China most exposed to the Europeans, already at this time took a negative view of the foreigners. Christianity was proscribed in 1724. Some churches were seized and other acts of persecution occurred, but the suppression of Christianity was not as thorough as that which had taken place in Japan. This was probably because there was no Chinese equivalent to the Shimabara Rebellion—at least not yet. Not until the nineteenth century did the potential of Christianity as an ideology of peasant revolt become evident in China. By the end of the eighteenth century, the number of Chinese converts had been reduced to about half their number at the beginning of the century.

## The Canton System

As with Japan, Europeans came to China to trade as well as to win converts, but, unlike the Japanese, the Chinese authorities were not attracted by the prospects of commerce. During the years when the Ch'ing was consolidating its power, there was little Sino-European trade. Then from 1685 to 1759 there was multiport trade, while the British East India Company and others tried out Chinese markets and the Chinese gradually developed the components of what became the Canton System (1760–1842). It is called the Canton System because trade was now confined to the single port of Canton where a special area was set aside for the warehouses (called "factories") of the foreign traders. The traders were allowed to reside there but were not allowed to bring their wives and settle down.

In all their transactions foreign traders were required to deal with a group of Chinese merchants who had been granted a monopoly of foreign trade. These merchants belonged to the Cohong, an association for firms (or hong) established for that purpose. In theory the Cohong was composed of a maximum of thirteen hong, but in practice there were only seven or eight such establishments, supervised by an imperial official who usually squeezed a good deal of personal profit out of his position. Each foreign ship was placed under the responsibility of a particular hong, which handled not only commercial matters but also saw to it that duties were paid and that the foreigners conducted themselves properly. Under this system, the foreigners were not granted direct access to Chinese officials, nor was allowance made for government-to-government relations. On the British side the prime agent was the East India Company, which enjoyed a monopoly of trade between England and China.

These arrangements suited the Chinese more than they did the English. In 1793 the English sent Lord Macartney to Peking to negotiate an expansion of trade and the opening of European-style diplomatic relations, but he failed to get the system changed and matters continued as before.

Much research remains to be done on the influence of early Western contacts on Chinese thought and civilization. There was certainly some stimulus from the West, but more frequently the Western influence seems not to have progressed much beyond the appreciation of European exotica, such as clocks and other mechanical devices. The influence was much stronger the other way, for the Jesuit reports on China were well received in Europe and helped to create the image of an ideal China dear to the *philosophes* of the European Enlightenment. In the arts there was an enthusiasm for things "Chinesy"—*chinoiserie*. Neither *chinoiserie* in Europe nor *namban* ("Southern Barbarian") art in Japan may have reached great aesthetic heights, but in their relative openness to foreign stimulus, there is a certain resemblance between Europe and Japan (but missing in China) in this period of first encounters.

## NOTES

1. C. R. Boxer, *The Christian Century in Japan* (Berkeley and Los Angeles: University of California Press, 1951), Appendix I, p. 401. Also quoted in Donald F. Lach, *Asia in the Making of Europe*, Vol. I, *The Century of Discovery* (Chicago: University of Chicago Press, 1965), p. 284, also pp. 663–64.

2. Boxer, *The Christian Century in Japan*, p. 74.

3. Lach, *Asia in the Making of Europe*, 1:728.

4. *Ibid.*

5. Quoted in Boxer, *The Christian Century in Japan*, p. 75.

6. Boxer, *The Christian Century in Japan*, p. 214.

7. Yoshitomo Okamoto, *The Namban Art of Japan* (Tokyo and New York: John Weatherhill, 1972), p. 77.

8. Boxer, *The Christian Century in Japan*, p. 441.

9. E. Kaempfer, quoted in Donald Keene, *The Japanese Discovery of Europe*, revised edition (Stanford: Stanford University Press, 1969), p. 4.

10. A. H. Rowbotham, *Missionary and Mandarin* (Berkeley and Los Angeles: University of California Press, 1942), p. 46.

11. Quoted in Jonathan Spence, *Emperor of China* (New York: Alfred A. Knopf, 1974), pp. 72–73.

12. *Ibid.*, p. 84.

13. Michael Sullivan, *The Meeting of Eastern and Western Art* (New York: New York Graphic Society, 1973), pp. 66–67.

# PART TWO
# China and Japan in the Modern World

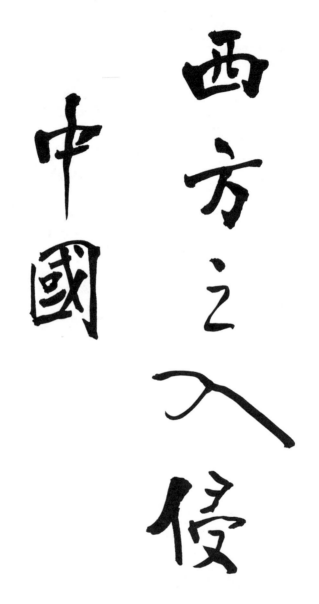

中國　西方之入侵

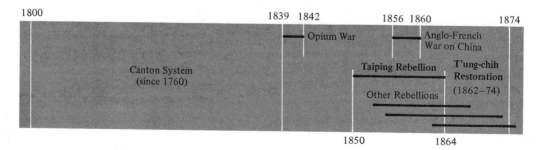

1800　　　　　　　　　　　　　　　　1839　1842　　　　　1856　1860　　　　　1874

Opium War　　　　　Anglo-French
　　　　　　　　　　War on China

Canton System
(since 1760)

Taiping Rebellion　　T'ung-chih
　　　　　　　　　　　Restoration
　　　　　　　　　　　(1862–74)
Other Rebellions

1850　　　　　　　　　　　1864

# 4 The Intrusion of the West: China

In the nineteenth century China and Japan had to deal with a world in which Europe was supreme. Intellectual, political, and economic forces at work since the Renaissance had steadily transformed European civilization and produced unprecedented wealth and power. The process was accelerated in the late eighteenth century by industrialization and the French Revolution, explosions that set off tremors reaching eventually all around the globe. During the century, the economic revolution created new wealth, new technology, new appetites, and new problems, first in England and then in other countries of Western Europe. The nation-state offered its citizens more, but it also made greater demands on them than had the old empires in Europe or elsewhere. It was also a tumultuous period of intense economic competition, stringent national rivalries, bitter class conflicts, and sharp clashes between old values and ideas and new. Yet few Europeans questioned the superiority—moral, intellectual, economic, and political—of their civilization.

The new Europe, powerful and aggressive, challenged all other civilizations. Ultimately it left its mark everywhere. Those areas which, like East Asia, did not become outright colonies still had to face the challenge of European intrusion. In the process, they initiated changes that ultimately were to be just as profound as those which took place in colonized lands. On the other hand, terms such as "the intrusion of the West" or "westernization" should not be allowed to obscure the fact that the "West" itself was changing, and that it was a pluralistic civilization differing in its various national manifestations.

To understand developments in China and Japan, it is necessary to bear in mind what was happening in Europe at the same time. Militarily the nineteenth century was the age of sea power, and Great Britain was the major sea power of the age. Thus Britain was able to create the largest of the European overseas empires, and it was Britain which took the lead in dealings with nineteenth-century China, and initiated a new era in Chinese history by forcing China to abandon the Canton System and to open her doors to the West. (See map, Figure 4-1). The pivotal event was the Opium War (1839–42).

## Breakdown of the Canton System: Sino-British Tensions

As already noted, Chinese contact with the West in the eighteenth century was limited to commerce; there were no diplomatic relations. Even commerce was strictly limited by the Canton System, that is, all Western commerce with China was carried out through the port of Canton (see Figure 4-2), Western residence in Canton was strictly regulated, and the terms of trade allowed Western merchants to deal with only a small group of Chinese firms (the Cohong), which had a monopoly on foreign trade. Western traders, used to more open commercial dealing in other parts of the globe, and chafing under the lack of respect shown to Westerners in China, became increasingly resentful. Thus, well before the actual outbreak of war, the limitations imposed by the Canton System seemed likely to lead to a clash between the increasingly aggressive Europeans and a Manchu-Chinese Empire past its prime.

Exacerbating political and economic tensions was the incompatibility of the Chinese and English views of themselves and their respective places in the world. Both were supremely self-confident and proud of their own civilizations. Both were narrowly culture-bound. Thus when the Macartney mission arrived in Peking in 1793 in the hope of broadening the terms of trade and initiating treaty relations with China, the presents sent to Emperor Ch'ien-lung

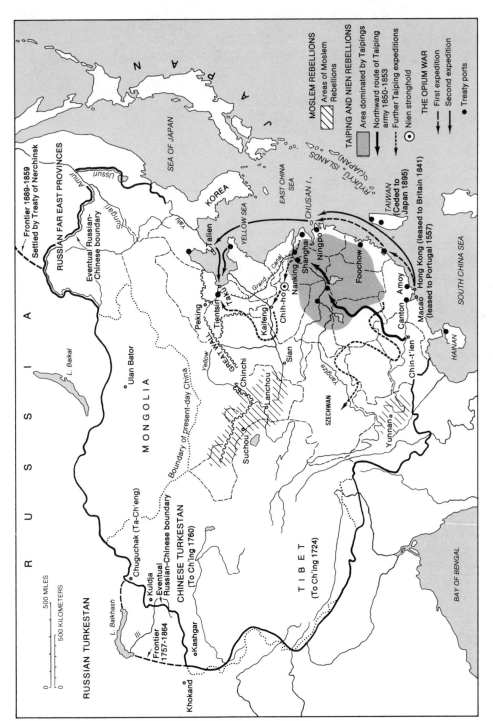

Figure 4-1 **China in the Nineteenth Century**

Figure 4-2 *Canton, ca. 1760.* Artist unknown. Gouache on silk, 47.7 cm × 73.7 cm. One of four creating a panorama of the waterfront. Peabody Museum, Salem.

by England's George III were promptly labeled as "tribute" by the Chinese. Ch'ien-lung responded to the English monarch by praising his "respectful spirit of submission"[1] and, in the gracious but condescending language appropriate for addressing a barbarian king residing in the outer reaches of the world, turned down all his requests, political and economic. He saw no merit in the English request for representation in Peking nor did he favor increased trade, "As your Ambassador can see for himself, we possess all things. I set no value on objects strange or ingenious, and have no use for your country's manufactures."[2]

On the English side, Lord Macartney refused to perform the ceremonial kowtow expected of barbarian envoys and performed by the Chinese themselves toward their superiors and by the emperor toward Heaven. Macartney was confident that the Chinese would perceive "that superiority which Englishmen, wherever they go, cannot conceal."[3] In the end, the Chinese allowed an informal audience that did not require the full kowtow (three kneelings and nine prostrations), but in their self-assessments the Chinese and the English remained as far apart as two peoples have ever been. The English sent another mission to China in 1816 headed by Lord Amherst, but he did not even get an audience at court.

The British motive for coming to China was and continued to be primarily economic. In contrast to China's self-sufficiency and Emperor Ch'ien-lung's disdain for foreign products, there was a Chinese product in great demand in Britain. This was tea. First imported in tiny quantities in the late seventeenth century, tea was initially taken up as an exotic beverage with medicinal properties, then popularized as a benign alternative to gin, and finally was considered a necessity of English life, with the East India Company required by Act of Parliament to keep a year's supply in stock at all times. Tea imports reached fifteen million pounds in 1785 and double that amount in the decade preceding the Opium War. Not only did the East India Company depend on the income from the tea trade, the British government also had a direct stake in tea, since about one-tenth of its entire revenue came from a tax on Chinese tea. Not until the 1820s did the Company begin experimenting with tea growing in India, and it was many years before Indian tea provided an alternative to the tea of China. The importance of Chinese tea extended even to American history: it was Chinese tea that was dumped from East India Company ships in the famous Boston Tea Party (1773).

The British problem was how to pay for this tea. There was no market for British woolens in China, and the "sing-song" trade in clocks, music boxes, and curios was insufficient to strike a balance of trade. Until the last third of the century, the sale of British imports covered 10 percent or less of the cost of exports, with the rest paid for in cash and precious metals. Unable to find anything European that the Chinese wanted in sufficient quantity, the English turned toward India and the "country trade." This was the term for trade between India and various places from the Indian Ocean to the China seas conducted under East India Company license by the private firms of British subjects. Money obtained in Canton by the "country traders" was put on deposit there for the Company against bills of exchange on London. In this way, England, India, and China were connected by a trade and payments triangle.

## The Opium Trade

Until 1823 the largest commodity imported to China from India was cotton, but this never reached the volume necessary to balance the trade. That was accomplished by opium. Opium had long been used for medicinal purposes, but the smoking, or more accurately, the inhaling of opium fumes through a pipe, began in the seventeenth century. The spread of the practice was sufficient to provoke an imperial edict of prohibition in 1729, but this and subsequent efforts to suppress the drug were unsuccessful and opium consumption continued to increase. Distributed by a network of illegal wholesalers and retailers with the connivance of dishonest officials, it spread among people of diverse occupations but proved particularly attractive to Chinese soldiers and government underlings. The drug was debilitating and habit forming. (See Figure 4-3.) Withdrawal was excruciatingly painful. Over time the addict developed a tolerance for opium and needed more and more of the drug to achieve a "high." The addict became a slave to opium. Thus, to pay for tea the Chinese were sold a poison. Since the opium was brought to China by country traders, the East India Company disclaimed responsibility for the illegal traffic in China. At the same time, however, it profited from the sale of opium in India where it monopolized the Bengal crop (Patna) and did what it could to control West Indian production (Malwa). In India itself, where the British as the paramount power felt a certain sense of responsibility, consumption of opium for nonmedicinal purposes was strictly prohibited.

The Chinese market for opium developed at such a pace that the balance of trade was reversed. During the 1820s and 1830s silver to pay for opium imports seems to have left China in large quantities. This, in turn, helped cause a decline in the exchange rate between copper coinage and silver, which upset the basis of the Chinese monetary system. Thus, what began as a public health problem now became a fiscal problem as well. In 1834, the Company's monopoly of the China trade was abolished by the British government. This opened the gates of trade still wider on the British side, resulting in an increased flow of opium to China, and an increased flow of silver out of China. Thus abolition of the Company's monopoly made the problem worse.

Abolition of the Company's trade monopoly was a victory for English advocates of free trade, who were as antagonistic to restraints on trade abroad as they were at home. The immediate effect in China was to put an end to the system of Cohong-Company relations in Canton. Now in place of the Select Committee of the East India Company, the British side was represented by an official of the crown. To initiate the new relations, Britain sent out Lord Napier as First Superintendent of Trade with instructions to establish direct contact with the Ch'ing viceroy, to protect British rights, and to assert jurisdiction

Figure 4-3   Opium Smokers.

over Englishmen in Canton. To accomplish these aims, he was ordered to use a moderate and conciliatory approach. Napier, however, more ambitious than diplomatic, immediately took an adamant stand on the issue of direct communication with the viceroy. He violated Chinese regulations by not waiting in Macao for permission to proceed to Canton and by sending a letter rather than petitioning through the hong merchants. With neither side willing to back down, the impasse developed into a showdown. All Chinese employees were withdrawn from the British community, food was cut off, and trade was stopped. Napier finally withdrew to Macao, where he died. This all took place in 1834. Unfortunately, in the ensuing lull no progress was made toward finding a new *modus vivendi* between the two sides.

For a brief moment the Chinese considered legalizing opium, but in 1836 the government decided on suppression instead. Dealers and addicts were prosecuted with great vigor, and imprisonments and executions were widespread, with the result that the price of opium dropped precipitously. This program was well under way when Lin Tse-hsü (1785–1850), a man of excellent reputation and demonstrated intellect and ability, arrived in Canton in March 1839. As imperial commissioner, he was charged with stamping out the drug trade once and for all.

In Canton, Lin Tse-hsü conducted a highly successful campaign against Chinese dealers and consumers. He also severely punished the corrupt officials who had connived at the trade. To deal with the foreign source of the opium, he appealed to Queen Victoria: "Suppose there were people from another country who carried opium for sale to England and seduced your people into buying and smoking it; certainly your honorable ruler would deeply hate it and be bitterly aroused."[4] He also admonished the foreign merchants, and he backed moral suasion with force.

What Lin demanded was that the foreigners surrender all their opium and sign a pledge to refrain from importing the drug in the future at the risk of confiscation and death. To effect compliance, he used the same weapons of isolating the foreign traders employed successfully in 1834 against Napier. Elliot, the British Superintendent of Trade, took a fateful step in response when he ordered the British merchants to turn their opium over to him for delivery to the Chinese authorities. By this act Elliot relieved the merchants of large amounts of opium they had been unable to sell because of the efficacy of the Chinese prohibitions, and he further made the British government responsible for eventual compensation. No wonder that the merchants enthusiastically dumped their opium: 21,306 chests were delivered to Lin Tse-hsü. It took the Chinese twenty-three days to destroy it all.

In England great pressures were exerted on the government by firms interested in the China trade demanding prompt and vigorous military action. Lin meanwhile, pleased with his victory, continued to press Elliot on the issue of the bonds or pledges, but here he did not succeed. The Superintendent of Trade argued that it was against British law to compel the merchants to sign the bonds and that the imposition of the death penalty without the benefits of

English judicial procedure was also contrary to British law. What was at stake here was the issue of British jurisdiction over British subjects, a source of Anglo-Chinese friction since 1784, when the British had refused to submit to Chinese justice. The issue came to the fore again in the summer of 1839 when a group of English sailors killed a Chinese villager in the Canton hinterland. Refusing to turn the men over to Lin Tse-hsü, Elliot tried them himself, but when they were returned to England the men were freed, since the home court ruled that Elliot had exceeded his authority.

The first clash of the war took place in November 1839, when the Chinese tried to protect one of the only two ships whose captains had signed the bond despite Elliot's stand and now wanted to trade. When a British ship fired a shot across the bow of the offending vessel, the Chinese intervened with twenty-one war junks, which, however, were no match for the foreign ships. In December trade with the British was stopped, and on January 31, 1840, a formal declaration of war was announced by the governor-general of India acting in the name of the home government.

## The Opium War (1839–1842)

In June 1840, the British force, consisting of sixteen warships, four armed steamers, twenty-seven transports, a troop ship, and 4000 Irish, Scottish, and Indian soldiers, arrived in China. First the British blockaded Canton and then they moved north. They were fired on at Amoy while trying to deliver a letter from Prime Minister Palmerston under a white flag of truce, a symbol the Chinese did not understand. They then seized Chusan Island, south of the Yangtze estuary, and Ting-hai, the chief city there. The main body of the fleet sailed another 800 miles north to Pei-ho, near Tientsin, where Palmerston's letter was accepted. By this time the emperor had lost confidence in Lin Tse-hsü whose tough policy had led to military retaliation. Lin was dismissed, disgraced, and exiled to Ili in Central Asia. His place was taken by the Manchu prince Ch'i-shan (d.1854), who pursued a policy of flattery and accommodation to get the British to return to Canton for further negotiations. This they did in September 1840.

When the negotiations with Ch'i-shan in Canton turned out unsatisfactorily from the British point of view, they resumed military operations, with the result that in January 1841 Ch'i-shan was forced to sign the Convention of Ch'uan-pi, which provided for the cession of Hong Kong, an indemnity payable to Britain, equality of diplomatic relations, and the reopening of Canton. Both Ch'i-shan for the Ch'ing and Elliot for the British thought they had done very well, but neither government accepted their work. The Chinese emperor was indignant at how much had been conceded while Palmerston fumed that Elliot had demanded too little. The reactions of the Chinese and British governments showed all too clearly how far apart they still were in their appraisal of the situation. Caught in the middle were the negotiators. Like Lin Tse-hsü earlier,

Figure 4-4  *Foreign Devil.*
A Chinese sketch, ca. 1839.

now Ch'i-shan came to feel the imperial displeasure: his property was confiscated and he was sent to exile on the Amur. Elliot too was dismissed; his next position was as consul-general in Texas.

In the renewed fighting Canton was besieged in February 1841, but the siege was lifted on payment of a ransom of 6 million Spanish silver dollars. However, before their departure the British experienced the growing hostility of the local population. They were attacked by a body of troops organized by the local gentry. Although militarily ineffective, the attack was an indication of popular sentiment. (See Figure 4-4.)

In August Elliot was relieved by Pottinger, and the last phase of the war began when the British moved north, occupying Amoy in August and Ting-hai in October. Reinforcements were sent from India, increasing the naval force and bringing troop strength up to 10,000. With this force Pottinger continued the campaign, advancing up the Yangtze until his guns threatened Nanking. In Nanking on August 29, 1842, the treaty was signed that brought the war to a close. It was a dictated peace imposed by the Western victor on the vanquished Chinese.

## The Treaty System

The Treaty of Nanking (together with the supplementary Treaty of the Bogue, October 1843) set the pattern for treaties China later signed with the United States and France in 1844, established the basic pattern for China's relations with the West for the next century, and supplied the model for similar treaties imposed on Japan. The Treaty of Nanking marked the end of the Canton System. The Cohong monopoly was abolished. Five ports—Canton, Amoy, Foochow, Ningpo, and Shanghai—were opened to Western trade. Britain received the right to appoint consuls to these cities, where British merchants were now allowed to trade and to reside together with their families. The treaty also stipulated that henceforth official communications were to be made on a basis of equality. This implied adoption, even if reluctant, of the European instead of the Chinese practice of international relations.

The Chinese were forced to pay an indemnity of 21 million Spanish silver dollars. Of this amount 12 million was for war expenses, in keeping with the normal European practice of forcing the loser to pay for the cost of a war. Another 6 million was paid as reparations for the opium handed over to Commissioner Lin, while the remaining 3 million went to settle the debts owed by the hong merchants to British merchants, thus liquidating another aspect of the old Canton System.

An important provision of the treaty established a moderate Chinese tariff of from 4 to 13 percent on imports, with an average rate of 5 percent. The Chinese, whose statutory customs levies had been even lower, did not realize that by agreeing to this provision they were relinquishing the freedom to set their own tariffs. On the British side there was the conviction that, as Adam Smith had taught, the removal of constraints on trade would benefit all by allowing everyone to concentrate on what he did best.

The British, having acquired an empire in India, with all the burdens of government that it entailed, did not seek to create another in China. Trade not territory was their aim. But they did demand and obtain a Chinese base. Hong Kong Island, at that time the site of a tiny fishing village, was ceded to them in perpetuity. Well-located and with an excellent harbor, it developed into a major international port.

The issue of legal jurisdiction over British subjects was settled by the Treaty of the Bogue, which provided for extraterritoriality, that is, the right of British subjects to be tried according to British law in British consular courts. The British, having only recently reformed their own legal system, were convinced of its superiority. There were precedents in Chinese history for allowing "barbarians" to manage their own affairs, but in modern terms extraterritoriality amounted to a limitation on Chinese sovereignty.

The Treaty of the Bogue also provided for most-favored-nation treatment. This obliged China to grant to Britain any rights China conceded in the future to any other power. Its effect was to prevent China from playing the powers off against each other. It meant that once a nation had obtained a concession it automatically was enjoyed by all the other states enjoying most-favored-nation status.

In the 1844 treaties the United States and France also received this status. In the American treaty China agreed to allow for the maintenance of churches and hospitals in the treaty ports, and to treaty revision in twelve years, while the French won the right to propagate Catholicism.

The status of the opium trade was left unsettled in the original treaties, and American agreement to outlaw smuggling did not slow down the growth of opium traffic, which was legalized under the next round of treaty settlements, 1858–60. From the annual 30,000 chests a year prior to the Opium War, this trade reached 87,000 chests in 1879 and then declined as native Chinese production of opium increased. British opium imports were down to about 50,000 chests when in 1906 the Ch'ing took strong measures against the drug. British imports finally came to a stop in 1917, but opium smoking remained a serious social problem until the early 1950s.

For China the treaties solved nothing. A particularly ominous development was the permission granted foreign gunboats to anchor at the treaty ports, for when additional ports were opened it gave foreign powers the right to navigate China's inland waterways. The cumulative effect of the treaties was to reduce China to a status of inequality, forcing her to relinquish powers that no European state would have surrendered.

## China and the West (1842–1860)

The Chinese were slow to realize the full implications of the Treaty of Nanking, and only a very few men at court had any inkling of the dimensions of the "barbarian" challenge. The best "barbarian" experts could suggest was for China to acquire "barbarian" arms and to employ the old diplomacy of playing off one "barbarian" against another. Less well informed officials suggested that future military operations take advantage of the supposed physical peculiarities of the "barbarians," for example, their stiff waists and straight legs, which made them dependent on horses and ships, or their poor night vision.

Negotiations were handled by the governor-general of Kwangtung and Kwangsi. The first governor-general managed the English by charm and conciliation, "sharing their cup and spoon to hold their hearts,"[5] but he was later replaced by a more hard-line, intransigent official. Frustrated in attempts at local negotiation, the British demanded direct representation in Peking. They also pressed for treaty revision because the opening of the new ports had not led to the anticipated increase in trade. Behind the demands for freer trade was the persistent belief that only artificial restrictions prevented the development of a giant market in China for British textiles and other products.

One cause for friction between the English and the Chinese was the repeated postponement of the opening of Canton in view of the strong antiforeign feeling of its people. The continuation of the opium trade did not help matters, and Chinese antagonism toward Europeans was reinforced by the development of a new commerce in Chinese laborers. These men were often procured against their will, crowded into dismal "coolie" vessels, and transported as contract laborers to work the plantations of Cuba and Peru. The boom set off by the discovery of gold in California in 1848 also brought Chinese immigrants to the United States, but they came as free laborers, their passage organized by Chinese merchants. By 1852 there were 25,000 Chinese in the American West, and by 1887 there were twice that number in California.

There were some efforts at cooperation during these years. With Chinese consent, the British set about suppressing piracy. More important was the establishment of the Foreign Inspectorate of Customs in Shanghai in 1854, after the Ch'ing officials had been ejected by rebels. The Inspectorate became responsible for the collection of tariffs and the prevention of smuggling. By the new treaties of 1858, its authority was extended to all treaty ports, and it became an important source of support for the dynasty.

Despite such collaboration, however, there remained more discord than harmony, and in 1856 war broke out once more. The immediate cause of the war was the Arrow Affair. The Arrow was a Chinese-owned but Hong Kong-registered lorcha, a vessel with a Western hull but Chinese rigging, which although flying the British flag was boarded by Chinese officials, who seized twelve Chinese men whom they charged with piracy. When the governor general returned the men but refused to apologize and guarantee there would be no repetition of the event, the British responded by seizing Canton. Then they withdrew, and there was a lull in the fighting while the British were occupied fighting a war in India set off by the Sepoy Mutiny of 1857 (sepoys were Indian soldiers). When the war in China was resumed in December 1857, however, the English were joined by the French.

As in the first war, the Europeans again moved north, and again the first attempt at peace failed, since the Ch'ing emperor refused to ratify the British and French Treaties of Tientsin negotiated in 1858. Hostilities then recommenced. This time the allies entered Peking itself in 1860, and Elgin, the British commander, vented his anger by burning down the imperial summer palace. In October the Conventions of Peking were signed to supplement the Treaties of Tientsin, which now also took effect. In addition to the usual indemnity, China was forced to open eleven new ports, to grant rights to travel in the interior, and to allow foreign envoys to reside in Peking. In 1860 the French also surreptitiously inserted into the Chinese text a provision granting missionaries the right to buy land and erect buildings in all parts of China.

## Russian Gains

The peace agreements were secured through the mediation of the Russian ambassador to Peking, who used the opportunity to consolidate the gains Russia had made to date and to obtain new concessions for his country. Under Peter the Great and Catherine the Great, Russia's land empire had expanded into the area west of the Pamirs known as Russian Turkestan, and in 1851 Russia obtained trading privileges and the right to station consuls at Kuldja and Chuguchak (Ta-ch'eng) in the Ili region of Chinese Turkestan east of the Pamirs. Now Kashgar, southwest of Kuldja, and Urga (Ulan Bator) in Outer Mongolia were also opened to them.

The most massive Russian gains, however, were in the Northeast. In the Amur region Nikolai Muraviev, governor-general of Siberia, had been putting pressure on the Ch'ing since 1847. Now, in 1860, the entire area north of the Amur was ceded to the Russians, who also received the lands east of the Ussuri River, which were incorporated into the Russian Empire as the Amur and Maritime Provinces. In the latter Muraviev founded Vladivostok ("Ruler of the East," in Russian). Russia also now received most-favored-nation status. The gains Russia made at this time remain a source of conflict between the Russians and Chinese today.

# Internal Crisis

The encroachments of the foreign powers, serious as they were, constituted only one of the threats facing the dynasty. An even greater danger to the regime developed internally as the government proved unable to deal with long-term problems that would have taxed the ingenuity and energy even of an honest and effective government. Foremost were the problems created by population pressures, for the population continued to increase in the nineteenth century as it had in the eighteenth. By 1850 the number of inhabitants in China had risen to about 430 million, without any comparable increase in productivity or resources. As ever, the poor suffered most, and they were legion, for the uneven distribution of land left many people landless, destitute, and in despair. The situation was made worse by government neglect of public works. The opium trade also contributed to the economic crisis, for silver continued to leave China, further disrupting the silver-copper ratio and thereby increasing the farmer's tax burden, which was calculated in scarce silver but paid in copper cash.

Government leadership was totally inadequate. Emperor Chia-ch'ing (1796–1820) tried to remedy the government's financial problems by cutting expenses but was unable to solve the underlying fiscal and economic problems. Sale of official posts and titles helped the treasury but did not raise the quality of the bureaucracy nor help the people who ultimately supplied the funds.

Emperor Tao-kuang (1821–50) continued his father's policy of frugality. It is said that he himself wore old and patched clothes. His partial success in reforming the official salt monopoly system did not compensate for his failure to reinvigorate the Grand Canal or Yellow River managements, however. The former was impassible by 1849, after which tax grain had to be shipped by sea. The abandonment of the canal cost thousands their jobs. Emperor Tao-kuang did not live to see the Yellow River disaster. Since 1194 the great river had flowed into the sea south of Shantung Peninsula but now, silted up, it shifted to the north, spreading flood and devastation over a wide area.

The next emperor, Hsien-feng (1851–61), was nineteen when he inherited the throne and proved equally incapable of dealing with an increasingly menacing situation. Even while rebellion threatened the dynasty, a major scandal involving bribery and cheating shook the examination system.

Famine, poverty, and corruption gave rise to banditry and armed uprisings, as had so often happened in the past. The most formidable threat to the dynasty came from the Taiping revolutionaries. To aggravate the crisis even further, the dynasty also had to contend with rebellions elsewhere. In the border regions of Anhwei, Kiangsu, Honan, and Shantung, there was the Nien Rebellion (1853–68) led by secret societies, probably related to the White Lotus Society. There was also a Muslim rebellion in Yunnan (1855–73) and the Tungan Rebellion in the Northwest (1862–75). Yet it was the Taipings who came closest to destroying the Ch'ing in a civil war that in terms of bloodshed and devastation was the costliest in human history. It is estimated that more than 20 million people lost their lives.

## The Taiping Rebellion (1850–1864)

The founder of the Taiping movement was a village school teacher named Hung Hsiu-ch'üan (1814–64) who belonged to the Hakka minority, which many centuries earlier had migrated from the North to the Southeast, where they remained a distinct ethnic group. Originally Hung hoped for a conventional civil service career and four times went to Canton to participate in the examination for the licentiate, only to fail each time. Shocked by his third failure he became seriously ill and for forty days was subject to fits of delirium during which he experienced visions. These visions he later interpreted with the aid of a Christian tract he picked up in Canton, where Protestant missionaries had made a beginning in their effort to bring their faith to China. He also received some instruction from an American Southern Baptist missionary. On the basis of his limited knowledge of the Bible and Christianity, he proceeded to work out his own form of Sinicized Christianity.

Central to Hung's faith was his conviction that in his visions he had seen God, who had bestowed on Hung the divine mission to save mankind and exterminate demons. He had also met Jesus and was given to understand that Christ was his own elder brother. This recasting of Christianity into a familiar familistic mode had its appeal for Hung's Chinese audience but dismayed Western Christian missionaries, who were further appalled by Hung's claims that he himself was a source of new revelation.

The emphasis in Taiping Christianity was on the Old Testament rather than the New Testament, on the Ten Commandments not on the Sermon on the Mount. Hung's militant zeal in obeying the first commandment by destroying Buddhist and Taoist "idols" and even Confucian tablets soon cost him his position as a village teacher. He became an itinerant preacher among the Hakka communities in Kwangsi, gaining converts and disciples as he went about spreading the word among the downtrodden and dispossessed, whom he recruited into the Association of God Worshippers. To the poor and miserable, he held out a vision of the "Heavenly Kingdom of Great Peace" (T'ai-p'ing t'ien-kuo), an egalitarian, God-ordained utopia.

In keeping with both Christianity and native traditions, Hung and his disciples laid great stress on a strict, even puritanical, morality. Opium, tobacco, gambling, alcohol, prostitution, sexual misconduct, and foot binding were all strictly prohibited. Women were put on an equal basis with men in theory and, to a remarkable extent, also in practice. Also, consonant with both the Christian belief in the brotherhood of man and native Chinese utopian ideas was a strong strain of economic egalitarianism, a kind of simple communism. Property was to be shared in common, and in 1850 the members of the Association were asked to turn over their funds to a public treasury that would provide for everyone's future needs.

What stood in the way of realizing this utopia were the demons, mostly Manchus. By July 1850 the Association had attracted 10,000 adherents, primarily in Kwangsi province. In defiance of the Ch'ing they now cut off their queues, the long braids of hair hanging down from the back of the head, which had been introduced by the Manchus as a sign of Chinese subjugation. Since they also refused to shave the forepart of their heads, the government called them the "long-haired rebels."

Millenarian religious beliefs, utopian egalitarianism, moral righteousness, and hatred of the Manchus proved a potent combination when fused into a program of organized armed resistance. At this stage the Taipings also enjoyed good leadership. One of the outstanding secondary leaders was Yang Hsiu-ch'ing, originally a charcoal burner, who was a talented organizer and strategist. Starting from their base in Kwangsi, the Taiping forces made rapid military progress. One of their favorite tactics in attacking cities was to use their contingent of coal miners to dig tunnels to undermine the defending walls. The incompetence of the government forces was also a help. As the Taiping armies advanced, they picked up strength. It has been estimated that their number reached over one million by the time they took Nanking in 1853.

After such a quick advance, with their ranks swollen by new adherents only partially versed in Taiping tenets, the leadership decided it was time to call a halt and consolidate. The "Heavenly Kingdom of Great Peace" had formally been proclaimed in 1851. Now, with its capital at Nanking, the attempt was made to turn it into a solid regime. To continue military operations, two expeditions were sent out. A small force was dispatched north and reached within twenty miles of Tientsin before suffering reverses and defeat. Large forces were sent west and enjoyed considerable success until 1856, but also were eventually defeated. The future of the rebellion depended in large part on the success of its planned consolidation.

## Taiping Programs and Policies

The Taipings proclaimed a revolutionary program of political and economic reorganization. They did not want simply to establish a new regime on the old pattern but to change the pattern itself. The source for their official terminology and many of their ideas was *The Rites of Chou*, long a source of radical thought in China.

The Taiping land program was based on a system of land classification according to nine grades found in *The Rites of Chou*. The idea was that everyone would receive an equal amount of land, measured in terms of productivity of the soil, so that all their personal needs would be met. Any production over and above what was needed by the assignees was to be contributed to common granaries and treasuries. The system did not recognize private property.

The basic political structure was a unit of twenty-five families consisting of five groups of five families each. The leadership of these and larger units was to combine civil and military duties and also to see after the spiritual welfare of the people. Taiping Christianity was propagated by Sunday services conducted by these leaders. It developed its own hymns and literature including *The Three Character Classic* written in the vernacular. Taiping writings also served as the subject matter for a new examination system open to women as well as to men. In other respects, too, women were made equal to men, and there were female military units. Marriages took place in church and were monogamous.

Taiping treatment of Westerners was cordial but clumsy. They lost much good will by employing condescending language and expressions of superiority not unlike those used by Peking. After the British failed to obtain Taiping recognition of their treaty rights, they decided on a policy of neutrality, and the other powers soon followed suit. This remained the policy of the foreign powers through the 1850s.

## Dissension and Weakness

A turning point for the Taiping regime came in 1856 in the form of a leadership crisis they could ill afford. Yang Hsiu-ch'ing, more ambitious than devout, had increased his power to the point of reducing Hung to a mere figurehead. To legitimize his position, Yang went into trances and claimed to be acting on God's orders, but he was unable to convince the other leaders. When he overreached himself, they turned on him. Yang, along with his family and thousands of followers, was killed, but no strong successor appeared to take his place. Meanwhile Hung Hsiu-ch'üan was preoccupied with his religious visions. By the time Hung's cousin Hung Jen-kan (1822–64) came into prominence in 1859, it was too late to restructure the regime. Hung Jen-kan was the most Westernized of the Taiping leaders but had neither the time nor the power to build the centralized and modern state he had in mind. His leadership lasted only until 1861.

Failure of the leadership was one source of Taiping weakness. Inadequate implementation of stated policies was another. Practice did not conform to theory. For example, Hung Hsiu-ch'üan and the other leaders kept numerous concubines despite the Taiping call for monogamy. Moreover, there were many missed opportunities: the failure to strike before the dynasty could regroup; the failure to cooperate with secret societies and other opponents of the regime who did not share the Taiping faith; the failure to cultivate good relations with the foreign powers.

To make matters worse, Taiping revolutionary ideas repelled all those Chinese who identified with the basic Confucian way of life and understood that the Taiping program was not merely anti-Manchu but anti-Confucian, and thus subversive to the traditional social order. Consequently the Taipings not only failed to recruit gentry support, but they antagonized this key element in Chinese society. To the literati, rule by "civilized" Manchus was preferable to rule by "barbarized" Chinese.

## Tseng Kuo-fan and the Defeat of the Taipings

What ultimately saved the dynasty was a new kind of military force organized by Tseng Kuo-fan (1811–72), a dedicated Confucian and a product of the examination system. Unlike the old armies organized under the banner system (see pages 326–27), Tseng's army was a strictly regional force from Hunan, staffed by officers of similar regional and ideological background personally selected by him. They, in turn, recruited soldiers from their own home areas or from members of their own clans. A paternalistic attitude of officers toward their men, a generous pay scale honestly administered, careful moral indoctrination, and common regional ties all helped to produce a well-disciplined force high in morale.

Ch'ing statesmen were aware that strong regional armies such as Tseng's threatened the balance of power between the central government and the regions, and were ultimately dangerous to the authority of the dynasty. But the traditional armies of the regime had proved hopelessly inadequate, and the Manchu rulers had no choice but to trust their defense to Tseng. Although organized in Hunan, where it began its operations, the army also fought the Taipings in other provinces. It was not always victorious: twice Tseng suffered such serious reverses that he attempted suicide. But in the long run a well-led and highly motivated army, honestly administered and true to its purpose, proved superior to the Taiping forces.

The dynasty also benefited from the services of two other remarkable leaders, Tso Tsung-t'ang (1812–85) and Li Hung-chang (1823–1901), whose armies were similarly organized on the new model. After the treaties of 1860 the Western powers also sided with the regime. There was direct British and French military intervention in defense of Shanghai, but what proved more important were the supplies of modern weapons, the training of Ch'ing soldiers, and the activities of "The Ever Victorious Army." This was a force of some 3000 to 4500 mercenaries led by a small staff of Western officers, first under the command of the American adventurer Frederick T. Ward and then under the English officer Charles George Gordon ("Chinese Gordon"). Both these men took their orders from Li Hung-chang, who valued the army's efficacy but was also concerned to keep the foreign role in the war from expanding.

After a series of victories the loyalist armies laid siege to Nanking, and when the situation became hopeless in the Taiping capital Hung Hsiu-ch'üan committed suicide. Shortly thereafter, on July 19, 1864, the city fell to an army commanded by Tseng Kuo-fan's brother. As had happened often in this bitter war on both sides, the fall of Nanking was followed by a bloodbath. Hung's son managed to flee but was discovered in Kiangsi and executed. The Taipings, once so close to victory, were completely eradicated, leaving only the force of their example to inspire future revolutionaries. For many years Tseng Kuo-fan was widely admired as a great Confucian statesman, steadfast in his loyalty to the dynasty when he could have used his provincial power base for his own personal ends. But a hundred years later the tables of historical evaluation were reversed, and in the new China led by another Hunanese, Mao Tse-tung, the Taipings were cast as heroes.

Although the other uprisings against the dynasty did not threaten the Ch'ing as severely as had the Taipings, it still took considerable fighting to suppress them. In the campaigns against the highly mobile mounted Nien bands and the Muslim rebellions, Tseng Kuo-fan, Li Hung-chang, and Tso Tsung-t'ang again played a prominent part.

According to Chinese political theory, force was merely an adjunct of government. The suppression of the Taipings, the Niens, and other rebels was only one aspect of the general effort to revitalize the dynasty.

## The T'ung-chih Restoration

The leading statesmen and scholars of the T'ung-chih period (1862–74) thought of themselves as engaged in a restoration (chung-hsing*), that is, a dynastic revival similar to the revival of the Han dynasty by the founder of the Later Han, or to the resurgence of the T'ang after the rebellion of An Lu-shan. From this sense of historical precedent they derived the confidence to initiate a broad program, which they hoped would revitalize the dynasty. Although their accomplishments fell far short of their goals, they achieved enough to induce modern scholars also to employ the term "restoration."

To cope with the dislocations wrought by warfare, the T'ung-chih leaders applied old remedies: relief projects were instituted, public works projects initiated, land reclaimed and water controlled, granaries set up, expenses cut, taxes reduced in the ravaged lower Yangtze Valley. As always, priority was placed on agriculture.

An aspect of the revival dear to the hearts of its Confucian sponsors was a strengthening of scholarship by reprinting old texts, founding new academies, opening libraries, and the like. Examination system reform was similarly high

* A different term (wei-hsin in Chinese, ishin in Japanese) was used by the Japanese to designate their Meiji Restoration. Although the Japanese term comes from the Chinese Book of Songs and has the meaning of "making new," or "renovation," it lacks the historical referents and programmatic content of the Chinese term.

on the list of priorities, as was the elimination of corruption from the bureaucracy. In the examinations, questions dealing with practical problems of statecraft were introduced, and attempts were made to limit the sale of degrees and offices. By such measures, the reformers sought to raise the level of honesty and elevate the moral tone of officialdom so as to reestablish the moral authority of the officials and the government they served. However, nothing effective was done about the solidly entrenched and notoriously corrupt subbureaucracy of clerks and other underlings.

Furthermore, the dynasty was powerless to reverse the trend toward regionalism, which ultimately had grave consequences for the center and the provinces alike. In the latter, the disruption of old bonds with the central government removed many of the political constraints on local wealth and power. It thus set in motion a restructuring of local society that ultimately was to prove dangerous both to the state and to the social order.

T'ung-chih was only six when he came to the throne, and the real leadership was in the hands of his uncle Prince Kung (1833–98) and his young mother, the Empress Dowager Tz'u Hsi (1835–1908). Foreign policy was largely under the direction of Prince Kung, who expressed the regime's order of priorities thus:

> The situation today may be compared (to the diseases of a human body). Both the Taiping and the Nien bandits are gaining victories and constitute an organic disease. Russia, with her territory adjoining ours, aiming to nibble away our territory like a silk worm, may be considered a threat at our bosom. As to England, her purpose is to trade, but she acts violently, without any regard for human decency. If she is not kept within limits, we shall not be able to stand on our feet. Hence she may be compared to an affliction of our limbs. Therefore we should suppress the Taipings and the Nien bandits first, get the Russians under control next, and attend to the British last.[6]

It was apparent to Prince Kung that new approaches to foreign policy would be required if these objectives were to be met. In 1861 he sponsored the establishment of a new agency to deal with the foreign powers and related matters. This was the Tsungli Yamen (Office of General Management), not an independent ministry but a subcommittee of the Grand Council supervising a number of offices. (See Figure 4-5.) As such its influence depended on that of its presiding officer and his associates. It was, accordingly, most influential during the 1860s, when Prince Kung was at the height of his authority. An important innovation introduced by the Tsungli Yamen was its appeal to international law, using Henry Wheaton's *Elements of International Law*, a standard text translated by the American missionary W. A. P. Martin.

Prince Kung, recognizing that Chinese officials would be at a disadvantage in dealing with foreigners unless they had a better understanding of foreign languages and learning, was instrumental in having the Tsungli Yamen establish a school (the T'ung-wen kuan) for foreign languages and other nontraditional subjects in 1862. The foreign language staff was foreign and included Martin, who became the school's president in 1869. By that time astronomy and math-

Figure 4-5 Three members of the Tsungli Yamen and statesmen of the T'ung-chih period. LEFT TO RIGHT, Shen Kuei-fen, President of the Ministry of War; Tung Hsün, President of the Ministry of Finance; Mao Ch'ang-hsi, President of the Ministry of Works.

ematics had also been introduced, despite the objections of the distinguished Mongol scholar, General Secretary Wo-jen who said: "From ancient down to modern times your slave has never heard of anyone who could use mathematics to raise the nation from a state of decline or to strengthen it in time of weakness."[7] Wo-jen (d. 1871) was not alone in his objections to this extension of "barbarian" influence.

Nevertheless, similar schools were established at Shanghai, Canton, and Foochow in association with arsenals and shipyards sponsored by Tseng Kuo-fan, Tso Tsung-t'ang, and Li Hung-chang. (See Figure 4-6.) Foreigners were relied on to run both the military and the educational establishments. In this way the foundations of "self-strengthening" and of modernization were laid, but the emphasis remained heavily military. This was true even of Feng Kuei-fen (1809–74), an advocate of learning from the barbarians, who had the audacity to propose that examination degrees, including the *chin-shih*, be presented to men demonstrating accomplishment in Western mechanical skills.

During the 1860s, following the close of hostilities, Chinese cooperation with the foreign powers brought certain advantages to the Ch'ing, although there were some on both sides who were opposed to cooperation. (For example,

Wo-jen and men of similar views felt that China should resist all foreign influence and seek the expulsion of all foreigners; while the British mercantile community frowned on the efforts of Rutherford Alcock, English minister in Peking, to work amicably with the government.)

An important area of cooperation was the Maritime Customs Service. The first director of the service, Horatio Nelson Lay, had acquired a fleet of eight gunboats for the Chinese in England. But although these were paid for by the Chinese, he arranged that the captain of the fleet should receive all his orders through and at the discretion of Lay himself! This was unacceptable to the Ch'ing. There were protests. China's first effort to acquire a modern navy ended with disbandment of the little fleet (known as the Lay-Osborn flotilla), and Lay was pensioned off.

Matters improved, however, when Robert Hart succeeded Lay in 1863. Hart's attitude was the opposite of Lay's. He insisted that the customs was a Chinese service, that Chinese officials were to be treated as "brother officers," and he gave the Ch'ing government well intentioned and frequently helpful advice on modernization while building the service into an important source of support for the dynasty.

Cooperation between the Ch'ing and the powers was further exemplified by the first Chinese diplomatic mission to the West, which was headed by the retiring American minister to Peking, Anson Burlingame. Accompanied by a

Figure 4-6   Scene at the Nanking Arsenal.

Manchu and a Chinese official, Burlingame left China in 1867 for a trip to Washington, several European capitals, and St. Petersburg, where he died. Somewhat carried away by his own eloquence he told Americans that China was ready to extend "her arms toward the shining banners of Western civilization."[8] In Washington he concluded a treaty rather favorable to China.

The most important negotiations for treaty revision, however, were conducted in Peking by the British. These culminated in the Alcock Convention of 1869 which included some concessions to the Chinese, among them the provision that British subjects under the most-favored-nation clause would enjoy privileges extended to other nationals only if they accepted the conditions under which those privileges were granted. It also allowed China to open a consulate in Hong Kong and contained provisions concerning duties and taxes. These concessions may not appear very far reaching, but the English merchant community felt threatened by them, and their opposition proved strong enough to prevent the ratification of the convention.

A fatal blow to the policy of cooperation came in 1870 in Tientsin. A Catholic nunnery there had made the mistake of offering small payments for orphans brought to the mission, and rumors spread that the children had been kidnapped and that the sisters removed the children's hearts and eyes to make medicine. The tense situation erupted into violence, and a mob took the lives of the French consul and twenty other foreigners, including ten nuns, in what came to be known as the Tientsin Massacre. The powers mobilized their gunboats. Diplomacy finally settled the issue, largely because France's defeat in the Franco-Prussian War the same year deprived France of military power and forced the French to concentrate on domestic problems. But the decade ended with demonstrations of the gap between the two civilizations and with feelings of mutual bitterness and disdain. Tseng Kuo-fan was given the difficult task of negotiating with the Westerners after the tragic Tientsin Massacre. Tseng died in 1872. As the T'ung-chih period came to an end, the internal reform also lost momentum.

Thirty years after the Opium War the dynasty had survived despite the maladies attacking it from within and without. The progress of the disease had been halted. But time was to show that there had been no genuine cure and that, in the long run, the medicine itself had potentially lethal side effects. In Japan, in contrast, the old regime had fallen, and work had begun on the creation of a new state and society.

## NOTES

1. John K. Fairbank, Edwin O. Reischauer, and Albert Craig, *East Asia: Tradition and Transformation* (Boston: Houghton Mifflin, 1973), p. 257.
2. Franz Schurmann and Orville Schell, *The China Reader: Imperial China* (New York: Vintage Books, 1967), pp. 105–13, which reproduce Harley F. MacNair, *Modern Chinese History, Selected Readings* (Shanghai: Commercial Press Ltd., 1923), pp. 2–9.

3. John K. Fairbank, *Trade and Diplomacy on the China Coast: The Opening of the Treaty Ports, 1842–1854* (Cambridge: Harvard University Press, 1953), p. 59, which quotes H. B. Morse, *The Chronicles of the East India Company Trading to China, 1635–1834,* 5 vols. (Oxford, 1926, 1929), 2: 247–52.

4. Ssu-yü Teng and John K. Fairbank, *China's Response to the West: A Documentary Survey, 1839–1923* (Cambridge: Harvard University Press, 1954), p. 26.

5. *Ibid.,* p. 38.

6. *Ibid.,* p. 48.

7. *Ibid.,* p. 76.

8. Quoted in Immanuel C. Y. Hsü, *China's Entrance into the Family of Nations: The Diplomatic Phase, 1858–1880* (Cambridge: Harvard University Press, 1960), p. 168.

西方之入侵日本

1800                    1868  1873

LATE TOKUGAWA       MEIJI

Reform Program    Ii Naosuke
(1841–43)     (1858–1860)  First
                   Phase

Ōsaka Uprising → 1837     1853 ← Perry's Arrival

# 5 The Intrusion of the West: Japan

Like China, Japan in the middle of the nineteenth century had to come to terms with vigorous and expanding Western powers that could no longer be contained by the old system of "barbarian" management. Also for Japan as for China, the threat from abroad came in a period of political weakness at home. However, despite these similarities, Japanese and Chinese history in the nineteenth century, as in the twelfth or twentieth, offers a study in contrasts. The similarities are just sufficient to make these contrasts meaningful.

# Problems at Midcentury

Japan differed from China not only in the rapidity of Japanese response to the West but also in the depth of the changes which this set off in Japanese society; a milder foreign challenge provoked a stronger domestic response. This happened not only because Japan was smaller than China and historically more open to foreign influence but because the internal dynamics of Tokugawa history had already produced the essential ingredients of change even though it took the threat from abroad to set them in motion.

A major source of trouble and distress during the late Tokugawa was the inability of the ruling class to cope with a money economy. The samurai who had to convert a substantial portion of his rice stipend into cash was constantly at the mercy of a fluctuating market which he could not understand and would not study. Even the daimyo, burdened with the heavy expenses of periodic attendance in Edo, and required to maintain separate establishments in the *bakufu* and *han* capitals, found themselves in financial difficulty. One way for a daimyo to improve his finances was to cut stipends, further aggravating the situation of the samurai. This hurt even the small minority of high-ranking men, but the effects were most serious, even devastating, on the bulk of samurai who ranked low in status and stipend.

Some samurai married daughters of wealthy merchants, but many lived in desperate circumstances. They pawned their swords, worked at humble crafts, such as umbrella making and sandal weaving, and tried to hide their misery from the world. A samurai was taught that he should use a toothpick even when he had not eaten.

The samurai were not dissatisfied with the basic social system in which, after all, they formed the ruling class. But they were unhappy at the discrepancy between the theoretical elevation of their status and the reality of their poverty. Not only was their poverty demeaning, but the spectacle of contrasting merchant wealth hurt their pride. It seemed the height of injustice that society should reward the selfish money-making trader and condemn to indigence the warrior whose life was one of service. This helps explain the rapidity with which men of samurai background eventually dismantled the system.

The immediate focus of samurai discontent was not with the Tokugawa order, however, but with the character and abilities of the men in power. There was deep resentment against incompetence and corruption in high places, and it was felt that government could be reformed by putting into office more capable men, including able men from the lower ranks of the samurai class. In staffing the *bakufu* and *han* bureaucracies, ability and competence should take precedence over family.

City merchants and rural entrepreneurs flourished economically and were acquiescent politically, but below them the rural and urban poor included many who earned barely enough to keep themselves alive. Crop failures in the 1820s and 1830s and a national famine in 1836 caused great misery and brought masses of displaced peasants into the cities. The government did supply relief but not enough to forestall violence. Four hundred incidents of violent protest were recorded between 1813 and 1868. One which made a great impression occurred in Ōsaka in 1837. It was led by Ōshio Heihachiro (1793–1837), a low-ranking *bakufu* official and follower of Wang Yang-ming's philosophy of action, but it was poorly planned and quickly suppressed. Peasant discontent during these years also found expression in the rise of messianic religious movements. But neither religious sects nor uprisings ever reached anything like the dimensions of the Taiping Rebellion in China. Tokugawa samurai, unlike Ch'ing gentry, were never called upon as a class to defend their regime against the masses nor did they experience a serious threat from below.

## Reform Programs

The *bakufu* itself faced financial problems. By 1800 its annual budget showed a small deficit, the beginning of a trend. For more than a century it had coped with fiscal crises by resorting to two devices: forced loans and currency devaluation. Now it did so again. Between 1819 and 1837 there were nineteen instances of currency devaluation. These brought temporary relief, but they did not effect long range improvements in the shogunate's finances. Nor did they free it from dependence on the market and on the merchants who understood and manipulated the market. There was in Tokugawa Japan no system or theory for regular deficit financing.

The reforms undertaken by Mizuno Tadakuni (1793–1851) during 1841–43 were reminiscent of earlier *bakufu* efforts and in spirit went back to Ieyasu himself. They included recoinage and forced loans, dismissal of officials to reduce costs, and sumptuary laws intended to preserve morals and save money. Censorship became stricter. An effort (by no means the *bakufu's* first) was made to force peasants to return to their lands. This was in keeping with the Confucian view of the primacy of agriculture as well as with the Tokugawa's policy of strict class separation but hardly solved any problems. A program to create solid areas of *bakufu* control around Edo and Ōsaka proved too ambitious. It called for the creation of a *bakufu*-controlled zone of twenty-five square miles around Edo and twelve square miles around Ōsaka by moving certain daimyo and housemen out of these areas, but the plan was never carried out. In the hope of fighting inflation, merchant monopolies were broken up, but the result was economic chaos and still further inflation. Despite the retrenchment policy, an expensive and ostentatious formal procession to the Tokugawa mausoleum at Nikkō was organized in an effort to shore up the *bakufu's* prestige. In the end Mizuno's program produced more resentment than improvement.

The various domains (*han*), faced with similar problems, attempted local reform programs of their own. Here and there *han* government machinery was reformed, stipends and other costs were cut, agriculture was encouraged, and commercial policies were changed. The results were often as disappointing as

Figure 5-1  **Japan on the Eve of the Meiji Restoration**

they were for the shogunate—often but not always. The political division of Japan allowed for local variations and experimentation so that some domains were more successful than others.

Two of the most successful *han* were Satsuma in Kyūshū and Chōshū in Southwest Honshū. (See map, Figure 5-1.) In interesting and important ways these were untypical domains. For one thing, they were both large, outside *han* (*tozama*), that is, *han* that had arisen independently of the Tokugawa, which prior to 1600 they sometimes opposed and sometimes supported, but as equals not subordinates. In the seventeenth century they accepted Tokugawa supremacy since they had no other alternative, but their commitment to the Tokugawa order was not beyond question. In line with Tokugawa policy, Satsuma and Chōshū had their domains transferred and reduced in size in the seventeenth century. One consequence was that they kept alive an anti-Tokugawa feudal tradition. Another result was that the reduction in the size of their domains left them with a much higher than average ratio of samurai to the land. In Satsuma this led to the formation of a class of samurai who worked the land (*goshi*) and a tight control of the countryside, which experienced not a single peasant uprising throughout the Tokugawa period. Satsuma backwardness was also an asset to the domain in the sense that it worked against the erosion of samurai values found in economically more advanced and urbane regions. Both Chōshū and Satsuma also had special family ties with the court in Kyōto, the most likely focus for any anti*bakufu* movement.

In both *han*, finances were put in order and a budget surplus was built up, although by different methods. In Chōshū a rigorous cost-cutting program was initiated, major improvements were made in *han* financial administration, and there was a reform of the land tax. Most *han* monopolies were abolished, since they were unprofitable for the government and unpopular among the people. Only the profitable shipping and warehouse monopolies at Shimonoseki were continued. Otherwise, commodity transactions were turned over to merchants for a fee. Satsuma, in contrast, derived much of its income from its monopolies, especially the monopoly on sugar from the Ryūkyū Islands (Liu-ch'iu, in Chinese), which were a Satsuma dependency. At the same time Satsuma directed the Ryūkyūs to continue sending tribute to China in order to foster trade between China and the islands, which thus became a source of Chinese goods for Satsuma. The sugar monopoly was strictly enforced: private sale of sugar was a crime punishable by death. The sugar was brought to market in Ōsaka in the *han*'s own ships, and at every stage from production to sale everything was done to insure maximum profit for the Satsuma treasury.

These programs required vigorous leadership, since they naturally ran up against the opposition of merchants and others who benefited from doing things the old way. Both Chōshū and Satsuma were fortunate in having reform-minded daimyo who raised to power young samurai of middle or low rank, men who tended to be much more innovative and energetic than conservative samurai of high rank. Particularly in Chōshū such differences in background and outlook within the samurai class led to bitter political antagonisms and produced a period of turbulence in *han* politics.

The fact that reform was more successful in Chōshū and Satsuma than in the *bakufu* suggests that it was easier to implement reform in a well-organized, remote domain than in the central region where the economic changes were most advanced and political pressures and responsibilities were far greater. Reform attempts in the other *han* varied in success, but the Chōshū and Satsuma cases are particularly important, since these two large and wealthy domains were to play a crucial role in the eventual overthrow of the Tokugawa.

## Intellectual Currents

Economic, social, and political changes were accompanied by intellectual restiveness and the continued development of potentially anti*bakufu* strains of thought. These, it will be recalled (see Chapter 2), included the Shinto revivalists of the School of National Learning, members of the Mito school who stressed the centrality of the emperor, and the proponents of "Dutch Learning."

Frequently, ideas from one or more of these currents were combined. For example, Aizawa Seishisai (1782–1863), of Mito, combined the values of Confucianism and of *bushidō* with Shinto mythology in his discussion of Japan's unique polity (*kokutai*). To reconcile the Japanese theory of imperial divine descent going back to the Sun Goddess with the Confucian doctrine of the Mandate of Heaven, Mito scholars developed the idea that the emperor ruled by virtue of his unique descent, but that the shogun's legitimacy was derived from a mandate he received from the emperor. The implication was that what the emperor granted he could also revoke if the *bakufu* failed in its duties and obligations.

An example of an influential writer who combined advocacy of an irrational and frequently naive nativism with a good understanding of, and appreciation for, Western medicine was Hirata Atsutane, whose long life straddled the eighteenth and nineteenth centuries. Hirata was himself a physician and had studied Dutch medical texts in translation. To reconcile his adulation of Japan with his appreciation for the foreign science, Hirata maintained that Japan had originally been pure and free of disease: the need for a powerful medical science arose only after Japan was infected by foreign contacts.

During the first half of the nineteenth century interest in such practical Western sciences as astronomy, medicine, and mathematics continued to grow. The *bakufu* itself, in 1811, set up a bureau that translated Dutch books into Japanese even while it maintained its seclusionist policies. Outstanding among the students of Western science was the Confucian scholar Sakuma Shōzan (1811–64), who conducted experiments in chemistry and glassmaking and later became an expert in the casting of guns; he was a serious thinker about the principles as well as the products of Western technology. Seeking to

Figure 5-2
*Commodore Perry.*
Artist unknown.
Woodcut print,
nineteenth century,
26 cm × 24.5 cm.

preserve Confucian values and at the same time to adopt Western technology, Sakuma sought a rationale with room for both. His solution was incorporated in the formula "Eastern ethics and Western science." This became a very influential slogan after the Meiji Restoration, but Sakuma did not live to see the day, for he was murdered by an antiforeign extremist from Chōshū in 1864.

Sakuma's intellectual strategy was essentially one of compartmentalization: the native and foreign traditions were assigned different functions. Each had its distinct role. Most students of Dutch painting would have agreed, for they valued Western techniques more for their practical results than for any aesthetic merit. Yet, like all generalizations, this demands qualification. Hokusai, who lived until 1849, once contrasted the use of shading for decorative purposes in Chinese and Japanese art with its employment to create an effect of three dimensionality in the West. He concluded, "One must understand both methods: there must be life and death in everything one paints."[1]

## The "Opening" of Japan

The "opening" of China to the West was a result of the Opium War and subsequent treaties with the European powers. In Japan, the "opening" resulted from an armed mission by Commodore Matthew C. Perry of the United States Navy (1853). (See Figure 5-2.) The treaties which followed that momentous event ended the Tokugawa policy of seclusion. They thus contributed to the growing instability of the Tokugawa system and helped to pave the way for a very different future.

Before 1853 there were a number of Western attempts to induce the Japanese to broaden their foreign policy, but these efforts were sporadic since they were not supported by substantial economic and political interests of the kind at work in China. Regarded as poor and remote, Japan was considered an area of relatively low priority by the great powers. The first approaches came from Japan's nearest Eurasian neighbor, the Russian Empire, and took place in the North, in the Kurile Islands, Sakhalin, and Hokkaidō. In 1778 and again in 1792 the Russians requested trade relations in Hokkaidō, and in 1804 a similar request was made in Nagasaki. All were refused. British ships seeking trade or ship's stores were also turned away. British whaling ships sometimes requested supplies, but in 1825 the *bakufu* ordered that all foreign ships should be driven from Japanese waters. In 1837 a private American-British attempt to open relations with Japan fared no better. But in 1842 the shogunate relaxed the edicts of 1825 and ordered that foreign ships accidentally arriving in Japan were to be provided with water, food, and fuel. China's defeat in the Opium War and the opening of new ports increased the number of Western vessels in East Asia and hence the pressure on Japan.

This changing situation could not be ignored. To begin with, the lessons of Chinese weakness and Western strength were not lost on Japanese observers. Information concerning Western science, industry, and military capabilities continued to be provided by scholars of "Dutch Learning." Information also came from China: Wei Yüan's *An Illustrated Gazeteer of the Maritime Countries (Hai-kuo t'u-chih)* was widely read after it appeared in a Japanese edition in 1847. Furthermore, the Japanese were making progress in mastering Western technology. By the 1840s the domains of Mito, Hizen, and Satsuma were casting guns using Western methods. In 1850 Hizen possessed the first reverberatory furnace needed to produce iron suitable for making modern cannons. As we have already noted, a few courageous students of the West had suggested abandoning the policy of seclusion well before the arrival of Perry. The Dutch, too, had warned the *bakufu* of the designs of the stronger Western nations.

In 1846 an American mission to Japan ended in failure, but with the acquisition of California in 1848 the interest of the United States in Japan increased, since Nagasaki, five hundred miles from Shanghai, was a convenient fueling stop for ships bound from San Fransisco to that port. Putting real pressure on Japan for the first time, the United States government sent out Commodore Perry with eleven ships, three of them steam frigates. Perry and his fleet reached Japan in July 1853, forced the Japanese to accept a letter from the American president to the emperor, and announced that he would return for an answer the following spring.

No match militarily for the American fleet, the *bakufu* realized that it would have to accede at least in part to American demands. In preparation for that unpopular move, it took the unprecedented step of soliciting daimyo opinion only to receive divided and unhelpful advice. The *bakufu* did not gain the backing it had hoped for but did reveal its own weakness.

When Perry returned in February 1854, an initial treaty was signed that provided for the opening of Shimoda and Hakodate to ships seeking provisions, assured that the shipwrecked would receive good treatment, and permitted the United States later to send a consul to Japan. Similar treaties with Britain and France followed in 1855, and the Dutch and Russians negotiated broader agreements in 1857. Still, there was no commercial treaty satisfactory to Western mercantile interests. The task of negotiating such an agreement was left to the first American consul, Townsend Harris, who arrived in Japan in 1856 and gradually succeeded in persuading the shogunate to make concessions. (See Figure 5-3.) The resulting treaty was signed in 1858, and another round of treaties with the Dutch, Russians, British, and French followed.

At the end of this process, Japan's international situation was similar to that of China. First there was the matter of opening ports. This began with Shimoda on the Izu Peninsula and Hakodate in Hokkaidō; it was extended to Nagasaki and Kanagawa (for which Yokohama was substituted); and dates were set for the opening of Niigata, Hyōgo (modern Kobe), and the admission of foreign res-

Figure 5-3  *Harris's Procession on the Way to Edo.* Artist unknown.
Watercolor, 53.5 cm × 38.8 cm. Peabody Museum, Salem.

idents but not trade into Ōsaka and Edo. As in the case of China, the treaties provided for most-favored-nation treatment and extraterritoriality. Japan also lost her tariff autonomy and was limited to relatively low import duties.

## Domestic Politics

For the *bakufu* these were very difficult years, for it was forced to accede to the foreign powers without enjoying support at home. Each failure in foreign affairs provided additional ammunition to its domestic enemies. The *bakufu* was itself divided by factionalism and policy differences. An attempt was made after Perry's arrival to broaden the shogunate's political base by drawing on the advice of nonhouse daiymo. The Lord of Mito, Tokugawa Nariaki (1800–1860), a persistent advocate of resistance to the West, was placed in charge of national defense. These measures, however, failed to strengthen the *bakufu*—too many men were pulling in opposite directions.

When the shogun died without an heir in 1858, a bitter dispute took place over the rival claims of two candidates for the succession. One of these was still a boy, but he had the strongest claim by descent. He also had the backing of most of the house daimyo (*fudai*) including that of Ii Naosuke, the greatest of the *fudai*. The other candidate was Hitotsubashi (later Tokugawa) Keiki, the capable son of the Lord of Mito. It will be recalled that Mito was a collateral house of the Tokugawa, eligible to supply shoguns if the main line failed to produce an heir.

The immediate issue in the succession dispute concerned control over the *bakufu*, for Keiki's accession was seen as a threat to the continued control over the shogunate by the *fudai*. At the same time, foreign policy was also involved, for the *bakufu* officials, as men on the spot, were more inclined to make concessions to the foreigners. The great lords, on the other hand, demanded a vigorous defense policy against the intruders from the West. Furthermore, the Lord of Mito and some of his peers envisioned their own *han* as playing important roles in building up military strength against the West. Thus his advocacy of a strong foreign policy was consistent with his desire to strengthen his own *han* at the expense of the center.

The split in the *bakufu* increased the political importance of the imperial court. Nariaki even appealed to Kyōto for support for his son's candidacy. And when the shogun tried to obtain imperial approval for the treaty negotiated with Harris, he failed.

The crisis of 1858 was temporarily resolved when Ii Naosuke took charge of the *bakufu*. He did so as Grand Councilor (*tairō*), a high post more often than not left vacant, and which had previously been held by several members of the Ii family. The effective power of this position depended on the authority of the incumbent, and the strong-minded Ii Naosuke used it to dominate the shogunate. He proceeded to sign the treaty with the United States without prior imperial approval, vigorously reasserted *bakufu* power, purged his enemies, forced into retirement or house arrest the daimyo who had opposed him and were on the losing side in the succession dispute, including the Lord of Mito, and punished some of the court nobles and Mito loyalists. For a moment the *bakufu* was revitalized. But it was only for a moment: In March 1860 Ii was assassinated by a group of samurai, mostly from Mito.

Before committing suicide Ii's assassins drew up a document expressing their devotion to the cause for which they had killed and for which they were about to die. It can be summed up in the two phrases that became the slogans for the movement against the Tokugawa: *Sonnō*—"Revere the Emperor"—and *Jōi*—"Expel the Barbarians."

## Sonnō Jōi

As we observed earlier, Mito was the home of an emperor-centered school of historiography and political thought, and its lord was one of the most fervent advocates of a strong military policy to "expel the barbarians." It is therefore not surprising that Mito thought influenced the passionate and brilliant young man who became the main spokesman and hero of the *Sonnō Jōi* movement. This was Yoshida Shōin (1830–59), the son of a low ranking Chōshū samurai. Yoshida was influenced by *bushidō* in the tradition of Yamaga Sokō, by books on military science, and by Confucianism. From Sakuma Shōzan he learned about the West. Then he became acquainted with Mito ideas on a study trip to northern Japan, which, since it was unauthorized, cost him his samurai rank. Apprehensive of the West and convinced of the importance of knowing one's enemy, he tried to stow away on one of Commodore Perry's ships but was caught and placed under house arrest in Chōshū. After his release he started a school there and attracted disciples, including Kido Kōin, one of the three leading statesmen of the Meiji Restoration, and the future Meiji leaders Itō Hirobumi and Yamagata Aritomo.

Yoshida condemned the *bakufu* for its handling of the foreign problem. Its failure to expel the barbarians, he felt, reflected incompetence, dereliction of duty, and a lack of proper reverence for the throne. Like many men of lower samurai origins, he was impatient with a system that rewarded birth more than ability or talent, and he saw the *bakufu*'s inability to eject the foreigner as a consequence of this system. What was needed to redress the situation, he believed, were pure and selfless officials who would act out of true loyalty rather than mindless obedience. Thus Yoshida's teaching combined elements of moral revival at home, opposition to the foreigner, and championship of the throne.

Initially Yoshida favored the appointment of new men to the *bakufu*, but after the signing of the treaty with the United States in 1858, he concluded that the *bakufu* must be overthrown. Both personal fulfillment and national salvation required an act of unselfish self-sacrifice by a national hero. Yoshida sought to achieve both aims himself. In 1858 he plotted the assassination of the emissary sent by the shogun to the imperial court to persuade the emperor to agree to the commercial treaty with the United States. Word leaked out. Yoshida was arrested and sent to Edo where he was beheaded the following year.

## Mixed Reactions to the West

In this turbulent era Japanese reactions to the West varied widely. Some Japanese, like the Confucian Shinoya Tōin (1810–67), had an absolute hatred of everything Western. He even belittled the script in which the foreigners wrote, describing it as:

> confused and irregular, wriggling like snakes or larvae of mosquitoes. The straight ones are like dog's teeth, the round ones are like worms. The crooked ones are like the forelegs of a mantis, the stretched ones are like slime lines left by snails. They resemble dried bones or decaying skulls, rotten bellies of dead snakes or parched vipers.[2]

It is not surprising that a culture which prized calligraphy on the Chinese model should find the strictly utilitarian Western script aesthetically unappetizing, but Shinoya's invective goes beyond mere distaste. Every word betrays, indeed is meant to express, horror and disgust at the beast that had now come among them.

But there were others who were determined to learn from the West, even if only to use that knowledge to defeat the foreigner. Their slogan was *kaikoku jōi:* "open the country to drive out the barbarians." The learning process continued. In 1857 the *bakufu* opened an "Institute for the Investigation of Barbarian Books" near Edo Castle. Not only the *bakufu* but also some of the domains sent men on study trips abroad; in the case of the *han* this was often done illegally. The process of adopting Western technology, begun as we have seen even before Perry's arrival, was accelerated. An indication of the people's receptivity to the new knowledge is provided by the popularity of the writings of Fukuzawa Yukichi (1835–1901), who went abroad twice in the early sixties and published seven books prior to the Restoration, beginning with *Conditions in the West (Seiyō jijō)*, the first volume of which appeared in 1866 and promptly sold 150,000 copies. Another 100,000 copies were sold in pirated editions. These works, written in a simple style (easy enough for Fukuzawa's housemaid to read), were filled with detailed descriptions of Western institutions and life: hospitals and schools, tax systems and museums, climate and clothes, cutlery, and beds and chamberpots. Fukuzawa went on to become a leading Meiji intellectual, but the turbulent years just prior to the Restoration were dangerous for men of his outlook.

In contrast to men like Yoshida Shōin, others hoped for a reconciliation of the court and *bakufu,* and there were some who still hoped the *bakufu* could take the lead in creating a more modern state. These issues, at work during the sixties, were finally buried in the Restoration.

## Last Years of the Shogunate: 1860–1867

After the assassination of Ii Naosuke in 1860 the *bakufu* leadership turned to a policy of compromise. An effort was made to effect a "union of the court and military" that was confirmed by the shogun's marriage to the emperor's sister. In return for affirming the emperor's primacy, the *bakufu* obtained assent for its foreign policy. It also sought to win daimyo support by relaxing the old requirements for attendance at Edo. However, this policy ran into the opposition of Kyōto loyalists, activists of the *sonnō jōi* persuasion, samurai, and voluntary *rōnin* who had escaped the bonds of feudal discipline by requesting to leave their lords' service. Psychologically this was not difficult, since their loyalty to their lords had become bureaucratized and since they now felt the claims of a higher loyalty to the throne. Men of extremist dedication, ready to sacrifice their lives for the cause, terrorized the streets of Kyōto in the early sixties and made the capital unsafe for moderates.

Foreigners, too, were subject to attack. The opening of the ports had been followed by a marked rise in the price of rice, causing great economic distress. Xenophobia, that is, intense patriotism coupled with hatred of foreigners, was reinforced by economic hardship caused by the Westerners. Several foreigners were assassinated by fervent samurai in 1859, and in 1861 Townsend Harris' Dutch interpreter was cut down, and the British legation in Edo was attacked. In 1862 a British merchant lost his life at the hands of Satsuma samurai. When the British were unable to obtain satisfaction from the *bakufu*, they took matters into their own hands. In August 1863 they bombarded Kagoshima, the Satsuma capital, in order to force punishment of the guilty and payment of an indemnity.

A similar incident involving Chōshū took place in the summer of 1863. By that time extremists had won control of the court and with Chōshū backing had forced the shogun to accept June 25, 1863 as the date for the expulsion of the barbarians. The *bakufu*, caught between intransigent foreigners and the insistent court, interpreted the agreement to mean that negotiations for the closing of the ports would begin on that day, but Chōshū and the loyalists interpreted it more literally. When Chōshū guns began firing on foreign ships in the Straits of Shimonoseki, the foreign ships fired back. First American warships came to shell the fortifications; then French ships landed parties which destroyed the fort and ammunition. Still Chōshū persisted in firing on foreign vessels, until in September 1864 a combined British, French, Dutch, and American fleet demolished the forts and forced Chōshū to come to terms. These losses, plus a defeat inflicted on Chōshū adherents by a Satsuma-Aizu force in Kyōto in August 1864, stimulated Chōshū to overhaul its military forces. It had already undertaken to purchase Western arms and ships. Now peasant militia were organized, and mixed rifle units were formed—staffed by commoners and samurai, a radical departure from Tokugawa practice and from the basic principles of Tokugawa society. One of these units was commanded by Itō Hirobumi, recently returned from study in England.

Satsuma's reponse to defeat, although not as radical as Chōshū's, was similar in its appreciation of the superiority of Western weapons. With British help the domain began acquiring Western ships, forming the nucleus of what was to become the Imperial Japanese Navy. The British supported Satsuma partly because they were disillusioned with the *bakufu* and partly because the French were supporting the shogunate with arms in the hope of building a strong French role in a reconstituted shogunate. In both Chōshū and Satsuma there was less talk about "expelling the barbarians" and more about "enriching the country and strengthening the army," at least among the leaders.

The politics of these years were even more than usually full of complications and intrigues, and as long as Chōshū and Satsuma remained on opposite sides the situation remained fluid. Traditionally unfriendly to each other, competing for power in Kyōto, and differing in their policy recommendations, they were nevertheless unified in their opposition to a restoration of Tokugawa power. There were two wars against Chōshū. In the first, 1864–65, a large *bakufu* force with men from many domains defeated Chōshū. This in turn set off a civil war in Chōshū from which the revolutionaries with their mixed rifle regiments emerged victors. This led to a second *bakufu* war against Chōshū, but before this second war began, in 1866, Satsuma and Chōshū made a secret alliance. When war did come, Satsuma and some other powerful *han* remained on the sidelines. Chōshū, although outnumbered, defeated the *bakufu.*

After this defeat by a single *han,* the *bakufu* (under the direction of Hitotsu-bashi Keiki, who inherited the position of shogun in 1866) tried to save what it could. There were attempts to work out a daimyo coalition and calls for imperial restoration. In November the shogun accepted a proposal that he resign in favor of a council of daimyo under the emperor. According to this arrangement he was to retain his lands and as the most powerful lord in Japan serve as prime minister. However, this was unacceptable to the *sonnō* advocates in Satsuma and Chōshū and to the restorationists at court, including the court noble Iwakura Tonomi (1825–83), a master politician. On January 3, 1868, forces from Satsuma and other *han* seized the palace and proclaimed the restoration. The shogunate was destroyed. Tokugawa lands were confiscated, and the shogun himself was reduced to the status of an ordinary daimyo. A short civil war ensued. There was fighting in Edo and in northern Honshū but no real contest. Last to surrender was the *bakufu* navy in May 1869.

## Formation of a New Government (Meiji Restoration)

The men who overthrew the Tokugawa in January 1868 did not subscribe to any clear and well-defined program. There was general agreement on the abolition of the shogunate and "restoration" of the emperor, but this meant no more than that the emperor should once again be at the center of the political system, functioning as the source of legitimacy and providing a sense of continuity. It definitely did not mean that actual power should be given to the sixteen-year-old Meiji Emperor (1852–1912; r. 1867–1912),* nor did it necessarily imply the destruction of feudalism, for there were those who envisioned the restoration in terms of a new feudal system headed by the emperor. On the other hand, Japanese scholars had long been aware that the Chinese system provided a bureaucratic alternative to feudalism. This, very likely, eased the shift to bureacratic centralization.

The new leaders did not always see eye to eye, but they did share certain qualities: they were all of similar age (35–43) and rank, and came from the victorious *han* or the court aristocracy, although the *han* coalition was soon broadened to include men from Tosa and Hizen. The three most eminent leaders in the early years of the restoration were Ōkubo Toshimichi (1830–78), Kido Kōin (1833–77), and Saigō Takamori (1827–77). Both Ōkubo and Kido had risen to leadership in their own domains (Satsuma and Chōshū), through their influence in the domain's bureaucratic establishment and among the loyalist activists. Of the two, Ōkubo was the stronger personality, disciplined, formal, and somewhat intimidating; completely dedicated to the nation; cautious and practical. Kido was more lively but also more volatile, less self-confident but more concerned than Ōkubo with strengthening the popular base of the government. But he was just as devoted to building a strong state.

Ōkubo's was the single strongest voice in government during 1873–78. One of his initial tasks was to retain the cooperation of Saigō, the military leader of the Satsuma forces which had joined with Chōshū to overthrow the Tokugawa. Saigō was a man of imposing physique and great physical strength. He was known for his outstanding courage, and possessed many of the traditional warrior virtues, such as generosity and contempt for money. More conservative than the others, he was devoted to Satsuma and its samurai but worked with the others at least until 1873. They were united in their conviction that the country must be strengthened to resist the West.

For the sake of national self-preservation the leaders were prepared to enact vast changes, but it took time to plan and carry these out, and indeed, to consolidate their own power in a land where, as Kido complained, "we are surrounded on four sides by little *bakufu.*"[3] To insure that the emperor would not become a focus of opposition to reform, Ōkubo argued that he should be moved to Edo, renamed Tōkyō (Eastern Capital) in September 1868. This took place the following year when the emperor moved into the shogun's former castle, which was finally, after much debate, renamed the "imperial palace" in 1871.

## The Charter

Even before the move, in April 1868 while the emperor was still in Kyōto, a Charter Oath was issued in his name to provide a general if vague statement of purpose for the new regime. It consisted of five articles:

* His name was Mutsuhito, but, as in the case of the emperors of Ch'ing China, it is customary to refer to him and to his successors by the names of their reign periods.

1. An assembly widely convoked shall be established and all matters of state shall be decided by public discussion.
2. All classes high and low shall unite in vigorously promoting the economy and welfare of the nation.
3. All civil and military officials and the common people as well shall be allowed to fulfill their aspirations, so that there may be no discontent among them.
4. Base customs of former times shall be abandoned and all actions shall conform to the principles of international justice.
5. Knowledge shall be sought throughout the world and thus shall be strengthened the foundation of the Imperial polity.[4]

Although the government was reorganized to provide for an assembly in keeping with the first article, power remained with the original leadership, and the attempt to implement this provision was soon abandoned. In contrast, the end of seclusion, the acceptance of international law, and the openness to foreign ideas conveyed by the last two articles did take place. Symbolic of this shift was the audience granted representatives of the foreign powers by the emperor in Kyōto just a month before the Charter Oath was issued. The document itself was drafted by two men familiar with Western thought; it was then revised by Kido. The ramifications of the Charter Oath were far from clear, but the last article, to seek for knowledge "throughout the world" was taken very seriously. Furthermore, the entire document illustrates the gulf between Japanese and Chinese leaders at this time. No Chinese government would have issued such a document in an attempt to gain political strength.

## Dismantling Feudalism

While the machinery of the central government underwent various reorganizations, the prime need was for the government to extend and consolidate its authority. Since the continued existence of the feudal domains was a major obstacle to this, the government leaders undertook the delicate but essential task of abolishing the *han*. In March 1869, Kido and Ōkubo were able to use their influence to induce the daimyo of Chōshū and Satsuma to return their domains to the emperor. They were joined in this act by the lords of Tosa and Hizen, and many others followed suit, anxious to be in the good graces of the new government and expecting to be appointed governors of their former domains, which they were. The real blow came in 1871 when, in the name of national unity, the domains were completely abolished and the whole country was reorganized into prefectures. This was made palatable to the daimyo by generous financial arrangements. The daimyo were allowed to retain a tenth of the former domain revenue as personal income while the government assumed responsibility for *han* debts and financial obligations. The daimyo were also assured continued high social standing and prestige. Finally, in 1884, they were elevated to the peerage.

By background and experience the new leadership was keenly sensitive to the importance of military power. Initially the new government was entirely dependent on forces from the supporting domains, but this would hardly do for a government truly national in scope. Accordingly the leaders set about forming a new army freed from local loyalties. Rejecting the views of Saigō, who envisioned a samurai army that would insure the warrior class a brilliant and useful role in Japan's future, the leaders decided in 1872 to build their army on the basis of conscription. In January 1873, the new measure, largely the work of Yamagata Aritomo (1838–1922), "father of the Japanese Army," became law.

The restoration had a profound effect on the samurai. The new army, by eliminating distinctions between commoners and samurai, cut right to the heart of the status system. Anyone could become a warrior now. Other marks of samurai distinctiveness were eliminated or eroded. In 1870 commoners were allowed to acquire surnames and were released from previous occupational and residential restrictions. In 1871 the wearing of swords by samurai was made optional—five years later it was to be prohibited entirely.

The samurai's position was further undermined by the dismantling of feudalism. The abolition of the *han* threatened their economic position because the *han* had traditionally been the source of samurai stipends, and the burden of continuing stipend payments at the usual rate was more than the central government could afford. In addition, without the old domains, the samurai no longer had any social or political functions to perform. Accordingly, they were pensioned off. But in view of their number, 5 or 6 percent of the total population, the government could not afford to treat them as generously as it did the daimyo. At first samurai stipends were reduced on a sliding scale from half to a tenth of what they had been, then they were given the right to commute these into twenty year bonds (1873), and finally they were forced to accept the bonds (1876).

Reduction and commutation of samurai stipends was only one of the measures taken to establish the new government on a sound financial basis. In addition to monetary and banking reforms, a tax system was created (1873). These fiscal measures were largely the work of Ōkuma Shigenobu (1838–1922), a man from Hizen who was to remain prominent in Meiji politics, and Itō Hirobumi (1841–1909), of Chōshū. The main source of government revenue was, as before, agriculture, but in place of the old percentage of the crop payable by the village to the daimyo, the tax was now collected by the government in money in accordance with the assessed value of the land. It was payable by the owner, and for this purpose ownership rights had to be clearly established. This was not done in favor of the absentee feudal interest long divorced from the land, nor did ownership pass equitably to all peasants. Instead, certificates were issued to the cultivators and wealthy villagers who had paid the tax during Tokugawa times. In this way tenancy was perpetuated, and since poor peasants were often unable to meet their taxes and thus were forced to mortgage their land, the rate of tenancy increased, rising from about 25 percent before the new system to about 40 percent twenty years later.

## Disaffection and Opposition

The creation of a modern political, military, and fiscal system benefited the state but hurt some of the people. The peasantry was unhappy, not only about the land system but also about forced military service, and showed its displeasure by staging uprisings with increasing frequency from 1866 to 1873. Many of the large merchant houses that had developed symbiotic relationships with the *bakufu* or daimyo also suffered during these years and some went bankrupt.

More serious for the regime was samurai discontent. The new government was itself led by former samurai, and for many men the new order meant a release from old restrictions and the opening of new opportunities. Since the samurai were the educated class with administrative experience, it was they who supplied the personnel for local and national government, provided officers for the army, teachers for the schools, and much of society's leadership. Yet there were many who did not make a successful transition, who were unable to respond positively to the new vocations now opened to them or to use their payments to establish themselves in new lines of endeavor. And among the leaders as well as the supporters of the Meiji government were men who firmly believed that its purpose was the restoration of the old, not the creation of the new. A split between conservatives and modernizers developed early in the Restoration and came to a head in 1873.

## The Crisis of 1873

The crisis centered on the issue of going to war with Korea in order to force that country to open her doors to Japan. Those who advocated war, such as Saigō and the Tosa samurai Itagaki Taisuke (1836–1919), did so not only out of nationalist motives but also because they saw war as an occasion to provide employment for the samurai, an opportunity to give them a greater role in the new society, a means to preserve their military heritage. Saigō, a military leader with great charisma and devotion to the way of the warrior, asked to be sent to Korea as ambassador so that the Koreans, by killing him, would provide a cause for going to war.

A decision for war was made in the summer of 1873, in the absence of Ōkubo, Kido, and other important leaders who were abroad, in America and Europe. They were on a diplomatic and study mission headed by Iwakura Tomoni, the noble who had played a leading role at court in bringing about the Meiji Restoration. The purposes of the Iwakura mission were to convey the Meiji Emperor's respects to the heads of state of the treaty powers and build good will, to discuss subjects for later treaty revision, and to provide its distinguished members with an opportunity to observe and study the West at first hand. Its major accomplishment was in fulfilling the last mentioned objective, for the trip made a deep impression on the Japanese leaders who were exposed for the first time to the West and saw at first hand the evidence of Western strength. They returned home with a new realization of the magnitude of the task facing Japan in her quest for equality, and a new appreciation of the importance and complexity of modernization. They were convinced of the urgent priority of domestic change.

When the mission returned Ōkubo led the opposition to the Korean venture on the grounds that Japan could not yet afford such an undertaking. Ōkubo, Kido, and Iwakura prevailed, with the support of many officials and the court. It was decided to abandon the Korean expedition and to concentrate on internal development. The decision split the government. Bitterly disappointed, the war advocates, including Saigō and Itagaki, resigned. In opposition they provided leadership for those who were disaffected by the new government and its policies, an opposition which would prove troublesome to those in power. But their departure left the government in the hands of a group of men unified by a commitment to modernization. Most prominent among them were Ōkubo, Itō, Ōkuma, and Iwakura.

By 1873 the Meiji government had survived the difficult period of initial consolidation. It had established the institutional foundations for the new state, had found a means of defense and national security, and with the resolution of the 1873 crisis, had charted the basic course of development at home and peace abroad that was to dominate Japanese policies during the next twenty years.

## The Meaning of the Restoration

A major aspect of the Restoration was increased openness to the West. Signs of at least superficial Westernization were already in evidence in the early 1870s, when the gentleman of fashion sported a foreign umbrella and watch and indulged in beef stew. Faddish Westernism was satirized in one of the bestsellers of the day, *Auguranabe* (*Idle Talks in the Sukiyaki House*) (1871–72) by Kanagaki Robun (1829–1904). Ōkubo ate bread and drank dark tea for breakfast and wore Western clothes even at home. In 1872 Western dress was made mandatory at court and other official functions. The Gregorian calendar was adopted the same year. After the Tokyo fire of 1872, Tokyo's main avenue, the Ginza, was rebuilt with brick buildings, colonnades, and gas lamps to provide lighting. (See Figure 5-4.) Supervising the work was an English architect, one of 214 Westerners employed by the government in 1872, over half of them English.

By contrast there was an effort to turn Japan into a Shinto state. In 1868 Shinto was proclaimed the basis for the government and a Department of Shinto was established with precedence over the other government departments. There was a drive to purify Shinto, to eliminate Buddhist influences that had steadily seeped into Shinto, and to make Shinto the only religion of

Figure 5-4  The Ginza, 1873.

Japan. This drive, however, ran into opposition from Buddhists and also conflicted with Western pressures for the legalization of Christianity. In 1872 the Department of Shinto was abolished, and in 1873 the old ban on Christianity was lifted.

The Restoration leaders opted for the new, and they were able to initiate far-reaching changes partly because they inherited from Tokugawa times a political system that reached much deeper and more effectively into society than did that of China. Furthermore, they introduced the new in the name of the emperor, a symbol of continuity with the old. This made it easier for them to innovate but also assured the survival of old values and ideas. In the light of hindsight they appear in the dual role of preservers of tradition and initiators of East Asia's first cultural revolution.

The Meiji Restoration bears very little resemblance to the contemporary T'ung-chih Restoration in China,* for it laid stress on innovation rather than renovation or renewal. In many essential ways the restoration was revolutionary: it destroyed the feudal system and created a centralized state; it eliminated the old class lines and legally opened all careers to all men; in all areas of human activity it prepared the way for the profound changes that during the next century were to transform the very countryside of Japan. But if it was a revolution, it was a revolution from above, an aristocratic revolution, to borrow a term from Thomas C. Smith.[5] If it was not a restoration in the nineteenth-century Chinese sense, neither was it a revolution as the term is applied to

---

* On the meaning of the Chinese and Japanese terms, see note, page 98.

twentieth-century China. Relatively peaceful, it was not the product of a mass movement nor of a radical social ideology, and it did not radically change the structure of village life or the mode of agricultural production. It eliminated the samurai as a legally defined, privileged class, but, led by men who were themselves samurai, did so gently and in terms samurai could understand.

## NOTES

1. Michiaki Kawakita, *Modern Currents in Japanese Art*, Heibonsha Survey of Japanese Art, Vol. 24, trans. Charles S. Terry (New York and Tokyo: Weatherhill/Heibonsha, 1974), p. 29.

2. Marius B. Jansen, ed., *Changing Japanese Attitudes Toward Modernization* (Princeton: Princeton University Press, 1969), pp. 57–58; quoting van Gulik, "Kakkaron: A Japanese Echo of the Opium War," *Monumenta Serica* 4 (1939): 542–43.

3. Albert Craig and Donald Shively, eds., *Personality in Japanese History* (Berkeley and Los Angeles: University of California Press, 1970), p. 297.

4. Ishii Ryosuke, *Japanese Legislation in the Meiji Era*, trans. William J. Chambliss (Tokyo: Pan-Pacific Press, 1958), p. 145. Frequently quoted, as in William G. Beasley, *The Meiji Restoration* (Stanford: Stanford University Press, 1972), p. 325.

5. See Thomas C. Smith, "Japan's Aristocratic Revolution," *Yale Review* 50 (Spring 1961): 370–83. Also see Marius B. Jansen, "The Meiji State: 1868–1912," in James B. Crowley, ed., *Modern East Asia: Essays in Interpretation* (New York: Harcourt Brace Jovanovich, 1970), pp. 95–121, which cites Smith on p. 103.

現代日本之形成

| 1868 | 1877 | 1889 1890 | 1894 1912 |

The Restoration

Satsuma
Rebellion

Promulgation of
the Constitution

Rescript on
Education

Start of the
Sino-Japanese War

M E I J I   J A P A N

# The Emergence of Modern Japan: 1874-1894

During the last thirty years of the nineteenth century the Western challenge to the rest of the globe became more intense, more formidable, and more complex. With continued progress in science and technology, the power of the economically advanced countries continued to grow while capitalism and nationalism fueled competition over the acquisition of colonies. As the area left for possible expansion diminished, the race gained momentum. In these thirty years Europeans expanded their colonial empires by over 10 million square miles, about a fifth of the world's land area, inhabited by nearly 150 million people, about 10 percent of the world's population. Much of this expansion took place in Africa, but new colonies were formed also in Southeast Asia. Northeast Asia came under imperialist pressure leading to the Sino-Japanese War of 1894–95 fought over Korea. Japan's victory in that war demonstrated that she had by that time become a participant in, rather than a victim of, the new imperialism.

The leading maritime power in the world continued to be Great Britain, which, as before, had the largest foreign commercial stake in China and Japan. Russia persisted in its overland expansion into and beyond Central Asia. Two other powers, France and the United States, maintained an interest in East Asian developments. In Europe, the emergence of Germany after the Franco-Prussian War (1870) provided a conservative alternative to England's liberal model for modernization. After the war the German Chancellor, Otto von Bismarck (1815–98), adopted a policy of encouraging France to compensate for her losses in Europe by building an overseas empire. This gave an impetus to France's ambitions in Southeast Asia that led to war between France and China in 1883–85. The world was becoming smaller, and, for the weak or weakened, more dangerous.

Relations between China and Japan during the twenty years discussed in this chapter began with a minor clash and ended with a war that had profound internal effects in both countries and changed the balance of power between them for the next half century. The minor clash occurred in 1874 when Japan sent an expedition to Taiwan ostensibly to punish aborigines who had killed some Okinawans shipwrecked on their shores. Its real purpose was to mollify those who resented the abandonment of the Korean expedition so earnestly advocated by Saigō and his friends. An expedition to Taiwan was a smaller and less dangerous undertaking. It was successful, and the result was that China was forced to pay an indemnity and to recognize Japanese sovereignty over the Ryūkū Islands, of which Okinawa is the largest. This ended the ties that the Ryūkyūs had maintained with China even while they were Satsuma vassals. Thus for China the war brought the first of a series of alienations of tributaries, but in Japan it did little to reconcile the samurai.

Statesmen in both China and Japan saw their primary task as that of strengthening their states against the predatory foreign powers, of stemming and if possible reversing the tide of humiliating concessions incorporated in the unequal treaties. But they differed not only in their methods and achievements, but also in their views of what had to be done and for what ultimate ends. In the process, Japan during these years changed more rapidly than China.

For Japan the years between the Restoration and the Sino-Japanese War were a period of conscious learning from the West in an effort to become a modern nation accepted as an equal by the powers of the world. It was a time of great changes: in government and politics, in the economy, in people's ideas, in education—a time of building national strength. These changes were neither smooth nor simple. In the intricate interplay of old and new, foreign and traditional, some old ways went the way of the samurai's sword and topknot, but others were retained and put to new uses. This is a process that still continues in the second half of the twentieth century, but the Sino-Japanese War marked the end of a crucial stage, for by then Japan had achieved many of her initial objectives: a centralized government, a modernizing economy, and sufficient military strength to warrant international respect.

## Political Developments

Acting in the name of the emperor, a small oligarchy (group of leaders) dominated the government during the 1870s and 1880s, but not without opposition. Embittered samurai resorted to arms, first in an uprising in Hizen in 1874 and then, more seriously, in 1877 in Satsuma. The Satsuma Rebellion was led by Saigō Takamori, who had withdrawn from the government after the 1873 decision against the Korean expedition. The number of those who threw in their lot with the rebellion rose as high as 42,000. Its suppression strained the military resources of the Restoration government, but after half a year the rebellion was crushed. The Satsuma Rebellion was the last stand of the samurai. When the military situation became hopeless, Saigō killed himself in the approved warrior manner. His was a martyr's death for a lost cause. Saigō died under official condemnation as a traitor, but the Meiji government soon rehabilitated him, and government leaders joined in expressions of admiration and acclaim for the man who came to be regarded as *the* hero of the Restoration. Not only conservatives but representatives of the most diverse political persuasions praised the magnanimity of his spirit and transformed Saigō into a legendary hero, celebrated in poems and songs (including an army marching song), portrayed on stage and in an extensive literature, depicted in portraits and prints, even identified with the planet Mars.

Protest against the government continued, on occasion, to take a violent turn. Less than half a year after Saigō's death, some of his sympathizers assassinated Ōkubo Toshimichi, also from Satsuma, who had worked so hard and successfully to create the new Japanese state. There were other assassination attempts as well, both successful and unsuccessful. More important in the long run, however, was the formation of nonviolent political opposition, animated not only by objections to one or another aspect of the government's policies, but also in protest against the political domination exercised by a few oligarchs from Chōshū and Satsuma, men who had exclusive control over the centers of power. Basing their position on the first article of the 1868 Charter Oath, opposition leaders early in 1874 demanded the creation of an elected legislature. Prominent among them was Itagaki Taisuke, the Tosa leader who, like Saigō, had left the government in 1873 over the Korean issue. In Tosa and then elsewhere antigovernment organizations voiced the discontent of local interests, demanding political rights, local self-government, and formation of a national assembly. The advocates of a constitution, and the leaders of what became known as the movement for popular rights, drew upon Western political theories for support. They argued also that the adoption of representative institutions would create greater unity between the people and the emperor. In their view a constitution was needed not in order to limit the emperor's powers but in order to control his advisers.

The men in power were not adverse to some kind of constitution as a necessary and even desirable component of modernization. By the end of 1878, Kido, Ōkubo, and Saigō were all dead. Of the older men only Iwakura remained important, and three younger men who had already contributed significantly to the Meiji state now gained major prominence: Itō Hirobumi and Yamagata Aritomo, both from Chōshū, and Ōkuma Shigenobu from Hizen. Yamagata was the creator of the new army while Itō took the lead in political modernization and Ōkuma served as Finance Minister. But there were tensions between Itō and Ōkuma. In 1881 the latter precipitated a break when he wrote a memorandum advocating the adoption of an English-style political system. His proposals that the majority party in parliament form the government, that the cabinet be responsible to parliament, and that the first elections be held in 1883 clashed with the conservative and gradualist views of his colleagues. First his proposals were rejected; then when he joined in public criticism of the government over its sale of a certain government project in Hokkaidō, Ōkuma was dismissed. At the same time the government announced that a constitution would be granted to take effect in 1890.

## Formation of Parties

In response Itagaki and his associates formed the Jiyūtō (Liberal party), and Ōkuma followed by organizing the Kaishintō (Progressive party). Both parties advocated constitutional government with meaningful powers exercised by a parliament, but they differed considerably in ideology and composition. The Jiyūtō, linked to Tosa, was influenced by the ideas of Rousseau and the French Revolution. It drew much of its support from the rural areas, where peasants and landlords were unhappy that their taxes remained as high as they had been under the Tokugawa and resented bearing a heavier tax burden than that required of commerce and industry. Ōkuma's party (linked to Hizen) was, in contrast, more urban and more moderate, advocating English-style liberalism. It had the backing of merchants and industrialists. Although they both opposed the government, the two parties fought each other energetically. At the same time the parties were troubled by internal factionalism; party splits were based on master-follower and patron-client relations rather than on differences in programs.

The organized opposition was further hampered by the need to operate under restrictive laws, including some promulgated to control political criticism before the parties were formed. Restrictive press laws enacted in 1875 and revised in 1877 gave the Home Minister power to suppress publications and provided fines or imprisonment for offenders. The 1880 Public Meeting Law placed all political meetings under police supervision. Included among those prohibited from attending such meetings were teachers and students. Nor were political associations allowed to recruit members or to combine or correspond with similar bodies. Finally the 1887 Peace Preservation Law increased the Home Minister's powers of censorship and gave the police authority to expel people from a given area: 570 were shortly removed from Tokyo in this fashion.

The Liberal party was hurt not only by differences among its leaders but even more by antagonism within its membership, including conflicts between tenants and landlords. It proved impossible to contain within one party both radicals who supported and even led peasant riots and the substantial land-owners who were the objects of these attacks. In 1884 the party was dissolved. At the end of the same year Ōkuma and his followers left the Progressive party, although others stayed to keep it in existence. Criticism of the government continued, but this initial attempt to organize political parties turned out to have been premature.

## The Meiji Constitution

While suppressing its critics the government was also taking steps to increase its effectiveness. A system of centralized local administration was established that put an end to the Tokugawa tradition of local self-government. Villages and towns were now headed by officials appointed by the Home Ministry in Tokyo, which also controlled the police. In the late seventies (1878–80), local assemblies were created as sounding boards of public opinion, but their rights were limited to debate and their membership restricted to men of means. The details of bureaucratic procedure were worked out and a civil service system fashioned. A new code of criminal law was enacted, and work was begun on civil and commercial codes.

To prepare for the promised constitution-making, Itō spent a year and a half in Europe during 1882–83, mostly studying German theories and practices, for he and his fellow oligarchs already had a general idea of the kind of conserva-tive constitution they wanted. After his return, a number of steps were taken in preparation for the constitution: a new peerage was created in 1884 com-posed of the old court nobility, ex-daimyo, and some members of the oligarchy; in 1885 a European-style cabinet was created with Itō as premier; and in 1888 the Privy Council was organized as the highest government advisory board.

In 1889 work on the constitution was completed, and it was promulgated as a "gift" from the Emperor to the people. It continued in force until 1945. To the Emperor was reserved the power to declare war, conclude treaties, and command the army. He also had the right to open, recess, and dissolve the leg-islature; the power to veto the latter's decisions; and the right to issue his own ordinances. The cabinet was responsible not to the legislature but to the em-peror. The Diet, as the legislature was called, consisted of two houses, the House of Peers and the House of Representatives. The latter was elected by a constituency limited to about half a million voters out of a total population of around forty million. The most consequential power of the Diet was the power of the purse, but, borrowing from the Prussian example, the constitution provided for automatic renewal of the previous year's budget whenever the Diet failed to pass a new budget. Only the emperor could take the initiative to revise the constitution.

The constitution favored the men who had been governing in the emperor's name and who viewed government, like the emperor in whose name it functioned, as operating on a level above the divisive and unedifying world of party politics. But the parties turned out to be stronger than the oligarchs had expected. In the first election of 1890 the reconstituted Liberal party (Jiyūtō) won 130 seats, the Progressives (Kaishintō) led once again by Ōkuma won 47, and only 79 members favoring the government were elected. As a result of this growing party strength there was a stiff parliamentary battle over the budget in the first session of the Diet, which was resolved only after the premier, Yamagata, resorted to bribery and force. When the budget failed to pass the following year, the Diet was dissolved. During the subsequent elections (1892) the government used the police to discourage the opposition but failed to obtain a more tractable Diet. Another election was held in 1894, but the constitution worked no better. It was the war with China over Korea that broke the political deadlock of that year and provided temporary unity in the body politic. During the war the government enjoyed enthusiastic support at home. By that time Japan was quite different from what it had been twenty years earlier when the oligarchs rejected intervention in Korea. The political developments were just one dimension of the transformation of Japan.

## Western Influences on Values and Ideas

Enthusiasm for aspects of Western science and technology went back, as we have seen, to Tokugawa proponents of "Dutch Learning," and from the very start of Meiji, there was a fashion for Western styles, including styles of dress. Representative of Japanese attitudes, the Meiji Emperor himself wore Western clothes and dressed his hair in the Western manner. See, for example, the emperor's portrait by Takahashi Yūichi (1828–94) shown in Figure 6-1.

Not only the subject, but also the artist, was influenced by Western styles. Takahashi was very conscious of his precursors: he revered Shiba Kōkan. Like Shiba and his own teacher, the prominent Western-style painter Kawakami Togai (1827–81), Takahashi placed great value on realism in his works. Most of these, unlike the emperor's portrait, were still-life studies of familiar objects, and his most famous work is a realistic painting of a salmon. A major difference between Kawakami and Takahashi is that whereas the former saw Western art as no more than a necessary component of Western learning to be mastered for technical reasons, Takahashi also valued it as art.

Figure 6-1
Takahashi Yūichi,
*Portrait of the Meiji
Emperor*. Oil, 1880.

Similarly men turned to the West in other fields, not only for practical reasons but because they were attracted by the intrinsic nature of Western achievements. Prominent among such men were the intellectuals who, in 1873, formed the Meirokusha, a prestigious society devoted to the study of all aspects of Western knowledge. These same men led what was known as the movement for "civilization and enlightenment" (*bummei kaika*). A leading theorist of this movement was Fukuzawa Yukichi, whose books on the West were mentioned earlier.

## "Civilization and Enlightenment"

In eighteenth-century Europe the intellectual movement known as the Enlightenment sought to put all traditional ideas and institutions to the test of reason. Impressed by the achievements of science as exemplified in the work of Sir Isaac Newton (1642–1727), such philosophers as Voltaire (1694–1778) and Diderot (1713–84) believed that reason could produce similar progress in solving human problems and that the main obstacles to truth and happiness were irrationality and superstition. Their greatest monument was the encyclopedia compiled by Diderot and his associates, a summation of the accomplishments of reason in all fields of human knowledge.

Japanese intellectuals like Fukuzawa Yukichi were strongly influenced by the heritage of the European Enlightenment, particularly the emphasis on reason as an instrument for achieving progress. Their faith in progress was also confirmed by such influential nineteenth-century Western historians as H. T. Buckle (1821–62) and François Guizot (1787–1874). Indeed, the belief in progress remained a major nineteenth-century conviction even after the faith in reason had faded.

A corollary to this new concept of historical progress, in Japan as in the West, was a negative reevaluation of Chinese civilization, now seen as unchanging and therefore decadent. No longer did the Japanese look up to China as the land of classical civilization; on the contrary, China was now a negative model, and as her troubles continued Japanese intellectuals tended to regard her with condescension as well as concern. Now the source of "enlightenment" was in the West.

One of Fukuzawa's prime goals in advancing the cause of "civilization and enlightenment" was to stimulate in Japan the development of an independent and responsible citizenry. "It would not be far from wrong," he once complained, "to say that Japan has a government but no people."[1] Tracing the lack of individual independence back to the traditional family, Fukuzawa advocated fundamental changes in that basic social institution. Ridiculing the ancient paragons of filial piety, he urged limitations on parental demands and authority. He also recommended greater equality between the sexes, championed monogamy, argued that women should be educated and allowed to hold property, and compared the Japanese woman to a dwarfed ornamental tree, artificially stunted.

According to Fukuzawa, history was made by the people not by a few great leaders, and he thought it wrong to place too much faith in government or to give the political authorities too much power. His view of the role of government resembled the concept of the minimal state held by early European liberals. Consistent with these ideas he did not enter government himself but disseminated his views in books and through a newspaper he founded. He also established what became Keiō University, a distinguished private university in Tokyo whose graduates played an important part in the world of business and industry.

In Fukuzawa's mind the independence of the people and the independence of the country were linked; indeed, the former was a prerequisite for the latter. This view was widely held among the proponents of "enlightenment." For instance, the translator of the best seller *Self-Help* by Samuel Smiles, whose Japanese version was published in Tokyo in 1871, explained that Western nations were strong because they possessed the spirit of liberty. John Stuart Mill's *On Liberty* appeared in Japanese translation the same year; Rousseau's *The Social Contract* was published in installments during 1882–84. Fukuzawa, with his faith in progress, believed that the ultimate universal movement of history is in the direction of democracy and that individual liberty makes for national strength.

# Natural Law

Fukuzawa's liberalism of the early seventies was based on the eighteenth-century Western concept of natural law, that is, that human affairs are governed by inherent concepts of right just as the physical world is governed by the laws of nature. This belief resembled the Neo-Confucian concept of *li* ("principle") in linking the natural and human orders, but the European doctrine, unlike the Chinese, included the affirmation of innate human rights. It postulated an affirmative body of law stating the inherent rights of man in society, in whose name societies could overthrow unjust governments and establish new ones. It was to natural law that the American colonists appealed when they declared their independence in 1776, and that the French revolutionaries appealed to when they promulgated their Declaration of the Rights of Man in 1789.

# Social Darwinism

The concept of natural law, however, was soon displaced by another more recent Western import: Social Darwinism. There were various versions of this doctrine, most notably those developed by the enormously influential Herbert Spencer (1820–1903), but all were based on the theory of evolution by natural selection presented in Darwin's famous *Origin of the Species* (1859). Darwin held that over time the various forms of life adapt to changing natural conditions and to competition with each other, and that those which adapt best are most likely to survive. This theory was summarized by the catch phrase "survival of the fittest." Social Darwinism was the application of these doctrines to human history, explaining the rise and fall of nations, for example, in terms of competition, adaptation, and "survival of the fittest."

Social Darwinism seemed entirely apropos to the Japanese experience. It explained why China and Japan had been unable to resist the Western powers, but held out the promise that a nation did not have to accept permanent inferiority. Instead it justified Japanese efforts to develop national strength by mastering the learning and techniques of the West. It purported to have a "scientific" basis. And, unlike natural law with its moralistic overtones, it turned strength itself into a moral criterion, and it provided a justification for imperialism to support the expansionism of any ambitious state. Relations among nations could thus be viewed as one vast struggle for existence in which the fittest survived.

In the mid-seventies Fukuzawa first became skeptical of natural law, and then abandoned it. One effect was a loss of confidence in international law and a new view of international relations as an arena in which nations struggle for survival. Already in 1876 Fukuzawa remarked, "a few cannons are worth more than a hundred volumes of international law."[2] By 1882 he was willing to accept even autocracy if it meant strengthening the nation. Furthermore, he favored imperialist expansion both to assure Japan's safety and to bring the benefits of "civilization" to neighboring countries such as Korea. Thus he welcomed the war when it came in 1894.

Fukuzawa found words of praise for some aspects of the Japanese tradition, including the samurai value of loyal service, but continued to look primarily to the West for his models and ideas. However, he avoided the extremes of Westernization. In early Meiji some thinkers allowed their enthusiasm to get the better of their judgment, and there were all kinds of extreme proposals for radical Westernization, including one to make English the national language. However, not all supporters of Western ways were genuine enthusiasts. Many desired to impress Westerners in order to be accepted as equals and to speed treaty revision. This was the motive behind a variety of movements, ranging from a drive to reform public morals to the revision of the legal code. It also accounts for one of the symbols of the era, the Rokumeikan, a hall completed in 1883 to accommodate mixed foreign and Japanese social gatherings. Designed by an English architect in the elaborate manner of the European Renaissance, it provided the setting for dinners, card parties, and fancy dress balls.

## The Arts

In the arts, Western influence was both audible and visible. It affected the music taught in the schools and that performed in military bands. In painting, we have already noted the work of Takahashi, but the impact of the West was

Figure 6-2   Kobayashi Kiyochika, *Train at Night.* Woodcut print.

Figure 6-3
Kuroda Seiki,
*Morning Toilet.*
Oil, 1893,
178.5 cm × 98 cm.

visible also in more traditional genres. Sometimes called the last of the major *ukiyo-e* artists was Kobayashi Kiyochika (1847–1915). He introduced Western light and shading into *ukiyo-e,* using the principles of Western perspective but retaining a traditional Japanese sense of color. (See Figure 6-2.)

Western styles of painting were advanced not only by foreign artists who taught in Japan but also by Japanese who studied abroad, particularly in France, and brought back new styles and ways of looking at the world. Kuroda Seiki (1866–1924) studied in France from 1884 to 1893, and it was there that he painted *Morning Toilet* (Figure 6-3), which caused a stir when exhibited in Tokyo in 1894 and created a storm of controversy when shown in more conservative Kyōto the following year. Japan had never had a tradition of painting the nude, and there were protests that Kuroda's painting was pornography, not art. But Kuroda won the battle and went on to become one of Japan's most influential Western-style painters.

The initial enthusiasm for Western art led to the neglect and even disdain of traditional art, which shocked the American Ernest Fenollosa (1853–1908) when he came to Japan in 1878 to teach at Tokyo University. Fenollosa did what he could to make the new generation of Westernized Japanese aware of the greatness of their artistic heritage. He, himself, was an admirer of the last of the masters of the Kano school, Kano Hōgai (1828–88), and together with the younger Okakura Tenshin (1862–1913) sparked a revived interest in traditional styles. The two men were assisted by a reaction, which set in during the late eighties, against excessive Westernization. Many were attracted to the formula, "Eastern ethics; Western technology," a concept earlier advanced by Sakuma Shōzan, and there was now more talk about a national "essence" but little agreement on how it should be defined. Some feared that acceptance of a foreign culture was a step toward national decline and sought for ways to be both modern and Japanese, to adopt the universalist aspects of Western culture while retaining what was of value in their own particularist past.

The educated and sensitive were especially troubled by the tensions inherent in a program of modernization under traditionalist auspices. Western scientific rationalism could, by questioning the founding myth, undermine the throne itself. In 1892 a Tokyo University professor was forced to resign after he wrote that Shinto was a "survival of a primitive form of worship."[3] That was sacrilege. Similarly, Western individualism, fostered by the policy of modernization, clashed with the old family values that, Fukuzawa notwithstanding, continued strong and remained in official favor. In Japan, as in other modernizing countries, individuals experienced the need to make difficult choices. For many the resolution of conflicts was eased by the national triumph in war, but the problems, as we shall see, were to remain.

# Education

Japanese intellectual and political leaders were quick to realize the importance of education in fashioning a new Japan capable of competing with the West. In this, as in other areas, they showed great interest in the practices and institutions of European countries and of the United States. For example, one of the members of the Iwakura Mission paid special attention to education and wrote fifteen volumes on the subject after his return home.

At the beginning of the Meiji period, Japan sent many students overseas to obtain the advanced training it could not provide at home. One-eighth of the Ministry of Education's first budget (1873) was designated for this purpose, and 250 students were sent abroad on government scholarships that year. Furthermore, many foreign instructors were brought to Japan to teach in various specialized schools. These, however, were temporary expedients to be used until Japan's own modern educational system was in operation. By the late 1880s the number of foreign instructors was down, and only some 50 to 80 students annually were being sent abroad by the government. A landmark in the history of higher education was the establishment of Tokyo University in 1877 with four faculties: physical science, law, literature, and medicine.

Considerable progress was made in building a complete educational system, yet actual accomplishments fell short of the ambitious plan drawn up in 1872. This called for 8 universities, 256 middle schools, and 53,760 elementary schools, but thirty years later, in 1902, there were only 2 universities, 222 middle schools, and 27,076 elementary schools. Similarly, the government had to retreat from its 1872 ordinance making four years of education compulsory for all children. Among the difficulties this program encountered were money problems (elementary education was locally financed), teacher shortages, and the reluctance of rural parents to send their children to school. However, by the time four years of compulsory education were reintroduced in 1900, the great majority of children who were supposed to be in school were in actual attendance, and in 1907 the government was able to increase the period to six years. By that time the teachers were predominantly graduates of Japanese Normal Schools (teacher training institutes, the first of which was established in Tokyo in 1872).

When the Ministry of Education was first established in 1871, the French system of highly centralized administration was adopted. Although local schools were locally financed, the ministry not only determined the general direction of education but prescribed textbooks, supervised teacher training, and generally controlled the curriculum of schools throughout the country. Government educational policy therefore was decisive in determining what was taught.

There was wide agreement among political leaders that an essential function of the educational system was to provide the people with the skills necessary for modernization. They realized that not only factories and businesses but also armies and navies require a certain level of literacy and a command of simple arithmetic among the rank and file, as well as higher education for managers and officers. Beyond that, the leaders recognized that schools foster values and looked to them to mold the Japanese people into a nation. On the question of specific moral content, however, there were intense disagreements reflecting different visions of Japan's future. In the seventies when enthusiasm for the West ran high, even elementary readers and moral texts were frequently translated from English and French for use in Japanese schools. But there were also critics who insisted that the schools should preserve traditional Confucian and Japanese values. Another influential position was opposed to both Western liberal values and to traditional ideals but looked to the schools to indoctrinate the populace with modern, nationalist values. An influential proponent of this last position was Mori Arinori (1847–89), Minister of Education from 1885 until he was assassinated by a nationalist fanatic in 1889.

Although Mori had a strong hand in shaping the educational system, the most important Meiji pronouncement on the subject was drafted under the influence of the emperor's Confucian Lecturer. This was the Rescript on Education, which was issued in 1890. For half a century it remained the basic statement of the purpose of education, memorized by generations of Japanese school children. It begins by attributing "the glory of the fundamental character of Our Empire" to the Imperial Ancestors who "deeply and firmly implanted virtue" and calls upon His Majesty's subjects to observe the usual Confucian virtues beginning with filiality toward their parents, enjoins them to "pursue learning and cultivate arts" for the sake of intellectual and moral development, and "to advance public good and promote common interests." Furthermore, "should emergency arise, offer yourselves courageously to the State, and thus guard and maintain the prosperity of Our Imperial Throne coeval with heaven and earth."[4] In this document, Confucianism is identified with the throne (no mention is made of its foreign origins), and a premium is placed on patriotic service to the state and the throne. These values were further drummed into school children in compulsory ethics classes. Education was to serve both to prepare Japan for the future and to preserve elements of the past, or rather, to prepare Japan for the future in the name of the past.

Meanwhile the religious orientation of the state had also been settled. In 1882 Shinto was divided into Shrine Shinto and Sect Shinto. Most Shinto shrines, including the most prominent such as Ise and Izumo, came under Shrine Shinto and were now transformed into state institutions supposedly patriotic rather than religious in character, operating on a higher plane than the merely "religious" bodies such as the various forms of Buddhism, Christianity (legalized in 1873), and Sect Shinto. This formula permitted the government to identify itself with the Shinto tradition from which was derived the mystique of the emperor, source of its own authority, while at the same time meeting the demands for religious tolerance voiced by Japanese reformers and Western nations.

## Modernizing the Economy

In the twenty years that followed consolidation of the Meiji regime, Japan laid the foundations for a modern industrial economy. The nation was still primarily agrarian, but Western experience had shown that capital accumulated through the sale of surplus agricultural production, and labor obtained through the migration of surplus rural population to the cities, were necessary conditions for industrial development. Both conditions existed in Meiji Japan.

Japanese agriculture had become more efficient due to the introduction of new seed strains, new fertilizers, and new methods of cultivation. New land for farming was being opened, especially in Hokkaidō. New applications of science to agriculture were being tried at experimental stations and agricultural colleges. In consequence, during the fourteen years preceding the Sino-Japanese War rice yields increased by 30 percent and other crops showed comparable gains; per capita rice consumption increased. Agriculture was further stimulated by the development of a substantial export market for silk and tea, and a growing domestic demand for cotton. Thus trade also helped generate capital needed for investment in manufacturing.

Increased agricultural production did not result in major changes for the cultivator, however. Village government and the organization of village labor remained largely the same. Rents remained high: it was not unusual for a peasant's rent to equal half his rice crop. Profits resulting from the commercialization of agriculture went to the landlord, who handled the sale, rather than to the tenant. Even the creation of factory jobs did little to relieve population pressure on the land. Much of the factory labor was performed by peasant girls sent to the city to supplement their families' farm incomes for a number of years before they were married. Housed in company dormitories and strictly supervised, they were an untrained but inexpensive work force. When times were bad and factory operations slowed down, they could be laid off and returned to their villages. It was a system advantageous to both the landlord and the industrialist.

In Western countries the industrial revolution had been largely carried out by private enterprise. In Japan, however, where it was government policy to modernize so as to catch up with the West, the government itself took the initiative. The Meiji regime invested heavily in the economic infrastructure, that is, those basic public services that must be in place before an industrial economy can grow: education, transportation, communications, and so forth. As previously mentioned, students were sent abroad at public expense, for example, to study Western technologies, and foreigners were brought to Japan to teach in their areas of expertise. A major investment was made in railroads. The first line was completed in 1872, running between Tokyo and Yokohama. By the mid-nineties there were two thousand miles of track, much of it privately owned, for government initiative was followed by private investment once the feasibility, and especially the profitability, of railroads had been established.

This sequence of state initiative followed by private development can also be observed in manufacturing. The government took the lead, for example, in establishing and operating cement works, plants manufacturing glass and tiles, textile mills (silk and cotton), shipyards, mines, and munition works. The government felt these industries were essential, but private interests were unwilling to risk their capital in untried ventures, with little prospect of profits in the near term. Thus, if such ventures were to be started, the government would have to start them and finance the initial period of operations. It did so.

## The Zaibatsu

The expenditure of capital required for this effort, the payments due to samurai on their bonds, the costs of the Satsuma Rebellion, and an adverse balance of trade combined to create a government financial crisis. Rising inflation damaged the government's purchasing power and also hurt the samurai, whose income depended on the interest paid on their bonds. These problems came to a head in 1880. The government's response was mainly to cut back on expenditures, and, thereby, it gradually brought the situation under control. As part of this economy move the government decided, late in 1880, to sell at public auction all its enterprises with the exception of the munitions plants. The

buyers were usually men who were friendly with government leaders and recognized the long-term advantages of buying the factories, which were selling at
bargain prices. These enterprises did not become profitable immediately, but
when they did the result was that a small group of well-connected firms enjoyed a controlling position in the modern sector of the economy. These were
the *zaibatsu*, huge financial and industrial combines.

The *zaibatsu* were usually organized by new entrepreneurs, for most of the
old Tokugawa merchant houses were too set in their ways to make a successful transition into the new world of Meiji. The outstanding exception to
this generalization was the house of Mitsui, originally established in Edo as a
textile house and also enriched by its banking activities. When it became apparent that government initiatives were creating new economic opportunities
in commerce and industry, Mitsui brought new men into the firm to take advantage of them. The new leadership was vigorous and capable, establishing
first a bank and then a trading company. These institutions became important factors in Japan's foreign commerce; they also engaged in domestic transactions, profiting handsomely from handling army supply contracts during the
Satsuma Rebellion. In 1881 Mitsui bought government coal mines, which ultimately contributed greatly to its wealth and power. By that time the traditional drapery business had been relegated to a sideline and delegated to a subordinate house.

A contrast to Mitsui is offered by the Mitsubishi *zaibatsu*, founded by Iwasaki Yatarō (1834–85), a former Tosa samurai bold and ruthless in the wars of
commerce. Iwasaki developed a strong shipping business by obtaining government contracts, government subsidies, and for a time even government guarantee of its dividend payments. At one point the government lent the company
ships, a loan that eventually became a gift. Mitsubishi also benefited greatly
during the Formosan expedition of 1874 and again during the Satsuma Rebellion from doing government business. The firm grew strong enough to displace
some of its foreign competitors, and around its shipping business it developed
banking and insurance facilities and entered foreign trade. It also went into
mining, and its acquisition of the government-established Nagasaki shipyard
assured its future as the leader in shipbuilding and heavy industry, although
Iwasaki did not live long enough to see the shipyard turn a profit. Iwasaki ruled
the combine like a personal domain, but he also recruited an able managerial
staff composed largely of graduates of Fukuzawa's Keiō University.

For Iwasaki personal ambition and patriotism were fused. As he conceived it,
his mission was to compete with the great foreign shipping companies, and he
was convinced that whatever benefited his company was also good for the nation. Not everyone, however, agreed with this assessment. For a time Iwasaki
had to face the competition of a rival company, one of whose organizers was
Shibusawa Eiichi (1840–1931), one of the great Meiji entrepreneurs and
bankers, founder of the Tokyo Chamber of Commerce and Bankers' Association, a believer in joint-stock companies, in competition, and in business independence from government. Iwasaki won this battle, but Shibusawa remained

enormously influential, not only because of his economic power but also because of his energetic advocacy of higher business standards and of the view that business could contribute most to the public good by remaining independent of government.

The success of such men as Iwasaki and Shibusawa should not obscure the fact that new ventures continued to entail risk. Not all new ventures were successful. For example, the attempt to introduce sheep raising into Japan was a failure. Initial attempts at organizing insurance companies were similarly ill-conceived, since they used rates and tables appropriate for European rather than Japanese conditions. But insurance companies were finally established, and altogether successes outnumbered failures.

One reason for the success of the *zaibatsu* and other new companies was their ability to attract capable and dedicated executives. Formerly, many capable members of the samurai class had refused to enter the business world because concern with money making was considered abhorrent. But this obstacle was largely overcome after the Restoration, not merely because the status of the samurai was changing, but because commercial and industrial development were required for the good of the state, and the member of a samurai family who helped build a strong bank, trading company, manufacturing industry, and so forth was rendering a service to the emperor and to Japan. Indeed, the government's initial sponsorship of many enterprises lent them some of the prestige of government service. The fact that many of the companies were created by men of samurai origins also helped make business socially acceptable.

The association of business with government also influenced business ideology in Japan. From the beginning, the ethos of modern Japanese business focused on its contributions to the Japanese nation, not on the laissez-faire notions of economic liberalism that prevailed in the West. The company did not exist only, or even primarily, to make a profit for its shareholders. Similarly, the internal organization of the business firm followed different lines in Japan; old values of group solidarity and mutual responsibility between the samurai and his lord were incorporated into the business structure to give all participants in the venture a strong sense of company loyalty.

In discussing the *zaibatsu* and other modern firms it should not be supposed that large-scale trading, mining, and manufacturing represented the whole of Japanese business. On the contrary, many small-scale traditional establishments continued to function well past the early Meiji era. But the new firms did represent a major growth and change in economic activity, and signaled a change in Japanese perceptions of their role in international affairs as well. This was reflected in economic terms by the government's efforts to preserve economic independence, for example, by protecting home markets, conserving foreign exchange, and avoiding dependence on foreign capital so as to assure Japanese ownership of railways and other large-scale enterprises. It was reflected, also, in Japanese foreign policy, and especially in the modernization and deployment of the Japanese military.

## The Military

Japanese military forces engaged in three major military operations in the twenty years following the Restoration: the Formosa expedition of 1874, the Satsuma Rebellion of 1877, and the Sino-Japanese War of 1894–95. The first two operations were fought primarily for domestic purposes, as the new Meiji government sought to consolidate its power. The Sino-Japanese War, on the other hand, was an outward looking venture from the start, a test of strength with China on the Korean Peninsula. An even more striking difference, however, was the difference in the quality of Japanese military organization, armament, and tactical skill in 1874–77 and 1894.

The Formosa expedition of 1874 was far from brilliant. The landing was poorly executed, hygiene was so defective that disease took a great toll, and equipment had to be abandoned because it was unsuitable for use in a tropical climate. Similarly, the force which suppressed the Satsuma Rebellion did so because of its superiority in numbers and equipment rather than because of its military excellence.

To improve the quality of the army, a major reorganization was carried out in 1878 under the direction of Yamagata. A general staff was established along German lines, and Germany became the overall model for the army, which had previously been influenced by France. By strengthening the reserves, the military potential was greatly increased. During the ten or fifteen years before the Sino-Japanese War, generous military appropriations had enabled the army to acquire modern equipment, mostly manufactured in Japanese arsenals and plants, while the creation of a Staff College and improved training methods further strengthened the army and made it more modern. Like Yamagata, most of the leading generals were from Chōshū.

Naval modernization was similar to that of the army except that England was the model and continued to be a source from which some of the larger vessels were purchased. In 1894 the navy possessed twenty-eight modern ships with a total displacement of 57,000 tons and also twenty-four torpedo boats. Most important, Japan had the facilities to maintain, repair, and arm her fleet. From the start most of the naval leadership came from Satsuma.

The military is a good example of the way in which the various facets of modernization were intertwined and supported each other, for the armed forces both benefited and contributed to the process. Not only did they stimulate new industries, ranging from armaments to tin cans, but it was also in the army that the rural conscript was for the first time exposed to a wider and more modern world. Indeed, when conscription was first introduced, many men from backward districts were quite bewildered by the accouterments of modern life. There are reports that some bowed in reverence to the stove in their barracks, taking it for some kind of god. For many men, the army provided the first introduction to shoes. Before the spread of education, some men learned to read and write in the army. All were exposed to the new values of nationalism and loyalty to the emperor. Most also learned to smoke (cigarettes were first reported in 1877) and to drink (native beverages and also excellent Japanese beer, first brewed in the 1870s), and they had their first experience with the modern city. Soldiers also enjoyed a better diet, receiving more meat than the average Japanese. But discipline was very harsh, and draft dodging was prevalent: in 1889 almost one-tenth of those eligible avoided conscription. Nevertheless, the vast majority did serve.

## The Test of War

For the country as a whole this was a period of crucial and remarkable change and of highly visible accomplishments. These accomplishments did not come cheap, but that they were genuine was demonstrated by Japan's impressive victory in the Sino-Japanese War. The triumph of Japan's army, which rapidly made its way north through Korea, crossed the Yalu River into Manchuria, and captured Port Arthur on the Liaotung Peninsula, was matched by the victory Japan's naval forces won over the Chinese at sea.

The events leading up to this conflict are discussed in the next chapter, but essentially Japan went to war to counter Chinese dominance in Korea. The motivations of Japan's leaders included alarm over the prospect of a weak Korea open to Western (particularly Russian) aggression as well as more positive empire-building sentiments. Many believed that bringing the peninsula under Japanese influence would foster needed reforms in a reactionary country, and there were Koreans who shared this view. As it turned out, the war did not assure Japanese security let alone Korean progress. But it did signal the beginning of the Japanese Empire. It did not resolve the tensions created during the preceding years, but it did usher in a new phase of Japan's modern history.

## NOTES

1. Quoted in Carmen Blacker, *The Japanese Enlightenment: A Study of the Writings of Fukuzawa Yukichi* (London: Cambridge University Press, 1964), p. 111.
2. *Ibid.*, p. 128.
3. Quoted in Kenneth Pyle, *The New Generation in Meiji Japan: Problems in Cultural Identity, 1885–95* (Stanford: Stanford University Press, 1969), p. 124.
4. "Rescript on Education," in John Lu, *Sources of Japanese History* (New York: McGraw-Hill, 1974), 2: 70–71.

中國之發奮自彊

1861          1872          1884          1894

THE SELF-STRENGTHENING MOVEMENT

(Phase 1)

T'ung-chih Restoration

(Phase 2)

Sino-French War
(1884—85)

(Phase 3)

Sino-Japanese War
(1894—95)

# 7 Self-Strengthening in China: 1874-1894

The Empress Dowager and the Government
Self-Strengthening
The Theory
Education
Economic Self-Strengthening
Missionary Efforts and Christian Influence
Endings and Beginnings
Foreign Relations
Vietnam and the Sino-French War of 1884-1885
Korea and the Sino-Japanese War of 1894-1895
The Treaty of Shimonoseki (April 1895)
China in Perspective

In China, the defeat of the Taiping Rebellion gave the Ch'ing dynasty a new lease on life. Other military victories over Muslim rebels in the West further bolstered the regime. On the other hand, as the impetus of the T'ung-chih Restoration slowed, the reform movement faded, and old abuses reappeared. For example, the purchase of examination degrees and government posts continued to be widespread.

In the twenty years preceding the Sino-Japanese War (1894-95) pressures from the Western powers—Russia in Central Asia, France and Britain in Southeast Asia—increasingly restricted the scope of Chinese influence among peoples traditionally considered tributaries of the imperial throne. These pressures, along with the intrusion into China's internal affairs represented by the treaty system, led Ch'ing statesmen to attempt selective modernization as a way to strengthen and preserve their state and society. This effort is known as the Self-Strengthening movement.

In Japan an ambitious modernization program succeeded, at least partly, because it was sponsored by a vigorous new government and accompanied by significant social and political change. For a number of reasons, "self-strengthening" accomplished less in China: contrasts in geographic scale, in historical traditions, and in social structure spring readily to mind. The political situation, too, was very different.

## The Empress Dowager and the Government

The dominant figure at court during the last phase of the Ch'ing dynasty (which outlasted her by only three years) was the Dowager Empress Tz'u Hsi (1835–1908). (See Figure 8-1.) The intelligent and educated daughter of a minor Manchu official, she entered the palace as a low-ranking concubine but had the good fortune to bear the Hsien-feng emperor his only son. After the Hsien-feng emperor died, she became co-regent for her son, the T'ung-chih emperor. Skillfully using her position to increase her power, she dominated her son and, it is rumored, encouraged him in the debaucheries that weakened his constitution and brought him to the grave at the youthful age of nineteen (1875). She then manipulated the succession in order to place on the throne her four-year-old nephew, the Kuang-hsü emperor (r. 1875–1908), and continued to make the decisions even when he ostensibly assumed the imperial duties in 1889. At first Prince Kung had provided a counterforce at court, but his power declined in the seventies, and in 1884 he was removed from government altogether.

The Empress Dowager was a strong-willed woman, an expert at the arts of political infighting and manipulation. One of her most reliable supporters was the Manchu bannerman Jung-lu (1836–1903), to whom she gave important military commands. Yet, it was an anomaly to have a woman in control of the court, and her prestige was not enhanced by rumors that she was responsible for the murder of her rivals. Corruption in very high places also took its toll. The very powerful eunuch Li Lien-ying (d. 1911) was totally loyal to his mistress but also totally corrupt, using his influence to amass a fortune. Tz'u Hsi herself accepted payments from officials and misspent government funds. The most notorious case of financial abuse was her use of money intended for the navy to rebuild the summer palace destroyed in 1860 by Elgin and his troops during the second war between Britain and China. Eventually the navy department, established in 1885, became a branch of the imperial household, and China's most famous and magnificent "ship" was made of marble. (See Figure 7-1.)

Tz'u Hsi's prime political aim was to continue in power. She had no profound aversion, but neither did she have any commitment, to the policy of se-

Figure 7-1    Marble Pavilion in the shape of a ship. Summer Palace, Peking.

lective modernization advocated by the champions of self-strengthening, and her understanding of the West was very limited. It was to her immediate political advantage to avoid dependence on any single group of officials and to manipulate a number of strong governors-general who had gained in power as a result of the Taiping Rebellion. These indispensable provincial administrators could no longer be controlled by the court at will, but fortunately for Peking, they remained absolutely loyal to the dynasty. The governors-general operated their own political and financial machines and commanded substantial military forces, but they were still dependent on Peking's power of appointment. Major policy decisions continued to be made in Peking. During this period, the central government was also strengthened financially by the receipts from the Maritime Customs. Thus the West helped to preserve the dynasty even as it was undermining its foundations.

Most powerful of the governors-general was Li Hung-chang, who from 1870 was firmly established in Tientsin, where he commanded an army, sponsored self-strengthening efforts, and successfully avoided transfer. A protégé of Tseng Kuo-fan, he shared his master's devotion to the dynasty but not his Confucian probity. From his headquarters, not far from Peking, Li was able to dominate China's policy toward Korea, but he could not control its foreign policy elsewhere. Arguing for the priority of maritime defense, he had unsuccessfully opposed the emphasis on inner Asia, which produced Tso Tsung-t'ang's campaigns of the 1870s, and in the eighties he failed again when he tried to prevent war with France (1884–85). His opposition earned him the denunciations of his enemies, who castigated him as an arch traitor comparable to Ch'in Kuei, always blamed for the Sung's failure to regain the North from the Juchen in the twelfth century. The war, along with other developments in foreign relations, is discussed below; but first, consideration of the Self-Strengthening movement is in order. It was a movement in which Li played a major part.

## Self-Strengthening

The Self-Strengthening movement is readily divisible into three stages. Initially, during the period of the T'ung-chih Restoration (1862–74), it was strongly military in orientation and produced arsenals, the Foochow dockyard, and schools offering instruction principally in subjects of military application. In its middle phase, 1872–85, interest in the military continued, but efforts were expanded to include projects in transportation (shipping and railways), communication (telegraph), and mining. The final period (from China's defeat by France in 1885 until the outbreak of the Sino-Japanese War in 1894) was one of continued concern for military modernization, but there was also a further broadening of industrial capacity, including the development of light industry. Since there was a good deal of continuity among the protagonists and in their projects, we will discuss their ideas and programs topically rather than chronologically.

## The Theory

A willingness to adopt new means to strengthen and reform the state animated the works of a long line of Confucian scholars, from the Sung through the Ch'ing. As it became apparent during the early years of the nineteenth century that the dynasty was in serious trouble, more scholars turned against the philological emphasis of the school of Han learning and focused on what today would be called policy studies. *Huang-ch'ao ching-shih wen-pien* (*A Compilation of Essays on Statecraft*), published in 1827, is a case in point. It is a collection of essays on social, political, and economic matters written by various Ch'ing officials and compiled by Ho Ch'ang-lin (1785–1841). Concern for reform and willingness to take a hard, critical look at financial and political institutions characterized the writings of leading intellectuals and, in the work of Wei Yüan, began to merge with an interest in the West, although Wei still proposed to apply the old formula of using barbarians against barbarians. Feng

Kuei-fen went further, seeing the West as a threat, to be sure, but also as a source for solving the dangerous problems it had created. He was the first in China to urge the use of "barbarian techniques" against the "barbarians", the hallmark of the Self-Strengthening movement.

Although the ideas of self-strengthening were well established by the 1870s, the classic theoretical formulation came in 1898 from the brush of Chang Chih-tung (1837–1909), a leading scholar-official and governor-general of the Late Ch'ing. Like Sakuma Shōzan earlier in Japan, Chang wanted to preserve traditional values while adopting Western science and technology. The idea was that Chinese learning would remain the heart of Chinese civilization, while Western learning would have a subordinate supporting and technical role. This was expressed in terms of the traditional Neo-Confucian dichotomy of *t'i* (substance) and *yung* (function): Western means for Chinese ends. The basic pattern of Chinese civilization was to remain sacrosanct, but it was to be protected by Western techniques. The techniques to be adopted were initially military but gradually, as already indicated, came to include a great deal more. In the process the details of the prescription were altered without changing the basic plan.

Conservative opponents of self-strengthening, on the other hand, feared that Chinese civilization would be contaminated by borrowing from the West, since, as they well knew, ends are affected by means. In the Confucian formulation, *t'i* and *yung* are aspects of a single whole. The Confucian tradition had always been concerned with means as well as ends, and generations of scholars had insisted that the Way did not consist merely of "empty" abstractions but was concerned with practical realities. There was no essence apart from application. And there was a great deal more to the West than mere techniques. It was fallacious to believe that China could merely borrow the techniques of the West without becoming entangled in manifestations of Western culture.

If China went ahead with efforts to adopt Western techniques while preserving traditional culture, the best that could be hoped for would be an uneasy compartmentalization. Individuals who came in contact with the West would have to separate the modern from the traditional elements in their lives. Those parts of the country that had the most direct experience with the West, such as the treaty ports, would have to be isolated from the traditional Chinese hinterlands. In others words, to preserve tradition in a period of modernization, the country would have to be protected from the kind of radical social reappraisal hailed in Japan by champions of "reason" like Fukuzawa Yukichi. The contrast with Japan is instructive, for there social change was sanctioned by an appeal to nationalism as symbolized by the throne, whereas in China Confucianism was much too closely associated with the social structure to allow for a similar development. Meiji Japan demonstrated that elements of Confucianism were compatible with modernization but also that modernization involved changes reaching into the very heart of a civilization.

An indication of the inadequacy of self-strengthening theory was China's failure to educate a new leadership, both fully Confucian and modern.

# Education

The Self-Strengthening movement was led by impressive and capable men, such as Li Hung-chang, but there was a lack of competent middle-echelon officers and managers, as well as technical personnel such as scientists and engineers. The fastest way to make up this deficit was to send students overseas for training, which the Chinese did. However, this approach had only mixed success. The most extensive effort of this sort was made between 1872 and 1881, when 120 students were sent to the United States under the supervision of Yung Wing (1828–1912), Yale class of 1854, and the first Chinese to graduate from an American university. The boys were between fifteen and seventeen years old, young enough to master new subjects, but also immature and easily swayed by their foreign environment. To assure continued Confucian training, they were accompanied by a traditional Confucian mentor. Nevertheless, they soon adopted American ways: participating in American sports, dating and in some cases eventually marrying American girls, and in a few instances even converting to Christianity. Yung Wing himself married an American and ended up making his home in Hartford, Connecticut.

The mission had been launched with the backing of Tseng Kuo-fan and Li Hung-chang, but Li withdrew his support when the students were denied admission to West Point and when they were fiercely attacked by Peking officials for neglecting their Confucian studies. The mission, poorly managed from the beginning, was abandoned. Among its participants were some of the first, but by no means the last, Chinese students who in the course of their overseas stay became alienated from their culture.

The obvious alternative to study abroad was to supply instruction in modern subjects at home. As we have seen, the advocates of self-strengthening were active from the start in doing just that, establishing the T'ung-wen Kuan in the capital and other schools in conjunction with several arsenals and the Foochow dockyard. By 1894 the government also operated a telegraph school, a naval and military medical school, and a mining school. These schools typically offered a curriculum encompassing both the classical studies required for success in the examination system and the new subjects for which they were established. Since command of traditional learning remained the key to entry into the civil service, students naturally tended to concentrate on that, for without an examination degree career opportunities were limited. The most famous graduate of the Foochow dockyard school was Yen Fu (1853–1921), who was sent to England to continue his studies at the naval college in Greenwich but after returning home to China was unable to pass the provincial examination. He became famous not as an admiral but as a writer and translator.

It did occur to some reformers to broaden the content of the examinations to allow candidates credit for mastering modern subjects, but suggestions along these lines encountered formidable opposition, since they were likely to affect the Confucian core of the civilization. A minor concession was finally made in 1887, which provided that 3 out of some 1500 provincial examination graduates might be granted that degree after being examined in Western along with (not in place of) traditional subjects. They would then be eligible for the *chin-shih* examination on the same terms as the other candidates. Creation of a leadership versed in modern subjects would have required major changes in the content and function of the examination system or its elimination altogether.

## Economic Self-Strengthening

In China, as in Japan, there were those who wished to adopt Western technology so as to build up their country's economic strength. In Japan a strong central government took the lead in modernizing crucial sectors of the economy and successfully involved members of the upper classes in this undertaking. In China, on the other hand, there was no major sustained national effort. Leadership came from political sponsors (usually regional strong men, typically, governors-general); central government involvement was half-hearted; and the upper classes were divided over whether or not the effort was worthwhile. These differences were reflected in the results achieved.

In the first phase of the Self-Strengthening movement, the focus was military. Early projects included gun factories in Shanghai and Soochow, the Kiangnan Arsenal in Shanghai and another arsenal in Nanking, the Foochow dockyard, and a machine factory in Tientsin. These enterprises, partly due, perhaps, to their political sponsorship and operation under official control, suffered from bureaucratic corruption and poor management. Furthermore, they depended on foreigners for expertise and supervision of operations, but the individuals hired to perform these crucial tasks were frequently unqualified for the job.

During the second phase of the Self-Strengthening movement, "government operated merchant enterprises" (*kuan-tu shang-pan*) became the rule. These were mixed companies established under the patronage of a political sponsor, with capital from both the public and private sectors. Private financing was very much desired, but capital was scarce in China and other forms of investment were more prestigious or more lucrative than modern business enterprises. Private investment came primarily from Chinese businessmen resident in the treaty ports. They had participated in the growth of these centers of international trade and were familiar with modern-style business ventures and techniques. However, their capital was limited; hence the need for public funds, usually provided by the political sponsor.

The new companies applied modern technology to a somewhat broader range of activities than had been true in the initial phase. The new Western-style establishments included a shipping company, textile mills, the beginnings of a telegraph service, and the K'ai-p'ing Coal Mines.

The shipping firm known as the China Merchants Steam Navigation Company is a good example of the *kuan-tu shang-pan*. Albert Feuerwerker's study of this concern is particularly interesting for the light it sheds on the role of the political sponsor in economic development at this time.[1] When private capital proved insufficient to finance the company, the sponsor Li Hung-chang put up the rest from public funds. To help the company make a go of it, Li secured the shipping line a monopoly on the transportation of tax grain and official freight bound for Tientsin. He obtained tariff concessions for the company and protected it from its domestic critics and enemies. In exchange, Li exercised a large measure of control, appointing and dismissing its managers, employing its ships to transport his troops, and using its payroll to provide sinecures for political followers. He also used its earnings to buy warships. To advance his policy in Korea, Li had the company lend money to the Korean government.

The overall record of this and similar companies was mixed. The investors made money and their political sponsors benefited. But after an initial spurt, the companies failed to establish a pattern of sustained growth. Instead, they stagnated. Moreover, they failed to train Chinese technical personnel. They were plagued by incompetent managers, by nepotism and corruption. Even their political sponsors, high officials in the areas where the enterprises operated, exploited the companies, regarding them as sources of patronage and revenue along the lines of the traditional salt administration, rather than as key investments for the modernization of the country.

During the last phase of the Self-Strengthening movement, attempts were made to decrease government participation by organizing joint government-merchant companies and to eliminate government influence entirely by founding private enterprises, but these had very limited success. Absent in China was the close relationship between business and government found in Japan. By the mid-nineties, there was a modern sector in the Chinese economy, but it was largely limited to the periphery of the empire (for example, the treaty ports and Hong Kong), where Chinese merchants were able to hold their own quite successfully against foreign competition.

The total economic impact of imperialism on China during this period is a subject of debate. Obviously tariff restrictions and other concessions forced on the Chinese were designed to benefit Western interests vis-à-vis the Chinese economy. Yet the balance of evidence to date suggests that the traditional Chinese economy, beyond the treaty ports and their immediate hinterlands, remained little affected during this period. Some of the traditional handicraft industries (for example, spinning) were damaged by foreign competition, while others (for example, weaving) held their own or even expanded slightly. Since labor was cheap but capital scarce (and therefore expensive), it did not pay to build factories to produce everything the people needed. Furthermore, the prospective owners of modern factories had to consider not only the cost of their products but also the cost of marketing, including high transportation charges.

To say that traditional economic patterns continued to prevail in China's interior is not to say that all was well. On the contrary. All that continuity implied was that China's economic and social problems had a familiar ring. As Kwang-Ching Liu has put it:

> The chief cause of rural tension continued to be excessive and unequal taxation, the tyranny of yamen underlings, landlordism and usury—social injustice reinforced by administrative abuse.[2]

# Missionary Efforts and Christian Influence

The Western presence in nineteenth-century China was no more confined to trade and politics than it had been during the Late Ming encounter. Once again missionaries were drawn to China as a promising area for their endeavors, but now there were Protestant as well as Catholic missionaries. An early Protestant arrival was Robert Morrison of the London Missionary Society. He reached Canton in 1807, learned the language, brought out a Chinese-English dictionary and a Chinese version of the Bible (later used by the Taipings), founded the school where Yung Wing received his early education, and set up a printing press. Other missionaries, many of them Americans, brought Western medicine and other aspects of Western secular knowledge to China.

The missionaries made a notable effort in education: by 1877 there were 347 missionary schools in China with almost six thousand pupils. Such schools helped spread knowledge about the West as well as helping to propagate the religion. A notable missionary-educator was W. A. P. Martin, who contributed to the Self-Strengthening movement. When Martin became head of the T'ung-wen Kuan, he greatly raised its standards and later was appointed first president of Peking University. Missionaries were also important as a major source of information about China for their home countries. The first foreign language newspaper published in China was a missionary publication, and missionaries also contributed to scholarship. Outstanding among the missionaries who became Sinologists was James Legge, a master translator who rendered the Chinese classics into sonorous Victorian prose. In this and other ways, missionaries with varying degrees of sophistication and self-awareness served as cultural intermediaries.

As indicated by the growth of their schools, the missionaries met with some success, but their strength was largely in the treaty ports, and the results were hardly commensurate with their efforts. By the end of the century, the number of Catholic missionaries in China had climbed to about 750, and there were approximately half a million Catholics in China, up from around 160,000 at the beginning of the century. (See Figure 7-2.) The Protestants had less success: in 1890 there appear to have been only slightly over 37,000 converts served by roughly 1300 missionaries, representing forty-one different religious societies. The Tientsin Massacre of 1870 had demonstrated the potential fervor of antimissionary sentiment, and nothing happened to reduce hostilities during the next quarter of a century.

The reasons for the poor showing of Christianity are many and various. They include difficulties in translation and communication analogous to those that plagued Buddhist missionaries a millennium and a half earlier. The most important concepts of Christianity such as sin or the trinity were the most difficult to translate, none more so than the most sacred idea of all, the idea of God. Agreement on how to translate "God" into Chinese was never reached; three versions, one Catholic and two Protestant, remained current. As before, differences in culture compounded the difficulties in communication.

Figure 7-2  The French Cathedral at Canton, built on the former site of the governor's yamen.

The nineteenth-century missionary, however, also encountered problems which he did not share with his predecessors, for the Chinese associated Christianity with both the Taiping Rebellion and the unequal treaties. The former showed Christianity as subversive to the social and political order, while the latter brought the missionaries special privileges. Both were resented. Furthermore, the aura of power also drew to Christian establishments false converts; individuals attracted by the possibilities of a treaty port career, and opportunists out to obtain missionary protection for their own ends. Popular resentment of the missions was fired by scurrilous stories and bitter attacks, such as those which employed a homonym for the transliteration of "Jesus" to depict Christ as a pig. (See Figure 7-3.) This hostility was encouraged by the elite who saw in Christianity a superstitious religion that threatened their own status and values. It was no accident that anti-Christian riots often occurred when the examinations were being held in the provincial capitals.

Here there is an interesting contrast with the situation in Japan, where 30 percent of Christian converts during the Meiji period were from samurai backgrounds. Christianity served the spiritual needs and provided a vehicle for social protest for samurai who found themselves on the losing side of the Restoration struggle. As a result in the 1880s and 1890s a prestigious native clergy was developing in Japan, and Christianity remained more influential than the slow growth of the churches would indicate. In post-Taiping China too, Christianity continued to appeal to people dissatisfied with the status quo, and it counted among its converts some notable protesters, including Sun Yat-sen (see below). But the elite remained hostile, and the real cutting edge of protest was to be elsewhere: too radical for the nineteenth century, Christianity turned out to be insufficiently radical for the twentieth.

In the meantime, missionaries contributed to the Western perception of China. Working in the treaty ports, dealing not with Confucian gentlemen but with people on the margin of respectable society, the missionaries frequently developed a very negative view of China and its inhabitants, an image the reverse of the idealistic picture painted earlier by the Jesuits:

> The universal practice of lying and dishonest dealings; the unblushing lewdness of old and young; harsh cruelty toward prisoners by officers, and tyranny over slaves by masters—all form a full unchecked torrent of human depravity, and prove the existence of a kind and degree of moral degeneration of which an excessive statement can scarcely be made, or an adequate conception hardly be formed.[3]

These words, dated 1848, were written by S. Wells Williams who, after his service in China, became an influential American expert on China. Similar sentiments were expressed throughout the century.

Figure 7-3   *The [Foreign] Devils Worshipping the Incarnation of the Pig [Jesus].*

## Endings and Beginnings

Perhaps the most interesting themes in the intellectual and artistic life of an era are those which reflect the end of a tradition and look toward a new future. Such a time had arrived in China. For some time sensitive men had been conscious that they were living in the last stages of a great tradition. The sense of ending was intensified by awareness of dynastic decay. For some, the sense of impending national change represented an exciting challenge. For the majority, however, the mood was one of uncertainty, apprehension, and regret. This mood is caught particularly well in a poem by Wang P'eng-yü (1818–97), an official who served as a Ch'ing censor:

*Tune: "The Fish Poacher"*

*In Reply to a Poem from Tz'u-shan, Thanking Me for the Gift of Sung and Yüan Lyrics I Had Had Printed*

Now that the lyric voice wavers in wind-blown dust
Who is to speak the sorrows of his heart?
Ten years of carving, seeking from each new block
The truest music of the string unswept,
Only to sigh now
Finding my griefs in tune
With every beat that leaves the ivory fret!
I sigh for the men of old
Pour wine in honor of the noble dead:
Does any spirit rhymester
Understand my heartbreak?

The craft of letters
Furnishes kindling, covers jars:
True bell or tinkling cymbal, who can tell?
Tu Fu, who lifelong courted the perfect phrase
—Did his verse help him, though it made men marvel?
Take what you find here,
See if an odd page, a forgotten tune
Still has the power to engage your mind.
My toiling over
I'll drink myself merry, climb the Golden Terrace,
Thrash out a wild song from my lute
And let the storms rage at will.[4]

Among those who welcomed the winds from the West were a small group of remarkable men, some with experience abroad in an official or unofficial capacity. An example of the former is Kuo Sung-tao (1818–91), China's first minister to England and the first Chinese representative to be stationed in any Western country. Another was Wang T'ao (1828–97), who spent two years in Scotland assisting James Legge in his translations and who also visited Japan. One of the founders of modern journalism in China, he favored the adoption of Western political institutions, not just their science and technology. There were other men like Kuo and Wang, for instance Cheng Kuan-ying (fl. 1884), a famous scholar-comprador, modernizer, and writer. Such men were interested in Western "substance" (not just "function"), while retaining their prime commitment to the Confucian tradition.

Still more important for the future were a number of younger men whose formative years fell into this period, although they did not become influential until the late nineties. There are three names in particular to which we will return: Yen Fu, born in 1853; K'ang Yu-wei, 1858; and Sun Yat-sen, 1866. The discussion of their ideas must wait, however, for it was not until China was jolted by her defeat in the Sino-Japanese War that they came to the fore.

## Foreign Relations

Western pressures continued to affect China's foreign relations in the twenty years prior to the Sino-Japanese War, but the nature of these pressures began to alter. The initial conflicts had been over Western efforts to open trade and diplomatic relations with China proper; in the 1870s and 1880s foreign intervention in lands constituting peripheral areas of the empire or traditionally tributary states were the major causes of friction. (See map, Figure 7-4.)

Even as Japan was engaged in the Taiwan expedition, the Ch'ing government was troubled by a dangerous situation in Central Asia. In 1871 the Russians used a Muslim rebellion in Sinkiang as a pretext for occupying the Ili region, where a lucrative trade had developed. In Sinkiang itself, Yakub Beg (1830–77), a Muslim leader from Kokand in Central Asia, obtained Russian and British recognition for his breakaway state. In response to these alarming developments, the Ch'ing court assigned the task of suppressing the rebellion to Tso Tsung-t'ang, who had just finished crushing Muslim rebellions in Shensi and Kansu. He carried out the task with great success. By 1877, the government's control over Sinkiang was being reestablished and Yakub Beg was driven to his death. After difficult and protracted negotiations, the Russians returned nearly all of Ili (1881).

This strong showing in Central Asia, an area to which the Chinese were traditionally sensitive, bolstered morale, and Chinese successes in the diplomatic negotiations which followed encouraged those who were opposed to accommodation with the West. Indeed, the success of China's Central Asian policy encouraged them to demand an equally strong policy in dealing with the maritime powers. Pressure from this source was too strong to be ignored and constituted a major factor leading to confrontation and then to war with France in 1884–85. At issue was French expansion into Vietnam.

## Vietnam and the Sino-French War of 1884–1885

North Vietnam had been annexed by the Han in 111 B.C., but after A.D. 939 native Vietnamese regimes prevailed, the major exception being the short period of Ming domination, 1406–26. The leader of the resistance against the

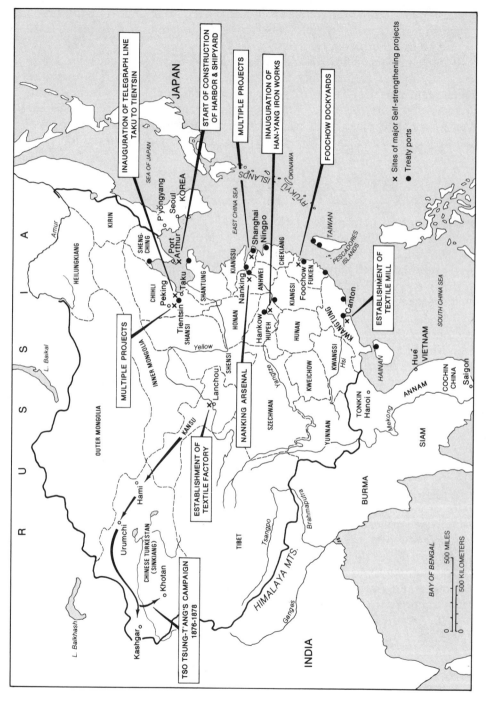

Figure 7-4  **China During the Self-Strengthening Period**

Ming, Le Loi, established the Later Li dynasty (1428–1789), with its capital at Hanoi and its government organized along Chinese lines. As in Korea, the determination to maintain political independence from China went hand in hand with admiration for Chinese culture and institutions. It is the Chinese influence on Vietnam which sets it apart from the other, more Indian oriented states of Southeast Asia.

China also served as the model for the Nguyen dynasty (1802–1945), which from its capital at Húe in Central Vietnam ruled the country through a bureaucracy modeled as closely as possible on that of China. The Chinese model was powerful, yet differences in size and culture between China and Vietnam required adjustments and compromises. To give just one example, Chinese influence was much stronger on civil government than on the military, for military theory and practice in Vietnam (as in the rest of continental Southeast Asia) centered on the elephant.

Vietnam's location in a cultural frontier area made for a rich and complex culture but was also a source of political weakness. One result was that the social and cultural gap between village and bureaucracy was greater in Vietnam than in China. Another result was the difficulty the Vietnamese state experienced in its efforts to incorporate the south, which had been gradually taken over from the Cambodians (regarded by the Vietnamese as "barbarians") during the century from roughly 1650 to 1750. Under the Nguyen dynasty this continued to be an area of large landlords and impoverished peasants, a region where the central bureaucracy operated inadequately. The area also suffered from educational backwardness, with the result that very few southerners were able to succeed in Vietnam's Chinese-style civil service examination system.

Vietnam's long coastline and elongated shape, as well as the presence of minority peoples within its boundaries, further hampered government efforts to fashion a strong unified state capable of withstanding Western encroachments. French missionaries and military men had early shown an interest in the area and had assisted in the founding of the Nguyen dynasty itself. Nearly 400 Frenchmen served the dynasty's founder and first emperor, Gia-long (r. 1801–20). Catholicism also made headway: it has been estimated that there were more Catholics in Vietnam than in all of China. For much the same reasons as had earlier animated anti-Christian policies in China and Japan, the Vietnamese authorities turned against the foreign religion, but their suppression of Catholicism gave the French an excuse for intervention.

French interest in Vietnam increased during the reign of Louis Napoleon. In 1859 France seized Saigon. Under a treaty signed three years later, the French gained control over three southern provinces, and five years later they seized the remaining three provinces in the South. These southern provinces became the French colony called Cochin China. During 1862–63 the French also established a protectorate over Cambodia. French interests were not limited to the South but included Central and North Vietnam (Annam and Tonkin). Treaties concluded in 1862 and 1874 contained various provisions eroding

Vietnamese sovereignty, and when disorders occurred in North Vietnam in 1882, France used the occasion to seize Hanoi.

Throughout this period of increasing French penetration, the Vietnamese court had continued its traditional tributary relations with Peking. When the French took Hanoi, the Vietnamese court responded by seeking both help from the Ch'ing and support from the Black Flags, an armed remnant of the Taipings which had been forced out of China and was fighting the French in Vietnam.

The Ch'ing responded by sending troops. Considerable wavering and diplomatic maneuvering followed in both Peking and Paris, but in the end no means were found to reconcile the Chinese wish to preserve their historic tributary relations with Southeast Asia and the French determination to create an empire in this region. The resulting war was fought in Vietnam, on Taiwan and the Pescadores, and along the nearby coast of China proper, where the Foochow dockyards and the fleet built there were among the war's casualties.

In the peace agreement that followed, China was forced to abandon her claim to suzerainty over Vietnam. The French colony of Cochin China, and the French protectorates of Annam and Tonkin, were joined by protectorates over Cambodia and (in the 1890s) Laos, to constitute French Indo-China.

Chinese influence in Southeast Asia was further diminished in 1886 when Britain completed the conquest of Burma, and China formally recognized this situation as well. Then in 1887, China ceded Macao to Portugal, officially recognizing the de facto situation there. Thus in the last third of the nineteenth century the foreign powers tried to gain further concessions and proceeded to establish themselves in tributary areas which had been part of the traditional Chinese imperial order, although not of China proper. In the face of this challenge, the Chinese made concessions where necessary and resisted where feasible. When areas of major importance were at stake, their policy was quite forceful. The struggle over Korea is an example.

## Korea and the Sino-Japanese War of 1894–1895

Like Vietnam, Korea had adopted Chinese political institutions and ideology and maintained a tributary relationship with China while guarding her political independence. Again, as in Vietnam, differences in size, social organization, and cultural tradition insured the development of a distinct Sino-Korean culture. In the nineteenth century, however, Korea was sorely troubled by internal problems and external pressures. The Yi dynasty (1392–1910), then in its fifth century, was in serious decline. Korea's peasantry suffered from "a skewered or concentrated pattern of landholding; small average per capita holdings; high rates of tenancy; a regressive tax structure; false registration of taxable land; extortion and illegal charges and gratuities at tax collection time; and usury, especially official usury in the management of the grain loan system."[5] There was a serious uprising in the North in 1811. In 1833 there were rice riots in Seoul. And in 1862 there were rebellions in the South.

During the years 1864 to 1873, there was a last attempt to save the situation by means of a traditional program of reform initiated by the regent, or Taewŏngun (Grand Prince, 1821–98), who was the father of the king. The reform program proved strong enough to provoke a reaction but was not sufficiently drastic, even in conception, to transform Korea into a strong and viable state capable of dealing with the dangers of the modern world.

That world was gradually closing in on Korea. During the first two-thirds of the century a number of incidents occurred involving Western ships and foreign demands. Korea's initial policy was to resist all attempts to "open" the country by referring those seeking to establish diplomatic relations back to Peking. This policy was successful as long as it was directed at countries for whom Korea was of peripheral concern, but this had never been the case for Japan. Japan, therefore, was the most insistent of the powers trying to pry Korea loose from the Chinese orbit. In 1876 Japan forced Korea to sign a treaty establishing diplomatic relations and providing for the opening of three ports to trade. The treaty also stipulated that Korea was now "independent," but this did not settle matters since China still considered Korea a tributary. Insurrections in Seoul in 1882 and 1884 led to increased Chinese and Japanese involvement in Korea, including military intervention, always on opposing sides. But outright war was averted by talks between Itō Hirobumi and Li Hung-chang, which led to a formal agreement between China and Japan to withdraw their forces and inform each other if either decided in the future that it was necessary to send in troops.

During the next years the Chinese Resident in Korea was Yüan Shih-k'ai (1859–1916), a protégé of Li Hung-chang, originally sent to Korea to train Korean troops. Yüan successfully executed Li's policy of vigorous assertion of Chinese control, dominating the court, effecting a partial union of Korean and Chinese commercial customs, and setting up a telegraph service and a merchant route between Korea and China.

Conflicting ambitions in Korea made war between China and Japan highly probable; the catalyst was the Tonghak Rebellion. Tonghak, literally "Eastern Learning," was a religion founded by Ch'oe Si-hyong (1824–64). In content it consisted of an amalgam of Chinese, Buddhist, and native Korean religious ideas and practices. As so often before in East Asian history, the religious organization took on a political dimension, serving as a vehicle for expressions of discontent with a regime in decay, and for agitation against government corruption and foreign encroachments. Finally outlawed, it was involved in considerable rioting in 1893, which turned to rebellion the following year when Korea was struck by famine. When the Korean government requested Chinese assistance, Li Hung-chang responded by sending 1500 men and informing the Japanese, whose troops were already on the way. The rebellion was quickly suppressed, but it proved easier to send than to remove the troops.

When Japanese soldiers entered Seoul, broke into the palace, and kidnapped the king and queen, Li responded by sending more troops and war was inevitable. It was a war which everyone, except the Japanese, expected China to win, but all parties were stunned when Japan defeated China on sea and on land. Begun in July 1894, the war was all over by March of 1895. In retrospect the reasons for the outcome are easy to see: Japan was better equipped, better led, and more united than China, a country which was hampered by internal division, corruption, and inadequate leadership in the field. Powerful governors-general considered it Li Hung-chang's war and were slow in participating; the southern navy remained aloof.

## The Treaty of Shimonoseki (April 1895)

The war was terminated by the Treaty of Shimonoseki. China relinquished all claims to a special role in Korea and recognized that country as an independent state (although its troubles were far from over). In addition, China paid Japan an indemnity and ceded it Taiwan and the Pescadores, thus starting the formation of the Japanese empire. A further indication that the Japanese had now joined the ranks of the imperialist nations was the extension to Japan of most-favored-nation status, along with the opening of seven additional Chinese ports. Japan was also to receive the Liaotung Peninsula but, after diplomatic intervention by Russia, Germany, and France, had to settle for an additional indemnity instead. The effects of the treaty on Korea, on domestic Chinese and Japanese politics, and on international relations in the area are discussed in the following chapters. Here it should be noted that the treaty marked an unprecedented shift in the East Asian balance of power, a shift from China to Japan that was to continue until Japan's defeat in the Second World War.

## China in Perspective

Japan's victory over China toward the end of the nineteenth century has helped to produce a stark and misleading image of contrasting Japanese success and Chinese failure. History is more complicated than that. For Japan the acquisition of empire brought at least as many problems as it did solutions: the history of Japan in modern times has hardly been smooth and easy. Furthermore, compared to any non-Western political entity other than Japan, nineteenth-century China comes off rather well, both in terms of the preservation of sovereignty and in fashioning a response to the onslaught from abroad. Since this book focuses on China and Japan, it naturally tends to view one in terms of the other and emphasize the contrasts between them, but it is necessary to bear in mind the limits of this perspective even while making the most of its advantages. A study devoted, for example, to China and India during the same period might show modern Chinese history in quite a different and more positive light.

## NOTES

1. Albert Feuerwerker, *China's Early Industrialization: Sheng Hsuan-huai (1844–1916) and Mandarin Enterprise* (Cambridge: Harvard University Press, 1958).

2. Kwang-Ching Liu, in Ping-ti Ho and Tang Tsou, *China in Crisis* (Chicago: University of Chicago Press, 1968), 1: 117.

3. Harold Isaacs, *Images of Asia: American Views of China and India* (New York: Capricorn, 1962), p. 136, quoting S. Wells Williams, *The Middle Kingdom* (New York: 1883), 1: xiv–xv.

4. Cyril Birch, ed., *Anthology of Chinese Literature* (New York: Grove Press, 1972), 2: 294.

5. James B. Palais, *Politics and Policy in Traditional Korea* (Cambridge: Harvard University Press, 1975), p. 63.

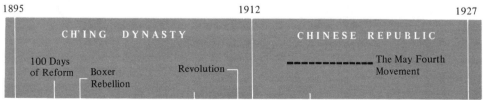

| 1895 | | 1912 | 1927 |
|---|---|---|---|
| CH'ING DYNASTY | | CHINESE REPUBLIC | |
| 100 Days of Reform | Boxer Rebellion | Revolution | ————————— The May Fourth Movement |
| 1898 1900 Death of Tz'u Hsi→1908 1911 | | 1916 ←Death of Yuan Shih-k'ai | |

# End of the Old Order and Struggle for the New: China, 1895–1927

8

China's defeat by Japan ushered in a period of profound change, accelerating at a pace that often bewildered the participants. As a result, the radical of one decade frequently found himself left behind by events in the next. Politically, intellectually, and in many other respects, the forces of reform, reaction, and revolution competed, interacted, and interlocked in complex patterns. The disintegration of the old was more apparent than the shape of the new. Bisecting the period chronologically and politically was the revolution of 1911, more an end than a beginning.

In foreign affairs the period began with a round of concessions forced on China by the imperialist powers, in a process that reached its greatest intensity during the first six months of 1898. Internally it began with a movement for reform, which also climaxed in 1898 when it culminated in a "hundred days" of intense reform (at least on paper) from June 11 to September 20 of that year. New foreign demands helped to spur the reformers in their efforts, but the defeat of 1895 was the major event that brought them to the fore and gave them an audience.

## K'ang Yu-wei and the "Hundred Days of Reform"

In 1895, a small group of reformers began an energetic campaign to urge major changes in China. Working primarily through study groups and journalism, they sought to spread their ideas in an intellectual climate newly receptive to radical ideas. A willingness to reexamine basic assumptions about the very nature of reality distinguished the men who emerged in the nineties from their modernizing predecessors. At the same time, the radicals of this generation, unlike those of the generation to follow, had received a thorough Confucian education and had a command of traditional learning. Steeped in the old culture, they felt the pull of the past even as they charted a bold course for a new future.

A major influence on a whole generation of reformers was Yen Fu, the one-time naval student at Greenwich. Now in his forties, he was emboldened by events to publicize his ideas, which he did first in a series of essays, and then in a number of very influential translations of Western works: Thomas Huxley's *Ethics and Evolution* (1898), Adam Smith's *Wealth of Nations* (1900), John Stuart Mill's *On Liberty* (1903), and others. Yen argued that Western learning was needed to release Chinese energies. He rejected much of the Chinese tradition while praising the West, particularly Social-Darwinism, with its dynamic view of history as evolutionary and progressive, and the high value it placed on struggle.

The leader of the reform movement was K'ang Yu-wei (1858–1927). Unlike Yen Fu, who was no political activist, theorists like K'ang Yu-wei and his younger followers, T'an Ssu-t'ung (1865–98) and Liang Ch'i-ch'ao (1873–1929), tried to implement programs as well as publish critiques. K'ang himself was a thinker who, deeply grounded in Buddhism as well as Confucianism, elaborated a highly original theory to provide a seemingly Confucian basis for ideas which went well beyond the Confucian tradition. Drawing on the Modern Text school of classical interpretation which, founded in the Han, enjoyed something of a revival in the late Ch'ing, K'ang argued that Confucius was not merely a transmitter of ancient teachings but a prophet who, ahead of his time, cast his message in subtle language full of hidden meanings. Confucius, according to K'ang, saw history as a universal progress through three stages, each with its appropriate form of government: the Age of Disorder (rule by an absolute monarch), the Age of Approaching Peace (rule by a constitutional monarch), and the Age of Great Peace (rule by the people). K'ang's Confucius was thus a seer and prophet not only for China but for the entire world. This was K'ang's solution to the problem of how to be modern without rejecting everything that was native and old, when modernization implied wholesale borrowing from abroad, not only of technology but of institutions and ideas. After the failure of his reform attempts, when K'ang was in exile, he elaborated on his vision of utopia. He portrayed a future when the whole world would be united in love and harmony under a single popularly elected government, which would operate hospitals, schools, and nurseries; administering a society in which all divisive institutions would have disappeared, including even the family.

Another radical reinterpretation of tradition came from T'an Ssu-t'ung, a brilliant man destined to become a martyr. T'an did not confine his radical vision to a distant utopia but argued that the monarchy should be replaced by a republic, and attacked the traditional Confucian family distinctions in the name of *jen*, the central Confucian virtue frequently translated "benevolence" or "humanity." Neo-Confucian thinkers had earlier given *jen* a cosmic dimension, but T'an drew on modern scientific concepts to develop his metaphysics of *jen* in which *jen* is identified with ether (*yi-t'ai*, a transliteration of the Western word). K'ang Yu-wei, too, equated *jen* with ether and electricity.

K'ang Yu-wei and his followers sought in their practical program to transform China into a modern and modernizing constitutional monarchy along the lines of Meiji Japan. Thanks to the patronage of a reformist governor, K'ang's disciples were able to carry out some of their program in Hunan, but their greatest moment came in 1898 when K'ang received the support of Emperor Kuang-hsü, who aided the reform movement in an attempt to assert himself and shake off the control of the Empress Dowager. (See Figure 8-1.) For a "hundred days" (actually 103 days), there was a flood of decrees reforming the examination system, remodeling the political apparatus, promoting industry, and otherwise modernizing state and society. It was an ambitious program, but the edicts are more significant as expressions of intent than indicators of accomplishment, for many of them were never implemented. Opposition was strong, not only among high-placed Manchu and Chinese officials but also from the Empress Dowager. She was not necessarily opposed to reform but was alarmed over the reformers' extremism. Furthermore, she was aware of the threat to her own position implied in the reform movement and was unwilling to be shunted into political oblivion. A showdown was inevitable. Realizing this, the emperor and the reformers turned to Yüan Shih-k'ai, formerly Li Hung-chang's representative in Korea, since Yüan was a reform-minded military man then training a modern military force. But at the crucial point, Yüan failed to execute the emperor's orders, which included putting to death Jung-lu, the Manchu general known for his loyalty to the Empress Dowager. Instead, Yüan confided in

Figure 8-1 The Empress Dowager seated on the Imperial Throne.

Jung-lu, and the outcome was a coup that placed the Empress Dowager again in command of the throne. Emperor Kuang-hsü continued as a figurehead.

K'ang Yu-wei and Liang Ch'i-ch'ao managed to flee to Japan, but T'an Ssu-t'ung remained behind to give his life for the cause. Although many of the reform edicts were rescinded, the Empress Dowager did give her approval to moderate reforms, including military modernization and reforms in education and the monetary and fiscal systems. That little was accomplished even then was due to the weakness of the central government and the enormity of the problems facing the dynasty. By no means the least of these was China's perilous international situation.

## The Scramble for Concessions

China's display of weakness in the war against Japan brought in its wake an imperialist scramble for special rights and privileges in which Russia, France, Britain, Germany, and Japan pursued their immediate national interests and jockeyed for position in case China collapsed completely. (See map, Figure 8-2.)

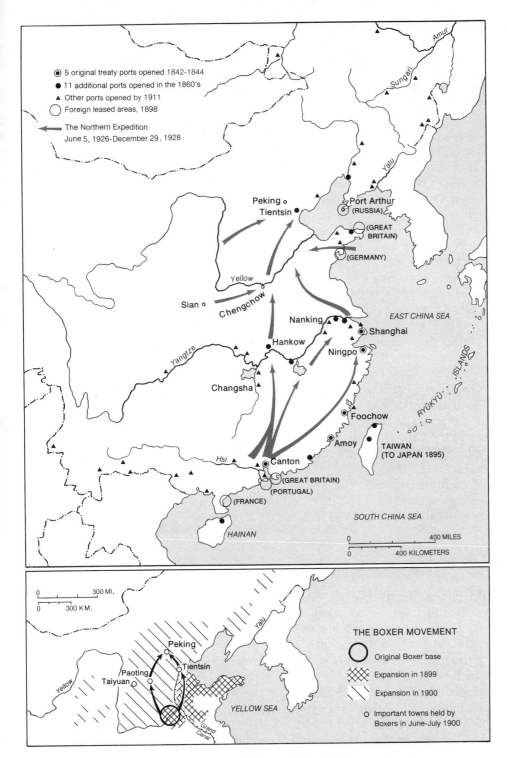

Figure 8-2 **China, 1895–1927**

The concessions extracted from China were economic and political. For example, the powers forced loans on the Ch'ing, which were secured by Chinese tax revenues, such as maritime customs. Long-term leases of Chinese territory were granted to the powers, including the right to develop economic resources such as mines and railroads. Thus Germany leased territory in Kiaochow and Shantung; Russia leased Port Arthur in the southern Liaotung Peninsula; France held leases on land around Kwang-chow Bay; and Britain obtained Wei-haiwei and the Kowloon New Territories, adjacent to the Kowloon area ceded in 1860. The powers also frequently obtained the right to police the areas they leased. Often the powers combined leaseholds, railroad rights, and commercial rights, to create a "sphere of interest," that is, an area in which they were the privileged foreign power, as, for example, Germany was in Shantung. Finally, there were "non-alienation" pacts by which China agreed not to cede a given area to any power other than the signatory: the Yangtze Valley to Britain, the provinces bordering French Indo-China to France, Fukien to Japan. In addition, Russia received special rights in Manchuria.

Britain, as the prime trading nation in China, pursued an ambiguous policy, concerned on the one hand to retain access to all of China and on the other to obtain a share of the concessions. The United States at this time was acquiring a Pacific empire. In 1898 it annexed Hawaii and, after war with Spain, the Philippines and Guam. At the urging of Britain, the United States then adopted an "Open Door" policy enunciated in two diplomatic notes. The first of these (1899) merely demanded equality of commercial opportunity for all the powers in China, while the second (1900) also affirmed a desire to preserve the integrity of the Chinese state and Chinese territory. This was a declaration of principle, not backed by force; neither its altruism nor its effectiveness should be exaggerated.

Resentment against the encroachments of the powers was strong, not only among conservatives in office and the exiled opposition, but also among the poor and illiterate. In 1900 it flared up in violence.

## The Boxer Rising

The Boxers, members of the *I-ho ch'üan* (Righteous and Harmonious Fists), developed in response to harsh economic conditions and resentment over the privileges enjoyed by missionaries and their converts. Passions were further fueled by alarm over the spread of railways, which cut across the land regardless of the graves of ancestors or the requirements of geomancy, railways along which stood telephone poles carrying wires from which rust-filled rainwater dripped blood red. As a counterforce the Boxers relied on rituals, spells, and amulets to endow them with supernatural powers, including invulnerability to bullets. In 1898 flood and famine in Shantung combined with the advance of the Germans in that province to create conditions which led to the first Boxer rising there in May of that year.

Originally antidynastic, the Boxers changed direction when they received the support of Ch'ing officials prepared to use the movement against the powers. Thus encouraged, the Boxers spread, venting their rage on Chinese and foreign Christians, especially Catholics. On June 13, 1900 they entered Peking. Eight days later the court issued a declaration of war on all the treaty powers. Officially the Boxers were placed under the command of imperial princes, and there followed a dramatic two-month siege of the legation quarter in Peking, where 451 guards defended 473 foreign civilians and some 3000 Chinese Christians who had fled there for protection. The ordeal of the besieged was grim, but they were spared the worst, for the Boxers and the Chinese troops were undisciplined, ill-organized, and uncoordinated. The city was full of looting and violence, but the legation quarter was still intact when an international relief expedition reached Peking on August 15 and forced the court to flee the capital.

During these dangerous and dramatic events, southern governors-general chose to ignore the court's declaration of war, claiming it was made under duress (forced by the Boxers); hence the term "Boxer Rebellion." The powers, nevertheless, demanded from the Ch'ing court a very harsh settlement. It included a huge indemnity (450 million taels, 67.5 million pounds sterling) to be paid from customs and salt revenues. Other provisions required the punishment of pro-Boxer officials and of certain cities, where the civil service examinations were suspended. The powers received the right to station permanent legation guards in the capital and to place troops between Peking and the sea. The Boxer rising also provided Russia with an excuse to occupy Manchuria, where some Russians remained until Russia's defeat by Japan in the war of 1904–05.

The failure of the Boxers meant a further decline in China's international position and struck a blow at the dynasty whose policies had led to ignominious flight. A convincing demonstration of the futility of the old ways, it propelled the Ch'ing government into a serious attempt at reform.

## Economic Developments

During the period 1895–1911, the modern sector of the Chinese economy continued to develop at a steady pace, but it was dominated by foreign capital. Not only were extensive railway concessions granted to the treaty powers, but Chinese railroads, like that linking Peking and Hankow, were financed by foreign capital. Foreign capital also controlled much of China's mining and shipping, and it was a major factor in manufacturing, both for the export trade (tea, silk, soybeans, and so forth) and for the domestic market (textiles, tobacco, and so forth). Modern banking was another area of foreign domination, prompting the Ch'ing government in 1898 to approve the creation of the Commercial Bank of China, a modern bank functioning as a "government operated merchant enterprise" (*kuan-tu shang-pan*). Two more banks were formed in 1905 and 1907.

Except for railways and mines, foreign investments were concentrated in the treaty ports, and it was there also that Chinese factories gradually developed, taking advantage of modern services and the security to be found in foreign concession areas. Chinese enterprises were particularly important in textile manufacturing. Most remained small (by 1912 only 750 employed more than one hundred workers), but they were an important part of China's economic modernization. It was also during this period that Shanghai became China's largest city, a status it retains today.

The development of a modern economic sector in Shanghai and, to a lesser extent, in other treaty ports, was accompanied by changes in social structure. A Chinese business class developed, as did a class of urban laborers who at times expressed their resentment over terrible working conditions by going on strike. In the city, too, the old family system lost its economic underpinnings, and there was an audience receptive to new values and ideas. Some of these were revolutionary, but government leaders too were now convinced of the need for extensive change.

## Eleventh-Hour Reform

Even while continuing to denounce K'ang Yu-wei, the Ch'ing regime after 1900 pursued a reform program similar to that of 1898. By making extensive changes, the Empress Dowager hoped to save the dynasty and transform the Ch'ing into a state capable of surviving in the modern world. The reforms were in earnest, and some, like the drive against opium, accomplished much, but frequently the measures taken to save the Ch'ing had a way of working against the dynasty instead.

The educational reforms, which received high priority, are an example. In 1905 the government took the radical step of abolishing the examination system, and by the end of the decade even remote provinces boasted new schools, teaching new subjects and ideas. Chinese students also studied abroad in record numbers, especially in Japan where by 1906 there were at least 8000 of them, many supported by their provincial governments. There, away from their families, they enjoyed a new personal and intellectual liberty. Even those who did not manage to complete their education drank in the heady wine of new ideas. The most influential intellectual of the decade was Liang Ch'i-ch'ao, from whose writings many learned about the major events of world history for the first time, and were introduced to Western social and political thought from Rousseau to the twentieth century. The example of Japan was itself a powerful influence, as were books translated from Japanese. More books were translated into Chinese from Japanese than from any other language, and many Japanese loan words entered the Chinese language, thus reversing the flow which had taken place over a millenium before.

In this way Chinese students learned about Western history and law, science and logic, and above all became convinced of the truths of evolutionism, with its positive evaluation of struggle, and of nationalism, with its shift of loyalty from culture to nation. The Japanese example showed that nationalism was compatible with the preservation of elements of traditional culture, but a commitment to nationalism did imply a willingness to jettison those elements of tradition which failed to contribute to national development. Toward the end of the decade students became increasingly restive and revolutionary. The new education was intended to mold the men who would save the dynasty, but it fashioned those who helped to bury it.

Manchu political reform included restructuring the government along modern lines and the development of a constitution. After a study mission abroad (1905–06) and subsequent deliberations, the government in 1908 announced a nine-year plan of constitutional reform beginning with provincial assemblies in 1909. Although elected on a limited franchise, these assemblies, as well as the central legislative council convened in 1910, became not sources of popular support but centers of opposition.

Nothing was more urgent than the creation of a modern military force, but here too the reform program backfired. The new forces proved unreliable because they were either influenced by new, subversive ideas or were loyal to their commanders rather than the throne. The main beneficiary of military modernization turned out to be Yüan Shih-k'ai, who as governor-general of Chihli from 1901 to 1907 built up an army with which he retained ties even after he was dismissed from the government in 1908.

The government had some foreign policy success, especially in reasserting Chinese sovereignty over Tibet, but failed to emerge as a plausible focus for nationalism. Not only was it handicapped by its non-Han ethnic origins, but during this very difficult and dangerous period of rapid change, there was a deterioration in the quality of dynastic leadership after the Empress Dowager and Emperor Kuang-hsü both died in 1908. The new emperor was an infant, and the regent was inept.

## The Revolution of 1911 and Sun Yat-sen

In its program of modernization the dynasty was seriously handicapped by its financial weakness. This became painfully apparent in its handling of the railway issue. In order to regain foreign railway concessions, a railway recovery movement was organized by provincial gentry and merchants who created their own railway companies. The Ch'ing government, however, wanted to centralize power, and in 1911 decided to nationalize the major railway lines. Lacking the necessary financial resources, it was able to do so only by contracting foreign loans, inevitably with strings attached. The loans and the subsequent disbanding of provincial railway companies caused a furor, nowhere more so than in Szechwan, where local gentry who had invested in the provincial railway company felt cheated by the price the government was willing to pay for their shares. Provincial interests resented the threat to provincial autonomy. Nationalists were indignant over the foreign loans that financed the transaction. This was the prelude to revolt. The insurrection which actually set off the revolution took place in Wuchang on October 10 and was conducted by men only very loosely connected with the Revolutionary Alliance, the main revolutionary organization in the land.

The Revolutionary Alliance (*T'ung-meng hui*, also translated "United League") was formed in Tokyo in 1905 when a number of revolutionary groups joined together under the leadership of Sun Yat-sen (1866–1925). Sun was born into a Kwangtung peasant family, received a Christian education in Hawaii, and studied medicine in Hong Kong. He founded his first revolutionary organization in Hawaii in 1894, and overseas Chinese communities remained an important source of moral and financial support. Over the years he elaborated his "Three Principles of the People"—nationalism, democracy, and the people's livelihood. His political program called for the toppling of the Ch'ing dynasty and the establishment of a republic. Sun was influenced by Henry George's "single tax" theory, which held that unearned increases in land values (as when farm land rises in value because it is sought for commercial development) should go to the community rather than to the individual landholder. Sun, however, did not work out a full-fledged economic program. This may have been just as well, since the Three Principles were broad enough to attract the varied and loosely organized membership of the Revolutionary Alliance; details might only have raised questions and disagreements.

## Yüan Shih-k'ai and the Warlord Era

After the October 10 incident, province after province broke with the dynasty, which turned for help to Yüan Shih-k'ai. Yüan's former army commanders stood to gain by supporting him and did so, but neither Yüan nor the revolutionaries were strong enough to impose their will on all of China. At the same time, all the contenders for power were anxious to achieve sufficient political stability to prevent foreign intervention and were thus ready for a compromise. The result was that the Manchu child-emperor formally abdicated on February 12, 1912, and after Sun stepped aside, Yüan accepted the presidency of a republic with a two-chambered legislature. Yüan agreed to move the capital to Nanking, but once in office he evaded this provision.

In the absence of well-organized political parties or deep-rooted republican sentiments among the public, there was little to restrain Yüan, who rapidly developed into a dictator. Elections were duly held in February 1913, but Yüan bullied the parliament. The leader of its largest party, the Nationalist party (KMT, Kuomintang), was assassinated in March 1913. That summer Yüan forced a showdown by ordering the dismissal of pro-Nationalist southern military governors. When they revolted in what is sometimes known as the Second Revolution, Yüan crushed them easily. However, his policy of centralization financed by foreign loans won little support.

During the First World War, Japan presented Yüan Shih-k'ai with the notorious twenty-one demands, divided into five groups: (1) recognition of Japanese rights in Shantung; (2) extension of Japanese rights in Mongolia and Manchuria; (3) Sino-Japanese joint operation of China's largest iron and steel company; (4) China not to cede or lease any coastal area to any power other than Japan; and (5) provisions which would have obliged the Chinese government to employ Japanese political, financial, and military advisers, given the Japanese partial control over the police, and obliged China to purchase Japanese arms. Yüan managed to avoid the last and most onorous group of demands, which would have reduced China to a virtual Japanese satellite. However, with the other powers preoccupied in Europe, Yüan was forced to accept Japan's seizure of Germany's holdings in Shantung, grant Japan new rights in Southern Manchuria and Inner Mongolia, and acknowledge her special interest in China's largest iron and steel works, which had previously served as security for Japanese loans. The domestic result was a wave of anti-Japanese nationalist outrage, which expressed itself in protests and boycotts. To reinvigorate his regime, Yüan set about restoring dynastic rule with himself as emperor. The new regime was proclaimed in December 1915 and was to begin on New Year's Day. At the time it was argued that China was not ready for a republic, and Yüan may have been right in his belief that a new imperial dynasty would meet the expectations of the great mass of the people. However, he did not draw the people into politics, and those who did have a political say were overwhelmingly hostile to the dynasty. In March 1916 Yüan gave way and officially abandoned his imperial ambitions. But he never regained his old prestige, and died a failure in June of that year.

The collapse of Yüan Shih-k'ai's plans demonstrated that it was impossible to return to the old order and revealed just how far the central government had disintegrated since it first lost the initiative to the provinces during the Taiping Rebellion. Now all that remained in the way of a national government was an empty shell, which served to provide a facade of legitimacy under presidents who were puppets of warlord forces controlling the capital region.

After the fall of Yüan Shih-k'ai, the pattern of Chinese politics became exceedingly complex. Although a national government ruled in Peking, actual power lay in the hands of regional strongmen (warlords) who dominated the areas under their control largely through force of arms, and who struggled with each other to enlarge or protect their holdings. They constantly entered into and betrayed alliances with each other, and the foreign powers (especially Japan and the Soviet Union), fishing in these troubled waters, sought to play the warlords off against each other, and against the central government, for their own benefit.

Some of the warlords had been generals under Yüan Shih-k'ai; others had begun their careers as bandits. In ideology they varied widely, ranging from advocates of Confucianism to one prominent general who adopted Christianity. In personality they ran the gamut from ruthless butchers to benevolent commanders, selfish despots to rulers interested in social welfare and education;

but those who oppressed and squeezed the people were the more numerous. Conditions varied in different regions, but "the terror, oppression, tax demands, bloodshed, intrigue, and pillaging of the warlord era made those dozen years a nightmare."[1] It was a period of bitter suffering, when the disintegration of the old values and institutions was more apparent than the growth of the new. It was also a period of great intellectual ferment and artistic creativity.

## Intellectual Ferment

Revolutionary ideas were current among Chinese students in Tokyo during the first decade of the century and were welcomed by the magazines and schools of China proper. Pedants were mocked and corruption was castigated. There were demands for improved social conditions, the education of women, and an end to footbinding. The defeat of 1895 elicited demands for more effective resistance to imperialism, but more than that, it gave rise to a wave of social commentary: critiques of the old and advocacy of the new. This tendency increased after 1900, and again after the government abolished the examination system. Abolition of the examination system was particularly significant because, without weakening the traditional respect accorded scholars and intellectuals, it removed the institutional prop for Confucianism and opened the way for new patterns of thought and new approaches to social and political problems. Moreover, by lifting the requirement of a Confucian education, it further encouraged the modernization of education for prospective scholars and office holders.

It was a sign of the times that the conservative Lin Shu (1852–1924), the most famous and prolific translator of Western fiction into classical Chinese, now translated *Uncle Tom's Cabin.* Furthermore, new ideas also led to new actions. A modern-style student protest took place as early as 1903 when the Russians delayed a promised evacuation of troops from Manchuria. The first antiimperialist boycott came in 1905 in protest against United States legislation excluding Chinese laborers from entering that country.

It did not take the fall of the Ch'ing to produce iconoclasm and protest, but these tendencies became deeper and more widespread after the dynasty collapsed. An important landmark was the founding of *New Youth* (1915) by Ch'en Tu-hsiu (1879–1942), just returned from Japan. In the first issue of this influential journal, Ch'en issued an eloquent call for the rejuvenation of China accompanied by an equally strong denunciation of the old tradition. A prime target for the new intellectuals was Confucianism, still advocated by, among others, K'ang Yu-wei, who tried to cast it in a new role as an official religion for the Chinese state. It was K'ang's great misfortune that in the late Ch'ing he could not construct a Confucian justification for modernization which was persuasive to scholars grounded in the classics, and that afterward he was equally unsuccessful in devising a modern justification for Confucianism acceptable to those whose primary loyalty was to the nation. Confucianism was not destroyed, but it was put very much on the defensive.

*New Youth* not only opposed the traditional teachings, it also opposed the language in which they were written. The journal opened its pages to Hu Shih (1891–1962), a former student of the American philosopher John Dewey, and China's leading champion of the vernacular language (*pai-hua*). Hu Shih argued that people should write the spoken language not the language of the classics, and that the vernacular should be taught in the schools. He praised the literary merits of the old novels written in the vernacular, which had long been widely read but never before enjoyed respectability. The campaign for the vernacular was a success. The transition did not come all at once: classical expressions had a way of creeping into the vernacular, and newly borrowed terms stood in the way of easy comprehension. Nevertheless, the new language was both more accessible and more modern than the old. Introduced into the elementary schools in 1920, it was universally used in the schools by the end of the decade.

*New Youth* was also the first magazine to publish Lu Hsün (Chou Shu-jen, 1881–1936) who became China's most acclaimed writer of the twentieth century. Lu Hsün had gone to Japan to study medicine but decided to devote himself to combating not physical ailments but China's spiritual ills. His bitter satire cut like a sharp scalpel, but a scalpel wielded by a humanist who hoped to cure, not kill. His protagonist in "A Madman's Diary" (*New Youth*, 1918) discovers the reality underneath the gloss of "virtue and morality" in the old histories: a history of man eating man. He ends with the plea, "Perhaps there are still children who have not eaten men? Save the children . . ."[2]

Many of the leaders of the new thought were on the faculty of Peking University, now directed by a tolerant European-educated intellectual, and their ideas found a ready following among the students at this and other Chinese universities. On May 4, 1919, some 3000 of these students staged a dramatic demonstration to protest further interference in Chinese affairs by the imperialist powers. China had entered the World War on the allied side, and sent labor battalions to France, in order to gain a voice in the peace settlement. But when the powers met at Versailles, they ignored China, and assigned Germany's former possessions in Shantung to Japan. The students were outraged. The demonstration became violent. There were arrests. These were followed by more protest: a wave of strikes and a show of merchant and labor support for the students. This was particularly significant because the growth of the modern-minded merchant and labor classes in China's large cities had been stimulated by the wartime withdrawal of European firms from East Asia. Imports fell, exports grew, and Chinese commercial and industrial concerns made the most of their opportunities.

In the end the government had to retreat. Those who had been arrested were released, and those who had ordered the arrests were forced to resign. China never signed the ill-fated Treaty of Versailles.

The May Fourth incident came to symbolize the currents of intellectual and cultural change first articulated in *New Youth* and gave rise to the term "May Fourth movement," usually used to designate the whole period from 1915 to the early 1920s. The incident gave intellectuals a heightened sense of urgency and turned what had been a trickle of protest into a tide. A flood of publications followed, introducing new and radical ideas. There was action as well as talk. In private life young men and women rejected arranged marriages and began to question the whole family system. There was also increased social action, particularly in the area of organizing labor unions.

The May Fourth movement had long-term revolutionary consequences. In the short term, however, the eddies of Chinese intellectual and cultural life were as confused as ever. There were intense disagreements concerning the future direction of Chinese culture and, in the absence of an official orthodoxy, a tremendous variety of competing ideas, theories, and styles.

## Intellectual Alternatives

In the wake of the May Fourth movement there was vigorous disagreement about basic values and directions. Among those who turned back to the Chinese tradition after witnessing the spectacle of Europe's self-destruction in the First World War was the former champion of the West, Liang Ch'i-ch'ao. Liang now hoped to combine the best of both worlds and achieve a synthesis in which the Chinese elements would predominate (just as Sung Neo-Confucianism had synthesized Buddhism into an essentially Confucian framework), but in the twentieth century this turned out to be an extraordinarily difficult task.

An important debate began in 1923 between the proponents of science and metaphysics, a debate which also involved differences over the interpretation and evaluation of Chinese and Western cultures. Among the advocates of the former were the proponents of scientism, that is, the belief that science holds the answers for all intellectual problems (including problems of value) and that the scientific method is the only method for arriving at truth. These tenets were challenged by those who argued that science is applicable only to a limited field of study, such as the study of nature, and that moral values have to be based on deeper metaphysical truths that by their very nature are beyond the reach of scientific methodology. Since similar problems agitated the West at this time, Chinese thinkers drew not only on the ideas of such classic European philosophers as Immanuel Kant but also on the thought of contemporaries as varied as John Dewey and Henri Bergson, the French exponent of vitalism. Those who identified with the Chinese tradition further drew on the insights of Neo-Confucianism and Buddhism, particularly the former.

Noteworthy among the defenders of tradition were Liang Shu-ming (Liang Sou-ming, 1893–), also well known for his work in rural reconstruction, and Chang Chün-mai (Carson Chang, 1887–1969) later the leader of a small political party opposed to both the Chinese Communist party (CCP) and the KMT. The most influential traditionalist philosophers whose most important works were written in the 1930s were Fung Yu-lan (1895–), a proponent of Chu Hsi's Neo-Confucianism, and Hsiung Shih-li (1885–1969), who developed the opposite, mind-centered stream of Neo-Confucian philosophy drawing on the thought of Wang Yang-ming.

Among the champions of science and Western values were the scientist Ting Wen-chiang (T.V. Ting, 1887–1936) and Hu Shih, the father of the vernacular language movement. Hu Shih was a leading liberal who advocated a gradualist, piecemeal problem-solving approach to China's ills in the face of attacks not only from the traditionalists on the right but also from the left. His message increasingly fell on deaf ears, for his approach required time, and time was precisely what China lacked. More often than not, this included time to digest the heady dose of new intellectual imports. Similarly, liberal individualism was another luxury which many felt a nation and a civilization in crisis could ill afford.

## Cultural Alternatives

It is a truism as applicable to modern China as elsewhere that painting reflects the times, yet the most beloved twentieth-century painter was singularly unaffected by either the impact of the West or the heady excitement of the May Fourth movement. This was Ch'i Pai-shih (1863–1957), already in his fifties at the time of the May Fourth incident. Ch'i began as a humble carpenter and did not turn to painting until his mid-twenties, but his industry and longevity more than made up for his late start. It is estimated that he produced more than 10,000 paintings. Ch'i was a great admirer of the seventeenth-century individualist Chu Ta but essentially followed his own inner vision. He was not given to theorizing but did express his attitude toward representation: "The excellence of a painting lies in its being like, yet unlike. Too much likeness flatters the vulgar taste; too much unlikeness deceives the world."[3] Although his work includes landscapes and portraits, he is at his best in depicting the humble forms of life, including rodents and insects, with a loving and gentle humor reminiscent of the haiku of Kobayashi Issa. (See Figure 8-3.) His pictures are statements of his own benevolent vision. They show, to quote a Chinese critic, "a loving sympathy for the little insects and crabs and flowers he draws," and have "an enlivening gaiety of manner and spirit," so that, "his pictures are really all pictures of his own gentle humanism."[4]

There were other painters and calligraphers in the twenties and thirties who remained uninfluenced by the West, but many felt that the new age required a new style. Among those who tried to combine elements of the Chinese and Western traditions were the followers of a school of painters established in Canton by Kao Lun (Kao Chien-fu, 1879–1951). Kao sought to combine Western shading and perspective with Chinese brushwork and was also influenced by

Figure 8-3 Ch'i Pai-shih,
*The Night Marauders.*
Hanging scroll, Chinese ink
on paper.

Japanese decorativeness. He also sought to bring Chinese painting up to date by including in his works new subject matter, such as the airplanes in Figure 8-4.

In Shanghai, meanwhile, a small group of artists tried to transplant French-style bohemianism into that international city. Hsü Pei-hung (Péon Ju) (1895–1953), for example, affected the long hair and general appearance popular in the artists' quarter of Paris when he returned from that city in 1927. Hsü also brought back a thorough mastery of the French academic style. The subject of the painting shown in Figure 8-5 comes from the Warring States Period (403–221 B.C.), but in style it is a typical product of a European art school of the

Figure 8-4  Kao Lun (Kao Chien-fu),
*Landscape with Airplanes.*
Hanging scroll. Art Gallery, Chinese
University of Hong Kong.

Figure 8-5  Hsü Pei-hung, *T'ien-heng Wu-pai Shih.* Oil.

time, although it is executed with great technical skill. Somewhat more contemporary in his Western tastes was Liu Hai-su (1895– ), founder of the Shanghai Art School (1920), where he introduced the use of a nude model for the first time in China. This was also one of the first schools to offer a full course of instruction in Western music. Liu drew his inspiration from French postimpressionists like Matisse and Cézanne. Later, however, Liu returned to painting in a traditional manner, and Hsü too abandoned his Western dress for a Chinese gown. Today Hsü is perhaps most appreciated for his later paintings of horses, which are modern, yet essentially Chinese.

The literature of the period is an excellent source for the student of social and psychological history, but more than that it mirrored the temper of the age. As Leo Ou-fan Lee has noted, "the May Fourth Movement had unleashed not only a literary and an intellectual revolution: it also propelled an emotional one."[5] While there were also experiments with form such as Hsü Chih-mo's (1896– 1931) effort to recast Chinese verse in an English mold, complete with rhyme, the dominant quality of the period was an unabashedly romantic outpouring of feelings released by the removal of Confucian restraints and encouraged by the example of European romanticism.

One strain, as analyzed by Lee, was the passive-sentimental, presided over by the hero of Goethe's *The Sorrows of Young Werther* read in China (as in Japan) as "a sentimental sob story." The subjectivism of these writers was not unlike that of the writers of "I" novels in Japan. Another strain was dynamic and heroic. Its ideal was Prometheus, who braved Zeus's wrath and stole fire for mankind. Holding a promise of release from alienation, it was compatible with a revolutionary political stance. For Kuo Mo-jo (1892– ), once an admirer of Goethe, Lenin became beyond all else a Promethean hero. Perhaps the strongest expression of Promethean martyrdom came from Lu Hsün, "I have stolen fire from other countries, intending to cook my own flesh. I think that if the taste is good, the other chewers on their part may get something out of it, and I shall not sacrifice my body in vain."[6]

Controversies and rivalries stimulated the formation of literary and intellectual societies as like-minded men joined together to publish journals for their causes and denounce those of the opposition. Revolutionaries were not alone in arguing that literature should have a social purpose, but as the years passed without any improvement in Chinese conditions, the attractions of revolutionary creeds increased. Writers of revolutionary persuasion such as Mao Tun (Shen Yen-ping, 1896– ) employed their talents in depicting and analyzing the defects in the old society and portraying the idealism of those out to change things. Such themes appeared not only in the work of Communist writers like Mao Tun but are found also in the work of the anarchist Pa Chin (Li Fei-kang, 1904– ), best known for his depiction of the disintegration of a large, eminent family in the novel appropriately entitled *Family* (1931), a part of his *Turbulent Stream* trilogy (1931–40). Such works provide important material for the student of social as well as literary history.

## Marxism in China: The Early Years

Marxism was not unknown in China, but it held little appeal prior to the Russian Revolution. The most radical Chinese, like their Japanese counterparts, were most impressed by the teachings of anarchism, which opposed the state as an authoritarian institution and sought to rely on man's natural social tendencies to create a just society. Those few who were drawn to socialism were attracted more by its egalitarianism than by concepts of class warfare. The writings of Marx and Engels offered the vision of a perfect society, but their thesis that socialism could only be achieved after capitalism had run its course suggested that Marxism was inappropriate for a society only just entering "the capitalist stage of development."

The success of the Russian Revolution (1917) altered the picture considerably. Faced with a similar problem in applying Marxism to Russia, Lenin amended Marxist theory to fit the needs of his own country, and thereby also made it more relevant to the Chinese. His theory that imperialism was the last stage of capitalism gave new historical importance to countries such as China, which were the objects of imperialist expansion. It also suggested that the imperialist nations were themselves on the verge of the transition to socialist states. Most significant for the Chinese situation, perhaps, was Lenin's concept of the Communist party as the vanguard of revolution, which showed a way in which party intellectuals could help make history even in a precapitalist state, and thus justified their efforts.

Furthermore, Marxism was modern and claimed "scientific" validity for its doctrines. It shared the prestige accorded by Chinese intellectuals to what was Western and "advanced," even as it opposed the dominant forms of social, economic, and political organization in the West. A Western heresy which could be used against the West, it promised to undo China's humiliation and to place China once again in the forefront of world history. Most important of all, it worked. The Russian Revolution demonstrated its effectiveness. To many, and not only in China, it seemed the wave of the future.

The appeal of Marxism in China was varied. Li Ta-chao (1888–1927), professor and librarian at Peking University and an ardent revolutionary, was attracted to it initially as a vehicle for national revolution. Ch'en Tu-hsiu (1879–1942), the editor of New Youth and, for a time, a champion of science and democracy, was attracted to Marxism as a more effective means of achieving modernization. Others were drawn to it for still other reasons. Whatever their reasons, a core of Marxist intellectuals was available as potential leaders by the time the Comintern* agent Grigorii Voitinsky arrived in China, in the spring of 1920, to prepare for the organization of the Chinese Communist party (CCP). Organization of the CCP took place in the following year.

---

* The Third International (Communist International) founded in Moscow in 1919 to coordinate Communist movements around the world.

At its first gathering in July 1921, the CCP elected Ch'en Tu-hsiu its Secretary General. Despite very considerable misgivings, the leadership of the fledgling party submitted to a Comintern policy of maximum cooperation with the Kuomintang, with which a formal agreement was reached in 1923. Under this arrangement, at the insistence of Sun Yat-sen, the two parties were not allied as equals with the CCP as a "block without," but CCP members were admitted into the KMT as individuals, forming a "block within," and subjecting themselves to KMT party discipline. The CCP leadership was suspicious of the KMT and found it difficult to accept the Comintern's theoretical analysis of the KMT as a multiclass party. But it submitted to Comintern discipline and the logic of the situation in China, where the few hundred Communists were outnumbered by the thousands of KMT members and had little contact with the masses they sought to lead. This initial period of CCP-KMT cooperation lasted until 1927. Although the CCP greatly expanded during these years, the KMT remained definitely the senior partner.

## The Nationalists (KMT) and Sun Yat-sen (1913–1923)

After the failure of the "second revolution" of 1913, Sun Yat-sen was once again forced into exile in Japan, where he tried to win Japanese support for his revolution. After the death of Yüan Shih-k'ai, he was able to return to China and establish a revolutionary base in Canton, where he retained a precarious foothold dependent on the good will of the local warlord.

Denied foreign backing despite his efforts to obtain support in Japan and elsewhere, Sun was also handicapped by the weakness of the KMT party organization, which was held together only loosely, and largely through loyalty to Sun himself. Meanwhile, the success of the Russian Revolution provided a striking contrast to the failure of the revolution Sun tried to lead in China. Further, Sun was favorably disposed to the U.S.S.R. by the Soviet Union's initial renunciation of Czarist rights in China. This corresponded to a new antiimperialist emphasis in his own thought and rhetoric. The end of Manchu rule had not led to marked improvement in China's lot vis-à-vis the foreign powers, and a stronger antiimperialist line seemed called for.

Sun was therefore ready to work with the Communists, and in 1923 he concluded an agreement with the Comintern agent Adolf Joffe, who concurred with Sun's view that China was not ready for socialism and that the immediate task ahead was the achievement of national unity and independence. Through this pact with Joffe, Sun received valuable assistance and aid. Under the guidance of the Comintern agent Mikhail Borodin (Grusenberg), the KMT was reorganized into a more structured and disciplined organization than ever before, while General Galen (Blücher) performed the same service for the KMT army. Sun Yat-sen made some minor ideological compromises but did not basically depart from his previous views. Of his Three Principles of the People, that of nationalism was now redirected so as to be antiimperialist rather than anti-Manchu. The principle of the people's livelihood now gave greater emphasis to farmers.

## KMT and CCP Cooperation (1923–1927)

For both sides, the agreement of 1923 was a marriage of convenience, and at first it worked to the advantage of both parties. The KMT gained guidance and support while CCP members rose to important positions in the KMT organization, and the party reached out to organize urban workers and made a beginning in rural organization. A good example of a CCP leader occupying an important KMT office is provided by Chou En-lai (1898–1976), who became head of the political department of the Whampoa Military Academy, headed by Chiang Kai-shek (1887–1975). At Whampoa the cream of the KMT officer corps was trained and prepared to lead an army to reunify China and establish a national regime.

In accord with Marxist principles, the CCP devoted its main efforts to organizing the urban labor movement, which had already won its first victory in the Hong Kong Seamen's Strike of 1922. Shanghai and Canton were particularly fertile grounds for the labor organizer, since in these cities the textile and other light industries continued their pre–First World War growth, assisted in part by the wartime lull in foreign competition. Of some 2.7 million cotton spindles in China around 1920, 1.3 million were in Chinese controlled factories, and 500 thousand were owned by Japanese. In Chinese and foreign plants alike, working conditions remained very harsh.

Under these circumstances, the CCP's work met with substantial success. It gained greatly by its leadership during and following the incident of May 30, 1925, when Chinese demonstrators were fired on by the police of the International Settlement in Shanghai, killing ten and wounding more than fifty. A general strike and boycott followed; in Hong Kong and Canton the labor movement held out for sixteen months. The strike did not achieve its goals, but CCP party membership increased from around 1000 in early 1925 to an estimated 20,000 by the summer of 1926.

Sun Yat-sen did not live to witness the May 30 incident, for he died of liver cancer in March 1925. In death he was glorified even more than he had been while alive, but his image as the father of the revolution did not suffice, in the absence of a clearly designated heir apparent, to keep the only-recently reorganized KMT united. Furthermore, his ideological legacy was open to a variety of interpretations. His last major statement of the Three Principles of the People, issued in 1924, stressed the first principle, nationalism, which included opposition to foreign imperialism and also provided for self-determination for China's minorities.

The second principle, democracy, contained proposals for popular elections, initiative, recall, and referendum, but full democracy was to come about only after a preparatory period of political tutelage. In terms of political structure, Sun envisioned a republic with five branches of government: the standard Western trilogy (legislative, executive, judicial), plus two contributions from traditional Chinese government: an examination branch to test applicants for government posts, and a censorial branch to monitor the performance of government officials and to control corruption.

Finally, the principle of the people's livelihood aimed at both economic egalitarianism and economic development. It incorporated a Henry Georgian plan to tax the unearned increment on land values in order to equalize land holdings. An additional refinement was a land tax based on each landholder's assessment of the value of his land. To prevent underassessment, the state was to have the right to purchase the land at the declared value. Sun also had a grandiose vision of Chinese industrialization, but this was unrealistic since it called for enormous investments from a Europe which could ill afford them. More realistic was a proposal for state ownership of major industries. He remained critical of Marxist ideas of class struggle, preferring an emphasis on the unification of the Chinese people.

Prominent among the leaders competing for KMT leadership after Sun Yat-sen's death was Wang Ching-wei (1883–1944), who had been associated with Sun in Japan and gained a reputation for revolutionary heroism when he attempted to assassinate the Manchu Prince Regent in 1910. Wang, however, could not dominate the party and had to work with various factions and other leaders. In 1926 it became apparent that the most formidable challenger for the leadership was Chiang Kai-shek. After the pact with Joffe in 1923, Sun had sent Chiang to Moscow to study the Soviet military. On his return to China, Chiang was appointed to head the newly formed Whampoa Military Academy, where he was highly successful, esteemed alike by the Soviet advisors and by the officer candidates, whom he exhorted to do their utmost for the KMT and the Three Principles of the People.

While Wang Ching-wei loosely presided over the KMT, the CCP steadily gained influence in the party, much to the alarm of the KMT right and of Chiang Kai-shek. In March, 1926, Chiang decided to act: he declared martial law, arrested Soviet advisors, and took steps to restrain the CCP influence in the KMT, while managing to retain the cooperation of both the CCP and of its Soviet supporters, since he required their assistance for the military unification of the country. This he began in the summer of 1926, when he embarked on the Northern Expedition (see map, Figure 8-2), setting out with his army from Canton. Although there was some heavy fighting against warlord armies, the force made rapid headway on its march to the Yangtze, and some warlords decided to bring their forces over to the Nationalist side. In the fall of 1926, the Nationalist victories enabled them to shift the capital from Canton to more centrally located Wuhan.* There Wang Ching-wei headed a civilian KMT government but lacked the power to control Chiang and his army.

---

* Wuhan refers to the three cities (Wuchang, Hanyang, and Hankow) where the Han River flows into the Yangtze.

## The Break Between the KMT and the CCP

On its march north to the Yangtze, the KMT army was assisted by popular support for the revolutionary cause, and nowhere was this support more enthusiastic than among the Communist-led workers of Shanghai, where the General Labor Union seized control of the city even before the arrival of the Nationalist troops. Elsewhere too there was an increase in labor activity. This alarmed Chinese bankers and industrialists who, ready to support a national but not a social revolution, financed the increasingly anti-Communist Chiang Kai-shek. In April, 1927, Chiang finally broke with the CCP completely by initiating a bloody campaign of suppression in Shanghai, which then spread to other cities. Union and party headquarters were raided; those who resisted were killed; suspected Communists were shot on sight. CCP cells were destroyed and unions disbanded in a devastating sweep that left the urban CCP shattered.

The CCP's work in organizing city factory workers was entirely consistent with Marxist theory, but the majority of the Chinese people continued to be peasants. Marx, as a student of the French Revolution, despised the peasantry. He referred to them as "the class which represents barbarism within civilization."[7] But Lenin, operating in a primarily agrarian land, assigned the peasantry a supporting role in the Russian Revolution. The CCP, although it concentrated on the cities, had not neglected the peasants. In 1921, China's first modern peasant movement was organized by P'eng Pai (1896–1929), and by 1927 the CCP was at work in a number of provinces, most notably Hunan, where the young Mao Tse-tung (1893–1976) wrote a famous report urging the party to concentrate on rural revolution and predicting, "In a very short time . . . several hundred million peasants will rise like a mighty storm, like a hurricane, a force so swift and violent that no power, however great, will be able to hold it back."[8] In another famous passage in the same report, he defended the need for peasant violence:

> A revolution is not a dinner party, or writing an essay, or painting a picture, or doing embroidery; it cannot be so refined, so leisurely and gentle, so temperate, kind, courteous, restrained, and magnanimous. A revolution is an insurrection, an act of violence by which one class overthrows another.[9]

In Hunan, as in other parts of China's rice producing region, tenancy rates were high, and the poorer peasants were sorely burdened by heavy rental payments and crushing debts. Tenants had few rights, and they faced the recurring specter of losing their leases. Furthermore, the demise of the old order helped to undermine the social functions and destroy the ideological moorings of the old rural gentry, now increasingly transformed from local elites into simple landlords. It was, as Mao saw, a volatile situation, fraught with revolutionary potential. But the Chinese party and its Soviet advisers remained urban minded.

After Chiang's April coup, the CCP broke with him but continued to work with the government at Wuhan, which also broke with Chiang. But here again the needs of the social revolution clashed with those of the national revolution, since the Wuhan regime depended for military support on armies officered largely by men of the landlord class, which was the prime object of peasant wrath. In this situation Comintern directives were wavering and contradictory, reflecting not Chinese realities but rather the exigencies of Stalin's intraparty maneuvers back in Moscow. The end result was that in June the CCP was expelled from Wuhan. Borodin and other Soviet advisers had to return to the U.S.S.R. For the CCP there began a difficult period of regrouping and reorganization.

## Establishment of the Nationalist Government

After Chiang Kai-shek's coup in Shanghai, he established a government in Nanking, which remained the capital after the completion of the Northern Expedition. The expedition was resumed in 1928, by which time the Wuhan leaders had bowed to the inevitable and made their peace with Chiang, as had a number of warlords whose forces now assisted the Nationalist army in its drive north and actually outnumbered the KMT's own troops. In June 1928, after a scant two months of fighting, Peking fell. China again had a national government, but the often nominal incorporation of warlord armies into the government forces meant that national unification was far from complete. Warlordism remained an essential feature of Chinese politics until the very end of the republican period in 1949.

During 1927 antiimperialist mobs attacked British concessions in two cities, and violence in Nanking in March left six foreigners dead, a number wounded, and foreign businesses and homes raided. Such incidents were officially attributed to Chiang Kai-shek's leftist rivals, and the foreign powers concluded that he was the most acceptable leader for China, that is, that his government would negotiate rather than expropriate their holdings. Thus Chiang's victory reassured the powers; except for the Japanese, who had plans of their own for Manchuria and Inner Mongolia. Japan had restored its holdings in Shantung to Chinese sovereignty after the American-sponsored Washington Conference of 1921–22 attended by nine powers with an interest in East Asia (Britain, the United States, France, Italy, Japan, China, Belgium, the Netherlands, and Portugal) to settle issues left over from the First World War. But now Japan sent troops to Shantung claiming that they were needed to protect Japanese lives and property, and there was fighting with Chinese soldiers in 1928. Still more ominous was the assassination that same year of the warlord of Manchuria, Chang Tso-lin, by a group of Japanese army officers who hoped this would pave the way for seizure of Manchuria. Acting on their own, without the knowledge or approval of their government, the Japanese officers did not get their way in 1928, but their act did serve as a prelude to the Japanese militarism and expansionism that threatened China during the thirties, even as the Nanking government tried to cope with warlords and revolutionaries at home, in its attempt to achieve a stable government.

## NOTES

1. James E. Sheridan, *China in Disintegration: The Republican Era in Chinese History, 1912–1949* (New York: The Free Press, 1975), p. 90.

2. Lu Hsün, "A Madman's Diary," in *Selected Works of Lu Hsün* (Peking: Foreign Language Press, 1956), pp. 8–21; reprinted in Ranbir Vohra, *The Chinese Revolution: 1900–1950* (Boston: Houghton Mifflin, 1974), pp. 62–71; quote p. 71.

3. See the biographical entry for Ch'i Pai-shih in Howard L. Boorman, ed., *Biographical Dictionary of Republican China* (New York: Columbia University Press, 1967–71) 1: 302–04. Ch'i's statement is quoted on p. 302.

4. Michael Sullivan, *Chinese Art in the Twentieth Century* (Berkeley and Los Angeles: University of California Press, 1959), p. 42.

5. Leo Ou-fan Lee, *The Romantic Generation of Modern Chinese Writers* (Cambridge: Harvard University Press, 1973), p. 265.

6. Quoted in Lee, *The Romantic Generation,* p. 291.

7. Karl Marx, quoted in Lucien Bianco, *Origins of the Chinese Revolution: 1915–1949,* trans. Murial Bell (Stanford: Stanford University Press, 1971), p. 74.

8. Mao Tse-tung, "Report on an Investigation of the Peasant Movement in Hunan," in *Selected Works of Mao Tse-tung* (Peking: Foreign Languages Press, 1967), Vol. 1; reprinted in Vohra, *The Chinese Revolution: 1900–1950,* p. 115.

9. *Ibid.,* p. 117.

日本

成功之限度

| 1895 | | 1912 | | 1926 | 1931 |
|------|------|------|------|------|------|
| LATE MEIJI | | TAISHŌ | | EARLY SHŌWA | |

# 9 The Limits of Success: Japan, 1895–1931

Japan could take great pride in her victory over China in 1894–95, a tangible measure of the success of Meiji modernization, and the years that followed brought further national achievements. But they did not bring stability in Japan's foreign relations or in her domestic life. The achievement of full status as a world power proved no easy task in a world dominated by Western superpowers: even Japan's triumph over China was laced with bitterness when France, Germany, and Russia interceded to force her to relinquish the

Liaotung Peninsula. Meanwhile, internally, political, economic, and cultural developments created problems as well as opportunities.

For Japan, as for China, the year 1912 provides an appropriate date for historical periodization, although in Japan it marked the demise not of a dynasty but of an individual, the Meiji emperor. However, since this was the emperor who had presided over Japan's transformation since 1867, his passing was felt at the time to signify the end of an era, a judgment in which modern scholars have generally concurred. We will therefore begin this chapter by considering developments from 1895 to 1912.

## Late Meiji Foreign Policy and Expansion

From the very beginning, the foreign policy goals of the Meiji leaders had been to achieve national security and equality of national status. But how were security and equality to be defined, and how were they to be attained?

A highly influential view of what constituted Japanese security was that of Yamagata Aritomo, architect of Japan's modern army, and an important political figure in or out of office. Yamagata was not a fanatical imperialist, but he was a hard-headed, realistic nationalist. The army's German advisor argued that Korea was the key to Japan's security, and Yamagata concurred in this analysis. In 1890 Yamagata propounded the thesis that Japan must not only defend its "line of sovereignty" but secure its "line of interest," which ran through Korea.

At the same time the Japanese navy was heavily influenced by the ideas of Admiral Mahan, an American advocate of the importance of sea power. From the navy's point of view, Japanese security demanded Japanese naval domination of the surrounding seas. The acquisition of Taiwan as a result of the Sino-Japanese War gratified the navy as a major step in this direction, but the army was very unhappy at having had to relinquish the strategic Liaotung Peninsula.

Equality was an equally elusive concept, but everyone agreed that at the very least it required the elimination of extraterritoriality and the restoration of tariff autonomy. Already in the 1870s work began on revision of the law codes to bring them into line with Western practices, so that the powers would no longer have reason to insist on maintaining jurisdiction over their own subjects. Even before the lengthy process of revising the codes had been completed, there was strong and vociferous public demand for an end to extraterritoriality. One result was that in 1886 the government was forced to back down from a compromise it had negotiated providing for mixed courts under Japanese and foreign judges. Appreciation of the intensity of public pressure was one of the factors that induced the British, in 1894 shortly before the start of the Sino-Japanese War, to relinquish extraterritoriality when the new legal codes came into effect (1889). Other countries followed suit. In return, foreign merchants were no longer limited to treaty ports. The treaties also secured tariff autonomy, and in 1911 Japan regained full control over customs duties.

By that time, Japan, under the most-favored-nation clause of the Treaty of Shimonoseki, was enjoying extraterritorial rights in China and benefiting from China's lack of tariff autonomy. As a result Japan's exports to China increased not only numerically but also in terms of the proportion of her total exports which went to China. This rose from less than 10 percent prior to 1894 to 25 percent by the First World War. A commercial treaty negotiated with China in 1896 gave Japan the right to establish factories in the treaty ports, spurring her investments in China.

During the Late Meiji period imperialism was a cause for national pride in the colonizing countries of the West, and in Japan, too, the acquisition of overseas colonies and interests was hailed as a sign of national fulfillment. Conversely, there was a sense of great public disappointment and outrage when French, German, and Russian intervention forced Japan to give up the Liaotung Peninsula. The government's reaction to this setback was to follow a prudent foreign policy while increasing military spending.

Accordingly, Japan exercised careful restraint during the Boxer Rebellion (1900). However, this stance was not emulated by Japan's chief rival in Northeast Asia, Czarist Russia, which had demonstrated its intent to become a major power in the area by undertaking the construction of the great Trans-Siberian Railway (1891–1903). In 1896 Russia had obtained permission to run tracks across northern Manchuria direct to Vladivostok, and the Boxer Rebellion was used to entrench Russian interests in Manchuria. Russia's lease of Port Arthur on the Liaotung Peninsula gave it a much needed warm water port, but it also grated on the Japanese, who had so recently been denied the peninsula. Nor did Russia refrain from interfering in Korea, where it allied itself to conservative opponents of Japanese-backed reformers. Agreements reached in 1896, 1897, and 1898 kept this rivalry from exploding into war, but the Russian moves in Manchuria furthered Japanese apprehension about Russian ambitions in Northeast Asia.

Japan was not the only nation concerned over Russian expansion in East Asia. Great Britain, which had not joined in the Triple Intervention following the Sino-Japanese War, had long been alarmed over Russian expansion in Central Asia and was also apprehensive over Russia's plans for China. In 1902 Britain cast aside its policy of "splendid isolation" to enter into an alliance with Japan. Great Britain now recognized Japan's special interests in Korea, and each nation recognized the other's interests in China. Furthermore, Great Britain and Japan agreed that each would remain neutral in the event the other fought a war against a single enemy in East Asia and would come to the other's assistance if either were attacked by two powers at once. This meant that in the event of a war between Japan and Russia, Britain would enter on the Japanese side if France or Germany supported Russia. Japan would not have to face a European coalition alone. Aside from strengthening Japan's hand vis-à-vis Russia, this alliance with the foremost world power gave Japan new prestige and confidence. At the same time, Russia showed every intention of wishing to maintain and expand its position in East Asia.

The conflicting imperialist ambitions of Russia and Japan led to the Russo-Japanese War of 1904–05, fought both on land (mostly in Manchuria) and at sea. For both belligerents the cost was heavy, but the victories went to Japan. Despite some hard fighting, Russian troops were driven back on land; while in two separate naval actions the Japanese destroyed virtually the entire Russian navy. The naval war was spectacular. Japan attacked the Russian Pacific fleet at Port Arthur, just before the declaration of war. Russia's Baltic fleet then sailed all the way around Africa because Britain would not allow it passage through the Suez Canal, only to be met and destroyed by the Japanese navy in the Tsushima Straits, which run between Japan and Korea.

In Russia these defeats had fateful consequences. The discredited government of the Czar, long the object of terrorist attacks, now faced full-scale rebellion. The Revolution of 1905 was a precursor of the Revolution of 1917, which overthrew the regime. For their part the Japanese, although victorious, were thoroughly exhausted. It was essential that the war be brought to a close. Thus both sides were happy to respond affirmatively to an offer from the United States to mediate their disputes, and a peace conference was subsequently held in Portsmouth, New Hampshire.

In the resulting treaty, Japan gained recognition of its supremacy in Korea, the transfer of Russian interests in Manchuria (the railway and the leasehold on the Liaotung Peninsula), and cession of the southern half of Sakhalin Island (north of Hokkaidō). Going into the negotiations Japan had demanded all of Sakhalin and also a war indemnity, but Russia successfully resisted these demands, much to the anger of the Japanese public, which, not informed of their country's inability to continue the war, expected more of the settlement. At home the treaty was greeted by riots. Elsewhere in Asia people were impressed by this first victory of a non-Western nation over a European power.

One immediate result of Japan's victory over Russia was economic expansion in Manchuria where the semiofficial South Manchurian Railway Company was soon engaged in shipping, public utilities, and mining as well as railroading. From the start the Japanese government held half of the company's shares and appointed its officers. Although private Japanese firms also entered Manchuria, it has been calculated that in 1914, 79 percent of all Japanese investments in Manchuria were in the South Manchurian Railway. Furthermore, 69 percent of all Japanese investments in China prior to the First World War were in Manchuria. The remainder was largely concentrated in Shanghai.

## Colonialism in Korea and Taiwan

In 1906 Itō Hirobumi was sent to Korea as Resident General with wide powers over the Korean government, but in 1909 he was assassinated by a Korean nationalist, and in the following year Japan annexed Korea outright. Korea was then placed under the control of a governor-general, always a military man, although after 1919 a civilian could legally have been appointed to this post.

Like other imperialist powers, Japan governed its colonies for the benefit of the homeland. In both Taiwan and Korea, Japan's policies were designed to control the local population and to exploit the local resources through selective modernization. Japanese rule over Taiwan and Korea, accordingly, shared certain characteristics: in both cases the police were prominent, and dissent was repressed; transportation and communications networks were developed; the landholding system was remodeled and agricultural production encouraged; public health was improved, leading to an increase in the population; schools were fostered, emphasizing Japanese studies and spreading the use of the Japanese language. In both cases too many of the benefits of modernization went to the Japanese who dominated the colonial administrative machinery and operated the larger colonial enterprises.

There were, however, also enormous differences between the two colonies— differences extending beyond such obvious factors as climate (Taiwan is suitable for sugar plantations, Korea not) or Korea's more strategic geographic location. From the beginning, Japanese rule over Taiwan, while vigorous and firm, was not as harsh as that over Korea. There were, no doubt, numerous reasons for this, but important among them was the difference in historical background between Taiwan and Korea. When Japan assumed control over Taiwan after the Treaty of Shimonoseki, it encountered only sporadic resistance, for the island had only recently been fully incorporated into the political and cultural life of the mainland; even though its residents were almost all Chinese (ca. 3 million Chinese as compared to ca. 120,000 aborigines), they were as yet uninfluenced by modern nationalism and lacked a deep-rooted tradition of local cultural and political independence.

Korea, by contrast, boasted a culture older than that of Japan and a tradition of fierce independence. It also contained an old hereditary elite resentful of Japanese intrusion, and after 1895, a small but dedicated group of nationalists. Although the leadership against the Japanese takeover was traditional in composition and organization, violence was widespread. Japanese retaliation (by burning villages and committing other acts of terror) enflamed it even more. Between August 1907 and June 1911, the Japanese recorded 2852 clashes involving 141,815 insurgents. Until 1919 Japanese rule remained totally uncompromising. On March 1 of that year, there was a massive nationalist protest which the Japanese repressed ferociously. Then, in the twenties, the colonial administration was partially relaxed, but this was followed by further severity in the thirties.

Under Japanese rule the average Korean suffered economically. The land survey conducted between 1911 and 1918 favored large landholders. Tenancy increased. The largest landholder in Korea came to be the Oriental Development Company, a semigovernment corporation originally chartered in 1908 with the intent of opening new lands for Japanese immigrant farmers. When that plan proved unrealistic, the company bought up Korean-worked paddy fields instead. This was a development consistent with Korea's role as a supplier of inexpensive rice for Japan. After the First World War, the Japanese greatly expanded rice production in Korea, but there was still not enough for both Japanese and Koreans, and Korean rice consumption declined. In the twenties and thirties a beginning was made in industrial development, especially in the north, which was suitable for hydroelectric plants.

As demonstrated by the 1919 protest, the Japanese built up a vast reservoir of ill will in Korea, and there were nationalists in exile yearning for an end to Japanese rule. Others, however, acquiesced and/or cooperated, and both Taiwan and Korea continued to contribute to the Japanese sense of national accomplishment as well as to the Japanese economy.

## Late Meiji Economic Developments

War against China in the 1890s, and against Russia during the following decade, stimulated the Japanese domestic economy. Both wars were followed by an outburst of nationalist sentiment that gave a strong boost to heavy industry (for example, the Yawata Steel Works, established in 1897) and to armaments, including shipbuilding. After 1906, Japan produced ships comparable in size and quality to any in the world. Japanese technology continued to progress and advances were made in new fields such as electrical engineering. Light industry, particularly textiles, continued to flourish and remained predominant in the modern sector. The single most important item of export, accounting for nearly half the total, was in partly finished goods, especially silk. (Because of superior quality control, Japanese silk was more in demand abroad than was the silk of China.) An index of the changing nature of the economy were trade figures which reveal an increasing emphasis on the import of raw materials and the export of manufactured goods. Other statistics indicate increases in productivity, in the labor force, and in urbanization, opening up a widening gulf between the city and the country.

Not everyone in the cities benefited from these developments. Those working in the numerous small traditional establishments experienced little change in their living conditions. Especially harsh were the working and living conditions of those who labored in the factories and shops. These were comparable to those in Western countries at a comparably early stage of industrialization. During the first decade of the twentieth century, 60 percent of the work force was still female, and efforts to improve the lot of women and children working in the factories made headway only slowly. Not until 1916 did a law take effect giving them some protection, such as limiting their working day to eleven hours. An act promulgated in 1900 outlawed strikes, but when conditions became too bad, male workers, for whom a factory job was not an interlude prior to marriage but a lifelong occupation, rebelled, sometimes violently. Thus in 1909, three infantry companies were required to quell violence in the Ashio Copper Mines. Another labor action which made a deep impression was the streetcar strike in Tokyo in 1911.

The distress of the workers was also of great concern to radical intellectuals. Beginning in the early nineties, there was a small radical movement composed of Christian socialists and anarchists. They exhibited great courage in oppos-ing the war with Russia. Even after the war had begun, they held antiwar ral-lies in the Tokyo Y.M.C.A. However, barred by the government from forming a political party and facing government repression, they were unable to expand their influence beyond the world of intellectuals and college students. In 1911, twelve of their leaders were convicted, on very flimsy evidence, of plotting the death of the emperor, and were executed.

Among the main beneficiaries of economic growth were the huge industrial-financial combines (*zaibatsu*), which retained their close ties with govern-ment. The dominant political party during this period, the Seiyūkai (Associa-tion of Friends of Constitutional Government), also had a stake in economic development, since projects for railway and harbor development were a major means by which it won regional support and built up its political power.

## Late Meiji Politics

During the Sino-Japanese War the oligarchs and the party-controlled Diet were united in pursuit of common national aims, but after the war the political struggles resumed. The oligarchs, enjoying the prerogatives of *genrō* ("elder statesmen"), advised the emperor on all important matters. As participants in the fashioning of the new state and architects of its major institutions, they enjoyed great prestige as well as the support of their protégés and associates in that process. The party politicians, on the other hand, resented the *genrō*'s ten-dency to perpetuate their power and to limit political decision making to a small group of hand-picked insiders. Their main weapon against a prime min-ister who defied them was that under the constitution only the Diet could au-thorize increases in the budget.

Complicating the political situation but also making for compromise rather than confrontation were divisions within both the oligarchy and the party leadership. Among the former, Yamagata, a disciplined rather austere military man, was committed to "transcendental government," dedicated to emperor and nation and above political partisanship. His main *genrō* rival was Itō, a more flexible conservative, the man who had supervised the writing of the con-stitution. Itō was more willing than Yamagata to compromise with the party forces.

Similarly not all Diet members were adamantly opposed to collaborating with the *genrō*. Some lost their enthusiasm for opposing a government which could dissolve the Diet and thereby subject them to costly campaigns for re-election. Furthermore, the oligarchs could—and did—trade office for support. Accommodation had its appeal to both sides, but initially it was an uneasy ac-commodation; there were four dissolutions of the Diet between 1895 and 1900.

Another political factor was the influence of the military. As stipulated in the constitution, the chief of the general staff reported directly to the emperor concerning command matters, thus bypassing the Minister of War and the cabinet. In 1900 the military's power was further strengthened when Yamagata obtained imperial ordinances specifying that only officers on active duty could serve as Minister of the Army or Minister of the Navy. This in effect gave the military veto power over any cabinet, for it could break a cabinet simply by ordering the army or navy minister to resign. However, control over funds for army expansion remained in the hands of the party politicians of the lower house.

Up to 1901 the oligarchs themselves served as prime minister, but after that date Yamagata's protégé Katsura Tarō (1847–1913) and Itō's protégé, Saionji Kimmochi (1849–1940) alternated as prime minister for the remainder of the Meiji period. Katsura, like Yamagata, was a general from Chōshū; Saionji was a court noble with liberal views but possessing little inclination to political leadership.

Katsura and Saionji were able to govern because they had the cooperation of the Seiyūkai, a party founded in 1900 by Itō who saw this as the way to obtain assured support in the Diet. In 1903 Itō turned the presidency of the party over to Saionji, but the real organizing force within the party was Hara Kei (1856–1921), an ex-bureaucrat who became the leading party politician of his generation. Hara greatly strengthened the party by building support within the bureaucracy during his first term as Home Minister (1906–08) and also used his power to appoint energetic partymen as prefectural governors. He further provided the party with sturdy local roots by freely resorting to the pork barrel, building up a constituency among the local men of means who constituted the limited electorate.

The financial and business community, including the *zaibatsu*, was interested in maintaining a political atmosphere favorable to itself, and political leaders for their part welcomed business support. Thus Itō, when he organized the Seiyūkai, obtained the support of Shibusawa Eiichi and other prominent business leaders, although many remained aloof. The head of Mitsui was so intent on establishing his firm's independence from government that he even discontinued the practice of extending loans to Itō without collateral. However, the trend was toward closer association between the *zaibatsu* and politics, as exemplified by the close relationship between Mitsubishi and Katsura after 1908. During Katsura's second ministry (1908–11), his chief economic advisor was the head of the Mitsubishi Bank.

The relative strength of the participants in the political process did not remain unchanged. The *genrō* enjoyed great influence as long as they remained active, but theirs was a personal not an institutional power, and it tended to diminish with time. As the participants in the original Restoration diminished in number, the power of the oligarchs to orchestrate politics decreased. Katsura as prime minister did not always follow Yamagata's advice. Furthermore, the *genrō* lost an important source of support when a new generation of bureaucrats came to the fore. These new officials did not owe their positions to *genrō* patronage, for after 1885 entrance to and promotion in the bureaucracy were determined by examinations. As servants of the emperor, the bureaucracy enjoyed high prestige and considerable influence.

Political compromise eroded much of the idealism found in the early movement for people's rights, but the Seiyūkai prospered. Indeed the increase of its strength in the Diet alarmed the party's opponents in that body, but this opposition was divided and diverse. It included not only those who opposed the Seiyūkai's compromise on principle, but also small and shifting groups of independents, and a series of "loyalist" parties that habitually supported the cabinet.

Decision making was complicated, and government policies were determined by the interaction of various power centers, none of which could rule alone. The system functioned as long as there were sufficient funds to finance the military's and the Seiyūkai's highest priority projects, and as long as none of the participants felt their essential interests threatened. When that ceased to be the case, it brought on the Taishō political crisis.

## Literature and Art

Early Meiji literature had largely continued Tokugawa traditions, but during the Late Meiji a modern literature developed under the influence of Western literature and literary theories. The beginning of the modern Japanese novel can be traced to Tsubouchi Shōyō (1859–1935), a translator of Shakespeare and an advocate of realism, that is, the view that literature should portray actual life. In his *The Essence of the Novel* (1885) Tsubouchi argued for the adoption of realism in place of the earlier didacticism or literature written solely for entertainment. Futabatei Shimei (1864–1909) then wrote the realistic novel, *Drifting Cloud* (1887–89), a psychological study of a rather ordinary man, told not in the customary literary style but in more colloquial form.

Following the introduction of realism, two other Western literary theories became particularly influential: romanticism, with its emphasis on the expression of feelings, and naturalism, which aimed at treating man with scientific detachment as advocated by the French writer Émile Zola. Although in Europe naturalism was hostile to romanticism, this was not necessarily the case in Japan, where Shimazaki Tōson (1873–1943) won fame both for his romantic poetry and for a naturalistic novel, *The Broken Commandment* (1906). This novel was an account of a member of the pariah class (*burakumin,* see Chapter 2) who tries to keep the pledge he made to his father never to reveal that he was born into this group (which was still the object of social discrimination and contempt even though not subject to any legal restrictions).

Two writers of the Late Meiji era stand out in particular, producing works of lasting literary merit that transcended their age, even as they reflected its concerns: Mori Ōgai (1862–1922) and Natsume Sōseki (1867–1916). Both men had a period of study abroad and were deeply influenced by the West, but both achieved greatness by drawing on their own Japanese heritage.

Ōgai's time abroad was spent mainly in Germany, where he studied medicine, and on his return to Japan he embarked on a distinguished career as an army surgeon, rising in 1907 to the rank of surgeon-general. His literary work was diverse, for he was a prolific and excellent translator as well as a writer of original works. Among his finest translations are his renderings of Goethe, including the full *Faust*, and of Shakespeare, which he translated from the German. He also translated modern German poetry, with the result that more modern German verse was available in Japanese translation than in English. Furthermore, he introduced German aesthetic philosophy to Japan and also had an influence on the development of modern Japanese theater: the performance of his translation of an Ibsen play in 1908 was one of the major cultural events of the Late Meiji.

Ōgai's first story, *Maihime* ("The Dancing Girl," 1890) recounts the doomed romance between a Japanese student sent by his government to Germany and a German girl named Alice. It became a precursor of the many "I novels," thinly disguised autobiographical works, which became one of the standard genres of modern Japanese fiction, although it also owes something to the old tradition of literary diaries.

After his initial romantic period, Ōgai went on to write works of increasing psychological insight and philosophical depth. He also turned increasingly to Japanese themes, as in his novel *The Wild Goose*. Ōgai was greatly moved when his friend General Nogi (1849–1912), hero of the Russo-Japanese War, followed the Meiji Emperor into death by committing ritual suicide along with his wife. After this event Ōgai published painstakingly researched accounts of samurai. One late work particularly acclaimed in Japan is his *Chibu Chūsai*, an account of a late Tokugawa physician with whom Ōgai identified.

Natsume Sōseki studied in England, where he was thoroughly miserable. A meager government stipend forced him to live in poverty, and he had virtually no friends. Later he described himself as having been "as lonely as a stray dog in a pack of wolves."[1] Both this experience of loneliness, and the extensive reading he did while in England, were reflected in his subsequent work. Sōseki returned from Europe to teach English literature at Tokyo Imperial University, before resigning this position to devote himself wholly to writing. He was acclaimed not only for his fiction but also for poetry in Chinese, haiku, and literary criticism. He once described his mind as half Japanese and half Western, and his early novels reflect English influence, particularly that of Meredith, but in his mature work the Japanese element predominates. Fortunately, much of his work is available in good English translations.

In his early novels *I Am a Cat* (1905) and *Botchan* (1906), Sōseki presents slices of Meiji life portrayed with affectionate good humor. Also in 1906, in a mere week, he wrote a remarkable painterly and diarylike book, *The Grass Pillow*, also translated as *The Three Cornered World*, for "An artist is a person who lives in the triangle which remains after the angle which we may call common sense has been removed from this four-cornered world."[2] The main theme of Sōseki's mature works is human isolation, studied in characters given to deep introspection. Like Ōgai, Sōseki was deeply moved by the death of the Meiji Emperor and General Nogi's suicide, which entered into *Kokoro* (1914), a novel concerning the relationship between a young man and his mentor, called "Sensei" ("master" or "teacher"). In the novel Sōseki links Sensei's personal tragedy and his suicide in 1912 to the death of the emperor and the general, and the larger tragedy of the passing of a generation and with it of the old ethical values, for Sensei perceives that he has become an anachronism.

Painters, like writers, were grouped in several schools. The disciples of Okakura Tenshin, for example, continued to avoid the extremes of formalistic traditionalism and imitative modernism, while seeking a middle ground that would be both modern and Japanese. One member of this school was Yokoyama Taikan (1868–1958). His screen, shown in Figure 9-1, depicts a perennial favorite of Chinese and Japanese scholars, the poet T'ao Ch'ien (366–427), whose blend of regret and relief at withdrawal from public life continued to strike a responsive chord in the complicated modern world.

Among the artists working in purely European styles was Kuroda Seiki, whose nude had so shocked Kyōto in the nineties. He continued to paint in an impressionistic manner and had many followers and imitators. Some attempts at rendering Japanese themes in Western style produced paintings which are little more than historical curiosities, but in other cases there was a happier result. The painting by Sakaki Teitoku (1858–1939) shown in Figure 9-2 was executed in oil around 1910. While the young men blow traditional bamboo flutes, two young ladies play violins.

Figure 9-1   Yokoyama Taikan, *T'ao Ch'ien*. Detail from one of a pair of sixfold screens, *Master Five Willows*. Color on paper, 1912, 169.4 cm × 361.2 cm. Tokyo National Museum.

Western influence on the visual arts was often direct and immediate. For instance, the noted Japanese artist Umehara Ryūzaburō (1888–) studied in France during the Late Meiji, met Renoir in 1909, and became his favorite pupil. The strongest influence on Japanese sculpture during this period was Rodin, who enjoyed a great vogue in Japan, especially after a major exhibition of his work in Tokyo in 1912. The Japanese continued to be informed, enthusiastic, and sensitive patrons of the visual arts.

There was also an interest in modernizing music. The Meiji government early on sponsored Western military music, and in 1879 the Ministry of Education agreed to a proposal made by Izawa Shūnji (1851–1917) to combine Japanese and Western music in the schools. Izawa had studied vocal physiology in the United States and persuaded the Ministry of Education to bring Luther Whiting Mason (1828–96) from Boston to Japan to help develop songs for use

Figure 9-2   Sakaki Teitoku, *Concert Using Japanese and Western Instruments*. Oil, 1910. Takakiyu Mitsui Collection.

in the elementary schools. The first of the song books to be completed (1881) consisted half of Western songs supplied with Japanese words ("Auld Lang Syne," for example, was turned into a song about fireflies) and half of Japanese pieces harmonized in the Western manner.

Meiji popular music was more freely eclectic than that taught in the schools. During the last decade of the nineteenth century and the beginning of the twentieth, Japanese composers began working with the forms of classical Western music (sonatas, cantatas, and so forth), and thanks to the efforts of the Tokyo School of Music good performers were available on the piano and violin, as well as on the koto and other traditional instruments also taught at the school. Actually, performers made greater progress than composers. The important compositions were still to come. Furthermore, as William P. Malm has suggested, "the training of generations of Japanese youth to harmonically oriented music has created a series of mental blocks which shut out the special musical potentialities of traditional styles."[3] The rediscovery of the latter, and their creative employment in original compositions, did not take place until after the Second World War.

## The Taishō Political Crisis (1912–1913)

The Meiji Emperor was succeeded, in 1912, by the Taishō Emperor (r. 1912–26). The transition was marked by a grave sense of unease in the country, not only due to the change in emperors, but also to social and economic conditions in the nation generally. Nevertheless, the crisis of 1912–13 was undoubtedly aggravated by the loss of the old emperor, who had given his people a sense of continuity even as he presided over the profound changes of the Restoration.

The crisis arose when it became apparent that Japan's financial condition required a cutback in government spending. The cutback brought two major interest groups into conflict. The dominant political party, the Seiyūkai, was determined to save its domestic spending program—in part because its political support depended on it, while the army, anxious to build two new divisions, pressed for increased military spending.

Although the Seiyūkai won support at the polls, Prime Minister Saionji was forced out of office in December 1912, when the army ordered the Minister of the Army to resign his post. While the *genrō* deliberated and sought for a successor to Saionji, a number of politicians, journalists, and businessmen organized a movement "to protect constitutional government," which led to mass demonstrations reminiscent of those greeting news of the Portsmouth Treaty in 1905. Called on to form a government once more, Katsura was no longer willing to compromise with the Seiyūkai, but he failed in an attempt to weld his bureaucratic followers and opposition politicians into a party strong enough to defeat the Seiyūkai. When the Seiyūkai threatened a vote of no confidence in the Diet, Katsura tried to save the situation by obtaining an imperial order forcing the Seiyūkai to give up its planned no-confidence motion. This was a stratagem employed previously by embattled prime ministers, but it did not work this time, for the Seiyūkai turned down the order. One consequence of Katsura's failure was to discredit such use of an imperial order, with the result that it was never attempted again.

Katsura died in 1913, but the coalition he had created held together under the leadership of Katō Komei (1859–1926), whose background included graduation from Tokyo Imperial University, service in Mitsubishi, and a career in the Foreign Office capped by an appointment as Foreign Minister at the age of forty. He enjoyed a financial advantage from his marriage into the family which controlled Mitsubishi. A capable and determined man, he was personally reserved. But this was no handicap, for there was no need for party leaders like Katō or Hara to cultivate mass support. The power of a party leader depended on his strength *within* his party, although this was influenced by the party's success at the polls.

The emergence of a strong second party meant that from now on the Seiyūkai faced a rival for control of the lower house. The parties represented a cross section of skills and resources needed to make participation in government viable. As Arthur E. Tiedemann observes, "Each party had associated with it the three essential ingredients for achieving political power: professional politicians to do the nitty-gritty of day-to-day party management; former bureaucrats who had the administrative talents required to form a viable alternative government acceptable to the genrō; and businessmen who could supply the funds and influence essential to successful election campaigns."[4] Thus Japan came to be governed by a two-party system that lasted until 1932.

The Taishō political crisis confirmed the importance of the Diet and of the parties, but it was not until 1918 (when Hara became Prime Minister) that the prime ministership went to a man who had made his career as a party politician. Meanwhile, there were three intervening prime ministers: Admiral Yamamoto Gombei, 1913–14, the first head of government from Satsuma since 1897; the septuagenarian Ōkuma Shigenobu, 1914–16, who was committed to destroying the Seiyūkai but failed; and Terauchi Masatake, 1916–18, a Chōshū general who had been governor-general of Korea. It was the Ōkuma and Terauchi governments which guided Japan during the First World War.

## Japan During the First World War

When the Western powers became immersed in the struggle which was to bring an end to Europe's predominance in the world, new opportunities were opened for the expansion of the Japanese empire and industry.

In August 1914 Japan declared war on Germany and within three months proceeded to seize German holdings in Shantung and the German islands in the Pacific. In January 1915 the Ōkuma government presented the Twenty-One Demands to China. Japan obtained additional rights on the continent but at the cost of stirring up strong Chinese resentment. A prominent critic of this policy was the pro-German Yamagata, who wanted an understanding with China in order to prepare for the war he anticipated against the West.

Much larger and more costly than Japan's military effort against Germany during the First World War was the country's effort against the Russians (1918–22). The Russian Revolution of 1917 had taken Russia out of the war and created disorder in Russia's East Asian territories. In Japan there was considerable disagreement over how to take advantage of a situation further complicated by the presence of Czech troops who were fighting their way out of Russia and were determined to continue the war against Germany. By mid-summer 1918 Japan controlled the eastern portion of the Trans-Siberian Railway and had seized Vladivostok. The United States then changed its earlier opposition to intervention, although President Wilson envisioned only a limited military operation. The Japanese, however, sent 75,000 troops, three times more than those sent by the Allies (United States, Britain, France, and Canada). In the light of Soviet victories and the absence of a viable alternative, the United States withdrew its forces in January 1919 and the other Allies soon did the same. This left only the Japanese, who continued their efforts in the vain hope of at least keeping the U.S.S.R. from controlling eastern Siberia.

Japan was able to pay for such a costly undertaking largely because of the great economic boom she experienced during the First World War, when there was an unprecedented demand for her industrial products and a withdrawal of the European competition. Old industries expanded and new ones grew up as exports surged. Japan earned enough foreign exchange to change her status from a debtor to a creditor nation. But while some prospered, others suffered. The sudden economic expansion produced inflation and workers' wages, as well as the income of men in traditional occupations such as fishing, failed to keep pace. Especially serious was the increase in the price of rice, which rose until people could no longer afford this most basic food. In August 1918, rice riots erupted in cities, towns, and villages all over Japan. Even as Japanese troops were setting off for Siberia other soldiers were firing on hungry people rioting at home. The bitter irony was not lost on Japanese radicals. The immediate effect of the turbulence was to bring down the Terauchi government. When the *genrō* met to choose a new prime minister, they settled on the Seiyūkai leader Hara Kei.

## Politics and Policies (1918–1924)

Hara Kei had spent his career building up the Seiyūkai in preparation for the day of party rule, but when he finally attained the prime ministership he was too set in his ways to embark on significant new policies or to devise meaningful changes in the structure of government. The changes he initiated from 1918 until he was assassinated by a demented fanatic in November 1921 were minor, and his concerns tended to remain partisan. Democratic intellectuals, the leaders of labor and farmer unions, and students were disillusioned when the government turned a deaf ear to their demands for universal suffrage, and instead passed an election law which retained a tax qualification for voting and reconstructed local electoral districts to favor the Seiyūkai. Abuse of office, financial scandals, and actions prompted by narrow partisanship had damaged the public image of the parties for years, and the record of the first party prime minister did nothing to alter this. Liberals who had placed their hopes in parliamentary reform either became cynical or looked elsewhere, while the public at large was apathetic.

In foreign affairs Hara's prime ministership began with the peace conference at Versailles, where Japan failed to obtain a declaration of racial equality but did have its rights in China and the Pacific confirmed. His government then adopted a policy of cooperation with the United States, the only possible source for capital badly needed by Japanese industry facing difficult adjustments after peace brought an end to wartime prosperity. The first product of the new policy was the Washington Conference of 1921–22, in which Japan's alliance with Britain was replaced by a Four Power Pact signed by France, Great Britain, Japan, and the United States. The conference also produced an agreement to limit construction of capital ships (that is, large warships) by the signatories, so as to maintain the existing balance of naval power. Under this agreement Japan promised to build no more than three capital ships for every five built by the United States and five built by Great Britain. In addition, Japan agreed to a Nine Power Treaty in February 1922, in which she acceded to the American Open Door policy. Also in the same month Japan reached an agreement with China that provided for the restoration of Chinese sovereignty over Shantung but retention by Japan of economic rights there. Finally, in October 1922, Japan agreed to withdraw from Siberia.

These actions were taken as part of a general policy of getting along with the United States and conciliating China, a policy followed by Shidehara Kijūrō when he served as foreign minister from 1924 to 1927 and again from 1929 to

December 1931. Its purpose was to avert another anti-Japanese outburst and costly boycotts of Japanese goods, in order to permit continuing Japanese economic expansion. After 1914 Japanese investments in China accelerated. By 1931 over 80 percent of Japan's total foreign investments were in China, where they accounted for 35.1 percent of all foreign investments in that country.* In 1930, 63 percent of Japanese investments in China were in Manchuria and another 25 percent in Shanghai, where Japanese engaged in trade, banking, and textile manufacturing. They were especially prominent in the latter: in 1930 Japanese owned 39.6 percent of the Chinese textile industry (calculated in spindles). They were also a very major factor in China's iron industry, with interests in Hankow and Manchuria.

Hara was initially succeeded by his finance minister, but this man lacked Hara's political skills and stayed in office only until June 1922. Three nonparty prime ministers followed, two were admirals (Katō Tomasaburō and Yamamoto Gombei) and one a bureaucrat (Kiyoura Keigo) who organized his cabinet entirely from the House of Peers but resigned when faced with a three-party coalition in control of the Diet. The leader of the strongest of these parties, the Kenseikai (Constitutional Government Association, established 1916) was Katō Kōmei, who had last served as foreign minister under Ōkuma during the war. He was now called upon to form a new government.

The most momentous event of the years between Hara and Katō was geological, not political: in September 1923 the Tokyo-Yokohama area was devastated by a severe earthquake followed by a conflagration, which came close to leveling the area. The red sky was visible all night from a hundred miles away. Around 150,000 people lost their lives. As so often in a disaster, the earthquake and fires brought out the best and the worst in the population. While some courageously and selflessly helped their fellows, others joined in hysterical mobs rampaging through the city killing Koreans. The police reacted to the emergency by rounding up socialists, anarchists, and Communists as a "security measure," and there were cases of police torture and killing.

## Party Government (1924–1931)

The main accomplishments of party government came during the two years Katō was prime minister (1924–26). Foremost among them was the passage of a "universal" suffrage act, which gave the vote to all males twenty-five and over. To still the fears of conservatives apprehensive over the possible spread of radical ideas, a Peace Preservation Law was also passed. This made it a crime to advocate change in the national political structure or to urge the abolition of private property. The Katō government never invoked the law, but it was available to later, less liberal regimes.

---

* Great Britain accounted for 36.7 percent of foreign investments in China, but this represented only 5 to 6 percent of all British overseas investments. Other countries accounting for over 5 percent of foreign investments in China were: U.S.S.R., 8.4; United States, 6.1; France, 5.9.

Katō also tried to reform the House of Peers (changing its composition and reducing its powers) but succeeded in making only minor changes. His government was more successful in introducing moderate social reforms, including the legalization of labor unions, the establishment of standards for factory conditions, the setting up of procedures for mediating labor disputes, and the provision of health insurance for workers. There was, however, no similar program to alleviate the problems of the rural poor.

Katō soon became embroiled in difficult political negotiations with other parties and the House of Peers among others. When Katō died in 1926, he had not transformed Japanese politics, but he did leave a record of accomplishment which might, under different circumstances, have served as a basis for building a strong system of party rule. That this did not happen is partly the result of the kinds of problems Japan had to face during the five years following Katō's death, but it also reflects the weaknesses of the parties themselves. Even the increased suffrage was a mixed blessing, for the larger electorate made election campaigns more expensive, so that politicians were more open to corruption.

From 1927 to 1929 the government was in the hands of Tanaka Giichi, a general from Chōshū who had entered politics and had been elected president of the Seiyūkai in 1925. During his term of office, Japan held its first election conducted under universal manhood suffrage. This took place in February 1928, but was followed by the large-scale arrest of radicals, many of whom were forced to spend long years in prison. Tanaka's administration was also marred by political irregularities and by his inept handling of the nation's economic problems. In his policy toward China, Tanaka departed from Shidehara's conciliatory approach. Under political pressure at home, Tanaka was also concerned over the safety of Japanese residents in Shantung during the Kuomintang's northern advance, yet unwilling to evacuate them. He therefore sent to Shantung the troops already mentioned in the preceding chapter. It was also during his tenure in office that Chang Tso-lin, the warlord of Manchuria, was assassinated. The collapse of the Tanaka government came when he incurred the displeasure of the Shōwa Emperor (r. 1926– ) and court by failing to obtain from the army suitable punishment for Chang Tso-lin's murderers. This was one of the rare instances in which the emperor personally intervened in a political decision. The episode was also a harbinger of future unilateral army action, but first, party government had one more chance.

In 1929, Hamaguchi Ōsachi became prime minister, and in 1930 his party, the Minseitō, product of a merger of the Kenseitō and another party, won the election. Shidehara once again became foreign minister and resumed his policy of reconciliation with China and cooperation with Britain and the United States, as signified in the London Naval Treaty of 1930, which included provisions extending the 5:5:3 ratio to other than capital ships. Ratification of the treaty was obtained only after heated debate and the forced resignation of the naval chief of staff. It generated much anger and bitterness among the military and members of patriotic societies, such as the young man who shot the prime minister in November 1930. Hamaguchi never recovered from his wounds, but he did not resign until April 1931. From April until December 1931, the Minseitō cabinet continued under Wakatsuki Reijirō (1866–1949), who earlier had served as Katō's home minister and as prime minister from January 1926 to April 1927. Wakatsuki was an experienced politician, but during 1931 the government lost control over the army.

The restlessness of the military was not Hamaguchi's only problem. During most of the twenties Japan was beset by persistent economic difficulties, including an unfavorable balance of payments, failure of employment opportunities to increase fast enough to keep up with population growth, and a sharp decline in the price of rice, which helped consumers but hurt farmers. The giant *zaibatsu* profited from new technology, the economics of large-scale management, and the failure of weaker firms, but the period was very hard on small operators and especially difficult for tenant farmers. To solve the balance of payments problem, there were at various times during the decade calls for the government to cut expenses and follow a policy of retrenchment in order to reduce the cost of Japanese goods and improve their competitive position in international trade. This was the policy followed by Hamaguchi, who also strengthened the yen by returning to the gold standard. Unfortunately, he initiated this program just as the world depression was getting under way and persisted in it despite great economic dislocations and suffering. From 1925 to 1930 the real income of farmers declined by about a third. The poorest were, as always, the hardest hit. As in earlier periods of famine, there were cases of peasants eating bark and digging for roots or maintaining life by selling their daughters into brothels.

The government's economic failure undermined the prestige of the political parties, which even in normal times had not enjoyed much public esteem. No mass movement arose directed against them, but there was also little in their record to inspire people to man the barricades in their defense. Their enemies included those dissatisfied not only with their policies and politics but with just about every facet of twenties liberalism and internationalism.

## The Arts

Internationalism was represented not only in politics but also in the arts. Tokyo was not far behind Paris or London in experimenting with the latest styles and techniques. Indeed it sometimes led the other capitals, as when in 1922 Frank Lloyd Wright built the Imperial Hotel in Tokyo, a break with Japan's own version of the European Art Nouveau. The American architect, himself influenced by the Japanese tradition, was not the only stimulating visitor from abroad during the Taishō and early Shōwa years. Japanese scientists, for example, could converse with Einstein on his visit to their country in 1919, and music lovers enjoyed concerts by eminent foreign performers: both Kreisler and Heifetz gave concerts in Tokyo in 1923. Bach, Mozart, and Beethoven were becoming as much a part of the musical life of Japan as of any other country, foreshadowing the time when, after the Second World War, the Japanese were acknowledged as the pioneers in teaching young children to play the violin and also became the world's foremost manufacturers of pianos.

A grand piano dominates the four panel screen (see Figure 9-3) painted in 1926 by Nakamura Daizaburō (1898–1947), which is representative of the followers of the Okakura school. Not only the traditional dress of the young lady playing by the light of an electric lamp but the technique and aesthetics of the painting recall the earliest Japanese art rather than contemporary Western styles. Conversely there were Japanese artists who, like Hsü Pei-hung in China, depicted traditional subjects in Western style, but the most successful modernists were modern in both subject and technique.

A major influence for modernism was the *White Birch* (*Shirakaba*) journal, which was published from 1910 to 1923, and was edited by a group of humanistic writers, including most notably Shiga Naoya (1883–1971). In contrast to the school of naturalism, the *White Birch* group was dedicated to the exploration of the inner self, the pursuit of deeper personal understanding and self-expression, as in the "I novel" or in individualistic art. International in their orientation, seeking to become "children of the world" (their expression), they introduced a host of European writers and published articles on the work and theories of such artists as Van Gogh, Cézanne, and Rodin, and sponsored art exhibits.

Much of the art produced during this period was merely imitative, but one artist who was able to go beyond imitation to develop his own style was Umehara Ryūzaburō, whom we have already encountered as a disciple of Renoir. However, his work also owes something to the Japanese tradition he absorbed while still a child in Kyōto, where he became thoroughly familiar with the

Figure 9-3    Nakamura Daizaburō, *At the Piano*. Fourfold screen, color on silk, 1926, 164.5 cm × 302 cm. Kyōto Municipal Museum of Art.

Figure 9-4  Umehara Ryūzaburō, *Cannes*. Oil, 1956, 32.5 cm × 49.5 cm.

styles of Sōtatsu and Korin as still practiced in his family's silk kimono business. The secret of his lively coloring lay in his use of semitransparent gold paint which allowed the color beneath to shine through. A prolific and long-lived artist, he is illustrated here by a work of his old age, painted when he was on his third visit to the French Riviera. (See Figure 9-4.)

European pointillism, cubism, futurism, dadaism, surrealism, and so on, all had their impact on the Japanese avant-garde, here represented by a painting dated 1926. (See Figure 9-5.) The artist, Tōgō Seiji (1897–1978), was in Europe at the time and was influenced by French and Italian futurism and dadaism, but here exhibits an inclination toward cubism. The title, *Saltimbanques*, is French for "traveling showmen." It is a cheerfully decorative picture, modern in style and subject matter. And it is just one of many works in which it would take a very keen eye, not to speak of considerable imagination, to detect a particularly Japanese element. The painter works in a medium which, for better or worse, is not bound to any particular national tradition, in contrast to the writer whose very language is linked to his historical culture.

## Popular Culture

Avant-garde art in Japan as elsewhere was produced by and for the few, but the flow of influence from abroad was by no means restricted to the sophisticated or wealthy. After the war there was a wave of Western influence on the pattern of life, affecting people's diet, housing, and dress, particularly in the great cities, where there was a boom in bread consumption, the wearing of Western dress in public became prevalent, and it became the fashion to include at least one Western-style room in a house.

On the Ginza the "modern boy" (*mobo*) and "modern girl" (*moga*) appeared, dressed and coiffured in the very latest styles imported from overseas. They might be on their way to the movies, for film was now coming into its own, throwing off the shackles of the theatrical heritage that had dominated the early years of Japanese film making, when the narrator was as important as the pictures and female roles were played by men. Although there was always an audience for films filled with melodrama and sword action, others dealt with the problems and joys of daily life. It was in the twenties that the foundations were laid for the great achievements to come in Japanese films.

There was also a great increase in sports activity, not least of which was baseball, although the formation of professional teams had to wait until the thirties. Another new sport was golf, including, in that crowded land, "baby" or miniature golf. After golf or tennis, one could relax in a café or a fellow could practice the latest steps with a taxi dancer at the Florida or another dance hall. The old demi-monde dom-

Figure 9-5   Tōgō Seiji, *Saltimbanques*. Oil, 1926, 114 cm × 71 cm. Tokyo National Museum of Modern Art.

inated by the geisha, a world so fondly chronicled by Nagai Kafū (1879–1959), was on the decline, and modern mass culture was in the ascendancy.

Although centered on the cities, the new popular culture was rapidly diffused now that even the remotest village was accessible by train and car, not to speak of the radio, which was introduced in 1925. Furthermore, mass circulation magazines, some directed at a general audience, others written especially for women or young people, turned out huge printings catering to the unquenchable thirst of the Japanese public for reading matter.

## Literature

Among the still active older writers whose reputations were established during the Late Meiji was Shimazaki Tōson, who after *The Broken Commandment* had turned to autobiographical writings published, as was so often the case, serially in magazines. Another master of the autobiographical form was Shiga Naoya, already mentioned as a member of the *White Birch* group, which rejected the pessimism of the naturalists. In the hands of the many lesser writers who indulged in the genre, the detailed examination of everyday life was apt to produce tedium rather than insight, but there was always a public for such works.

A highly gifted writer who rejected the autobiographical mode was Akutagawa Ryūnosuke (1892–1927), author of some 150 short stories between 1917 and 1927. Many of these are modern psychological reinterpretations of old tales. In the West he is probably best known for "Rashomon," a tale in which the story of a murder and rape is told from the viewpoint of three protagonists and a witness. This story inspired one of the finest films of Kurosawa Akira, released in 1950. Akutagawa's carefully crafted stories are frequently eerie, but they are saved from being merely macabre by the keenness of his psychological portrayals. Pessimistic, given to self-doubt, and distressed at the changing world about him, he committed suicide in 1927 citing "a vague unease."

In poetry as in art some dedicated themselves to new experiments while others continued working with the old forms. In the nineteenth century, Shiki Masaoka (1867–1902), known primarily as a haiku poet, made notable contributions toward revitalizing traditional poetry, and many *tanka* and haiku continued to be written and published in every decade of the twentieth century. Others, however, looked to the West for models of poetry for a modern age. Some even employed the Roman alphabet (*rōmaji*). Foreign influence did not necessarily produce timeless verse; one poet proclaimed, "my sorrow wears the thin garb of one-sided love."[5]

The most admired master of free verse was Hagiwara Sakutarō (1886–1942), who employed the colloquial language to compose poems intensely personal both in their music and in their symbolism. The following is from a collection entitled *Howling at the Moon* (*Tsuki no hoeru*, 1917):

### Bamboos

Out of the shimmering earth
The bamboos grow, the green
Bamboos; and there, below,
Their growing roots grow lean
As thinlier they grow
Until their tiny tails,
A glitter of hairlets make
Veined meshes, flimsy veils
Incredible a-quake

Out of the frozen earth
The bamboos grow, the tough
Intent bamboos that flow
Sky-tall with an almost rough
Interior rage to grow.
To grow. In hardening frost
Their knots swell hard with ooze.
To grow. The blue sky crosses
With growth, with green bamboos.[6]

A major prose writer was Tanizaki Junichirō (1886–1965), who began with a fascination with the West but gradually returned to the Japanese heritage. His artistic journey was paralleled by his physical move from Tokyo to Kyōto after the great earthquake of 1923. In 1919 he published *Some Prefer Nettles*, a title taken from a line in a poem by Yüan Mei, "some insects eat sugar, some prefer nettles."[7] The protagonist in this novel is unhappily married to a "stridently" modern wife. He finds comfort in the arms of a Eurasian prostitute, symbolic of the West, but, as the novel unfolds, he is increasingly attracted to a traditional Kyōto beauty representing the old culture of Japan. Some of Tanizaki's best work still lay in the future, including his masterpiece, *The Makioka Sisters*, which was written during the Second World War. One theme in this long, panoramic novel is the contrast between two of the sisters, one traditional in appearance and mentality, the other modern. Tanizaki's devotion to tradition also led him to translate *The Tale of Genji* into modern Japanese. An identification with tradition was also to characterize the work of Kawabata Yasunari (1899–1972), but during the twenties this famous writer was just at the beginning of his brilliant literary career.

## Intellectual Trends

Japanese students of philosophy were for many years under strong German influence, predominantly that of Kant and Hegel and their later elaborators. After the war, along with German idealism, the phenomenalism of Husserl and Heidegger and the vitalism of Bergson and Eucken also attracted a Japanese audience. Outstanding among the philosphers who digested Western philosophy and assimilated it into their own original work was Nishida Kitarō (1870–1945), strongly steeped in Buddhism and best known for his philosophy of transcendent nothingness. Other theorists exploring subjects as seemingly far apart as aesthetics and politics grappled with the relationship between the universal principles valid everywhere and accessible to the intellect, and the particularist values imbedded in the unique culture of Japan, which must be apprehended by direct experience. In theoretical as in literary writings, the emphasis tended to be on the latter.

Nishida is said never to have discussed politics in his many years as a professor of philosophy at Kyōto University, but some of the most influential thinkers of the time were also important political theorists. Most widely read were Minobe Tatsukichi (1873–1948) and Yoshino Sakuzō (1878–1933), both deeply versed in German thought. Minobe was a legal scholar who followed his teacher at Heidelberg, Georg Jellinek, in making a distinction between sovereignty, which belongs to the whole state, and the power to rule, which is supervised by the emperor. In this sense, the emperor becomes the "highest organ" of the state, limited by the other components of the state and by the constitution. The constitution, furthermore, in Japan as elsewhere (according to Minobe) allows, and indeed requires, continuing change in the direction of increasing rationality, responsible government, and popular participation.

Minobe's work gained wide currency, and his book was the most frequently assigned text in courses on constitutional law. In 1932 he was appointed to the House of Peers.

Yoshino did not obtain such Establishment approval, but his many articles were widely read. A Christian populist and a democrat, he was a philosophical idealist who argued for democracy as an absolute rather than on utilitarian or pragmatic grounds. He also held an idealistic view of the nation and rejected any suggestion that democracy was incompatible with the Japanese tradition: "Those who argue that democracy is not compatible with the national spirit believe in the anachronistic and erroneous notion that the Emperor and people are mutually exclusive of each other."[8] Democracy would fulfill, not diminish, the emperor's role.

The postwar world also witnessed a revival of interest in anarchism and socialism, suppressed in 1911, and Japanese intellectuals were drawn to Marxist ideals even as they were impressed by the Russian Revolution. After a brief period of political activity, Yoshino returned to academic life, but more radical intellectuals continued to seek political involvement. This they could find in the labor movement, which conducted a dramatic dockyard strike in Kobe in 1921. By 1929, there were 300,000 workers in labor unions, but the labor parties formed after passage of the universal suffrage act suffered from an excess of factionalism and a lack of mass participation. This was also true of the Japanese Communist party, which was dominated by intellectuals. Some of these Marxists were people of great personal stature, but none was able to create a Marxism suitable to the particular conditions of Japan, nor did any have theoretical influence on international Marxism. Also more important for its program than for its literary accomplishment was a proletarian literary movement exemplified by such novels as *The Cannery Boat* (1929) by Kobayashi Takiji (1903–33), in which the workers revolt against a brutal captain. Even though much of this literature was propagandistic, it did serve to make the reader and writer more sensitive to social conditions, thereby opening up new terrain for Japanese literature.

These years also saw the beginning of a feminist movement, which campaigned for women's rights at a time when they were minors under the law and were completely excluded from the political process. Despite the efforts of several organizations and some dedicated leaders, change in this area was very slow.

While leftists were dissatisfied with what they considered the slow pace of progress in Japan, there were also ideologues who rejected much of the modern world and envisioned a very different future for their country. Among them were men who, conscious of the hardships suffered by the countryside, condemned the life and values of the cities and called for a return to virtuous agrarianism. Among the most severe critics of the parties and *zaibatsu* was Kita Ikki (1883–1937), who combined advocacy of imperialistic assertiveness abroad with a call for egalitarianism at home to bring emperor and people together. Unhappy with Japan's political organization as well as her stance in the world, he looked not to the electorate or mass popular movements for salvation, but placed his faith in change from above enacted by a few dedicated men. Accordingly, his ideas found a friendly reception in small societies of superpatriots and among young army officers who saw themselves as continuing in the tradition of the *rōnin* who had selflessly terrorized Kyōto during the closing days of the Tokugawa; he also found more recent exemplars among post-Edo "patriots," including the ex-samurai who after Saigō's death had founded the Genyōsha (Black Ocean Society, 1881) in Fukuoka (Northern Kyūshū) and the related Kokuryūkai (Amur River Society, also translated Black Dragon Society, 1901), one dedicated to expansion in Korea, the other concentrating on Manchuria, both employing intimidation and assassination among their techniques.

The story of the attempts made by these men to effect a "Shōwa Restoration" belongs in the thirties, but Kita Ikki's most influential book was written in 1919. The seeds planted in one decade bore fruit in the next. The rejection in the thirties of party government and the general internationalism that had prevailed in the twenties revealed that these had as yet shallow roots. Whether they would have flourished in a gentler international climate, we do not know, but their later reemergence after the Second World War suggests, at the very least, that the possiblity existed.

## *NOTES*

1. Quoted in Sōseki Natsume, *Ten Nights of Dream—Hearing Things—The Heredity of Taste*, trans. Aiko Itō and Graeme Wilson (Rutland, Vt. and Tokyo: Charles E. Tuttle, 1974), p. 12.

2. Natsume Soseki, *The Three Cornered World*, trans. Alan Turney (Chicago: Henry Regnery, 1965), p. iii.

3. William P. Malm, "The Modern Music of Meiji Japan," in Donald H. Shively, ed., *Tradition and Modernization in Japanese Culture* (Princeton: Princeton University Press, 1971), p. 300.

4. Arthur E. Tiedemann, "Big Business and Politics in Prewar Japan," in James W. Morley, ed., *Dilemmas of Growth in Prewar Japan* (Princeton: Princeton University Press, 1971), pp. 278–79.

5. Quoted in Donald Keene, ed., *Modern Japanese Literature: An Anthology* (New York: Grove Press, 1956), p. 20.

6. Hagiwara Sakutarō, *Face at the Bottom of the World and Other Poems*, trans. Graeme Wilson (Rutland, Vt. and Tokyo: Charles E. Tuttle, 1969), p. 51.

7. Arthur Waley, *Yüan Mei, Eighteenth Century Chinese Poet* (New York: Grove Press, 1956), p. 150.

8. Tetsuo Najita, "Some Reflections on Idealism in the Political Thought of Yoshino Sakuzō," in Bernard Silberman and H. D. Harootunian, eds., *Japan in Crisis: Essays on Taishō Democracy* (Princeton: Princeton University Press, 1974), p. 40.

國民黨之中國

軍閥主義之日本與

第二次世界大戰

| 1931 | 1937 | 1941 | 1945 |
|---|---|---|---|
| Japan Seizes Manchuria | Start of Second Sino-Japanese War | December 1941 Start of Pacific War | August 1945 End of Pacific War |

# 10

# Nationalist China, Militarist Japan, and the Second World War

For much of the world the 1930s were bleak and somber years. In the capitalist nations of the West, the Great Depression ushered in an economic crisis that deepened the rifts in society and threatened existing institutions. In the Soviet Union, struggling to catch up with the West economically, the decade was marred by the brutalities of forced collectivization and Stalin's purge trials. To many people desperate for vigorous action, dictatorship of one kind or another seemed the most effective way of pulling a nation together, and it was not in Italy and Germany alone that fascism was viewed as a non-Communist means to achieve national unity and greatness. The crisis of Western democracy was not lost on observers in East Asia, where traditions of liberal constitutionalism were shallow at best.

During most of the decade those nations which preserved democratic government were preoccupied with domestic problems and the strongest, the United States, was committed to a policy of isolationism. International statesmanship was at a low ebb; national leaders gave only lip service to the principles of collective security embodied in the League of Nations. The weakness of the League was first revealed by its failure to mount an adequate response to Japan's seizure of Manchuria in 1931; the League's condemnation of Japan for aggression was not followed by sanctions. Those who had relied on the community of nations to provide collective security had been proved wrong. Japan withdrew from the League (1933), and China realized that it could not expect aid from that quarter. The League itself emerged from the episode seriously damaged; the lesson was not lost on Hitler or Mussolini.

## The Manchurian Incident and Its Aftermath

Party government as it developed in the 1920s derived its legitimacy from the emperor, but there were those in Japan who believed that it was failing its sacred trust. In the name of the emperor, the enemies of constitutional government criticized the political manipulations of the Diet leaders, their ties with business, and the lackluster conduct of foreign affairs—especially the policy of accommodation with the West and conciliation of China, exemplified by the Washington Conference of 1921–22. These sentiments animated the members of various patriotic organizations in Japan. They also prevailed in the army, which considered itself an independent agent of the imperial will and resented cuts made in its budget during the twenties. In the army, dissatisfaction with the political ethos and government policies was thus combined with resentment against restrictions imposed by a civilian government and a sense of a separate mission for which the army was responsible to the emperor alone.

Among the most vehement critics of party government were radical egalitarians like Kita Ikki, who favored nationalizing industry, and radical agrarians like Gondo Saikyo (1866–1937), who would have abolished industry altogether and returned Japan to rural simplicity. Although their visions of the future might differ, such men agreed on two things: that the existing government obtruded on the imperial will and must be swept away, and that Japan had a divine mission overseas.

Such ideas formed the rallying point for small societies of extremists given to direct action. Some, like the Cherry Society, which planned an unsuccessful military coup in Tokyo in March 1931, were composed entirely of army officers, none higher in rank than lieutenant colonel. Indeed, the army was a major source of extreme right-wing patriotic discontent. When the government lost control of the army, the gates to imperialist adventurism were flung open.

The assassination of the Manchurian warlord Chang Tso-lin in 1928 was the work of men such as these. They hoped that Chang's murder would lead to a war in which this vast, strategically important and potentially wealthy area would be conquered for Japan. The attempt failed, but the extremists were not discouraged. Indeed, another attempt in this direction appealed to the superpatriots, not only because it might gain Manchuria, but also because it would strengthen their support in the army, increase the army's power and popularity at home, and undermine the government by political parties they so detested. For these champions of a "Shōwa Restoration" felt that party government was a betrayal of the divine emperor, whom they regarded as the very embodiment of Japan's "national polity" (*kokutai*), a term which became an "incantatory symbol,"[1] all the more powerful for being rather vague.

The shift of attention to Manchuria was consistent with the aggressive Pan-Asianism popular in "patriotic" circles. Others, in the army and also in the Seiyūkai, were well disposed toward overseas expansion under army auspices. In the fall of 1931 the time seemed ripe, for China was hampered by floods in the Yangtze Valley, and the Western powers were neutralized by the depression.

The seizure of Manchuria was masterminded by officers below general rank serving with the Kwantung Army on the Liaotung Peninsula. It was these officers, none with a rank higher than colonel, who fabricated an excuse for hostilities: a supposed Chinese attempt to sabotage the South Manchuria Railway Company. And they saw to it that the fighting continued until the army controlled the entire area. Although certain high army officials in Tokyo very likely knew of the plot, it was carried out without the knowledge, let alone the authorization, of the civilian government in Tokyo, which, once informed, tried to halt the operations but found itself powerless to do so. An attempted military coup in Tokyo in October did not immediately topple the government but did succeed in intimidating civilian political leaders. The Wakatsuki government, divided and helpless, resigned in December. It was followed by a Seiyūkai government under Inukai Ki (1855–1932), which for another half year tried to maintain a semblance of party control.

Events moved swiftly on the continent and at home. In Manchuria the army consolidated its hold and established a puppet state, which early in 1932 declared its independence from China. Manchukuo, as it was known, was placed under the titular rule of P'u-yi who, as an infant, had been the last emperor of China, but it was actually the army's domain. Meanwhile the fighting had spread to China proper; for six strenuous weeks, Japanese and Chinese fought around Shanghai until a truce was finally arranged. Japanese efforts to make a general settlement with China and obtain recognition of Manchukuo were rebuffed, and, condemned by the League of Nations, Japan found herself isolated in world diplomacy. In May 1933 Japan and China concluded a truce that left Japanese troops in control of the area they had seized in China north of the Great Wall, but this did not prevent Japanese soldiers from interfering in the adjacent Chinese demilitarized area nor from exerting continuous pressure in that area. The arrangement lasted for an uneasy four years, but a truce is not a peace, nor necessarily even a prelude to peace, as became clear when full-scale war broke out in the summer of 1937. In the meantime in Manchuria, and now also in Korea, the Japanese concentrated on the development of heavy industry, building up an industrial base on the continent under army control.

At home, 1932 was also an eventful year as members of the patriotic societies continued to implement their schemes by assassinating prominent men, including the head of the house of Mitsui. On May 15 they raided the Tokyo power station, a bank, Seiyūkai headquarters, and the official residence of the prime minister. They failed to provoke a military takeover but did succeed in killing Inukai and bringing an end to party cabinets. The next two cabinets, in office from May 1932 to March 1936, did include party men but were headed by admirals, who were considered more moderate than certain potential prime ministers from the army.

## Japanese Domestic Politics and the Road to War

When the fanatic and inexperienced men who staged the May 15 incident were brought to trial, they were treated with great respect. They were allowed to expound their doctrines for days at a time and given a national podium from which to proclaim the selflessness of their patriotic motives. In this way they largely succeeded in creating for themselves an image of martyrdom that won considerable public support. The light sentences that were meted out after the trials were at last completed further discouraged those who hoped for a return to civilian rule. The political parties continued to function, and in 1936 the leftist Social Mass Party managed to win half a million votes. The following year that party's total climbed to 900,000 votes, and it captured 37 seats in the lower house of the Diet. In that same election the Seiyūkai and Minseitō together polled some 7 million votes, giving them 354 out of a total of 466 seats. But their showing in the polls was to little avail. The parties were too weak to serve as a counterweight to the military. Those who wished to preserve constitutional government chose to compromise with the military establishment in the hope of averting a complete overthrow of the existing order, as envisioned by the military extremists. Those who compromised included Saionji, last of the *genrō*, who also hoped to protect the throne from involvement in divisive politics.

In this situation the most important immediate issue concerned not the balance between military and civilian power so much as the control of the military itself, for the actions in Manchuria and the violence at home demonstrated not only the decline of civilian control but highlighted a breakdown in military discipline made possible by the lack of unity within the army. The lines of army factionalism were very complex; for example, there was a division between those officers who studied at the Central War College and those who attended officers' training school. However, two main groups stood out. The more extreme faction, led by Generals Araki Sadao (1877–1966) and Mazaki Jinzaburō (1876–1956), was known as the *kōdōha* or "Imperial Way faction," since it emphasized the imperial mystique and advocated an ill-defined doctrine of direct imperial rule. Like the radical civilian theorists of the right, it opposed existing political and economic institutions, but it placed its faith not in institutional change but in a moral and spiritual transformation which would assure a glorious future for both army and country. In contrast the *tōseiha*, or "Control faction," led by General Nagata Tetsuzan (1884–1935), was much more ready to work with the *zaibatsu* and bureaucracy in order to turn Japan into a modern militarist state prepared for total war. Both factions envisioned a forceful foreign policy, but the *kōdōha* put greater stress on fighting communism and therefore was more adamantly opposed to the U.S.S.R. than were the more pragmatic *tōseiha* leaders.

For a few years after late 1931, the advantage lay with the Imperial Way faction, but it suffered a setback in 1935 when General Mazaki was dismissed from his post as director-general of military education. A lieutenant colonel retaliated by assassinating General Nagata, and the Control faction reacted to this by arresting the officer and laying plans for the transfer of other firebrands to Manchuria. The lieutenant colonel's trial was still in progress when, on February 26, 1936, a group of junior *kōdōha* officers, commanding over a thousand men, seized the center of the capital and killed a number of prominent leaders, although some of their intended victims managed to elude them, including Admiral Okada Keisuke (1868–1952), the prime minister, who escaped by a fluke (his brother-in-law, who looked like Okada, was killed instead). The young officers hoped that their action would bring down the old system and that generals Araki and Mazaki would take the lead in restructuring the state, but these senior generals remained aloof. As in 1928, the emperor intervened, and the navy responded to the crisis with vigor. On the third day of the insurrection, the rebels surrendered. This time the leaders were tried rapidly and in secret. One of those who perished at the hands of a firing squad was Kita Ikki, who had not participated in the mutiny but was too closely associated with the young officers and their movement to escape punishment.

The elimination of the Imperial Way faction left the Control faction in command of the army and increased the army's power in government, since it could now threaten a second mutiny if it did not get its way. One consequence of these events was a substantial increase in the military budget for the army and navy. Japan now withdrew from the naval limitation agreement. This opened the possibility that she might have to compete with the combined might of the Western powers and the U.S.S.R. To cope with the latter, Japan signed, in December 1936, an anti-Comintern pact with Germany.

Domestically there ensued an intensification of propaganda and indoctrination, coupled with a continuation of repression directed at the radical left and also victimizing those whose ardor for emperor and national polity (*kokutai*) was deemed insufficient. The most notorious case took place in 1935 when Minobe, the distinguished legal theorist, was charged with demeaning the emperor by considering him merely "the highest organ of the state." Minobe defended himself with spirit but was forced to resign from the House of Peers. Even then, in 1936 while living in seclusion, the old man suffered an attempt on his life which left him wounded. By that time his books had been banned. Censorship increased in severity, and expressions of intense national chauvinism filled the media.

The abandonment of the gold standard and the military buildup largely paid for by deficit financing enabled Japan to recover from the depth of the depression, but agriculture remained depressed and small firms benefited much less than did the *zaibatsu*. The international situation was also very problematic. The great powers refused to recognize Manchukuo or agree that Japan was entitled to an Asian version of the Monroe doctrine. Nor was anyone able to devise a formula regarding China acceptable to both the Japanese army and the Chinese government.

During 1936, the Chiang Kai-shek government, as noted below, showed a new firmness in its attitude toward Japan, whose army, after the conquest of Manchuria, was steadily moving into "autonomous zones" in North China. Until the summer of 1937, Japanese pressure was primarily economic and political, but there was the danger than an unplanned military incident might escalate into a major war. This is, in effect, what happened after a clash between Chinese and Japanese soldiers in July on the Marco Polo Bridge outside Peking, when the Chinese drew the line and refused further concessions. The ensuing hostilities signified the beginnings of a war that in 1941 became part of an even more extensive and destructive war (the Second World War), although this is not what the Japanese intended in 1937.

# China under the Nationalists

For a decade, from 1927 to 1937, the Nationalist government in Nanking maintained peace with Japan, but it was, as we have seen, a tenuous peace made possible by concessions and requiring military preparedness to resist further demands. Underlying the initial policy of appeasing Japan was the conviction on the part of Chiang Kai-shek and the Kuomintang leadership that China's most pressing need was for internal unification, for even after the completion of the northern expedition in 1928, the government actually controlled only the lower Yangtze Valley. Elsewhere it was dependent on the questionable, self-serving allegiance of local power holders.

In 1930, in a costly campaign with heavy casualties on both sides, the government defeated the combined warlord armies of Feng Yü-hsiang and Yen Hsi-shan and thereby secured its authority in the North. Nanking was strengthened by this victory but lacked the power to subdue the remaining warlords once and for all. Instead it temporized with them, tried to prevent the formation of antigovernment warlord coalitions, and settled for expressions of warlord allegiance until such time as it could establish central control. The power and prestige of the Nanking regime were increased when it defeated a rebellion in Fukien in 1933–34, and especially after it obtained control over Kwangtung and the submission of Kwangsi in 1936. Its campaigns against the

Communists (see below) provided occasions for the dispatch of central government troops into warlord provinces, especially after the Communists began their Long March in 1934, and similarly the Japanese threat proved useful in eventually bringing certain warlords into line. Thus the trend was in favor of Nanking, but the actual balance between central and local power varied widely in different parts of China. The tenacity of the warlord phenomenon in certain regions is illustrated by Szechwan, in parts of which warlords remained powerful even after the Nationalists moved their wartime capital to that province. Similarly, remote western provinces such as Sinkiang remained virtually autonomous.

The need to unify the country and to withstand the menace of Japan, as well as his own background, were among the factors influencing Chiang Kai-shek to make the military his first priority. This was reflected in the government's expenditures, for its budgets consistently favored the army. Military considerations were paramount also in such projects as road and railway construction. Taking the place of the ousted Russian military advisors were a series of German military men, who tried to introduce German military doctrines (including concepts of military organization not necessarily suitable to the Chinese situation) and also helped to arrange for the import of German arms and munitions. In 1935, at the height of their influence, there were seventy German advisors in China. After the anti-Comintern pact between Germany and Japan, their number decreased until the last men were recalled in 1938. Noteworthy within the army were the graduates of the Whampoa Military Academy, particularly those who completed the course during Chiang Kai-shek's tenure as director, for they enjoyed an especially close relationship with their supreme commander.

It was also Whampoa graduates who during 1931 formed the Blue Shirts, a secret police group pledged to complete obedience to Chiang Kai-shek. They and the so-called CC clique (led by two Ch'en brothers trusted by Chiang) were influenced in ideology and organization by European fascism. The Blue Shirts were greatly feared because of their spying and terrorist activities, including assassinations. The CC clique, too, had considerable power but it failed in its prime aim, which was to revitalize the Kuomintang. After the split with the Communists, the KMT purged many of its own most dedicated revolutionaries. This discouraged those who remained from entertaining potentially dangerous ideas and created an atmosphere attractive to men who, concentrating on their own personal careers, would not rock the boat.

The deterioration of the party was a particularly serious matter because the Nanking government suffered from factional politics and favoritism as well as from bureaucratic overorganization, which spawned departments with overlapping functions and countless committees grinding out lengthy reports and recommendations, detailing programs that consumed vast quantities of paper but were rarely implemented. Coordination was poor. It sometimes happened, for example, that government censors suppressed news items deliberately issued by the government itself. The conduct of official business lumbered along unless quickened by the personal intervention of Chiang Kai-shek, whose power was steadily on the increase. It was power based on the loyalty of the military and the Blue Shirts, core partisans such as the CC clique, the financial backing of bankers and businessmen (including the relatives of Chiang's wife), and on a semblance of balance of various political cliques and factions manipulated by Chiang himself. It was a power that made Chiang indispensable to government, but he lacked the charisma to inspire his officials, who feared rather than loved him. Nor did he have the gift of eloquence with which to rouse the people had he so desired. Negative sanctions, such as the executions sporadically ordered by Chiang when an exceptionally flagrant case of corruption was brought to his attention, were not enough: the regime lacked drive and direction.

One problem was that the regime was ideologically weak. Sun Yat-sen became the object of an official cult, but his ideas were not further refined or developed. Instead emphasis was shifted toward a revival of Confucianism. In contrast to Sun's admiration for the Taipings, Chiang sought to emulate Tseng Kuo-fan, who in his day had successfully stemmed a revolution by revitalizing Confucian values. Chiang's regard for Confucius and Tseng was already apparent during his days at Whampoa but became even more obvious in 1934 when he launched an extensive program to foster traditional values known as the New Life movement. This movement exhorted the populace to observe four vaguely defined Confucian virtues and spelled out the criteria for proper behavior in detailed instructions. The people were to sit and stand straight, eat quietly, refrain from indiscriminate spitting, and so forth, in the hope that they would thus acquire discipline. It did not work. Officials and commoners continued to act much as before. The government never did devise an ideology able to arouse the enthusiasm of its own personnel, command the respect of the people, or convince intellectuals. Censorship clearly was not the answer, although even foreign correspondents were subjected to it, some complaining that it was worse in China than in Japan.

Ineffectiveness also characterized Nationalist economic policies, as when exports were subjected to the same tariffs as imports, and the imports of raw material were taxed as heavily as those of finished goods. Thus China's industry failed to draw much profit from the government's success when, during 1928 and 1929, it at last regained the tariff autonomy China had lost in the Opium War. It was the modern sector of the economy that supplied the great bulk of Nanking's revenue in a period when military expenses and debt service added up to between 60 and 80 percent of the government's annual expenditures. But despite its early links with the business community, the Kuomintang regime retained the traditional government attitude toward private business as a source to be exploited for revenue rather than as an asset to be fostered as a component of national strength. In 1933, embroiled in heavy borrowing from the banks, the government took control of the banking system in a move which benefited the treasury but not the modern private sector. Overall, the modern sector did grow during the decade but only at roughly the same pace as during the years between the fall of the Ch'ing and the establishment of the regime in Nanking.

During the early thirties the traditional agrarian sector of the economy, which accounted for most of China's production and employed the vast majority of its people, was sorely hurt by the fall of prices produced by the depression. The agrarian sector was further afflicted by severe weather conditions, including the Yangtze flood of 1931, and by the exactions of the tax collector who piled surtax on surtax (later changed to special assessments), with the result that the taxes on agriculture continued to increase despite the decline in farm prices. Taxation, like the climate, varied widely, making generalization very risky. Even in the same province, the tax burden paid by one district was often much more than that paid by another, and this was true even in provinces like Kiangsu and Chekiang, which were firmly controlled by the government. The same difficulty applies to attempts to generalize about the prevalence or burdens of tenancy, which was much more frequent in the south than in the north. Nevertheless, since the government did nothing to change the status quo in the village and on the land, the poorest and the weakest suffered most. Like so much legislation promulgated during those years, the law passed in 1930 limiting rents to 37½ percent of the harvest was not enforced. Payments of 50 percent were common and 60 percent was not unusual. Programs for developing cooperatives and fostering rural reconstruction were organized, but their benefits rarely filtered down to the rural poor. In 1937 there was a price recovery, and harvests were good, but by that time millions had suffered bitter poverty and despair.

Chiang Kai-shek and his supporters wanted to unify the country and to stabilize society. They wished to consolidate the revolution that had brought them into power, not to expand it. Therefore they put a premium on suppressing those forces which would lead to further and continued revolution. The regime was intent on destroying communism and the Communists, who maintained that the revolution was unfinished and proclaimed their readiness to lead it to completion. To Chiang Kai-shek nothing was more urgent than the elimination, once and for all, of his old enemies, the Chinese Communist Party. For the CCP too these were crucial years.

## The Chinese Communists (1927–1934)

The Shanghai massacre and the subsequent suppression of the CCP and its associated labor movement had effectively eliminated the party as an urban force and thereby altered its geographical distribution and profoundly affected its strategy and leadership. For some years it remained unclear just what direction the movement would take. Neither the Comintern nor its Chinese followers was willing simply to write off the cities. After urban insurrection failed, as in the Canton Commune established for four days in December 1927 and greeted by the populace with profound apathy, an attempt was made to capture cities by armed force, as in the case of Changsha in Hunan in 1930. But this also failed. Although no one was ready to say so, at least in public, Moscow clearly did not have the formula for success. Meanwhile in China various groups and factions contended for power and the adoption of their policies.

One of these groups was the CCP military force, which underwent a crucial reorganization in the Chingkang Mountains on the Hunan-Kiangsi border, where, in the spring of 1928, Chu Teh (1886–1976) joined Mao Tse-tung, who had arrived the previous fall. In command of some 2000 troops, the two leaders laid the groundwork for the Red Army, with Chu Teh taking military command and Mao in charge of political organization and indoctrination. As Mao was to say in 1938: "Political power grows out of the barrel of a gun. Our principle is that the Party commands the gun; the gun shall never be allowed to command the Party."[2] Through indoctrination, the recruitment of soldiers into the party, and the formation of soldiers' committees, Mao secured the control of the party over the army, while on the military side Chu and Mao emphasized guerrilla warfare, which put a premium on mobility and surprise, rapid retreats to avoid battle with superior enemy forces, lightning strikes to pick off small contingents of the enemy, and constant harassment to keep the enemy off balance. Essential to this type of warfare is popular support to provide intelligence, supplies, and recruits, as well as cover for guerrillas under enemy pursuit. Peasant participation and support were secured by redistributing land and furthering the revolution in the countryside.

This strategy focused on the development and expansion of rural CCP controlled bases, and in the early thirties there were a number of such areas. The largest were in Kiangsi, where in December 1931 the founding of the Chinese Soviet Republic was proclaimed. The basic agrarian policy was "land to the tiller," involving the confiscation of large holdings and their reassignment to the poor, with "middle peasants" left largely unaffected, but there was a good deal of disagreement over definitions as well as wide variations in the degree of local implementation of the program. During the Kiangsi period, Mao and Chu were influential leaders, but they had by no means won complete acceptance of either their programs or their leadership, even after party headquarters were moved to Kiangsi from Shanghai, a shift which signified recognition of the new power center in the CCP and a defeat for those oriented toward the Comintern in Moscow. Factionalism continued to undermine party unity, but the most severe challenge was external.

Chiang Kai-shek's first three "annihilation campaigns" came in 1930–31 and helped strengthen rather than weaken the CCP as the Red Army employed its tactics to good effect and captured weapons, men, and land. The fourth campaign, 1932–33, again ended in defeat for the Nationalists. In the fifth campaign, begun late in 1933, Chiang, on German advice, changed his strategy. Deploying some 750,000 men supported by 150 airplanes, he surrounded the Kiangsi Soviet and gradually tightened the circle of his blockade. When in the fall of 1934 their situation became untenable, the Communist forces abandoned their Kiangsi base, broke through a point in the KMT blockade manned by former warlord armies, and began their Long March. (See map, Figure 10-1.)

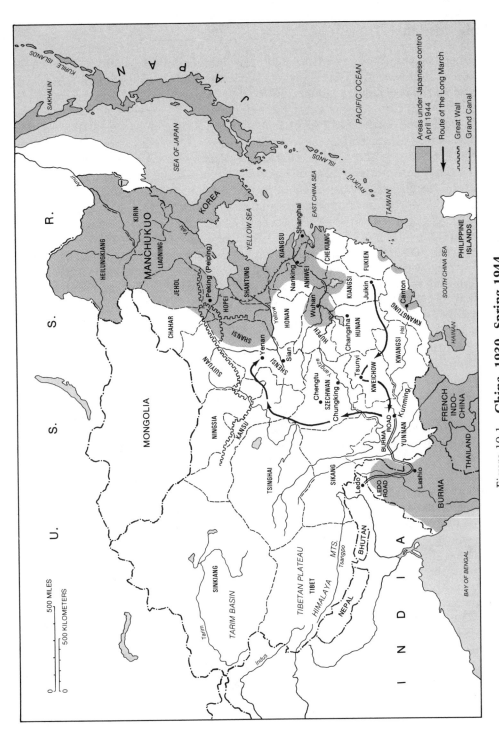

Figure 10-1  **China, 1930–Spring 1944**

(For Japan's maximum occupation of China, see Figure 10-4.)

Areas under Japanese control
April 1944

Route of the Long March

Great Wall

Grand Canal

# The Long March

When the Communists left Kiangsi, their first priority was survival, and their destination was not clear. That was settled at an important conference held at Tsunyi in Kweichow in January 1935, when it was decided to proceed to Shensi, where a small soviet was already in existence. In Shensi the CCP would be out of easy reach of the KMT armies. They would be able to act on their earlier declaration of war against Japan and might even hope for some assistance from the U.S.S.R. At the Tsunyi conference Mao gained a new prominence, although he did not actually control the party until the forties.

The march itself, was a heroic accomplishment, a vindication of Mao's belief in the power of the human will and determination. In just over a year, the marchers covered some 6000 miles, traversing snow-covered mountain passes where they froze in their thin clothes and crossing treacherous bogs and marshes. To the hardships provided by nature was added the hostility of man, for there was rarely a day without some fighting. At one point they had no alternative but to cross a mountain torrent spanned by a thirteen-chain suspension bridge from which the enemy, armed and waiting on the other side, had removed the planks.

A terrible ordeal was the six- or seven-day crossing of the grasslands of Chunghai in the Chinese-Tibetan border region. Here heavy rainfall and poor drainage had created a waterlogged plain in which green grass grew on multiple layers of rotting grass beneath. First a vanguard was sent to chart the way, and in the central grasslands they could find no place dry enough to sleep so the men had to remain standing all night long, leaning against each other. The rest of the army followed through the slippery, treacherous terrain, trudging on despite hunger and fatigue, trying to ward off rain and hail and survive the unbearable cold of the nights. Since the men carried only a very small amount of grain, they subsisted mostly on wild grasses and vegetables eaten raw because there was no firewood for cooking. Sometimes the vegetables turned out to be poisonous, and the stagnant water reportedly smelled of horse's urine.

The marchers succeeded in overcoming this and other obstacles but at great cost. Of about 100,000 who set out from Kiangsi, less than 10 percent completed the march. Some were left behind to work in various areas, but many more perished. The loss was only partially offset by new recruits who joined along the way. After completion of the march, including the men already in Shensi, the Communists were about 20,000 strong.

The survivors of the march emerged toughened and filled with a sense of solidarity forged by shared hardships and common suffering. There was also a heightened self-confidence, a conviction that the movement would surmount all obstacles. Something of this spirit is conveyed in a poem Mao wrote shortly before reaching Shensi:

> Lofty the sky
>  and pale the clouds—
> We watch the wild geese
>  fly south till they vanish.

We count the thousand
  leagues already travelled.
If we do not reach
  the Great Wall we are not true men.

High on the crest
  of Liup'an Mountain
Our banners billow
  in the west wind.
Today we hold
  the long rope in our hands.
When shall we put bonds
  upon the grey dragon?[3]

The saga of the Long March continued to be celebrated in poetry and prose. It remains today a source of heroic inspiration.

## United Front and War

With the Communists in Shensi, Chiang remained as determined as ever to crush them, but their call for a united front against Japan had special appeal for the troops of Marshal Chang Hsüeh-liang, son of Chang Tso-lin, the former warlord of Manchuria. Although assigned to the task, Chang's forces were less than enthusiastic in fighting the CCP. To breathe some life into the anti-Communist campaign, Chiang Kai-shek flew to Sian in December. But he had misjudged the situation. Instead of pledging themselves to renewed anti-Communist efforts, Marshal Chang and some of his men seized Chiang Kai-shek and held him prisoner for two weeks while his fate was being negotiated. Exactly what transpired is not clear, but, after Communist intercession, Chiang was finally released, having agreed to terminate his campaign against the Communists and lead a united front against Japan. He was at the time China's most distinguished military man, the leader of the government recognized as legitimate at home and abroad, the heir to the mantle of Sun Yat-sen. Even his enemies saw him as the only man possessing the political, military, and ideological authority to lead China in an effort to stop the Japanese.

The Sian incident led to the formation of a united front in 1937. Following the KMT's 1936 success against Kwangtung and Kwangsi, formation of the united front was viewed with dismay by Japanese army officers intent on dominating North China. As already noted, matters came to a head after the Marco Polo Bridge clash in early July 1937. This rapidly expanded into large-scale fighting. By the end of July the Japanese were in possession of Peking and Tientsin, and in August Japanese forces attacked Shanghai, where Chiang used some of his best German trained troops in three months of bloody fighting, with heavy casualties. After Shanghai came Nanking, which fell in December, followed by the notorious "Rape of Nanking," during which Japanese soldiers terrorized the inhabitants, killing and raping, burning and looting, leaving an estimated 100,000 dead. The Japanese acquired a reputation for terrible cruelty, which stiffened the determination of the Chinese people to resist.

Japan's prime minister at this time was Prince Konoe Fumimaro (1891–1945), a nobleman of most distinguished lineage and a protégé of Saionji. He was to hold office from June 1937 to January 1939 and from July 1940 to July 1941. Japanese policy making continued to be a very complicated process, since there was no centralized, coordinated, long-range planning. The general staff, for example, did not share the optimism of the armies in the field, yet the government continued to expand the war, encouraged by a string of victories. As the war escalated so did the Japanese government's aims and rhetoric. What had begun as a search for a pro-Japanese North China turned into a holy crusade against the West and Communism. Unable to obtain Chinese recognition of Manchukuo, the Konoe government in 1938 declared Chiang's regime illegitimate and vowed to destroy it. Japanese troops continued their advance, taking Canton in October, Wuhan in December. Chiang still showed no inclination to submit. In November Konoe proclaimed Japan's determination to establish a "New Order in East Asia" to include Japan, Manchukuo, and China in a political, economic, and cultural union, a bastion against (Western) imperialism and against Soviet Communism. Those who did not see the light were to be brought to their senses by force. The military fracas of July 1937 had been transformed into a holy war suffused with a mystic belief in Japan's mission to create a new East Asia.

By this time the Nationalist government, following a strategy of "trading space for time," had moved its capital to Chungking in Szechwan, where it was joined by many refugees from occupied China. Not only universities but hundreds of factories were transported piecemeal to the wartime capital to help produce for the war effort. In Chungking, Chiang held on gamely, on the defensive. Before the Japanese attack on Pearl Harbor, the Chinese did obtain some financial assistance from outside, and beginning in August 1941, they were also aided by the Flying Tigers, volunteer American pilots later incorporated into the Fourteenth U.S. Air Force, commanded by General Claire L. Chennault. However, the West's support remained primarily moral, and the U.S.S.R. alone sent some official assistance. Although Chungking suffered repeated bombings during 1939–41, at the battlefront these two years were marked by skirmishes rather than massive campaigns, as both sides worked to consolidate their positions. In 1940 the Japanese established a puppet regime in Nanking headed by Wang Ching-wei, the erstwhile follower of Sun Yat-sen and leader of the left wing of the KMT.

## Expansion of the War into a Pacific War

A major Japanese foreign policy concern during the thirties was Japanese relations with the U.S.S.R. During 1938–39 there were several military clashes in the border area along Russia's frontier with Korea and Manchukuo. In these operations, quite large in scale and involving the deployment of armor, Japan was not successful. Furthermore, the Japanese were caught off guard diplomatically when Germany, without any warning, came to terms with the Soviet Union in August 1939. Japan was therefore neutral when the Second World War began in Europe shortly afterward. However, the dramatic success of the German blitzkrieg strengthened the hands of those in Tokyo who favored a pro-German policy, and in September 1940, Konoe signed the Tripartite Pact forming an alliance with Germany and Italy.

The Germans again surprised the Japanese in June 1941 when Hitler invaded Russia. While some in Japan maintained that Japan should join the attack on the U.S.S.R., others argued that, with the Soviet Union preoccupied in Europe, the time was ripe for Japan to move into oil- and mineral-rich Southeast Asia and thereby advance its mission, now expanded into the creation of a "Greater East Asia Co-Prosperity Sphere." Without the resources of Southeast Asia, it was argued, Japan would never achieve naval supremacy in the Pacific.

Konoe hoped that, armed with the Tripartite Pact, he would be able to reach his aims without going to war with the United States, but the American government was becoming increasingly alarmed over Japanese expansion. When in the summer of 1941 Japan moved troops into southern Indo-China, the United States, Britain, and Holland (then in control of the East Indies, modern Indonesia) retaliated by applying the economic sanctions they had withheld in 1931. The principal and crucial product cut off from Japan by this action was oil.

The United States was now determined that Japan should withdraw from China as well as Indo-China. For Japan this would have meant a reversal of the policy pursued in China since 1931 and the relinquishment of the vision of Japanese primacy in East Asia. Dependent on oil and rubber from Southeast Asia, the Japanese were in no position to carry on protracted negotiations. Their choice was to fight or retreat. When it became clear to Konoe that the situation had reached an impasse, he resigned, to be followed by General Tōjō Hideki (1884–1948), prime minister from October 1941 to July 1944. (See Figure 10-2.) When last minute negotiations proved fruitless, the Japanese decided on war as the least unpalatable alternative. It began on December 7, 1941, with a surprise attack on Pearl Harbor, in Hawaii, which destroyed 7 American battleships and 120 aircraft, and left 2400 dead.

## China During the War

The conviction that eventually the United States would enter the war against Japan sustained Chiang Kai-shek during the long years when China faced Japan virtually alone. When as a result of Pearl Harbor this did happen, it naturally buoyed the spirit of the Chinese, now allied to the one country powerful enough to crush Japan. More material forms of support were also soon forthcoming, although there was never enough because in 1942 Japan cut off the government's last land route to its allies by seizing Burma and closing the Burma Road. Thereafter, supplies had to be flown in from India to Yunnan over

Figure 10-2   General Tōjō.

the Himalaya Mountains (the "hump"). In addition, China ranked low in the American war effort. The Allies decided first to concentrate on the defeat of Germany, and the island-hopping strategy adopted against Japan largely by-passed China, although the Allies appreciated the fact that China tied down vast numbers of Japanese troops that otherwise might have been used elsewhere.

The top American military man in China was General Joseph Stilwell, who in 1942 became Chiang's chief-of-staff as well as commander of American forces in the China-Burma-India theater. Stilwell was a fine soldier but no diplomat. He had high regard for the ordinary Chinese fighting man but scarcely concealed his irritation and impatience with the inefficiencies and corruption he encountered in Chungking, and his disgust at Chiang's policy of preparing for a postwar showdown with the CCP rather than joining in a single-minded effort against the Japanese enemy. The relationship between the two men deteriorated until Chiang requested and received Stilwell's recall in 1944.

Stilwell was replaced by General Albert Wedemeyer, who was more friendly to Chiang, but also was critical of conditions in the Chinese army, which were, by all accounts, horrendous. Induction was tantamount to a death sentence. Those who could possibly afford to do so bribed the conscription officer. The remainder were marched off, bound together with ropes, to join their units, often many miles and days away. Underfed and exhausted, many recruits never completed the trip. Those who did found that food was equally scarce at the front and medical services almost completely lacking.

Misery and corruption were not unique to the military. Even in times of famine (as in Honan during 1942–43) peasants were sorely oppressed by the demands of the landlord and the tax collector, while the urban middle class suffered from mounting inflation. This had already reached an annual rate of 40 to 50 percent between 1937 and 1939, climbed to 160 percent for 1939–42, and mounted to an average of 300 percent for 1942–45. By 1943 the real value in terms of purchasing power of the salaries paid to bureaucrats was only one-tenth what they had received in 1937, while teachers were down to 5 percent of their former earnings. The result was widespread demoralization of the Chinese military and civilian populations under Nationalist control. The secret police were unable to root out corruption. Government exhortations and the publication of Chiang Kai-shek's book *China's Destiny* (1943) did not suffice to reinvigorate ideological commitment to the government and the KMT.

A major reason for the wartime deterioration of the KMT was that Japan's seizure of the eastern seaboard and China's major cities had deprived the Nationalists of their usual sources of support, the great business centers of east China. In Szechwan they became critically dependent on the local landlords, precisely the elements in society that were most resistant to change and reform. Moreover, Chiang was unwilling to commit his troops to battle with the Japanese more than was absolutely necessary, or to do anything which might strengthen the armies of the CCP, because he was convinced that after the war with Japan there would be an all-out confrontation with the Communists that would determine China's future. As a consequence, he missed whatever opportunity might have existed for building a modern Chinese force with American assistance, and for translating anti-Japanese nationalism into support for his own regime.

The shortcomings of the Chungking government were highlighted by the accomplishments of the Communists, headquartered in Yenan. (See Figure 10-3.) During the war years, from 1937 to 1945, the party expanded its membership from roughly forty thousand to over one million, and its troop strength increased tenfold to an estimated 900 thousand, not counting guerrillas and militiamen. Furthermore, the Communists enjoyed widespread peasant support in North China, where they established themselves as the effective government in the countryside behind the Japanese lines. The Japanese, concentrated in the cities and guarding their lines of supply, did not have the manpower to patrol the rural areas constantly and effectively.

In the areas nominally under Japanese control, the Communists were often able to fuse social revolution and national resistance, for example, redistributing to the peasants land owned by landlords collaborating with the Japanese. Similarly, the lands of men who had fled to KMT areas were available for reassignment. In accordance with arrangements under the united front, the CCP did not follow a radical program of land confiscation and redistribution, but by enforcing limits on rents and interest payments and by restructuring the tax system, they favored the poor. In addition, they reorganized village government so as to give the people a larger voice in decision making and formed mass organizations for such groups as women and young people. All of these steps had the effect of liberating important segments of the population from oppressive conditions of life. Poor peasant farmers were released from the exactions of landlord and tax collector; village government was freed from the tyranny of local landlords and elites; women and youth were liberated from the Confucian familial tradition. The result was a tremendous unleashing of new enthusiasms and, of course, support for the CCP. Thus, the Communists were succeeding precisely where Chiang and the KMT had failed.

The Communist role in providing effective resistance against the Japanese was particularly important in those areas which felt the full force of Japanese attempts to terrorize the countryside into submission, as in the notorious "kill all, burn all, destroy all" policy implemented in parts of North China in 1941 and 1942. Areas were selected where this policy was literally implemented, with the effect that previously apolitical peasants, equally distrustful of all government, were turned into determined fighters. The twin lessons of nationalism and revolution were further brought home to the people through indoctrination programs and, particularly, through a campaign to combat illiteracy, conveying new ideas to the peasantry even as it gave them access to the written word, shattering the old elite monopoly on learning.

The social and national policies attracted many; not only peasants but also intellectuals from the cities joined the Communists. To insure discipline and preserve the cohesion of the movement, swollen by new adherents, the party under Mao (now firmly established as leader) organized a rectification cam-

Figure 10-3   Yenan in 1960. After the Long March and during the war, the CCP leaders lived and worked in the Yenan caves.

paign to assure "correct" understanding of party ideology and to bring art and literature into line. Art for its own sake or for the purpose of self-expression was condemned, and those guilty of being insufficiently mass oriented were induced to confess their faults. Many were sent down to work in villages, factories, or battle zones to "learn from the masses."

From the war, the CCP emerged stronger than it had ever been before, although the outcome of the civil war that followed was by no means obvious to observers at the time (see below). It is one of the ironies of the war that the Japanese, who proclaimed that they were combating communism in China, instead contributed to its ultimate success.

## Japan at War

Well before Pearl Harbor the effects of the continued war in China were felt by the Japanese people as militarization and authoritarianism increased at home. The National General Mobilization Law of 1938 strengthened the prime minister at the expense of the Diet, and the government began to place the economy on a war basis, with rationing, economic controls, and resource allocations. In October 1940, the political parties were merged into the Imperial Rule Assistance Association, which, however, did not become a mass popular party along the lines of European facism but served primarily as a vehicle for the dissemination of propaganda throughout Japan. Similarly labor unions were combined into a single patriotic organization. Great pressures were exerted to bring educational institutions and the public communications media into line so that the whole of Japan would speak with one collective voice. To effect the "spiritual mobilization" of the country, the government tried to purge Western influence from Japanese life. Not only were foreign liberal ideas banned, but such elements of popular culture as permanent waves and jazz, so popular during the twenties, were now suppressed. Efforts were made to remove Western loan words from the language, and the people were bombarded with exhortations to observe traditional values and revere the divine emperor. To mobilize the public down to the ward level, the people were formed into small neighborhood organizations.

Before the war was over the people were to suffer a great deal, but at first the war went spectacularly well for Japan. By the middle of 1942 Japan controlled the Philippines, Malaya, Burma, and the East Indies, and was assured of the cooperation of friendly regimes in Indo-China (controlled by Vichy France) and in Thailand. However, Japan's attempt to win over the population of the conquered areas by encouraging their native religious traditions, exploiting their resentment against Western imperialism, and teaching them the Japanese language was more than offset by Japan's own imperialistic exploitation, by the harshness of its rule, and by the cruelty of its soldiers, brutalized by the treatment meted out to them in the Japanese army. The slogan "Asia for the Asians" did not disguise the realities of Japanese rule.

In June 1942 Japan was checked at the battle of Midway. (See map, Figure 10-4.) The American use of aircraft based on carriers and the extensive employment of submarines, which took a tremendous toll of vital Japanese shipping, were two of the factors contributing to Japan's ultimate defeat. Another was the island-hopping strategy whereby the American forces seized islands selectively for use as bases for further advances, bypassing others with their Japanese forces intact but out of action. The closer the American forces came to the Japanese homeland, the easier it was for them to bomb Japan itself. Such raids were aimed not only at military and industrial installations, but also at economic targets and population centers. Incendiary bombs were dropped in order to sap the morale of the people, who by the last years of the war, were suffering from scarcities of all kinds, including food and other daily necessities, many of which were available only on the black market. The last year of the war was especially terrible; on one night in March 1945, some 100,000 people died as the result of a firebomb raid on Tokyo, and a similar raid in May devastated another large part of Japan's capital city. Short of resources, and with its cities in ruins, Japan during the last months of the war was reduced to desperate measures, such as the use of flying bombs directed by suicide pilots, called kamikaze after the "divine wind" that once had saved the land from the Mongols.

While internal propaganda persisted until the end in urging the people to ever greater efforts, it was clear to some political leaders that Japan could not win. After the fall of Saipan, largest of the Mariana Islands, General Tōjō was forced out of office in July 1944, but there was no change either in the fortunes of war or in policy under his successor General Koiso Kuniaki (1880–1950). Koiso remained in office until April 1945, when he was succeeded by Admiral Suzuki Kantaro (1867–1948). Some civilian leaders sent out peace feelers to the Allies, but their efforts were hampered by the noncooperation of the Soviet Union, anxious to have the war continue long enough to allow it to participate, and by the demand issued at Potsdam in July 1945, insisting on Japan's unconditional surrender. The demand for unconditional surrender reflected the Allied belief that it had been a mistake to allow the First World War to end in an armistice rather than in a full capitulation. The Allies felt that the armistice had permitted Hitler to claim that Germany had been "betrayed" into defeat, not beaten on the field of battle, and that he had been able to use this emotionally charged argument to generate the popular support that brought the Nazi party to power. Determined not to commit a similar mistake in the Second World War, the Allies demanded an unconditional surrender. But the insistence on an unconditional surrender actually stiffened Japanese resistance because it left the fate of the emperor in doubt, and this was impossible for the Japanese to accept.

The end came in August 1945. On August 6 the United States dropped an atomic bomb on Hiroshima (see Figure 10-5) in southwestern Honshū, razing over 80 percent of the buildings and leaving some 200,000 people dead or injured and countless others to continue their lives under the specter of radiation sickness. This holocaust added a new chapter to the horrors of war.

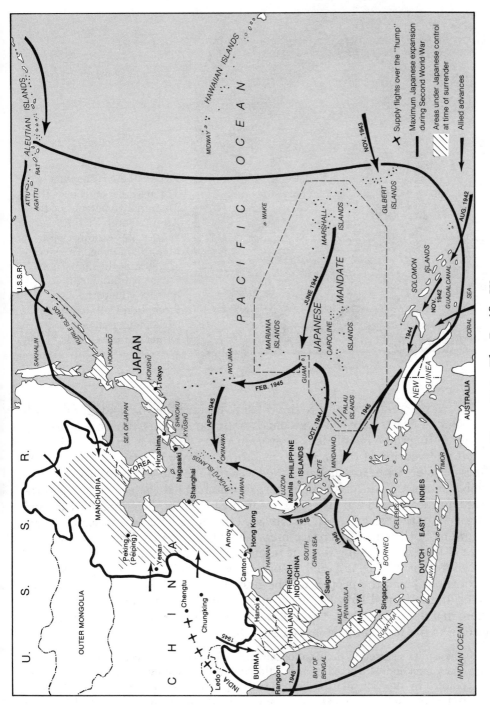

Figure 10-4  The Pacific War

Figure 10-5 Hiroshima. Through the vault over the Memorial Cenotaph for the Atomic Bomb Victims can be seen the Atomic Bomb Memorial Dome. The steel skeleton of the dome and the gutted building (formerly the city's Industrial Promotion Hall) have been left standing unaltered, in witness to the tragedy.

Two days later, on August 8, the U.S.S.R. entered the war, and on the ninth the United States dropped a second atomic bomb, this time on Nagasaki. Twice during these fateful days a government deadlock was broken by the personal intervention of the emperor, each time in favor of peace. Even after the final decision for peace, diehards tried to continue the war by a last resort to violence in the tradition of the terrorists who had first helped steer Japan toward militarism and war. They set fire to the homes of the prime minister and president of the privy council and invaded the imperial palace in search of the recording of the emperor's peace message, but they failed. When all was lost, several leaders, including the war minister, committed ritual suicide.

On August 15 the imperial recording was broadcast over the radio, and throughout Japan the people, for the first time, heard the voice of their emperor. In the formal language appropriate to his elevated status, he informed them that the war was lost. This is how Ōe Kenzaburō, ten years old at the time, recollects the impact of the broadcast:

> The adults sat around their radios and cried. The children gathered outside in the dusty road and whispered their bewilderment. We were most confused and disappointed by the fact that the Emperor had spoken in a *human* voice, no different from any adult's. None of us understood what he was saying, but we had all heard his voice. One of my friends could even imitate it cleverly. Laughing, we sur-

rounded him—a twelve year old in grimy shorts who spoke with the Emperor's voice. A minute later we felt afraid. We looked at one another; no one spoke. How could we believe that an august presence of such awful power had become an ordinary human voice on a designated summer day?[4]

## East Asia at the End of the War

Defeat brought an end to the half century during which Japan was the dominant military and political power in East Asia. It marked the dissolution of the Japanese Empire, for Japan was made to relinguish not only Manchuria and other areas seized since 1931, but all gains since 1895. It thus opened a new phase in the history of Taiwan and Korea. The defeat of Japan also initiated a new phase in the history of South and Southeast Asia, where former colonies resisted the return of Western colonial masters. Indeed, it marked the beginning of the end of colonialism throughout the world.

For Japan itself defeat brought a sharp break with the past, for it thoroughly discredited the militarists who had brought the country to disaster, and it opened the way for new departures. For China, in contrast, the end of the war did not bring with it an immediate change, for there the shape of the future was still a subject of contention between forces locked in civil war. The end of the great war brought no peace to that long-suffering country. Nor would it permit a peaceful determination of the future of Korea and Vietnam.

On the broad international scene, the war left the United States and the Soviet Union as the two giant powers who maintained a presence in East Asia and had the capacity to influence events in that part of the world. And Hiroshima and Nagasaki had demonstrated just how dangerous a place that world could be.

## NOTES

1. The term "incantatory symbol" comes from Masao Maruyama, in Ivan Morris, ed., *Thought and Behavior in Modern Japanese Politics*, Expanded edition (New York: Oxford University Press, 1969). p. 376.
2. Stuart R. Schram, *The Political Thought of Mao Tse-tung* (New York: Frederick A. Praeger, 1963), p. 209.
3. Jerome Ch'en, *Mao and the Chinese Revolution* (New York: Oxford University Press, 1965), p. 337.
4. Ōe Kenzaburō, *A Personal Matter*, trans. John Nathan (New York: Grove Press, 1968), pp. vii–viii.

# PART THREE

# East
# Asia
# since
# the Second
# World War

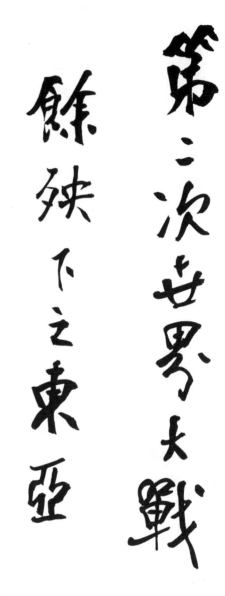

**Key Dates**

# 11
## The Aftermath of the Second World War in East Asia

Throughout East Asia, the third of a century following the Second World War was a period of change unprecedented in its rapidity and scope, affecting the direction of civilization, economic systems and social structure, and the very rhythm of the lives of millions of people. Two wars fought in Korea and Vietnam present grim proof that change did not always come peacefully nor without outside interference.

In China, Korea, and Japan the basic parameters of postwar history were decided during the years immediately following the Second World War. The triumph of the Chinese Communists, the war in Korea, and the remolding of Japan under the Occupation all fell into those years. This is not the case with the history of Vietnam, but since it too developed out of problems left unsettled by the Great War, it also is treated in this chapter.

The Second World War destroyed the Japanese Empire and, in the world at large, confirmed the eclipse of the Western European powers, thereby completing a process begun by the First World War. In Asia the once great British Empire was steadily dismantled as India and Burma attained independence in 1947 and the Malay Peninsula followed suit ten years later. Hong Kong alone remained a Crown Colony. The Dutch in Indonesia and, especially, the French in Indo-China did not yield as gracefully as did the British, but everywhere old-style colonialism was on the decline. Only two world powers remained in a position to exercise major influence over events in East Asia: the United States and the Soviet Union. During the immediate postwar years they developed a bitter Cold War rivalry that remained the prime fact of international relations for a whole generation and has yet to be resolved.

## Civil War and Communist Triumph in China (1945–1949)

For China the end of the Second World War brought not demobilization and peace but a rapid transition from an anti-Japanese war to civil war. The country, which had been at war for four years before Pearl Harbor, did not attain peace until four years after Japan's surrender.

When Japan surrendered in August 1945, its generals in China were ordered to submit only to Nationalist forces. To enable the KMT armies to accept the Japanese surrender, the United States undertook to transport them by water and by air to those parts of the country up to then occupied by Japan. However, they were not allowed into Manchuria until January 1946. Manchuria had been occupied by the U.S.S.R. during the last days of the war, and the Russians did not completely withdraw their troops until May 1946, by which time they had allowed the CCP to gain substantial control of the countryside there. Chiang Kai-shek, determined to retain the area where the Japanese had begun their aggression, disregarded American warnings against overextending his forces and stationed almost half a million of his best troops in Manchuria.

During the year or so immediately after the war, the Nationalists appeared to have formidable resources, at least on paper. Recognized as the legitimate government of China by all the Allies, including the Soviet Union, they had three or four times as many men under arms as their Communist rivals and enjoyed a similar superiority in armament. They were, therefore, in no mood to make concessions to the CCP. The Communists, on the other hand, had come through the war battle hardened, with well-established bases of support in the countryside, and high morale. Their leaders, too, were convinced that victory would be theirs in the coming struggle. It was against this background that the United States sought to mediate between the KMT and CCP. In December 1945, President Truman sent General George C. Marshall to China to help the parties compose their differences. Given their history of conflict, divergence of views, and confidence in their respective causes, there was little chance that American mediation could bring about a genuine meeting of minds between the bitter Chinese antagonists. The American initiative was probably doomed from the start. Marshall's efforts were also hampered by general American support of the Nanking government, even though President Truman stipulated that large-scale aid to China was contingent on a settlement. As during Mao's visit to Chungking in August–October 1945 (see Figure 11-1), there was a show of cordiality, but the Marshall mission produced only a brief breathing spell before fighting broke out in earnest in mid-1946.

Initially, until July 1947, the KMT armies enjoyed success, even capturing the wartime CCP capital at Yenan. However, these were hollow victories. Like the Japanese before them, in North China and Manchuria the KMT controlled only the cities in the midst of a hostile countryside. Moreover, the military efficacy of the armies was undermined by the rivalries between their commanders; by Chiang Kai-shek's penchant for personal decision making even when he was far removed from the scene; and by his abiding concern to prevent any possible rival from amassing too much power. Also much in evidence were the harshness and corruption that had sapped the soldiers' morale during the war against Japan and were even more demoralizing now that they were supposed to fight fellow Chinese.

In other respects too, far from stimulating reform, the defeat of Japan resulted merely in the transfer to the rest of China of the ills that had been incubating in wartime Chungking. A nation badly in need of political, economic,

Figure 11-1   Chiang Kai-shek and Mao Tse-tung exchanging toasts, Chungking, August–October 1945.

and social reconstruction was subjected to a heavy dose of autocracy and to a galloping inflation. There was talk of reform, but the assassination, in the summer of 1946, of the poet and professor Wen I-to (1899–1946) disheartened intellectuals who shared his liberal ideas and hoped for greater freedom to criticize the government. But intellectuals and students were not the only ones disenchanted with the regime, for many suffered from the arrogance of the Nationalist soldiers and the rapacity of those with political connections.

The situation was particularly bad on Taiwan, where carpetbaggers from the mainland enriched themselves at the expense of alleged Taiwanese "collaborators"—a convenient charge against any noncooperative Taiwanese who had done at all well during the preceding half century of Japanese rule. When the Taiwanese rioted in protest in 1947, the Nationalist government responded with brutal and bloody repression. The exact number of casualties is not known—Taiwanese leaders in exile claim that over 10,000 were killed.

The government, inefficient as well as autocratic, proved unable to halt rapidly accelerating inflation that threatened all those whose incomes did not keep up with rising costs. Toward the end, people in the cities had to carry enormous bundles of paper money on their daily rounds of shopping for the necessities of life.

In the CCP areas, in contrast, the political and military leadership offered models of earnest dedication to their cause based on the conviction that this cause was just and would ultimately triumph. Unlike the KMT, which promised reform only after the fighting was finished, the CCP offered immediate change, instant liberation from the exactions of local authorities, landlords and usurers. As they gained new territory, the Communists organized the poor and oppressed, convincing people, by deed as well as by word, that their military organization deserved its name: the "People's Liberation Army."

In July 1947, the Communists turned the tide of war decisively against Chiang Kai-shek and the Nationalists. Communist armies attacked along several fronts in North China. In Manchuria, General Lin Piao (1907–71) organized a campaign that put the KMT forces on the defensive and ended, in October 1948, by completely routing them. During that same month and into November, the last great battle of the war was fought at the strategic city of Hsuchow on the Huai River where the Peking-Nanking Railway line joined the Lunghai line, which runs from Shensi to the sea. Around half a million men on each side were involved in this battle, generally known as the battle of Huai-Hai after the Huai River and the Lunghai Railway. When it was all over, the Nationalists, under Chiang Kai-shek's personal command, had lost 200,000 men and no longer had any way to supply their forces to the north. In January 1949 Nationalist generals surrendered Peking and Tientsin. Throughout the campaigns the Communist army gained not only military advantages from its victories, but also captured valuable military equipment and supplies and increased its manpower as Nationalist soldiers defected or surrendered and were incorporated into the People's Liberation Army.

During 1949 the Communists continued their advance. They crossed the Yangtze in April, took Nanking the same month, and were in control of Shanghai by the end of May. On October 1 Mao Tse-tung, in a great ceremony in Peking, formally proclaimed the establishment of the People's Republic of China. (See map, Figure 11-2.) There was still some fighting in the south, but clearly the CCP had won control of the Chinese mainland. Meanwhile, Chiang Kai-shek and other Nationalists took refuge on Taiwan and vowed continued resistance.

The triumph of the Communists in 1949 began a new chapter in China's long history. It was the result of a long revolutionary process that had begun well before the founding of the CCP, but in terms of the party's own programs and goals the revolution had only just begun. The story of China's continuing revolution is told in Chapter 13. First, however, let us consider its immediate international ramifications and its indirect influence on Japan.

## The International Situation

Although hailed with enthusiasm in Moscow and bitterly deplored in Washington, the Communist victory of 1949 was a Chinese achievement very little affected by the plans or proposals of the two great powers. Just as Mao disregarded Stalin's prognosis that the Chinese revolution had little prospect for early success, Chiang turned a deaf ear to American counsels. Neither leader was amenable to foreign direction or inclined to accept unwelcome foreign advice. Nevertheless, partly for ideological reasons and partly in response to continued although unenthusiastic American support for the Nanking government, the CCP aligned itself with the U.S.S.R. in a policy of "leaning to one side" enunciated by Mao in July 1949.

Although some American observers had taken the measure of Chiang Kai-shek's regime, large sectors of the American public continued to view him as China's savior, a view fostered by wartime propaganda and the efforts of ex-missionaries, politicians, and others who argued that China had been betrayed and that continued support for the KMT was best for the Chinese people as well as in the interest of the United States. Yet, there may well have been room for diplomatic accommodation between the People's Republic and the United States had not war broken out in Korea in June 1950.

The Korean War brought the United States into conflict with China on two fronts. First, President Truman ordered the American Seventh Fleet to patrol the Taiwan Strait, creating a buffer between the Communist government on the mainland and the Nationalist regime on Taiwan. This prevented Chiang Kai-shek from trying to invade the mainland, but it also prevented the Communists from extending their rule to the island. Indeed, the Communists viewed the move as extending American protection to the KMT in order to prevent reassertion of historic Chinese sovereignty over Taiwan under CCP

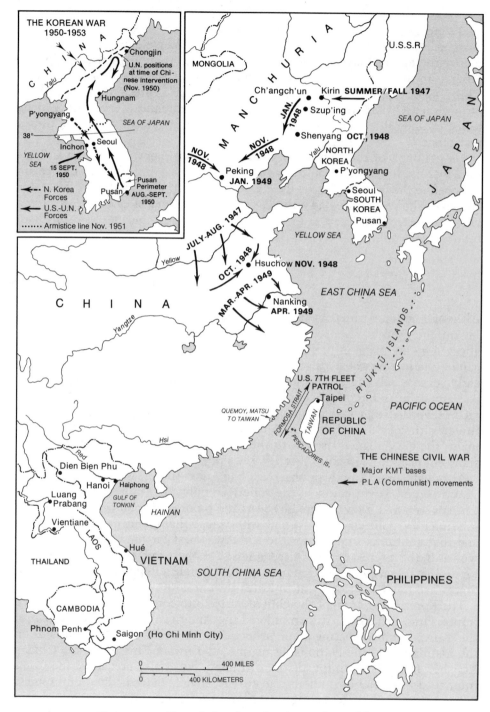

**THE KOREAN WAR
1950-1953**

Chongjin

U.N. positions
at time of Chi-
nese intervention
(Nov. 1950)

Hungnam

P'yongyang

*SEA OF JAPAN*

38°

Inchon · Seoul

*YELLOW
SEA*

15 SEPT.
1950

Pusan
Perimeter
AUG.-SEPT.
1950

Pusan

←--- N. Korea
Forces
← U.S.-U.N.
Forces
······· Armistice line Nov. 1951

*CHINA*

*Yalu*

MONGOLIA

Ch'angch'un · Kirin **SUMMER/FALL 1947**

**JAN. 1948** · Szup'ing

Shenyang **OCT. 1948**

**NOV. 1948**

*Yalu* **NORTH
KOREA**

· P'yongyang

· Seoul
**SOUTH
KOREA**
Pusan·

*SEA OF JAPAN*

**JAPAN**

**U.S.S.R.**

**M A N C H U R I A**

**NOV.
1948**

Peking
**JAN. 1949**

**JULY-AUG. 1947**

**OCT. 1948** · Hsuchow **NOV. 1948**

*YELLOW SEA*

**MAR.-APR. 1949**

Nanking
**APR. 1949**

*EAST CHINA SEA*

**C H I N A**

*Yangtze*

*Hsi*

U.S. 7TH FLEET
PATROL
· Taipei

*QUEMOY, MATSU
TO TAIWAN*

**REPUBLIC
OF CHINA**

*FORMOSA STRAIT*

*TAIWAN*

*PESCADORES IS.*

*RYŪKYŪ ISLANDS*

*PACIFIC OCEAN*

**THE CHINESE CIVIL WAR**

· Major KMT bases

← P L A (Communist) movements

*Red*

Dien Bien Phu

Hanoi · Haiphong

Luang
Prabang

*GULF OF
TONKIN*

Vientiane

*HAINAN*

· Hué

**THAILAND** **VIETNAM**

**LAOS**

*SOUTH CHINA SEA*

**PHILIPPINES**

**CAMBODIA**

Phnom Penh

· Saigon (Ho Chi Minh City)

0 ————— 400 MILES
0 ————— 400 KILOMETERS

Figure 11-2  **East Asia after the Second World War**

auspices. Second, as we shall see below, Chinese and American troops clashed head-on in Korea, after United Nations forces under General Douglas MacArthur approached the Yalu River, China's boundary with North Korea. After the Korean War, antagonism between Communist China and the United States hardened into the established foreign policy of both nations.

The United States came to the military assistance of the government of South Korea partly as a result of its worldwide policy of resisting the expansion of what American leaders then considered a monolithic Communist empire directed from Moscow. But what gave Korea its special importance, now as earlier, was its strategic location in respect to Japan. Therefore, before considering the Korean War further, it is important to consider what had been happening, in the meantime, in Japan.

## Japan under the Occupation

Japan was in ruins, cities largely destroyed, the economy wrecked. The devastation extended also to the psyche of the Japanese people, for whom the known world had ended in a cataclysm of destruction. Unprepared for defeat, they could not turn to their own history for guidance, for never before in historic times had their country been occupied by a foreign victor. They had no inkling what the future held in store for them. The whole nation now found itself in a psychological position not unlike that of the rare Japanese soldier who during the war, despite his best efforts and contrary to all expectation, found himself an American prisoner. Such men, their old orientations and expectations shattered, were usually most cooperative toward their former enemies, and the Japanese people too were disposed to cooperate with the Occupation authorities. In both cases, decent treatment of the defeated also helped. Thus, when defeat came, the Japanese evacuated many women to the countryside and even the government ordered its female employees out of town. It is not difficult to imagine people's relief when such measures turned out to have been unnecessary.

In theory the Occupation was placed under the authority of the Far Eastern Commission, which sat in Washington and whose members included representatives of all the countries that had fought Japan, but actual control was in American hands. The Japanese government continued to function but did so according to the directives and suggestions of the Occupation authorities, who assumed ultimate responsibility for governing Japan. At the head of the Occupation was General MacArthur, Supreme Commander for the Allied Powers (SCAP). Despite the reference to Allies in the title and the presence of some British and Commonwealth officials, the Occupation was essentially an American undertaking. In MacArthur it had a leader who won easy credibility among the Japanese, for he was a commanding figure, confident in his sense of historical mission, a military man who commanded respect and exuded confidence.

Among the initial and pressing tasks of the Occupation was the disarming of the Japanese military and the provision of relief to prevent famine. The widespread destruction of capital goods and industrial plants, a soil starved for lack of fertilizers, the loss of the natural resources from the former empire and of the entire mercantile fleet, and the need to provide for six million Japanese expatriates and refugees from overseas threatened economic catastrophe. In this situation, suffering was unavoidable. By supplying food and medical supplies, the Occupation authorities helped to avert the worst. But it was not until around 1947 that the Occupation, in the light of the emerging Cold War, became seriously concerned with rebuilding the Japanese economy, particularly Japanese industrial strength.

The basic long-term policy of the Occupation was to demilitarize Japan and turn the country into a peaceful and democratic state; or, we might say, "a peaceful because democratic state," reflecting the optimistic American belief that the one equaled the other. The American conviction of the righteousness of their political values, as well as confidence in the problem-solving powers of American "know-how," were important ingredients in the history of the Occupation.

Demilitarization entailed the dismantling of the military establishment and a purge of militarists from positions of leadership in government and business. Individuals charged with wartime brutality were placed on trial. At the top, twenty-eight leaders were charged with responsibility for the war and were brought to trial before an international tribunal in Tokyo, which sat from May 1946 to April 1948. When the sentences were handed down in November 1948, seven leaders were condemned to die. Foremost among them was Tōjō, the rather colorless general who had headed Japan's wartime government. His role during the war had been more like a chairman of the board than a dictator, but wartime propaganda had cast him as a Japanese Hitler, and it was as such that he was tried and condemned. The lengthy judicial proceedings produced voluminous records but never attained the legal clarity nor the moral authority achieved by the trial of Nazi leaders at Nuremberg.

The emperor was not charged with war crimes, but his person was subjected to a process of demythification. He was required to substitute a more open life style (akin to that of the British monarch, for example) for the secluded and ritualized existence traditionally led by Japanese emperors. An example of the demythification process was the emperor's unprecedented visit to MacArthur at his headquarters. The resulting photograph (Figure 11-3) showing the stiffly formal emperor standing next to the open-shirted general caused considerable shock and dismay throughout Japan. In his New Year's message of 1946 the emperor publicly and explicitly denied his divinity, and under the new constitution he became a symbol of the nation.

This constitution, which went into effect in May 1947, was practically dictated by the Occupation. It stipulated that sovereignty belongs to the people, placed the highest political authority in the hands of the Diet (to which the executive was now made responsible), and established an independent judi-

Figure 11-3  General Douglas MacArthur and the Emperor of Japan.

ciary. Another noteworthy set of political changes were those decreasing the power of the central government, particularly the Home Ministry, and fostering local self-government. Accompanying these structural changes were provisions for universal suffrage and human rights, including the equality of women. A unique feature was the renunciation of war that became Article IX of the constitution. This stipulates, "The Japanese people forever renounce war as a sovereign right of the nation and the threat or use of force as a means of settling international disputes" and goes on to say, "land, sea, and air forces, as well as other war potential, will never be maintained."[1] In this way the authors of the constitution hoped to incorporate peacefulness into the very framework of the new Japanese state.

The authorities at SCAP headquarters knew that Japan could not be turned into a democracy simply by changing the political system. Consequently they tried to change Japanese society itself and to do so in the relatively short time allotted to them. Since many American officials lacked previous study or experience in Japan and high military officials could be quite narrow in their outlook, there was a tendency to rely excessively on American prototypes without taking into sufficient account Japan's own experience and situation.

An example of limited success was the Occupation's reforms of the educational system. This was restructured to conform to the American sequence of elementary school, junior high school, high school, and college. The Japanese were forced to eliminate their old technical schools and special higher schools, which previously covered the eleventh to thirteenth years of education and prepared students for university study. Under the old system, only the student elite had access to a university education, but under the new, all students were to be given equal educational opportunities through high school. In an effort to expand opportunities for higher education, many of the old technical and higher schools were upgraded to become universities. But these new universities were not of a quality comparable to the old established schools like Tokyo University. Competition for admission to this and other prestigious universities remained brutal. Entrance examinations confronted students with an "examination hell" comparable to that which once faced the Chinese degree candidates; in both cases passing the examinations opened entry into the elite.

In order to reform the content of education, the Occupation abolished the old ethics courses and purged textbooks fostering old militaristic and authoritarian values. Its attack on these old values was rather successful, especially since they had in any case been largely discredited by defeat. It was rather less successful, however, in its attempt to create a positive sense of individual civic responsibility and citizenship.

Social change entails a transformation of values and thus naturally takes longer than institutional change, but changes in the legal system can encourage social change. Among the Occupation's notable efforts in this area were measures to enhance the status of women and limit the powers and privileges of the family's male head. The new constitution stated explicitly, "Marriage shall be based upon the mutual consent of both sexes, and it shall be maintained through mutual cooperation, with equal rights of husband and wife as a basis."[2] The presence of many thousands of Americans in their country also gave the Japanese an unusual opportunity to observe foreign mores. It may have encouraged them to become somewhat more relaxed toward authority and also stimulated a measure of cosmopolitanism.

It was generally recognized that the political and social changes desired by the Occupation demanded an economic foundation, and the authorities set about restructuring the Japanese economy. Most successful in this respect was the Occupation's program of land reform. This prohibited absentee landlordism and restricted the amount of land a resident landowner could hold to a maximum of 7½ acres to work himself and another 2½ acres to rent out (except in Hokkaidō where the average farm is twelve and one-half acres because the climate precludes intensive rice cultivation). Anything in excess had to be sold to the government, which resold it to former tenants. There was provision for compensation for the landlords, but inflation made this meaningless. The old inequity in the countryside was eliminated. In terms of productivity too, the land policy was a success, for the agrarian sector was the first to recover.

In the urban industrial sector, the Occupation tried to eliminate or at least to reduce the concentrations of economic power, which Americans viewed as a major component of Japanese authoritarianism. One policy was to foster labor unions. The constitution guaranteed "the right of workers to organize and to bargain and act collectively."[3] As intended, a vigorous union movement developed, but contrary to American wishes, the Japanese unions did not, like the American AFL and CIO, limit themselves to economic demands. Much like European unions, they were political in orientation, developing into labor arms of the Socialist and Communist parties. In February 1947, the Occupation banned a planned general strike and thereafter was less friendly toward the unions.

On the management and ownership side, the Occupation did break up the old holding companies and purged the old *zaibatsu* families from positions of economic leadership. Contrary to initial expectations, however, this did not lead to genuine decentralization. Where old systems were broken up, new and equally pervasive patterns of trade and finance developed, bearing a marked resemblance to the old. Furthermore, a plan to break up operating companies petered out: of 1200 companies initially considered, only 28 were, in the end, broken up. Economic power and decision making remained concentrated. The reasons for this are instructive for understanding the accomplishments and failures of the Occupation as a whole, for they include both a Japanese and an American component.

On the Japanese side, strong support for land reform contrasted with a marked lack of enthusiasm for American-style trust busting. Few shared the American faith in the ultimate benefits of maximum competition. Instead, the feeling was that Japanese companies needed to be large in order to compete in the international market. Radicals and conservatives disagreed about ownership and control, not about the structure of industry and commerce.

Decentralization of the economy also faltered because of a change in American policy. By 1948, developments in Russo-American relations and the turn of events in China made the rebuilding of Japanese economic strength a more important goal of American policy than economic reform. As the Cold War developed, the United States increasingly looked upon Japan (as on Germany) as a potentially valuable ally. Since an armed ally, capable at least of self-defense, would be more valuable than one unarmed, the United States now also had second thoughts about Japan's total renunciation of military force.

The United States also sought to end the Occupation—an idea MacArthur broached as early as 1947. In 1947 the United States approached the Far Eastern Commission to draft a peace treaty, but this diplomatic move failed largely because of Russian opposition.

The Occupation continued, but by July 1950, when MacArthur took command over the United Nations Forces in Korea, the work of the Occupation was practically complete. The next two years were little more than a holding operation awaiting the conclusion of peace. This was finally accomplished after the signing of a peace treaty in September 1951, an event which took place without Russian participation. (Relations with Russia were normalized in 1956.)

An assessment of the Occupation must naturally take into account the history of the post-Occupation years (see Chapter 12) when the Japanese could again make their own decisions concerning their society and its institutions. However, it is possible to draw a few preliminary conclusions. Perhaps the most significant of these is that the Occupation was most successful where Japanese precedents and Japanese support were available for its programs. Although the Occupation authorities failed to realize it, this was true of much of their political program, their plan for land reform, and their advocacy of liberal values. Representative institutions, after all, went back to the early Meiji period, and demands for land reform, for equality, and for a rejection of authoritarianism all predated the rise of Japanese militarism. Thus, despite the Occupation's misconceptions and mistakes and despite the contradiction inherent in a plan to foster democracy by command, much of what the Occupation attempted did actually take hold.

The Occupation also had unplanned side effects, including the influx of foreign culture. Intellectuals eager to catch up with the recent Western developments devoured translations of Western books, and popular culture was equally open to foreign influence. In some respects the scene resembled that after the First World War, and it is well to remember that it did not take the Occupation to introduce the Japanese to baseball and jazz. However, this time change went deeper, and there was to be no radical turning away such as took place in the thirties.

The constitution has remained in effect, and if Japan did not develop exactly along the lines envisioned by the Occupation authorities, neither was there a reversion to authoritarianism. Whether the Occupation merely hastened inevitable changes or served as a catalyst without which Japanese history would have developed very differently remains a subject of scholarly disagreement and dispute. What we might note here, however, is the contrast between the comparative American success in Japan and the total failure of United States policy in China. In both countries, the Korean War confirmed the direction of internal development as well as international orientation.

## Postwar Korea

Korea's last decade under Japanese rule was in many ways a bitter one. The Japanese relentlessly stamped out Korean nationalism, sending its leaders into prison, exile, or underground activities. In the late thirties the Japanese expanded their suppression of political nationalism into an attack on Korean cultural identity. In line with a policy of total forced cultural assimilation, they stopped Korean language instruction in all secondary schools in 1938, and soon elementary schools followed suit. No longer could Korean children learn their own language in school; the use of Japanese was mandatory. In 1940 the Korean press was closed down. The Japanese made strong efforts to propagate the official State Shinto. To help the war effort they first launched a movement of voluntary conscription. Then, in 1943, military service became compulsory. At the same time, the Koreans had to bear the hardships and deprivations of war.

During the war, the United States and the Soviet Union agreed on the 38th parallel as a dividing line: north of this line the Japanese forces would surrender to Soviet troops; south of the parallel they would submit to the United States. Perhaps the 38th parallel was selected by Pentagon officers in order to assure the inclusion of Seoul in the American zone. In any case when the Soviet army entered the peninsula three weeks before the Americans, they abided by the agreement. What was not clear at the time was that this was to become a semipermanent dividing line.

In the north the Soviet army backed the creation of a Communist state under Kim Il-sung (1912–), a former leader of Korean guerrilla fighters in Manchuria who had spent some time in the U.S.S.R. and now entered Korea as a major in the Soviet army. Gradually Kim overcame factionalism among Korean revolutionaries and fashioned a party and government along Soviet lines. Officials and policemen who had served the Japanese were purged. Industry was nationalized with minimal opposition, since it had mostly been owned by Japanese. Land reform followed, and a start was made in economic planning. And a military force was created.

In the south the American army did not arrive until three weeks after the end of the war. The American military government then refused to recognize an existing interim government, suspecting it of pro-Communist or pro-Japanese leanings. The initial American policy was to await the outcome of negotiations for unification, and there seemed hope that these would reach an early settlement when the United States and the Soviet Union agreed on a joint commission to supervise a five-year period of transition to independence of a unified Korea. This plan, however, ran into the vociferous opposition of a group of Korean nationalists who demanded immediate unification, and when the Soviet Union wanted to bar such men from participating in scheduled elections, Soviet-American cooperation came to an end.

The United States then initiated moves to give South Korea a representative government and in the meantime allowed the economic status quo to persist. Since the Japanese had effectively suppressed organized political activity, there was at the end of the war something of a political vacuum. The victor in the battle over who was to fill that vacuum was Syngman Rhee (Yi Sung-man, 1875–1965), a longtime Christian Nationalist who had suffered seven years' imprisonment as a young man. Forced to leave Korea in 1911, he had lived in exile (mostly in Hawaii) before returning to his native land after Japan's defeat. A strong advocate of immediate unification, Rhee was an eloquent speaker and a capable organizer. He was also strongly antileftist. In August 1948, the septuagenarian Rhee became president of the Republic of Korea, and American military government came to an end. Thus Korea was divided into two mutually hostile parts.

# The Korean War

Increasing international tensions between the United States and the Soviet Union as well as bitter hostility between the governments of North and South Korea reduced the chances for unification by negotiation. Both the Communist state in the north and the anti-Communist government in the south harbored the ambition to rule over the entire country. These ambitions erupted into war in June 1950, when North Korea attacked the south.

The period of intense fighting can be divided into three main phases, each with its own subdivisions. First, from June to September 1950, the North Koreans were on the offensive, pushing the South Korean and American forces back until they established a defense perimeter around Pusan from which they could not be dislodged. The second phase began with MacArthur's amphibious landing at Inchon in September, which led to the recapture of Seoul and then to an offensive intended to unify Korea by force. Then, in November, the Chinese, alarmed by the American advance to the Yalu River, and having had their warnings ignored, sent massive "volunteer" armies into Korea. These succeeded in regaining the north but were unable to win control over the south. This became clear in late May 1951, and in July of that year truce talks began. Earlier, in April, President Truman had dismissed General MacArthur, thereby making it clear that America would not extend the war beyond Korea. His dismissal of the eminent and popular general also demonstrated the American system of civil control over the military, a demonstration which had considerable impact in Japan.

Casualties in this war were heavy on both sides. They included over 800 thousand Koreans (approximately 520 thousand North Koreans and 300 thousand South Koreans) and probably as many or more Chinese soldiers. The southern forces were sanctioned by the United Nations and fought under a United Nations command, but approximately half of the ground troops in addition to most of the air and naval forces were supplied by the United States, which suffered 142 thousand casualties. South Korea supplied two-fifths of the remaining United Nations troops, and thirteen other countries combined to make up the remainder.

The truce talks dragged on for two years until an armistice was signed in July 1953. Although marred by incidents, this armistice still remains in effect today. For the long-suffering Korean people, so recently freed from very harsh Japanese rule, the cruel war accomplished nothing: their country remained divided essentially as before, only more bitterly.

# International Relations after the Korean War

The Korean War did not alter the international configuration of power in East Asia, but it did considerably embitter Sino-American relations. Both sides were now more convinced than ever of the enmity of the other. In the United

States, proponents of a moderate China policy were removed from influence and subjected to slander. The American commitment to the Nationalist regime was confirmed. Taiwan was given economic and military assistance, and in 1954 the United States signed a mutual defense treaty with the government of Chiang Kai-shek. Meanwhile, American troops remained in Korea. The United States also retained bases in Japan and on Okinawa, for the conclusion of a peace treaty with Japan was accompanied by the signing of a defense agreement. The Chinese, alarmed by these developments, were convinced of their wisdom in allying themselves with the U.S.S.R. The formal basis of the relationship between the two countries was provided by a treaty of friendship and alliance they had signed in February 1950 directed at preventing a revival of Japanese aggression. While the Chinese viewed America as an imperialist aggressor, throughout the 1950s many people in the United States, even those in high places, considered the People's Republic to be little more than a Soviet satellite.

If the Korean War merely solidified alliances already in the making and froze the participants into their Cold War postures, it did enhance China's international status by demonstrating the ability of her peasant army, a bare year after the triumph of the revolution, to resist the formidable armed might of the United States. Among those impressed with the caliber of the Chinese military were the authors of the official U.S. Marine Corps history, who found much to admire in the Chinese style of semiguerrilla warfare, with its emphasis on infiltration, deception, and surprise. Within China, the Korean War helped the government to mobilize the people under the banner of national resistance, and it created its share of national heroes. Above all, it meant that the revolution had now been tested in foreign as well as domestic war.

For Japan the war brought profitable orders for equipment and supplies, which provided a substantial stimulant to what was still a faltering economy. Even after the war, orders to supply American troops and bases continued to benefit the Japanese economy. Under American encouragement, Japan also created a paramilitary force of 75,000, a first step toward limited rearmament. In the peace treaty, signed with the United States in San Francisco in September 1951 and ratified the following April, Japan was restored to full sovereignty. The basic pattern of internal economic growth and dependence on the United States for ultimate military protection was set. During the fifties and sixties Japan continued to take its foreign policy cues from the United States.

During the years after the Korean War, both China and Japan were able to concentrate on domestic development, although this always took place within the parameters of the Cold War. The two leading countries of East Asia, of course, remained keenly aware of each other, but they had little to do with each other. Kept apart by Japan's alliance with the United States, oriented toward contrasting models of social and economic development, influenced by different ideologies, they interacted only sporadically and then in a limited way.

# Korea after the Truce

On both sides of the 38th parallel, the mutually hostile Korean governments maintained large military establishments. In the north, with about 55 percent of Korea's land area and a population which is now around 16 million, there are about 495 thousand men in the well-equipped military establishment (army, navy, air force), and this does not include paramilitary personnel such as the security forces and border guards. For South Korea, with a population of 34 million, the comparable figure is 670 thousand men under arms (army, navy, marines, air force). In both states the possibility of renewed hostilities also provided a rationale for the concentration of power in the hands of political strongmen.

The government of North Korea remained under the firm control of Kim Il-sung, who became the focus of a personality cult as intense as any in world history. When relations between China and the Soviet Union deteriorated, North Korea was able to pursue an independent line between them, and it remains an intensely nationalistic state. In keeping with its ideological objectives, the government in 1958 restructured agriculture, organizing cooperatives of about three hundred families and one thousand acres each. Industrialization, begun by the Japanese, continued to expand. Despite heavy military expenses, material conditions gradually improved for the people of North Korea. However, for many years, North Korea remained virtually closed to non-Communist outsiders, and even under the less strained international situation of the 1970s, it remains a country little known to the outside world.

South Korea was under the authoritarian rule of Syngman Rhee for a total of twelve years (1948–60), until he was overthrown by widespread and persistent student riots provoked by outrage at government repression and corruption, including dishonest elections. A brief ten months of multiparty liberal government came to an end in 1961 when the military carried out a coup under the leadership of General Park Chung-hee (1917–1979), who had been a second lieutenant in the Japanese army in Manchuria at the end of the Second World War. (Despite Rhee's bitter hostility toward Japan, in South Korea there had been no purge of Koreans who had served the Japanese.) In 1963 a constitution was enacted, elections were held, and Park became president. This initiated a system of presidential rule backed by military force, but the government frequently resorted to the suppression of dissent and the repression of its critics, including the imprisonment of political opponents. Park's assassination in 1979 was followed by a brief period of political liberalization, but then a new military strongman emerged. General Chun Doo Hwan (1931–) assumed the presidency in 1980 and put the country under martial law, with dissenting views suppressed once again.

Economically the new regime, which, like its predecessor, is allied to big business, hopes for a resumption of economic growth. During the first ten years or so following the Korean War, the economic priority of the South Korean government was reconstruction and rehabilitation, which was accomplished with American assistance. In the mid-sixties this was followed by a period of rapid economic growth. In 1965, Park, despite student opposition, signed a treaty of recognition and reparations with Japan, and since then Japan has played an increasingly important role in the South Korean economy, supplying capital and goods and marketing Korean-made products. When wages rose in Japan, many labor-intensive plants were attracted to Korea. Economic growth did not benefit all equally. Fast growing cities suffered from poor urban planning, and centralized administration from Seoul did not help. Land reforms carried out in the late forties and fifties left many rural poor with insufficient land for self-support.

After more than thirty-five years of division, peaceful reunification appears as much out of reach as ever. In the North, Kim Il-sung, although a professed Marxist, is grooming his son to succeed him, while in the South, the government rules with little regard for the sensibilities of its American allies. Both governments maintain large armies but ultimately rely on their powerful allies to extend military assistance in case they are attacked, for Korea's strategic importance is clear to all concerned.

# Vietnam

Comparison of Vietnamese history with that of Korea reveals significant similarities as well as differences and may help to put their postwar histories into perspective. In both countries the traditional rulers and elite looked to China as a model of organization and a source of high culture, but in both cases political independence from China was jealously guarded and cultural identity maintained. In modern times both Korea and Vietnam, after unsuccessful Chinese intervention, experienced a period of colonial rule (under the Japanese and the French) that strained and distorted traditional society and failed to prepare the countries for independence. Then, after the Second World War, both suffered division into two mutually hostile states, each supported by rival international power blocks. In both cases bitter warfare between northern and southern divisions ensued, and in each case massive American participation in aid of the south was a major factor.

On the other hand, Korea and Vietnam differ in climate, terrain, and internal geographic configuration; and in their wider cultural and regional settings. Korea's neighbors are China, Japan, and the Soviet Union, whereas Vietnam is a major power in Southeast Asia. Furthermore, there were differences in their experiences under colonialism. For one thing, the Japanese were much closer to the Koreans culturally, geographically, and even in physical appearance than were the French to the Vietnamese. And Japan and France were, of course, countries with very different histories and traditions. The present situation of the two lands is also different: Korea remains divided whereas Vietnam is now a unified nation.

French policy in Vietnam was not consistent over the years, and it also differed in the north and the south, but in neither area did it provide a viable fusion of either the modern and the traditional or the foreign and native. In the center (Annam) and the north (Tonkin) the French maintained "protectorates" with parallel French and Vietnamese systems of administration, although the French had superior authority. Under this arrangement the French maintained the Nguyen emperor in Hue with the result that the throne failed to become a symbol of Vietnamese nationalism. Even the examination system, modeled on that of China, was retained until 1919 by what Alexander Woodside has aptly termed, "the embalming agency of colonialism."[4] The south (Cochin China), in contrast, was governed as a full colony on French lines by French and French-oriented officials.

The difference between north and south extended also to economic organization. In the south, plantations (rice and rubber) developed, creating great economic inequities and dependence on the vagaries of the international market. The northern lowlands were an area of small fragmented holdings, but here too life became very hard as population growth created great and increasing pressures on the land.

In the beginning, resistance to the French came from members of the traditional elite, and it is noteworthy that men of mandarin (elite) background continued to figure prominently in the leadership of Vietnam's national and social revolutions. An important nationalist leader who shared this background was Phan Boi Chao (1867–1940), who studied with Liang Ch'i-ch'ao in Japan and hoped to transform Vietnam into a modern state along the lines of Meiji Japan. Japan was also admired by the founders of the Free School of Tonkin, in Hanoi, modeled on Keiō University. Here a romanized script was used in place of Chinese characters, the examination system was attacked, and modern political and social ideas were disseminated. Opened in 1907, it lasted less than a year before it was forcibly closed by the French.

The French could repress radical ideas, suppress insurrections, arrest, imprison, or execute their enemies, but they could not breathe life into moribund social and political structures. Nor could they restrict the import of Western ideas to Catholicism: Paris itself was, after all, a major center of Western radicalism. During the First World War 100,000 Vietnamese served in France as soldiers and laborers. Many returned to their native land ready to question the continued legitimacy of colonial rule. The most famous Vietnamese to be influenced by a stay in France was Ho Chi Minh (Nguyen That Thanh, 1890–1969). Ho was already a nationalist before he arrived in France, but it was in Paris that he complemented his nationalism by fusing it with Marxism.

Ho's status in the Vietnamese Revolution is comparable to that of Mao Tse-tung in China, but the Vietnamese leader differed from the Chinese not only in having extensive overseas experience but also in coming from an impoverished but nonetheless distinctly scholar-official family. His father eventually became a district magistrate. In 1911 Ho left Vietnam as a seaman and after a period of travel spent a crucial six years (1917–23) in France, supporting himself as a gardener, sweeper, waiter, photograph retoucher, and oven stoker. He also became a convinced Marxist and assisted in the founding of the French Communist Party. Subsequently he went to Moscow and was then sent by the

Comintern to assist Borodin in Canton. However, Ho's interest always remained focused on his native Vietnam. In 1930 he succeeded in fusing various groups into the Communist Party of Vietnam (soon changed to Indo-China).

Strong ideological foundations, powerful international models, and especially dedication to organizing grass-roots support in the villages were some of the factors that gave the Communists an advantage in their competition for leadership of Vietnam's national revolution. However, in the south, highly organized syncretic religious movements such as the Cao Dai and Hoa Hao sects supplied many of the same social, organizational, and psychological needs. Furthermore, on the eve of the Second World War in the Pacific, the Communists were beset by factionalism.

But this changed after 1941 when Ho organized a broad anticolonial movement known as the Viet Minh (more formally, the League for the Independence of Vietnam). The purpose of this organization, established with Nationalist Chinese support, was to resist both the Japanese who occupied Vietnam in 1941 and the French (adherents to the puppet regime established by the Germans at Vichy), whom the Japanese kept in office until they removed them in March 1945.

From a base along the Chinese border, the Viet Minh expanded their military and political influence to the Red Delta and beyond. They built up an effective military force under the command of General Vo Nguyen Giap (1912–), who had studied guerrilla warfare techniques in Yenan. During the war the demands of Vietnam's new masters created increased economic hardships. In Tonkin, in 1940, between 400,000 and 2 million people starved to death, having been deprived of the rice reserves necessary to combat famine.

When Japan surrendered in August 1945, the Viet Minh were the most effective force in the land. On August 26 Ho Chi Minh proclaimed an independent Vietnam in Hanoi. The French, however, had other ideas, and Ho lacked the resources to prevent them from reestablishing their presence in Vietnam.

## The Vietnam War (1946–1975)

The Vietnam War can be divided into two wars: one fought against the French (1946–54) and a second in which the United States became a principal party.

The first war began in 1946 after negotiations had revealed the gulf separating the Viet Minh, dedicated to achieving national independence, and the French, seeking to recover former glory and adamant in their refusal to relinquish their empire. As the fighting continued, the Cold War developed, and the Communist character of the Viet Minh came more to the fore while the French tried to attract non-Communist nationalist support by sponsoring a regime under the former emperor Bao Dai. This, however, won little support from the Vietnamese people. Furthermore, the French made little military headway against an enemy who knew the terrain and had the support of the civilian population. They committed 420,000 troops to Vietnam not counting another

200,000 in the Vietnamese army, but the end came in April-May 1954 when Giap, with the aid of artillery laboriously transported over the mountains, vanquished the French at the famous battle of Dien Bien Phu.

Negotiations at Geneva led to the partition of Vietnam at the 17th parallel into a Communist dominated state with its capital at Hanoi and a southern state ruled from Saigon. Nationwide elections were agreed upon for 1956.

The elections, however, were never held, for they were blocked, with American support, by the head of the Saigon government. This was Ngo Diehm Diem (1901–63), a Catholic Nationalist whose government lacked popular roots and administrative efficacy. In 1963 his government was overthrown and Diem* himself was killed in the coup. By that time the United States had 17,000 troops in Vietnam to assist in what the American government viewed as the containment of world communism.

The removal of the unpopular and aloof Diem and his corrupt family did not result in any marked improvements in government, which beginning in 1965, was in military hands. While the Saigon government remained autocratic, ineffective, and corrupt, the insurgents gained ground. Leadership of the southern revolutionaries was now exercised by the National Liberation Front (NLF), organized in December 1960.† The NLF was supported by the North Vietnamese, and there was logistic aid from the Soviet Union and China.

The Chinese continued to give moral and material support to their Vietnamese allies but, unlike the United States, did not send troops. American involvement meanwhile increased. Leading American policymakers justified this by drawing historical analogies from the appeasement of Germany and Japan in the thirties, when they might better have drawn lessons from the Japanese experience in China or the fall of Chiang Kai-shek. An elaboration of this approach was the "domino theory," which held that if Vietnam fell to communism the other countries of Southeast Asia would follow suit, toppling one by one like a row of dominoes. Furthermore, the United States government treated the war not as a civil war but as a case of combating "northern aggression." After gaining Senate support in the Tonkin Gulf Resolution (1964), President Johnson ordered the bombing of North Vietnam (February 1965). By July 1965, there were 70,000 American troops in Vietnam. The number continued to increase until early in 1968, when there were 510,000. In addition, Vietnam underwent the most massive bombing in history. As American involvement in Vietnam increased, the horrors of the war were brought home to the American people by casualty lists and by the sight of gruesome destruction of Vietnamese people and villages, which they witnessed daily on their television screens. At the same time, the American government was increasingly unable to justify

---

* Like Chinese, Japanese, and Korean names, Vietnamese names are written with the surname first. However, probably because certain surnames are extremely frequent, it is customary to refer to people by their personal names. An exception is made for Ho Chi Minh, actually a pseudonym.

† In the United States both the Front and its supporters were known as "Vietcong," an abbreviation of "Vietnamese communism" or "Vietnamese Communist."

the war to its own people. And the bombings and destruction reinforced the will of Vietnamese revolutionaries on both sides to persist in their struggle.

In February 1968 it became apparent that the American effort, despite its greater destructiveness, had destroyed neither the will nor the ability of the revolutionaries to continue to fight. That month they launched an offensive in which they attacked over one hundred cities. This show of strength prompted a reexamination of American policy, and the United States began to withdraw its troops from Vietnam. However, apparently in an attempt to bolster the Saigon regime, President Nixon in 1970 widened the war to include Cambodia and Laos. It was not easy for an American president to withdraw without "victory," but strong domestic pressures as well as the situation in Vietnam left him little choice. Finally an agreement was reached in Paris, and the last American military personnel left Vietnam in March 1973.

The war continued for another two years, but the outcome was a foregone conclusion to anyone who calculated military strength, not in terms of official statistics and armaments, but in terms of such factors as the participants' will to fight, the political credibility of the leadership, and the attitude of the people. Saigon fell in April 1975. In 1976 the establishment of the Socialist Republic of Vietnam, with its capital in Hanoi, was proclaimed. Saigon was renamed Ho Chi Minh City.

The early years of the unified state were difficult. Faced with the prospect of transfer to the countryside, numerous city dwellers, many of them ethnic Chinese, fled the country. This was just one factor in the deterioration of relations between China and a Vietnam that looked toward the Soviet Union for international support. Sino-Vietnamese relations were further strained by hostilities between Vietnam and the Chinese-supported Khmer Rouge regime established in 1975 in Cambodia (now called Kampuchea). In December 1978 Vietnam invaded Cambodia, proceeded to occupy most of the country, and installed a client government in Phnom Penh. This regime placed highest priority on subduing the remnants of the Khmer Rouge forces, who continued to wage guerilla warfare with the help of arms supplied by China. Meanwhile, the people of Cambodia, already decimated by the hardships and brutalities inflicted on them during the Khmer Rouge years, faced starvation on a massive scale while the world looked on in horror and international relief agencies did what they could. Thus, by a cruel twist of history, millions of Cambodians became the ultimate victims of a chain of events that had originated beyond their borders and over which they had little influence.

## NOTES

1. Article IX of the Constitution. A convenient source is David John Lu, *Sources of Japanese History* (New York: McGraw-Hill, 1975), 2:193–97. Article IX is reproduced on p. 194.

2. Article XXIV of the Constitution. Lu, 2:195.

3. Article XXVIII of the Constitution. Lu, 2:195.

4. Alexander B. Woodside, *Community and Revolution in Modern Vietnam* (Boston: Houghton Mifflin, 1976), p. 3.

**Key Dates**

# 12 Contemporary Japan: 1952–Present

The Economy
Politics
Social Change and the Quality of Life
The Japanese Film
The Visual Arts
Literature
The Seventies

In the quarter century following the end of the Occupation, Japan achieved phenomenal economic growth and became one of the world's industrial giants. By the 1970s Japan possessed the most advanced technology. Unfortunately the country also possessed some of the most characteristic problems of the modern industrial state: most notably, the widespread pollution that contaminated what was once pure air and clear water.

Industrialization and urbanization on an unprecedented scale have left their mark on every aspect of Japanese life. The forces of modernity are testing old values and ideas, traditional forms of social organization, long-accepted patterns of life, and previously unquestioned beliefs. At issue over the past quarter century has been the ultimate identity of Japan. To what extent would new social, political, and economic forces ultimately reshape Japanese society in the image of other economically advanced countries? Would Japan once again display an ability to work out creative adaptations of foreign borrowings?

The answers to these questions are not yet available, but during the period under consideration Japan did not become a "typical" modern society, if such exists, for its people continued to respond in new and interesting ways to the challenge of working out a satisfactory blend of new and old; a challenge which characterizes the entire period since Japan first embarked on extensive change in Meiji times. Indeed, it is the juxtaposition and interweaving of old and new that continues to make Japan both fascinating and unique.

# The Economy

The Japanese economy made tremendous gains during the Korean War, largely through producing goods and services needed to support the American war effort there. By 1953, economic production had practically returned to pre–Second World War levels, although the country's trade volume was still only half of what it had been previously. After 1954, the economic surge continued, transforming recovery into growth. The annual GNP (gross national product—the total goods and services produced by a nation) rose an average of roughly 9 percent per year from 1954 to 1961, followed by an even higher rate (over 11 percent) during the 1960s. GNP figures are admittedly very rough indices, but they are useful for measuring broad trends in national economic activity, and for comparing the performance of national economies. For example, in the United States, an advanced industrial nation with a mature economy, a more modest annual growth rate in the GNP is considered quite satisfactory; most economists would probably agree that an 11 percent growth rate would be inappropriate for the United States. But the comparison is a useful way of underscoring the truly remarkable vitality of Japan's "economic miracle."

Not only did Japan's industrial output increase in quantity, it also changed qualitatively, as old industries were transformed and new ones developed. During the fifties, with government support, great strides were made in heavy industry—despite the fact that Japan lacks raw materials and is poor in energy resources. For example, by building manufacturing plants in port cities, which provided the advantage of low-cost ocean transport, and through the sophisticated application of modern technologies, Japan was able to become the world's leading shipbuilder and the third largest producer of iron and steel (after the United States and the Soviet Union). With heavy industry well established, Japan then concentrated on such high-technology fields as electronics and developed a host of strong modern industries. Cars and television sets, computers and cameras, watches and even pianos—it is difficult to think of a major branch of consumer technology in which Japan has failed to excel.

Some of these products were built by new companies, such as Sony or Honda, founded by entrepreneurs who took advantage of the opportunities offered by postwar economic dislocation to build up new enterprises from scratch. Other ambitious men reorganized or rejuvenated older companies, often importing technology by buying rights to foreign patents. In the dominant position in the economy, however, familiar old names reappeared, including Mitsui, the world's oldest major firm, as well as Mitsubishi, Sumitomo, and others.

The names were old, but they now designated a new kind of economic grouping rather than the family centered *zaibatsu* of the prewar period. Each group included financial institutions (a bank, insurance company, and so forth), a real estate firm, and a cluster of companies engaged in every conceivable line of business, where the main competitor was most likely a member of a rival group. The activities of the various member firms of each group were coordinated in periodic meetings of their presidents in presidents' clubs. Interlocking directorships, mutual stock holdings, and internal loans further held the organizations together, although more loosely than in the old *zaibatsu*. However, the enterprise groupings continued to grow in size and strength until in the mid-seventies a study by Japan's Fair Trade Commission found that the six major groupings, composed of a total of 175 core companies, held 21.9 percent of all the capital in Japan and had a controlling interest in another 3095 corporations that held 26.1 percent of the nation's capital. To this must be added their substantial investments in other companies that they can influence without controlling.

Among the member firms of these enterprise groupings the most spectacular were trading companies (*shōsha*) that conducted their business not only at home but all over the world: exporting and importing, transporting and storing, financing and organizing a host of multifarious projects—an airport in Kenya, a large commercial farm on Sumatra, a petrochemical industry for Iran, or copper mining in Zaire. One of the greatest assets of these companies is their command of information gathered from throughout the world. Thus the Mitsui trading company has computers in Tokyo, New York, and London that exchange information automatically and are connected with 112 Mitsui offices in 75 countries plus another 44 offices in Japan. It is an information gathering network more extensive than that of any other private organization and larger than those operated by most governments. Furthermore, Mitsui, Mitsubishi, and the others have their own research organizations analyzing information, charting future trends, and drawing up plans to provide for future project recommendations. Their experts are engaged in city planning, energy research, research into the world's oceans and other major investigations that are likely to influence the future lives of people not only in Japan but in many parts of the world.

At the other end of the size scale from the trading companies and the huge economic groupings are the small concerns, which had for so long given the Japanese economy its dual, semitraditional, semimodern, structure. During the sixties and seventies, the small traditional enterprises steadily lost ground. They found it difficult to compete for labor with the larger firms, which could afford to pay higher wages and offer greater job security, paid for out of the increased productivity achieved by workers in modern well equipped plants.

Similar to the decline of the traditional small firms was a dramatic drop in the agricultural labor force without any corresponding decrease in production. Instead, technological improvements, including mechanization and the development of new seeds, made possible an increase in yield even as fewer people toiled in the fields. Much of Japan's rice was now grown by women and the elderly while a family's prime wage earner went to work in an urban factory.

The transformation of the Japanese economy would not have been possible without the dedicated efforts of the nation's blue- and white-collar workers. Labor unions, organized into two large confederations, did subscribe to radical theories. They did send their members into the streets with red headbands and Marxist slogans during the annual spring offensives for higher wages. However, most unions were also enterprise unions, that is, they were composed of all the workers employed in a single firm rather than all those in the same industry or line of work. Such unions included office as well as production workers and tended to be more cooperative with management than unions in most other industrialized countries.

Worker identification with individual firms was furthered by a pattern of lifetime employment, although companies did hire temporary workers when needed. The expectation of lifelong employment was also an important factor securing the loyalty of managerial personnel. On both the worker and the management level, loyalty to the firm was quite frequently strengthened by feelings of personal obligation, as, for instance, between an employee and a more senior man who had helped him to obtain his position. In contrast to the situation in most industrial countries, even highly trained men in Japan tended to think of themselves not as members of a particular profession (engineers, accountants, and so forth) but rather as members of a particular firm.

Japanese companies provided varied services and facilities for their employees, including company dormitories for the unmarried. There were company athletic teams and a host of recreational activities, such as organized outings to mountain retreats. These were intended to foster not only the health and well-being of the employees but also to strengthen feelings of group solidarity and identification with the sponsoring firm, which used them to convey an image of paternalistic solicitude. It was, of course, in the companies' interest to keep alive as long as possible the old values that had assured Meiji enterprises as well as Tokugawa merchant houses of the loyal devotion of their servants. Yet, it is important not to exaggerate their effectiveness nor to overemphasize the traditional aspects of Japanese labor relations, for company extras increasingly became matters not of traditionalistic paternalism but rather of contractual rights subject to collective bargaining, like fringe benefits in other countries.

Other signs indicated that, gradually, non-work-related activities and relationships were gaining in importance in the workers' lives even as industry's quest for economic efficiency was weakening the nexus of personal relationships which had long prevailed at work. At the same time, managerial personnel continued to receive intensive training and indoctrination in order to imbue them with company ways and spirit. Thus at Toyota, Japan's leading automobile manufacturer, white-collar men are given an entire year of training, including a month in a company camp. Recruitment patterns centered on certain universities, ties between men entering a company in the same year, an emphasis on longevity in promotions, the practice of extensive consultation, and a strong preference for decision by consensus all helped foster management solidarity.

For the most part, Japanese companies, especially the large modern concerns, retained the loyalty of their employees, who were made to feel that what was best for the company was also best for Japan. This business ideology gained credence from management's practice of plowing earnings back into the firm so that it could continue to grow and hopefully surpass its rivals. Since that rather than any increase in payouts to stockholders was the company's objective, management was long able to persuade workers to moderate their demands for wage increases and fringe benefits. Naturally, the threat of foreign competition was also used to good effect, and for many years Japanese companies enjoyed a lower labor bill and greater labor peace than many of their competitors in Europe and America. The threat of foreign competition helped to motivate employees to work harder at a time when the quest for increased GNP gave Japan a sense of national purpose.

Government in many ways helped to advance that purpose. Because of popular sentiment, constitutional constrictions, and the country's reliance on an American "nuclear umbrella," Japan was now freed from the burden of supporting a large and costly military establishment. Funds and energies were thus released for economic development.

More positively, the government fostered growth through its own policies. It did this not only by establishing a political climate favorable to economic expansion and by adopting appropriate fiscal and monetary policies but also by setting production targets, assigning priorities, and generally orchestrating the economy. At the center of the government's economic apparatus were the Finance Ministry and the Ministry of International Trade and Industry. The importance of the latter reflects the crucial role of foreign trade in Japan's economy and the determination of the government to oversee the country's economic as well as political relations with other countries. By deploying foreign exchange allocations, manipulating quotas, and establishing barriers protecting native capital from foreign competition, the government could channel the flow of investment funds according to its priorities. It could also extend or deny tax privileges. It thus had at its disposal a variety of weapons to bring recalcitrant firms into line if and when persuasion and/or pressures exerted by adverse publicity failed. Generally, however, it preferred to rely on discussion and to act as much as possible on the basis of a shared government-business consensus.

Such a consensus was possible because government and business shared common aims, and government support was a major asset for firms engaged in international competition. It was facilitated by business concentration and also by ties between government and the business community. Some of these ties were personal, for the men at the top in the private sector and those heading the influential and prestigious government ministries tended to share similar backgrounds (both included a high proportion of Tokyo University graduates). Some of the ties were ideological, since Japan was ruled during these years by conservatives. And some of the links were financial, for elections were costly and business constituted a major source of funds for conservative politicians.

# Politics

Under the Occupation electoral politics was reintroduced, and political parties representing a broad range of ideas and a variety of interests battled for votes. The Diet again became the central arena for national politics. The general trend favored conservatives.

The leading political personality to emerge during the Occupation was Yo-shida Shigeru (1878–1967), a former diplomat who had opposed the military leadership in Japan during the thirties. Yoshida dominated Japanese politics for the better part of a decade, serving as prime minister in 1946–47, and again from 1948 to 1954. A coalition of conservatives and socialists of various shades of radicalism held power briefly in 1947–48, but it was unable to create a viable government, partly because of divisions within its own ranks, and partly because of Occupation hostility toward socialism. Upon reassuming the prime ministership, Yoshida called a new election. Held in 1949, it provided his Liberal party with an absolute majority. He remained in office until he was forced to resign in 1954 in the wake of a scandal involving the shipping industry.

In foreign affairs Yoshida's policy was pro-American and anti-Communist. In 1951 he signed the San Francisco peace treaty for Japan, officially terminating the state of belligerancy between Japan and the United States. In domestic affairs Yoshida was a conservative. His policies favored business and economic development. In 1950 he received permission from the Occupation to form a National Police Reserve of 75,000 men, a paramilitary force that assumed responsibility for internal security, thus releasing American troops for duty in Korea. In 1953 this was expanded to form the Self-Defense Forces.

Ever since the resumption of party politics under the Occupation there had been rival conservative parties, and Yoshida as prime minister had his conservative critics. However, the main opposition to Yoshida's policies came from the Socialists, who in 1951 divided into left- and right-wing parties. In 1955, after Yoshida's downfall, they reunited in their quest for political power, but again split into two parties in 1959. In the elections of 1955 the conservative Democratic party won a plurality of seats in the Diet but required the cooperation of the Liberal party to govern. Negotiations between the two parties led to their merger in November 1955 to form the Liberal Democratic party (LDP), which continues to this day.

Since 1955 the LDP has been opposed by the two Socialist parties (Japan Socialist party and the Democratic Socialist party), by the "Clean Government party" (Kōmeitō, formed in 1964, first ran candidates for the lower house in 1967), by the Communist party, and by independent politicians. This opposition was too divided to constitute a serious alternative to conservative rule, but it was sufficient to prevent the LDP from gaining the two-thirds majority in the Diet needed for revising the constitution. Some conservatives, concerned about Japan's security, favored the revocation of Article IX so as to enable Japan to acquire her own military power. In the light of a dangerous world and in response to American urgings the Self-Defense Forces were expanded to include well-equipped naval and air arms and the defense budget continued to increase. However, Japan continued to forego offensive weapons or capabilities, and total defense expenditures remained limited to approximately 1 percent of GNP.

Once the LDP was entrenched in power, the party's internal politics had a decisive influence on Japanese politics and government. Dominating the internal dynamics of the LDP, and thus determining the composition of Japan's government and influencing its policies, has been the interplay of political factions. These are formal, recognized political groupings built around a leader, usually a man with prospects of becoming a prime minister. From his faction a member derives political as well as financial support in his election campaigns and backing in his attempts to gain high government or party office. In return he owes his faction leader political support, especially during the complicated political maneuvering that determines the party presidency and thus Japan's prime ministership. Since the occupant of this post is elected by a limited number of national and prefectural politicians, the men who have presided over Japan's government have generally been seasoned politicians skilled in the art of assembling votes and working out combinations rather than leaders with wide voter appeal. What has counted has been skill in political manipulation, not popular charisma.

This kind of factionalism was not a new phenomenon in Japanese politics. The LDP's origin as an association of independently based politicians also helps to account for the strength of the factions. Also helping to perpetuate it was Japan's system of multimember election districts. In these districts there were frequently more conservative candidates than could reasonably expect to win election. For example, in a five-member district, there might be four LDP candidates with only three likely to win. In such cases, the conservative politicians would be backed by rival factions within the LDP.

The power of the factions set limits on the prime minister's authority. Factionalism also weakened the party itself, which remained weak, particularly at the grass-roots level where each politician cultivated his own local support organization composed of various groups within his constituency. This local political machine was kept oiled by the politician's ability to further the interests of the community by obtaining public works and other special interest legislation, by his support for various community activities, and by his personal assistance to constituents. In seeking to fulfill these expectations, politicians naturally found political clout and a full purse to be obvious assets. Although some politicians were solidly entrenched, there were enough shifts in political fortunes on both the local and the national level to provide for political interest during two decades of single-party rule.

For the opposition parties of the left these were years of frustration. The two Socialist parties were closely associated with labor, each linked to one of the labor confederations. They depended on organized labor for votes, and labor leaders figured prominently in their leadership. Many of their Diet members also came from a labor background. Ideologically the Socialists ran the gamut from Maoist radicals calling for revolution to moderate reformists. During the fifties the Communist party was very weak, but it picked up strength in the late sixties after adopting pragmatic policies. However, even had they been able to unite, the three leftist parties lacked the strength to topple the LDP regime.

Domestically the opposition parties viewed with special alarm LDP measures that seemed to represent a retreat from Occupation reforms and a return to the past. These included measures to recentralize the police and education functions and to give Tokyo greater control over local government. Socialist fears of LDP intentions may have been exaggerated, but they were fortified by the prominence in the conservative leadership of men who had held cabinet offices in the thirties and had been purged from politics by the Occupation authorities.

The left was adamantly opposed to government moves to recreate a military establishment and did what it could to block or at least delay the expansion of the Self-Defense Forces. They also objected to the government's consistently pro-American foreign policy, protested against the continued presence of American bases, and protested against American nuclear weapons and tests.

Unrestrained by expectations of forming a government themselves, the Socialist parties did not conduct themselves like a loyal opposition but engaged in bitter struggles, including boycotts of the Diet and physical disruptions of Diet proceedings leading to police intervention. The LDP for its part did not refrain, on issues it considered important, from using its majority to ram legislation through the Diet with little regard for the niceties of parliamentary procedure let alone any attempt to conduct a genuine exchange of views.

Political animosity reached its greatest intensity in 1960 over the issue of renewing the Security Treaty with the United States, first signed in 1952 along with the peace treaty. Opponents of the renewal were not limited to advocates of revolutionary ideologies. Many felt that instead of providing for Japanese security it endangered Japan, threatening to involve the country in American wars. The specter of nuclear war was particularly terrifying to a people who had experienced the holocausts at Hiroshima and Nagasaki. The Socialists mustered impressive support for their opposition to the renegotiated treaty. Union workers, housewives, students, professors, and members of diverse organizations took to the streets in mass demonstrations in which hundreds of thousands of people participated. There was also a one-day general strike. All this activity did not block ratification or enactment of the treaty, but it did lead to the resignation of Prime Minister Kishi (in office, 1957–60), who had pushed the treaty through the Diet in what many thought was an undemocratic manner.

After the 1960 confrontation, politics simmered down to less violent exchanges as the success of Japan's economic progress became apparent and the government concentrated on providing more of the same. This was the policy under Prime Minister Ikeda (1960–64) who announced a plan to double income in ten years—it actually was exceeded in seven. Ikeda was succeeded by Satō Eisaku, who continued in office from 1964 to 1972, longer than any other prime minister since the promulgation of the Meiji Constitution. During the Satō years, the government continued to work closely with the business community and to follow the American lead on major foreign policy issues. In 1970 the Security Treaty was renewed with little trouble.

In 1964 the political scene was complicated by the appearance of the new Clean Government party formed by the Sōka Gakkai (Value Creation Society), a religious sect. As implied by its name, the party program opposed corruption, but it was vague on other issues. After obtaining 10.9 percent of the vote in the 1969 election, it declined to 8.5 percent in 1972. The LDP for its part aroused little enthusiasm and was particularly weak in the cities. Before 1967 its candidates had received over 50 percent of the vote, but in the election of that year its percentage declined to 48.8 percent. However, it remained by far the largest vote getter and was also helped by an electoral system that favored rural areas. The party was therefore able to continue in power despite the erosion of its voting strength.

## Social Change and the Quality of Life

The growth of the economy brought with it an unpredecented degree of affluence. The very physiognomy of the Japanese people was affected as an improved diet produced a new generation taller and healthier than their parents. People now ate more fish and meat, although the proportion remained modest by American standards. Dairy products became a staple of the daily diet. Changing tastes were reflected in a steadily rising consumption of wheat at the expense of rice, which, thanks to the government's price support policy, was in overabundance. While traditional cuisines continued to flourish so did Western foods and beverages. Japan became a nation of coffee as well as tea drinkers. During the seventies, the influx of Western foods continued apace as the arch of McDonald's hamburgers spread from Tokyo's Ginza to less likely places, where it was soon joined by the figure of Colonel Sanders inviting passersby to partake of Kentucky Fried Chicken, and Mr. Donut and Dairy Queen did their part to propagate popular fast-food culture American style.

Japan became a nation of Western-style consumers. The washing machine, vacuum cleaner, and refrigerator of the fifties were soon joined by the television set (preferably and increasingly color) and the air conditioner. Meanwhile, the worsening traffic jams that clogged Japan's roads demonstrated that many a family had realized its dream of owning a private automobile. Thus a solid domestic market supported Japan's major consumer-export industries.

Figure 12-1    The bullet train passing Mt. Fuji

Ownership of the new products was not confined to the cities, for the countryside also participated in the general prosperity. This was partly because the economic boom produced a labor shortage, so that wage scales were set and plant locations determined in such a way as to draw rural manpower into the factories. At the same time, as already noted, agricultural production nevertheless increased. Another source of rural well-being was the LDP's policies, including the support of rice that the government purchased from farmers at several times the price current in the international market. Thus the stark economic distinction between city and country, which had existed in prewar years, was eliminated. At the same time, the spread of television accelerated the process, begun by radio, of diffusing the culture of the cities to the countryside. However, despite the omnipresence of the television set, the Japanese remained the world's most avid consumers of the printed word, supporting a flourishing newspaper and magazine industry as well as more bookstores per capita than any other country in the world.

Japan also led the world in the excellence of its public transportation system, including the bullet trains which by the mid-seventies connected Tokyo and Northern Kyushu, whisking passengers past Japan's greatest mountain at 125 miles per hour. (See Figure 12-1.) Experiments are under way for a futuristic linear propulsion train, which, riding on a magnetic cushion, is envisioned as making the trip from Tokyo to Kyōto in an hour. Within the cities, public transport is frequent, punctual, and efficient, although in Tokyo's rush hour ("crush hour" would be more appropriate) "pushers" are needed to cram the people quickly into the overflowing subways.

Public transportation, communication, and security were excellent, but in other areas the state did little, preferring to leave matters to the private sector. While this worked quite well in certain respects, in others it proved highly inadequate. An example of the latter was the government's laxity in pollution control. As a result Tokyo became enshrouded in a semiperpetual screen of smog while elsewhere chemical pollution made some waters downright poisonous. Most notorious was the "Minamata Disease" caused by people eating fish contaminated by methyl mercury discharged by a fertilizer plant in Kyūshū. Over 200 people died. The company has acknowledged responsibility, and in 1977 a ten-year, multi-million dollar program was begun to clean up the pollution. Japan's long industrial area, running along its Pacific coast, became one of the most ugly and noxious to be found anywhere. While the Japanese people continued to cherish nature in miniature, lovingly tending tiny gardens on the most unlikely bits of land, Japan's leaders, in their rush to modernize, sacrificed much of the larger beauty of the natural landscape that had once been Japan's beloved heritage.

A serious social and economic problem was the constantly escalating price of land and housing in Japan's large cities. Young married people, despite their modern wish for independence, found themselves forced to live with their in-laws because they could not afford separate establishments. Others were crowded into tiny apartments in drab and monotonous buildings made of reinforced concrete. Raising a family in such confined quarters was no easy task. Although the small apartments reduced women's household chores, releasing time for other activities, the residents of such buildings were slow to develop a sense of community, since they regarded these quarters as temporary expedients marking a stage of their lives and careers soon to be surmounted. This outlook was not unreasonable, since in Japan promotion, particularly in the early career stages, was generally by seniority.

The absence of grandparents in the new housing was but one of the factors making for discontinuity between the generations. Such discontinuity was not unique to Japan, for in other countries too, rapid changes during the postwar years created a "generation gap." Indeed, the presence of this phenomenon in Japan can itself be regarded as one more sign of Japan's modernity. However, in Japan the gap was particularly severe. Not only did the younger people grow up in a society that had suddenly become very different from that of their parents, but a whole generation of leaders had been thoroughly discredited and the old values blamed for leading the nation to catastrophe. Included were many of the old values that long had helped to provide Japanese society with its cohesiveness.

New life styles and values appeared in the factories as young workers preferred to spend their leisure time manipulating pachinko (vertical pinball) machines or listening to rock music rather than going on company outings, and their valuation of skill over length of service, although very much in tune with the new technology, set them apart from their elders. Furthermore, they tended to regard the factory not so much as a second home but merely as a place of work.

Meanwhile, those fortunate enough to survive a brutal entrance examination system found themselves admitted to universities oriented largely to research and graduate work. Ostensibly paternalistic, the universities demonstrated their supposed concern for the youngest members of the academic community by virtually guaranteeing graduation to all matriculants. Neglected after having worked so hard for university entrance, the students expressed their discontent in radical political activities. Their dissatisfaction helped fuel widespread demonstrations and disruptions in the later sixties, their protest directed against both national and university policies. In this, again, Japanese young people were, of course, not alone.

In other ways, too, the postwar generation resembled their counterparts in other industrialized countries, and there is hardly a mode of dress, a style of music, or a social or political movement from consumerism to terrorism that did not attract at least a modest following in Japan. Thus, just as Japanese designers were scoring their first major triumphs in the sophisticated world of international haute couture, stores specializing in jeans began mushrooming in Japanese cities. In the meantime, the kimono, although still worn for special occasions, was losing ground. In other respects too, particularly in the practice of the old crafts, traditional elegance was giving way to modern practicality.

The general loosening of traditional patterns and values presented contemporary Japanese with a wide range of choice but within what remained, by and large, a closely knit society. For example, young people increasingly insisted on making their own selection of a spouse, and they were now always consulted before a marriage was arranged. Nevertheless, even in love marriages, most young people still asked their employer or teacher to serve as an official matchmaker. Others continued to leave the initiative to their parents. Under the postwar legal system, wives as well as husbands could now initiate divorce proceedings; however, the divorce rate remained low.

Most wives remained content with their traditional roles, which gave them a predominant influence over their children and firmly established the home as their field of authority. Although submissive to their husbands in public, most wives controlled the family budget and ran the household. Many treated their husbands as they would an older, somewhat difficult, and rather special child. They accepted their exclusion from much of their husbands' social lives, which the husbands spent largely in the company of their fellow workers. Like their Tokugawa predecessors, wives also tolerated visits to bars and overlooked occasional frolics with female playmates as long as nothing serious developed and their husbands continued to look after their families.

However, as in all periods of social change, there were some who suffered because change was too rapid and others for whom it was too slow. Among the former were old people bewildered and distressed by the whirl about them. One of the strengths of the old society had always been the dignity and security afforded to the aged, but now cramped quarters and new ideas ate away at old values and threatened traditional comforts. These were people who found that the social rules had changed just when it came to be their turn to reap the rewards the system offered to those who played by the rules. While the erosion of respect for the aged diminished the traditional attractions of longevity, forced retirement at an early age (usually 55) and the devaluation of savings because of continual inflation, deprived the old of a sense of economic security. Most families did manage to take care of the elderly one way or another. Most old people were not shunted off into nursing homes or set up in special retirement communities, but the social arrangements made for the elderly by their children were often grudging and poisoned by resentment. Niwa Fumio's short story "The Hateful Age" (1947), a revolting portrait of senile selfishness, was an early expression of the new attitude.

At the other end of the spectrum were those who felt that change was coming too slowly, such as the young and middle-aged adults who felt constrained to maintain and live with their parents. They felt stifled rather than supported by a social system that still expected the individual to be subordinate to the group whether it be family or company. They also balked at conforming to a social hierarchy that had lost much of its theoretical support. The discontented were a disparate group. They included women who wanted to make a career of work and found themselves discriminated against and artists and intellectuals seeking to fill the vacuum left by the passing of the old values with something more solid than consumerism and the race for increased GNP. This discontent was frequently shared by students and by radicals impatient for a more egalitarian society. Meanwhile, some of the young men who had no prospects for university study vented their frustrations by joining motorcycle gangs. However, most of the disaffected worked out a *modus vivendi* for themselves, and many, especially among the young, gradually came to terms with society.

The great majority of the population, however, neither mourned the passing of the old nor were impatient for the arrival of the new. Appreciative of the increase in material wealth, they were nevertheless unsure of the future. Many turned to new religious sects, seeking to satisfy their spiritual hunger and to cure a psychological malaise brought on by the loss of community entailed by moving from traditional village to modern city. Attracting the largest membership was Sōka Gakkai, which we have already encountered as the sponsor of the Clean Government party. Doctrinally based on Nichiren Buddhism, which originated in thirteenth century Japan, it denounced all other faiths and insisted that its members proselytize relentlessly. One of the obligations of the faithful was a pilgrimage to the head temple at the foot of Mt. Fuji, where an average of ten thousand people a day came to pay their homage. By passing a series of examinations, the faithful could rise in an academic-like hierarchy of ranks. For the devoted members, the sect provided not only spiritual community but a sense of personal worth and of belonging to a large, integrated, purposeful group.

## The Japanese Film

If, as is often said, the film is the characteristic art form of the twentieth century, then the worldwide acclaim accorded Japanese films is but one more indication of Japan's full participation in the culture of that century. All Japanese films were by no means masterpieces: Japanese film companies were second to none in turning out ephemeral entertainments—samurai movies that were the artistic equivalents of American westerns, lachrymose melodramas with torrents of tears intended to induce a similar flow in the audience, horror and monster films, and, in the seventies, a wave of erotica with little artistic or social value but much sexual action. Such films, reflecting social stereotypes and people's daydreams, are of considerable interest to psychologists and social scientists, but it is important to remember that the stereotypes they contain—the self-sacrificing but self-centered mother, the wife finding herself, daughters in various degrees of revolt—are never simple mirror images of society. The more ambitious and truly fine films also reflected the times and the society, but, beyond that, they provided new insights into the Japanese and the human reality. And they did this while drawing an enthusiastic mass audience as had the kabuki and *bunraku* (puppet theater) in their day.

The major films were the creations of fine actors, sensitive cameramen, and above all great directors. While some fine directors were remarkably versatile, the most outstanding were able to use the medium to create their own personal styles, conveying their own personal visions. If they had anything in common, it was a superb visual sense employed to create an atmosphere. Some may be said to have used the camera to paint their vision on the screen. Many are best viewed as one would view a painting—with a contemplative eye.

Exercising classic restraint in his insistence on a strict economy of means (empty spaces, simple objects, minimal plot) and avoiding anything superficial or artificially clever was Ozu Yasujirō (1903–1963), whose traditionalism also extended to his subject matter, for he was the film maker par excellence of the Japanese family. Describing the tone and effect of Ozu's films, Donald Richie refers to "a kind of refined sadness, a calm and knowing serenity which persists despite the uncertainty of life and the things of this world," a quality associated with *mono no aware*, one of the oldest terms of Japanese aesthetics. Richie went on to say that Ozu's "emphasis on effect rather than cause, emotion rather than intellect" and "his ability to metamorphose Japanese aesthetics into terms and images visible on film" made Ozu "the most Japanese of all directors."[1]

Other directors did not take as positive a view of Japan's social tradition and the old values. For example, in *Harakiri* (*Seppuku*, 1962), directed by Kobayashi Masaki, the hero sets out to avenge his son who had been forced to commit an unimaginably painful *seppuku* (ritual suicide) using a sword with a bamboo blade, but in the end the whole system is revealed as founded on hypocrisy. Or there is Night Drum (*Yoru no Tsuzumi*, 1958), directed by Imai Tadashi, in which a samurai kills the wife he loves and thereby deprives his own life of meaning, because this is what society demanded. Such vivid and moving historical films were among the triumphs of the postwar cinema, a part of a continuing and sometimes bitter dialogue with a still living past.

Outstanding as a truly great director is Kurosawa Akira (1910–), who, while remaining Japanese in his aesthetic and historical vocabulary, displays a concern for truly universal themes. Thus his world famous *Rashomon* (1950) suggests the relativity of all truth through a demonstration of the power of human subjectivity and self-interest. In *Ikiru* (1952) the viewer is taken through a Faust-like quest for meaning in life. The main character, a petty bureaucrat dying of cancer, in the end finds fulfillment in one meaningful social act—surmounting endless red tape and bureaucratic obstructionism, he gets a small park built. A gripping, powerful film, filled with action and drama, is *Seven Samurai* (1954), the story of seven warriors who agree to defend a village against its bandit enemies. It is one of those rare films in which powerful and sensitive acting, beautiful visual composition and realistic detail, story line and structure, friction and harmony, violence and stillness, blend into a major artistic statement, a masterpiece. Masterpieces are rare in any art form, but the productions of the gifted "New Wave" directors during the 1960s and 1970s attested to the continued vitality of the Japanese cinema at its best.

## The Visual Arts

Not only Japanese films but also the work of Japanese painters, potters, and architects won international recognition for their contributions to the world of art. As in the prewar years, some artists found their inspiration in, and took their cues from, the latest trends, so that Japan had its practitioners of abstract expressionism, action painting, pop art and the various other international art movements that at their best reflected the search for a style appropriate to a bewildering age and at their worst degenerated into fads. The cacophony of the art scene may be suggested by the disjointed ears in Figure 12-2. What are they listening to? No doubt their metallic color is appropriate for the age of the machine. Do they symbolize modern (Japanese?) man? Are they all that is left of humankind—disembodied ears?

More in keeping with the Japanese aesthetic tradition was the work of artists who strove to create beauty without attempting to convey a symbolic message. Japanese potters, both innovators and traditionalists, continued to blend shapes, textures, and colors to create works worthy of the great tradition to which they were heirs.

Another area of excellence was architecture. Although many opportunities for architectural excellence were missed in the surge of postwar reconstruction

Figure 12-2
Miki Tomio (1937–),
*Ear 201*. Bronze, 1965,
41.4 cm × 34.7 cm.

and some of Japan's industrial centers are among the ugliest cities in the world, there were also new buildings of great distinction. The architect Tange Kenzō (1913–), designer of the Hall Dedicated to Peace at Hiroshima, won a deserved international reputation as one of the great masters of his art. His work can be seen not only in numerous structures in his own country (the Swimming Pool and Sports Center he designed for the 1964 Tokyo Olympics is one of the most famous) but also in Europe, North Africa, the Middle East, and in the United States, where the Arts Complex in Minneapolis (1970–74) has been completed, and he is involved in the Inner Harbor Residential Redevelopment project in Baltimore. As illustrated by the latter, not only has Tange designed superb buildings, he has also been deeply involved in urban planning. Also in the interior design of modern buildings, the Japanese aesthetic of simplicity, of clean lines and uncluttered spaces, proved most compatible with modern tastes and sensibilities.

An area of major artistic achievement was the modern woodcut. Unlike the earlier *ukiyo-e* artists, those who now worked in this medium took responsibility for the entire process of print making. They did their own cutting and printing, although they might have students assist them in the more routine aspects of the process. Among the finest was Munakata Shikō (1903–75), a gifted painter as well as print artist, whose style was influenced by traditional Japanese folk art but who also developed new techniques. One was to add color to his prints by hand, applying color on the back of the print and letting it seep through the paper to create gentle, diffused coloring. This helped Munakata create a general decorative effect. Munakata's concern with decoration is well illustrated by his rendition of the clothing in *Lady in Chinese Costume,* shown in Figure 12-3. The lines marking the folds in the cloth and suggesting its ornamentation are repeated in the remainder of the print, giving the picture its rhythm. Strong black areas and lines contrast pleasingly with soft blues and browns.

A similar love for the decorative is evidenced by Munakata's frequent use of written characters for ornamentation. In subject matter his work ranges from the religious to the sensuous and the whimsical (for example, a nude with the artist's eyeglasses resting on her belly). In tone his art is positive and life

Figure 12-3
Munakata Shikō,
*Lady in Chinese Costume.*
Woodcut, 1946,
45.5 cm × 32.6 cm.

affirming—there is no echo here of the agony of the century. There are strong hints of Persia and India, but in the vigor of his lines, his gentle eroticism, and the decorative qualities of his art, Munakata resembles Matisse while his coloring is also reminiscent of Chagall.

# Literature

The literature of the postwar period continued to sound many themes pursued in a variety of styles, as older novelists published manuscripts they could not release during the war and new writers appeared to sound new themes. An outstanding example of the former is the long novel by Tanizaki translated as *The Makioka Sisters* in which the author of *Some Prefer Nettles* examined an Ōsaka family and the contrast between the old, traditional, and Japanese on the one hand and the new, modern, and Western on the other.

In 1947 Kawabata published the last installment of *Snow Country*. Previous segments of the novel had been published in various journals over the course of the preceding twelve years, each part appearing as though it might be the conclusion, as though each part were a stanza in a *renga* (linked verse) rather than a building block for a novel. Characteristically Kawabata's novels sacrifice structure and plot for the sake of naturalness and poetry. *A Thousand Cranes* (1948) and *The Sound of the Mountain* (1951) followed, each imbued with the author's visual sensibility and with his concern for beauty and sadness, inseparable as ever in Japanese literature, and evoking what one critic termed a "vibrant silence."[2] The essential Japaneseness of Kawabata's method and vision was clearly demonstrated in his Nobel Prize acceptance speech (1968). Translated as *Japan, the Beautiful, and Myself*, it is an evocation of the Japanese tradition, a string of poems and images held together by a shared perception of beauty and truth.

In his youth Kawabata had been influenced by Western literary theories, but his work and its themes were classically Japanese. For the younger Mishima Yukio (1925–1970), however, the classically Japanese had been lost and could be regained, if at all, only through great effort. Brilliant, prolific, versatile, and uneven, Mishima, in a series of well-constructed novels, developed his ideas on such universal themes as the relationship between art and life, warrior and poet, and the nature of beauty. One of his most compelling novels was *The Temple of the Golden Pavilion* (1956). Based on the actual burning down of the Golden Pavilion (Kinkakuji) in postwar Kyōto, it includes powerful psychological and philosophical explorations. A noted dramatist and critic as well as novelist, Mishima's work defies summarization. And it went beyond literature, for he tried to mold his life and his body as he did his art. Wishing to be both athlete and artist, he took up body building and succeeded in developing a strong torso (but on spindly legs). Seeking to achieve a unity of knowledge and action as in the philosophy of Wang Yang-ming whom he admired, Mishima's culminating act was a public *seppuku* committed after the completion of his final work, a tetrology entitled *The Sea of Fertility*. His ritual suicide was both a protest against what he perceived as contemporary Japanese decadence and an act fulfilling his life's work.

Among Mishima's contemporaries, a writer with a substantial national and international reputation is Abe Kōbō (1924–) perhaps best known for his novel, *Woman in the Dunes* (1962), subsequently made into a well-known film. In this work as well as later novels such as *Face of Another* (1964) and *The Boxman* (1973), and in such plays as *Friends* (1967), Abe explored some of the universal themes found in existentialist writers and thinkers of the postwar period in many countries. Although one of these themes is the search for identity (and for Abe this includes identification with place and community), he did not, like Mishima and others, draw on his specifically Japanese heritage but set out to make artistic statements valid for his time rather than only or even primarily for his place. The search for identity and for roots also infuses the work of Ōe Kenzaburō (1935–), two of whose novels, *A Personal Matter* (1964) and *The Silent Cry* (1967), have been translated into English. Insight into psychological complexities of modern people, including the sources of violence, a concern for social morality, a strong personal symbolism, and his grapplings with basic problems of existence in the second half of the twentieth century mark him as a major writer and one who speaks to the central problems of his age.

# The Seventies

During the early and mid-seventies there were no sharp breaks with the preceding decades, but there were signs of longer-term change as well as a series of short-term economic and political shocks. The latter began in 1971 when the United States, Japan's largest trade partner, placed a 10 percent surcharge on imports and effectively devalued the dollar by floating it, that is by allowing the international monetary market to determine its value vis-à-vis the yen and other currencies rather than maintaining a fixed rate of exchange. Both of these American actions were aimed at reducing, if not eliminating, a mounting United States trade and payments deficit in its dealings with Japan. They demonstrate the way in which Japan's economic success created new problems.

A political blow followed these economic acts when, still in the same year, Washington announced the impending visit of President Nixon to China, an act on which Japan was not consulted and which undercut Prime Minister Satō, who, primarily to please Washington, had been following the unpopular policy of maintaining the fiction that the Nationalist regime on Taiwan was the government of China.

Other shocks followed. The Arab oil boycott in 1973 reminded Japan of her dependence on imported energy and was followed by a quadrupling of the price of this vital import. Then, early in 1976, the Lockheed scandal ("Japan's Watergate") shook the political world as it was revealed that millions of dollars of the American company's funds had been used to corrupt the highest Japanese government officials. Among those indicted was Tanaka Kakuei, prime minister 1972–74. The case reached the courts in 1978 for what promised to be lengthy legal proceedings. The 1970s closed with intensified uncertainties over oil, as world prices kept rising and Japan worried over events in Iran, its major supplier. When Iran and Iraq went to war in 1980, it threatened to reduce to a total loss the 3.5-billion-dollar Mitsui petrochemical plants, which represented Japan's largest single overseas investment.

Both the economy and the LDP survived these shocks without serious restructuring. In the 1976 election for the lower house, the LDP declined to 41.8 percent of the popular vote and achieved a one-vote majority only by including eight independent conservatives. It did only marginally better in the 1979 elections, but in 1980 was able to reverse the trend and won a majority (284 out of 511) of seats in the lower house while retaining control of the upper chamber (135 out of 252 seats). Part of the party's success was attributed to a vote of sympathy for the recently deceased Prime Minister Ohira Masayoshi (1910–80), but it came at a time when conservatives were showing strength in other countries as well. Meanwhile, despite efforts to strengthen the party internally, the LDP remained essentially a coalition of factions. The new prime minister, sixty-nine-year-old Suzuki Zenko, resembled his predecessors in temperament and background. Thus the LDP continued to provide Japan with continuity and seasoned leadership. But only time will tell whether it will also be able to provide the statesmanship and vision the nation will need in coping with future problems.

On the international front, Japan recognized the People's Republic of China after Prime Minister Tanaka's visit to Peking in 1972, and relations have remained friendly since then. There were also efforts to broaden Japan's trade pattern, to increase trade with China and Southeast Asia and diminish the country's dependence on trade with the United States. There was, however, no major change in the general direction of foreign policy nor much enthusiasm for any shift away from reliance on American atomic protection. When the Soviet Union invaded Afghanistan in 1980, Japan joined the United States in economic sanctions and in boycotting the Moscow Olympics. In general, Japan continued a cautious, "low profile" foreign-policy stance, aware of its dependence on the international economic system.

Technological progress continued and advances were made in automation, with management and labor sharing in the benefits accruing from increased productivity. However, after achieving economic success, the Japanese government was increasingly prevailed upon not only to open new home markets to foreign companies but to restrain the country's exports of cars, television sets, steel, and other products to the United States and the European Common Market countries. Japanese companies were urged also to build factories in the United States. Most significant was the fact that Japan's economy had reached a size that made its trade and monetary policies important factors in the operation of the international economy. Thus any action undertaken by Japan affected the whole system and brought repercussions back to Japan itself.

During 1974–76 Japan suffered a severe recession, but on the whole the economy weathered the shocks of the seventies remarkably well. Now the prospect is one of continued economic growth but at a lower rate. This is in keeping not only with the economic realities but also with a change in the climate of opinion that developed in the seventies when people became disillusioned with the single-minded pursuit of economic growth as the social costs of such a policy became apparent. There was now an emphasis on the need for cleaning up air and water, for improving housing and social services, and there were those who were ready to abandon growth for these ends. Others argued that some growth was necessary in order to finance the needed improvements without increasing the tax load.

The new goals were generally supported by the public but were not capable of generating an enthusiastic sense of national purpose. In addition to those who had all along been unhappy over Japan's previous national purpose, there were now those who felt that the country lacked any such purpose at all. Many turned from company to home for personal satisfaction, but others felt that the pursuit of private goals (*maihōmushugi*, that is, "my-homeism") was an unsatisfactory solution.

Perhaps this was yet another sign of Japan's full participation in the international culture of the industrialized non-Communist world. Compared with the countries of Western Europe and with the United States, Japan continued to demonstrate comparatively greater social cohesion, although the breakdown of old patterns of behavior and old values was also apparent. Whether Japan would be able to achieve a creative synthesis between the new and old remained very much an open question, but the people's continuing quest for the answers gave the land much of its vital excitement.

## NOTES

1. Donald Richie, *Japanese Cinema* (New York: Doubleday, 1971), p. 69–70.
2. Masao Miyoshi, *Accomplices of Silence: The Modern Japanese Novel* (Berkeley and Los Angeles: The University of California Press, 1974), p. 120.

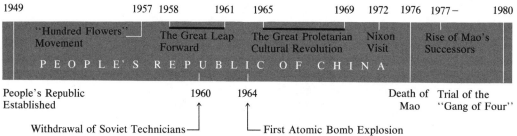

| 1949 | | 1957 | 1958 | | 1961 | 1965 | | 1969 | 1972 | 1976 | 1977 – | 1980 |
|---|---|---|---|---|---|---|---|---|---|---|---|---|

''Hundred Flowers''
Movement

The Great Leap
Forward

The Great Proletarian
Cultural Revolution

Nixon
Visit

Rise of Mao's
Successors

PEOPLE'S  REPUBLIC  OF  CHINA

People's Republic
Established

1960

1964

Death of
Mao

Trial of the
''Gang of Four''

Withdrawal of Soviet Technicians⏌    ⌐ First Atomic Bomb Explosion

# 13 The New China

When Mao Zedong (Mao Tse-tung)* proclaimed the existence of the People's Republic on October 1, 1949, it marked a watershed in the history of modern China. After a century of suffering because of foreign aggression and internal disintegration, China made a new beginning under leaders deeply committed to the revolutionary transformation of the nation. Mao and his associates were determined to create an egalitarian society at home and to make China a power respected abroad. While the road to these goals was to prove neither smooth nor easy, clearly China was moving in a new direction.

* As indicated in the Note on Names and Romanization (pages ix–xiii), Pinyin Romanization is introduced in this chapter so that the reader will become familiar with it.                                    **289**

In taking control of the entire country and then restructuring Chinese society, the new leaders faced problems as immense as China itself, but they brought to their task some powerful assets. These leaders were tempered by long years of struggle. They could draw on their experience of leading a mass movement and of actually governing, an experience not found in the history of any other Communist party prior to its seizure of power. In Mao, the Chinese had a leader who was both a dedicated Marxist and a man convinced of the necessity to adapt that foreign ideology to China. In retrospect, this dual commitment to China and to Marxism seems so obvious that it is hard to understand how the United States and the Soviet Union failed to perceive it. For many years, the United States saw only *Communist* China, while today the U.S.S.R. denies that the Chinese are genuine Marxists at all. As was true of Taiping Christianity, what from a Chinese vantage point appears as a creative adaptation of a foreign faith is seen from a different perspective as the abandonment of that faith. But what is important in the present context was the conviction of Mao and his associates that the interests of nation and ideology were one and the same, that the one could be served only by serving the other.

## The First Phase (1949–1958)

The first nine years of the new regime were marked by considerable continuity. These years can be subdivided into an initial period, 1949–52, during which the regime consolidated its rule and forged the basic framework of a new sociopolitical order, followed by a period of Socialist Construction (1953–58), initiated by the publication of the first Soviet-style five-year plan—begun in 1953, although not published until 1955.

Politically, the years after 1949 saw the establishment of the basic machinery for governing China. A characteristic feature of the Chinese system (as it was, also, in the Soviet Union) was the creation of parallel government and party structures, and the practice of appointing high party officials to top government posts. Thus Mao was head of the party (that is, Chairman of the CCP Central Committee) and, until 1959, also officially head of state. Party control was also exercised in other sectors by the same means. High party members held positions of leadership in various quasi-official organizations such as trade unions, and, as during the pre-1949 years, party members served as political commissars in the army. An important factor in the smooth functioning of this system was the ability of the CCP leadership to maintain its general cohesiveness. The only political conflict that erupted openly was the purge of Gao Gang (Kao Kang) and his followers. Gao, the head of the Communist Party in Manchuria, was accused of separatist ambitions. Also a factor were Gao's ties with the Soviet Union and the whole question of Russian influence in Manchuria. Gao's suicide was reported in 1955. Another prominent leader purged at the same time was Rao Shushi (Jao Shu-shih), who was based in the Shanghai region. Rao, like Gao, was charged with operating "an independent kingdom." These two leaders, in charge of China's two prime industrial centers, were also accused of forming a political alliance.

Administratively China was divided into provinces, and these remained the primary political subdivisions after an additional governmental level between the provinces and the central government was tried but discarded. The three most highly populated metropolitan areas, Shanghai, Beijing (Peking), and Tianjin (Tientsin), were placed under the central government, and "autonomous regions" were created in areas inhabited by a significant number of minority people. These "autonomous regions" were Guangxi (Kwangsi), Inner Mongolia, Ningxia (Ningsia), southeast of Inner Mongolia, and the vast western regions of Xinjiang (Sinkiang) and Tibet. Tibet was incorporated into the People's Republic after Chinese troops entered that mountainous land in October 1950, the same month in which Chinese "volunteers" intervened in Korea, but Tibet did not receive "autonomous region" status until 1965. (See map, pp. xx–xxi.) Aside from their strategic importance, the Inner Asian territories were significant because the Chinese government had to begin to deal with the interests and sensitivities of various ethnic minorities.

The People's Republic was clearly determined to guard China's frontiers and to reassert Chinese sovereignty over outlying areas. However, the Chinese recognized the independence of Outer Mongolia, where the Mongolian People's Republic had been established in 1926 under Soviet sponsorship. Mao's visit to Moscow, his first trip abroad, resulted in the February 1950 treaty with the U.S.S.R. Relations between the two allies were not easy, however, for the U.S.S.R. drove a hard bargain and was slow to relinquish special interests in Manchuria and Xinjiang. Still, the relationship with the Soviet Union remained very important to the Chinese leadership during these years because the U.S.S.R. provided a working model for social, economic, and governmental development; it provided moral, political, and economic support for the Chinese regime; and its alliance with China was the mainstay of Chinese foreign policy.

After the Korean War, the People's Republic gained in international standing, and Beijing's representatives played an important role in the Geneva Conference on Indo-China (1954) and at the conference of Asian-African states held at Bandung (Indonesia) in 1955. However, the People's Republic was not accorded membership in the United Nations, nor was it recognized by the United States and many of its allies. The United States-supported buildup of Nationalist strength on Taiwan rankled the mainland Chinese. However, with the U.S. Seventh Fleet patrolling the Taiwan Strait, actual fighting was limited to sporadic shelling of two Nationalist held islands off the coast of Fukien Province.

Internally during 1951–52, there was a "three anti" campaign against waste, corruption, and bureaucratism aimed at disciplining the greatly enlarged CCP membership, and a "five anti" campaign against bribery, tax evasion, fraud, the stealing of state property, and the theft of economic secrets. During this campaign, aimed particularly against businessmen such as those of Shanghai, many wealthy men had to pay heavy fines. In accordance with Mao's "On the

New Democracy" (1940), members of the national bourgeoisie were initially tolerated, and only capitalists with KMT or foreign ties were considered enemies of the revolution. Gradually, however, private companies were turned over to the state, although their former owners often remained as managers. The owners continue to receive some dividends to this day, although payments were interrupted during the Cultural Revolution.

Not all drives were directed against human evildoers; there was also a concerted Attack on the Four Pests: a war against rats, sparrows, flies, and mosquitoes. Partly by campaigns such as this, the People's Republic achieved enormous improvements in public health. Furthermore, by involving all the people in these campaigns, the leadership not only made use of China's most precious asset (manpower) but also gave the people a sense of participation and pride in the resulting accomplishments.

## Economic Policies

Economic matters were of central concern to the new government right from the start. It had inherited a land ravaged by war and floods, with both agricultural and industrial output badly down from prewar levels and the monetary system wrecked by inflation. Furthermore, the underlying economy had serious structural weaknesses. In the agrarian sector, the prevalence of small, uneconomic, scattered landholdings and uneven land ownership helped to perpetuate traditional farming techniques and discouraged capital formation and investment in agriculture. China's industrial sector, on the other hand, consisted primarily of light industry concentrated around Shanghai and heavy industry in Manchuria, much of which had been removed by the Soviet Union in 1949. It had been developed to meet the requirements of foreign capital rather than the needs of China and its people.

Any government would have had to restore and strengthen the economy to increase production, but as Marxists, China's new leaders were also committed to a complete restructuring of the entire system, including the transfer of the means of production from private to public ownership and the creation of an egalitarian system of distribution. Their aim was to create a socialist state with a strong proletarian (working class) base. The necessary precondition for this was vigorous industrialization. Since this was also required for the attainment of national strength, economic ideology and patriotism pointed to the same end and the Soviet example indicated the means.

By 1952, despite the strains of the Korean War, the economy had been restored to prewar levels. Factories had been put back into operation, railway lines had been repaired, and a sound monetary system established. In the cities, the private economic sector was temporarily retained and even encouraged, but control over materials and marketing, as well as wages, prices, and working conditions, was in the hands of the state. Meanwhile, in the countryside, a program of land redistribution was carried out not by government decree but by mobilizing the suppressed fury of the rural poor. Landlords were denounced and humiliated in public trials and at mass "speak bitterness" meetings. The more fortunate ones were allowed to retain enough land to support themselves, but many lost their lives. The campaign became associated with a general suppression of potential counterrevolutionaries during the Korean War. The end result was not only a more equitable distribution of land but a change of village leadership, which was now in the hands of activists drawn from the poor peasantry.

The achievements of the first three years of the People's Republic were viewed as merely a necessary stage for further socialization and economic development. China was now ready to embark on planned economic growth. A planning organization was established, as was a statistical bureau, and in 1953 China took its first modern census, which registered a total population of 582,600,000 on the mainland. Although demographers have questioned its accuracy, this figure is accepted as a general indication of the size of China's population at the time.

China's First Five-Year Plan followed the model of the Soviet Union's economic development in stressing heavy industry, with some 85 percent of total investments going into this sector. The role of the Soviet Union was important also in other ways. Russia supplied technical assistance (plans, blueprints, and so forth), helped train Chinese technicians (28,000 Chinese technicians and skilled workers went to the U.S.S.R. for training during the fifties), and sent about 11,000 of its own experts to work in China. Development was also accelerated by importing entire plants from the Soviet Union. Structurally, most of what was left of the private sector was eliminated. Control over the plants was given to professional managers, many of them technocrats. As in the Soviet Union, the prime responsibility of these managers was to carry out government economic directives. To enable them to do this, they were placed firmly in charge of their factories.

Since loans advanced by the Soviet Union amounted to only 3 percent of China's total state investments, the financing of this industrialization effort was predominantly Chinese. These funds came out of the government's budget. The government, in turn, derived much of its revenue from taxes and from the income of state enterprises. Ultimately, a considerable portion of investment capital was supplied by the agricultural sector, for agriculture remained the heart of the Chinese economy. To increase output and channel agricultural surplus more effectively into capital formation, the government in 1953 began a program of more radical transformation of the pattern of land management. To replace the existing system of small fields, individually owned and worked, the government planned to collectivize agriculture by pooling land, labor, and other resources. The change was not to be accomplished all at once. At first, "mutual-aid" teams, which shared labor, tools, and work animals, were organized. The next stage was to create village producers' cooperatives in which land also was pooled. Initially, agricultural collectivization was planned as a gradual program, because the Chinese leadership wanted to avoid the terrible bloodshed and suffering that had accompanied Stalin's rapid collectivization in the Soviet Union. Mao, however, in an important speech he delivered in July

1955, drew on the experience of the Chinese Revolution rather than the Russian Revolution and reaffirmed his faith in the revolutionary spirit of the Chinese peasantry. Just as the peasantry had been in the vanguard of the revolution that gave birth to the People's Republic, it would now lead the nation to socialism. In Mao's view it was the party, not the people, that was dragging its feet. The immediate effect of Mao's speech was an acceleration in the agricultural collectivization program, so much so that it was largely accomplished within a single year (1955–56); and the timetable for full collectivization was set ahead. A long-range effect of the speech was the emergence of a Maoist strategy of economic development distinct from that of the Soviet Union. In 1957 the process of collectivization was completed.

When the First Five-Year Plan came to an end, the Chinese viewed the results with considerable satisfaction. The government was now firmly in control of the industrial sector, and agriculture had been reorganized. In such key areas as iron, coal, and steel, the production targets set by the plan had been exceeded. Industrial production doubled between 1953 and 1957, and, altogether, remarkable progress had been made on the road to industrialization. There were problems, to be sure. One was the widening gap between the city and the country, a problem that has plagued all industrializing countries but was of special concern in China, where the peasantry remained the majority and where the party leaders identified with them. Another problem was the reappearance of bureaucracy. As Maurice Meisner put it, "Once leaders of the masses in a revolutionary situation, party cadres were becoming state administrators governing the masses."[1]

## Thought Reform

The leaders of the People's Republic were convinced not only of the scientific correctness of their doctrine but also of its moral rightness, and they believed that virtually everyone could be brought to share their vision and act accordingly. They were optimistic not only about the course of history but also about the nature of human beings, and they retained a traditional Chinese faith in the moral perfectibility of man as they set about creating an ideal socialist man to replace the traditional models. It was their belief that given the proper environment and correct guidance, people would become selflessly devoted to revolution and community.

Naturally the most promising were the young, uncontaminated by the old society, and the government saw to it that they were educated in the new values. Special attention was paid to the political awareness of Communist party members and cadres, who were relied on to set examples of personal conduct and lead ordinary people. Not only were the masses of peasants and workers to be educated, even the most unpromising human material was considered redeemable. In the Chinese view, the elimination of undesirable social classes required the reeducation, not the liquidation, of their members.

To further the thought reform and moral transformation of such people, the authorities devised techniques of group discussion, self-criticism, and public confession. By using the individual's own feeling of moral inadequacy and guilt, and by applying external pressures, the authorities induced people to renounce old values and prepared them for conversion to the new faith. Perhaps the most famous example of such a change of heart, accomplished in the controlled environment of a correctional institute, was provided by Puyi (P'u-i; Henry Pu-yi). As an infant he had been the last occupant of the Qing (Ch'ing) throne, and more recently he had served the Japanese as puppet ruler of Manchukuo. After undergoing thought reform, he reemerged in Beijing as a citizen in good standing.

Not only prominent personages but also ordinary people spent a good deal of time in small discussion groups, analyzing their lives as well as problems or incidents at their places of work. In this way the new ideology was transmitted to the people, and they were taught to use it in analyzing everyday problems. At the same time, social pressures were applied to everyone to conform to generally accepted standards of behavior.

## Policy Toward Intellectuals: The "Hundred Flowers"

The thought reform of intellectuals presented special problems. Highly trained and educated people were rare. They constituted a precious resource for a nation bent on industrialization and modernization. Yet few came from peasant or worker backgrounds. More serious than the question of class background was the persistence of traditional elitist attitudes among intellectuals, as well as their critical habits of mind. They tended to resent taking directions from party cadres who lacked expertise and were less well educated than themselves. Their special knowledge and skills were needed, but could they be trusted? The integration of intellectuals into the new society remained a difficult problem.

The extent of dissatisfaction among intellectuals was revealed when Mao invited writers and thinkers to "let a hundred flowers bloom; let a hundred schools contend." When this invitation was first issued in May 1956, there was little response, for writers and intellectuals had grown wary of exposing themselves to attack. Then, in February 1957, Mao delivered a speech, "On the Correct Handling of Contradictions Among the People," in which he said that nonantagonistic contradictions should be resolved by persuasion rather than force. He particularly stressed contradictions between the leaders and the masses, emphasized that party leaders might be wrong and the people right, and warned of the need for continuing ideological struggle. After some further reassurance, the floodgates of criticism were opened.

Criticism was directed not only against the behavior of individual party functionaries and at specific party policies but also at the CCP itself for seeking, as one editor declared, "to bring about the monolithic structure of a one-family empire."² Intellectuals and writers asked for independence from the party's ideological control. Academic problems should be left for professors to solve: "Perhaps Mao has not had time to solve these problems for us," one history professor suggested.³

Mao had intended to use the campaign to rectify the party, but the criticism was more than he had bargained for. Weeds grew where he had invited flowers, and soon criticism exceeded acceptable limits. In the resulting suppression of the Hundred Flowers some prominent intellectual and literary figures, most notably the revolutionary writer Ding Ling (Ting Ling), disappeared from the public scene. The intellectuals sent to do physical labor in the countryside were soon joined by many thousands of conservative or bureaucratic party members, targets of an antirightist campaign that began in June 1957 and by December of the same year had quickened into a massive purge of party members and cadres. This new move against the bureaucratization of the party was a direct reflection of the populist views of Mao Zedong, views that were to find their next expression in the Great Leap Forward.

The underlying issues remained. One of these was how to insure right thinking and moral dedication to the revolution. Another was how to balance the requirements for ideological purity essential for the achievement of the aims of the revolution with the professional competence required to operate a modern state and build an industrial system. Without ideological purity, the revolution would be jeopardized and a new elite of experts, technocrats, and managers would pursue its own aims. At issue was the emphasis to be placed on Redness over expertise. Beyond this, since it involved everyone, was the tension between spontaneity and control: how to encourage individual initiative and foster enthusiasm without disrupting social and economic progress, how to create disciplined spontaneity and spontaneous discipline.

## The Great Leap Forward

The Great Leap Forward was initiated in January 1958 but lost momentum the following year; after fall 1959 it was continued, but without vigor, until it was terminated in January 1961. Earlier, the government had intended to implement a Second Five-Year Plan; but now, on Mao's initiative, the Soviet model of development was abandoned. As in his 1955 speech, Mao placed his faith not in the gradual programs of Soviet-style central planners and experts but in the human energies of the masses imbued with revolutionary consciousness. A voluntarist as well as a populist, Mao believed that ideology was a force that could motivate people to heroic accomplishments. History was not confined to a series of well-defined objective stages of economic and sociopolitical development but instead was a constant process of "permanent revolution," with the subjective will transforming the objective world. The revolution had made extensive use of massive manpower in labor-intensive projects all along, projects such as the building of waterways, roads, and other giant construction works. Now all of China's human resources were to be focused in a giant leap. By emphasizing Redness and revolutionary fervor, Mao hoped to accelerate China's economic development and progress toward socialism. The spirit of the people was to be the driving force for China's continued economic growth and social transformation.

As the prime vehicle for this effort, rural communes were formed by combining the already existing cooperatives. By the end of 1958 there were 26,000 rural communes in which 98 percent of China's rural population lived. Each averaged about 25,000 people. The communes themselves were divided into production brigades, each corresponding roughly to the traditional village, and these were in turn divided into production teams. The communes were intended to function as China's basic political as well as economic and social units, integrating all aspects of the lives of their members. As economic units the communes supervised agricultural production and distribution, provided banking services, and also established small factories and machine shops operated on the commune or production brigade level, depending on the size and degree of specialization of the plant. The communes were further responsible for police functions, and they operated schools and hospitals, provided day care facilities and mess halls, took care of the aged, and staged plays and other entertainments. They represented an ambitious attempt to create new, large-scale communities. But they turned out to be too large. Their size was therefore reduced, so that by the end of the Great Leap Forward the original number of communes had almost tripled to 74,000 with a corresponding decrease in the size of their memberships. Later the communes lost many of their functions to the smaller production brigades.

There was also a movement to establish communes in the cities by combining or transforming earlier street associations, but this movement was briefer and accomplished less than its rural counterpart, perhaps because of the greater complexities of cities or because it ran into opposition. The street associations, which included the inhabitants of one street (or of several small streets, or of a portion of a large street), had originally been organized for security and welfare purposes. They were now given additional responsibilities for economic enterprises as well as for educational and medical facilities. In general, the formation of urban communes involved the transfer of authority over factories from central and provincial ministries to the local party committee that controlled the communes. Some of the communes consisted of workers in one large factory, others included the residents of one part of a city, still others, located on the outskirts of cities, included some farmland along with an urban sector. Whatever the form of urban organization, an effort was made to release women for work by establishing mess halls, nurseries, homes for the aged, and service facilities such as laundries.

To enlist the enthusiasm of the people and encourage initiative, local authorities were granted substantial leeway in deciding how to implement government directives. The central government still set general economic policy and retained control over the largest heavy industrial plants, but 80 percent of all enterprises were decentralized. No longer was there to be reliance on experts in far-off Beijing making all the decisions and operating with a centralized bureaucracy such as that of the U.S.S.R. This new policy was consistent with Mao's belief in mass participation and in the power of the human will.

High social as well as economic expectations were raised by the creation of the communes. According to Communist theory, the achievement of a truly communist society entails a change from paying people according to their productivity to paying "each according to his needs." In line with this, experiments were conducted in paying people approximately 70 percent of their wages in kind (produce to satisfy their needs) and the rest in cash according to their productivity. Meanwhile, impressive production targets were announced, including the goal of catching up with British industrial production in fifteen years. To the Chinese leaders, the social and economic goals seemed entirely compatible.

A major accomplishment of the Great Leap Forward was in furthering the emotional involvement of numerous people in the creation of a new order through the catharsis of intense participation. They were made to feel that the making of a strong China was not something to be left to the experts and technocrats; it was to be done by, as well as for, the people. People and government were to join in one vast common effort.

If the Great Leap Forward achieved some of its political and psychological goals, it was less successful economically. The initial statistics concerning production were impressive, but they turned out to have been grossly inflated. One unanticipated consequence of the Great Leap Forward was a breakdown in China's statistical services and central planning; serious mistakes were made because the government accepted the exaggerated figures forwarded by overenthusiastic local authorities. As a result, the government stopped publishing statistics after 1960.

Some projects originally pursued with enthusiasm later had to be abandoned as unworkable. Perhaps the best known was the campaign to build backyard furnaces for making iron and steel. The plan was vigorously implemented. All over China small furnaces were set up, but they proved incapable of turning out iron of acceptable quality let alone steel. Still, even the failures helped to spread an understanding of modern technology to the countryside, and the Great Leap Forward helped to introduce machine shops and other useful small operations into the country.

The most serious failure of the Great Leap Forward was in agriculture. Here too the government worked with misleading statistics, as local units vied with each other in reporting productivity gains. The harvest of 1958 was seriously exaggerated, leaving China poorly prepared for 1959 when bad weather harmed the crops and for the harvest of 1960, which was still worse. The gravity of China's economic situation increased when in July of 1960 the Soviet Union withdrew all of its technicians.

# The Sino-Soviet Split

From the founding of the People's Republic on, there were areas of tension and potential conflict between China and the Soviet Union. As we have seen, the CCP was not successful in achieving power until it went its own way, forging its own policies in accord with Chinese realities rather than with Moscow's theories. Furthermore, the Chinese leadership was as determinedly nationalistic as the Russians, who, ever since Stalin first came to power, had operated on the principle that what was good for the Soviet Union was also good for the cause of world communism. This was an equation with some plausibility as long as there was only one great Communist power in the world, but it was a thesis that the Chinese, sooner or later, were bound to challenge.

Initially, the forces holding the alliance together were stronger than those pulling it apart. These included not only the ties of a common ideological heritage but also a set of common Cold War enemies. However, around the mid 1950s the first cracks in the alliance began to appear.

One cause of friction and potential antagonism was territorial. The Chinese reluctantly accepted the independence of Outer Mongolia, but they were very unhappy about their northern and western boundaries with the Soviet Union. These borders had been drawn in the nineteenth century and thus formed part of the history of imperialism that China's new government was pledged to undo. As early as 1954 Chinese publications indicated the country's refusal to accept vast regions of Central and Northeast Asia as permanently belonging to the U.S.S.R.

Another source of friction was the Chinese desire for recognition as leaders within the Communist world. After Stalin's death in 1953, the Chinese expected that Mao would be honored as the leading living contributor to Marxist ideology. Instead, Khrushchev went his own way, first shocking the Marxist world by denouncing Stalin in a famous speech in 1956, and then by developing his theories of peaceful coexistence. Neither the rejection of Stalinism nor the U.S.S.R.'s new international stance accorded with Chinese needs, nor had the Chinese leaders been consulted before these major shifts in Soviet policy were announced.

Khrushchev's denunciation of Stalin sent shockwaves throughout the Marxist world and loosened the reins of Russian control over the Communist states of Eastern Europe. This gave the Chinese an opportunity to play a more important role within the Communist alliance. Even when they backed the U.S.S.R., as in supporting the Soviet suppression of the Hungarian uprising in the fall of 1956, the Chinese demonstrated a potential for independent action.

Despite signs of renewed friendship, including Mao's visit to Moscow in 1957, the strains in the alliance continued to mount. One reason for this was the U.S.S.R.'s unwillingness to exploit its temporary supremacy in rocketry to support a possible attack on Nationalist Chinese Taiwan, an attack that would have had no hopes for success unless the United States were neutralized by Soviet threats. Khrushchev's relatively unbelligerent stance toward the United

States seemed to the Chinese like a cowardly betrayal, while Mao's belittling of the dangers of nuclear warfare made him appear to the Russians as a dangerous adventurer gambling with the lives of millions. Consequently, the Russians were hesitant about sharing nuclear secrets with the Chinese, and that, in turn, increased the tension between the two nations.

The dispute also had a strong ideological dimension. The U.S.S.R. could hardly be expected to welcome Chinese claims, made during the Great Leap Forward, that their communes represented a higher stage on the road to the ideal society than anything achieved in the Soviet Union forty years after the revolution.

Khrushchev's visit to President Eisenhower in the fall of 1959 confirmed Chinese suspicions that the Russians were ready to come to terms with the United States. The CCP leaders did not mince their words, and relations deteriorated. When the Russians withdrew their technicians in the summer of 1960, they even took their blueprints with them. The split was final.

## Sino-Soviet Relations after 1960

Despite occasional attempts to settle their differences and despite limited cooperation on specific issues, such as supporting the North Vietnamese during the Vietnam War, efforts to reconstitute the Sino-Soviet alliance failed, and relations between the two countries worsened.

One aspect of this situation was the U.S.S.R.'s support of India in its disputes with China. Relations between China and India had generally been friendly during the 1950s, but in 1959, after the Chinese suppressed a revolt in Tibet, the Indians welcomed Tibetan refugees, including the Dalai Lama, the spiritual and sometime secular leader of Tibet. Furthermore, China and India, the world's two most populous nations, were natural rivals for Asian leadership. The resulting tensions would not have led to outright hostility, however, had it not been for Indian intransigence over border disputes. The result was a short border war in 1962 in which the Chinese quickly humiliated the Indian troops. The Soviet Union continued its policy of friendship for India, and China cultivated good relations with India's arch rival, Pakistan. Meanwhile, within the Communist world, China defended and allied itself with the bitterly anti-Soviet regime of Albania.

The Chinese continued to challenge Soviet claims to ideological leadership, insisting that Mao's thought constituted the guidelines for revolution in the underdeveloped countries of the world. Going a step further, they denied the Marxist validity of the U.S.S.R.'s own development and charged both Khrushchev and his successors with deviation from the true revolutionary path. In doing so they struck a responsive chord among those revolutionaries in various parts of the world who were dismayed by the U.S.S.R.'s domestic bureaucratism and the Soviet Union's comparative lack of zeal for world revolution. Russian and East European ideologues, for their part, responded in kind, explaining Chinese aberrations as arising from their lack of a firm proletarian base and an inadequate understanding of the principles of Marxism.

Militarily the Soviet Union remained much the stronger of the two powers, but the People's Republic was also developing its armed strength. A milestone was reached in 1964 when it exploded its first atomic bomb. Numerous clashes along the border between the U.S.S.R. and China endangered the peace between them, and both sides feared that the situation might evolve into a full-fledged war. Peking invested in an extensive system of underground shelters for use in case of an attack by air. The hostility of the Soviet Union continued to be a basic reality in China's international situation. It was one of the principal factors that led to a gradual rapprochement between China and the United States during the 1970s.

## Domestic Developments (1961–1965)

The failure of the Great Leap Forward led to retrenchment in domestic policies, a willingness to accept, for the moment, more modest interim social and economic goals. It also led to a decline in Mao's personal authority, not only because of the economic depression that had followed the Great Leap, but also because political and economic processes were becoming institutionalized and bureaucratized. The new system was settling down.

Mao was still chairman of the party, but in December 1958 he had resigned as head of the government. That post was filled by Liu Shaoqi (Liu Shao-chi, 1898–1969), a hard-working organization man long associated with Mao. Liu had a number of supporters in high party and government positions, but the supervision of the state's administrative machinery, including the various ministries, remained under the direction of the head of the State Administrative Council, who had the title of Premier. This position had been filled since 1949 by another trusted party veteran, Zhou Enlai (Chou En-lai). Zhou also served as Foreign Minister until 1959, and continued even after he left that post to serve as China's main spokesman in foreign affairs. By all accounts, Zhou was one of the most capable and versatile of all the CCP leaders, a superb political and military strategist, a truly gifted administrator and negotiator.

Another important government position was that of Minister of Defense. In 1959 a veteran general was ousted from this post for going too far in criticizing Mao and the Great Leap Forward, for pro-Soviet tendencies, and for overemphasizing professionalism, allegedly at the cost of failing to imbue the troops with sufficient ideological spirit. His successor as Minister of Defense was another distinguished general, Lin Biao (Lin Piao).

Under the direction of Liu Shaoqi, the government relaxed the tempo of social change and launched a policy of readjustment. There was now greater appreciation of expertise and less reliance on the revolutionary enthusiasm of the masses. There was an increased use of economic rather than ideological incentives: in the communes the more productive workers could earn extra work points, and in the factories there were wage increases, bonuses, and promotions to be earned—measures later castigated as "economism." Peasants were also allowed now to have small private plots and to sell on the free market whatever they could grow on them, while still under the obligation to produce a fixed amount of grain for the state.

After the great exertions and the disappointments of the Great Leap Forward, there was a natural slackening not only of the pace of change but also of revolutionary fervor. This alarmed Mao, who sought to combat this trend by initiating a socialist education movement in 1962 without, however, much effect. Furthermore, there now appeared in print thinly veiled attacks on Mao himself. Among them was the historical play, "Hai Rui (Hai Jui) Dismissed from Office," written by the Deputy Mayor of Beijing, a distinguished historian well known to Mao. In this play a sixteenth-century official was portrayed sympathetically as an honest minister who stood up for the peasants and was dismissed by a foolish and autocratic emperor. What was implied was a critique of Mao's own dismissal, in 1959, of the then Minister of Defense. In November 1965 an article was published in the Shanghai press denouncing this play. Thus began the Cultural Revolution.

## The Great Proletarian Cultural Revolution (1965–1969)

The Cultural Revolution was, from the beginning, both profoundly ideological and strongly political. In its intentions and consequences it was cultural in the broadest meaning of that term, since it sought to remold the entire society and to change the consciousness of the Chinese people.

At the center of the Cultural Revolution was Mao himself, determined not to allow the revolution that had been his life's work to drift into Soviet-style revisionism, resolved to combat the reemergence of old patterns of bureaucratic arrogance and carreerism, convinced that drastic measures were necessary to prevent the entrenchment of new vested interests in the state and party apparatus so that the people would not be robbed of their revolution. Now an old man, Mao was unwilling to rest on his laurels and enjoy the acclaim of his people as the father figure of the revolution. Instead, he actively involved himself in the Cultural Revolution and displayed great physical as well as mental energy. He demonstrated the former dramatically in July 1966 when, five months before his seventy-fourth birthday, he publically swam the Yangtze, covering some ten miles at remarkable speed.

The obstacles to the Cultural Revolution were formidable because it affected the vested interests of a majority of party functionaries both at the center and in the provinces. But among Mao's assets were not only his unequaled prestige but also the support of the People's Liberation Army, which under Lin Biao, emphasized guerrilla-style revolutionary spirit and fostered solidarity among officers and men by deemphasizing and reducing the importance of rank. In the summer of 1965, insignia of rank were abolished. Nor were there any other differences in uniform to differentiate officers and men. Mao and the other leaders of the Cultural Revolution hoped similarly to reduce or, if possible, to eliminate the distinctions and privileges of rank in society at large.

To accomplish this, required the destruction of the Establishment. A popular image of the Cultural Revolution was that of Monkey, the beloved hero of the Ming-dynasty novel, *Journey to the West* (*Xiyou-ji, Hsi-yu chi*).

> The Golden Monkey wrathfully swung his massive cudgel,
> And the jade-like firmament was cleared of dust.[4]

The author of the article in which these lines appeared in May 1966 went on to explain that the cudgel was Mao's thought. To carry on the battle, the country was inundated with copies of *Quotations from Chairman Mao*, the omnipresent Little Red Book cited on all occasions as the ultimate source of authority. Similarly, Mao himself was glorified as never before.

By all accounts the most enthusiastic wielders of the cudgel were the Red Guards, young people mostly born since the founding of the People's Republic. Mao hoped that their youthful spirit would revitalize the revolution and keep it from sinking into comfortable revisionism. In Mao's view it was not enough for these young people merely to read theoretical and historical works and to sing revolutionary songs. They must actually live and make revolution, so that they would be molded by direct personal revolutionary experience, much as Mao and his generation of leaders had been. Thus the youthful Red Guards were to form the vanguard of the Great Proletarian Cultural Revolution. To some they represented the wave of the future, but others suffered as their uncontrolled spontaneity got out of hand, and they administered public humiliation to prominent men, administered beatings and took captives, ransacked houses, and destroyed art.

Opposition to the Red Guard and the Cultural Revolution was considerable. In many places the local authorities were able to draw on popular support. There was rioting, and pitched battles were fought between rival groups, each claiming to represent the thought of Mao Zedong. Much of the information on these struggles comes from the posters written in large characters that were the prime means of public communication during the Cultural Revolution. Mao himself, in August 1966, wrote such a poster, "Let Us Bombard the Headquarters."

Many party headquarters were indeed attacked, and the party was crippled. Leaders of the government from Liu Shaoqi down were made to confess their sins in public and then disappeared from public view. Universities were closed, scientific and scholarly journals ceased publication (although nuclear development went on apace), intellectual and cultural life were disrupted, and there was turmoil in the cities. However, Zhou Enlai managed to keep the basic machinery of government working and was able to protect some from attack. Meanwhile, Mao's wife, Jiang Qing (Chiang Ch'ing, ca. 1915–), and Mao's secretary, Chen Boda (Ch'en Po-ta, 1904–), emerged as leaders of the Cultural Revolution group.

The Cultural Revolution reached its most radical phase in 1967. At the beginning of that year a dramatic series of events in Shanghai, China's largest city, led to the triumph of a workers' movement that was able to overthrow the local party apparatus by overcoming factional divisions. In February the workers formed a People's Commune, which lasted only nineteen days, since it did not receive the endorsement of Mao Zedong, who thought it too radical. He preferred the formation of "revolutionary committees" in which the army played a leading role. With the CCP out of commission and the country badly divided, the army grew in importance as the single organized and disciplined institution capable of forceful action on a national scale. However, the revolution developed a new "ultraleft" intensity before the army was called in to calm things down. In the summer of 1967, hundreds of thousands demonstrated in Beijing against Liu Shaoqi and Zhou Enlai. Radicals even occupied the foreign ministry for two weeks. Outside of the capital the most dramatic events took place in July, when the army intervened to suppress local anti-government insurgents. In September, fearing that China was on the brink of anarchy, Mao ordered the army to restore order.

Military men were prominent on the various revolutionary committees set up to administer provinces, factories, and communes as the Cultural Revolution continued, increasingly under army auspices. The revolution came to an end in 1969. In April of that year, a party congress officially confirmed the new prominence of the army by promoting Lin Biao to become Mao's successor, having been officially so designated in the constitution.

During the Cultural Revolution, party cadres and intellectuals were frequently "sent down" (xiafang, hsia-fang) to work the land among the peasants, and now thousands of Red Guards were similarly removed from the cities for a stint of labor in the fields. This was not only a practical measure for restoring order but also had a theoretical basis in the "mass line," which embodied Mao's conviction that the people were the source of valuable ideas and that the function of leaders was to obtain these ideas from the masses, to concentrate and systematize them, and then to take them back to the masses. Mao thus envisioned "an endless spiral, with the ideas becoming more correct, more vital and richer each time."[5] The function of party members and other leaders in this process was humbly to learn from the masses and also to teach them. Whatever else the procedure may have accomplished, was there any better way for leaders to achieve identification with the masses?

Economically the Cultural Revolution saw the resumption of Great Leap Forward programs that had been dismantled by the moderate leaders during the early 1960s. Again ideology was emphasized over expertise and personal economic incentives. Again the focus was on the rural sector, which benefited from programs that extended medical care and education. Plants were built in rural areas to manufacture and repair farm machinery, produce fertilizer, or process local products, thereby diminishing the distinction between city and country. After the cultural revolution, experiments in calculating work points for farm work on the basis of political criteria rather than in terms of an individual's productivity were abandoned. Similarly, in urban factories there were provisions for greater worker participation in factory management and programs to lessen the distinction between workers and managers and between mental and manual labor. But few of these survived the periods of consolidation and stabilization that followed the end of the Cultural Revolution.

## From the Cultural Revolution to the Death of Mao (1969–1976)

During the seven years between the end of the Cultural Revolution and the death of China's greatest revolutionary leader, the Communist party was rebuilt and became dominant once more. While leaders who had been denounced during the Cultural Revolution reappeared in prominent positions, the most eminent victim of the new political turn was Lin Biao. His downfall came in the autumn of 1971. The official account is that he tried to save himself by staging a coup, and that when those plans did not work out, he attempted to flee in an airplane, which crashed in Outer Mongolia killing all aboard. Lin Biao appears to have resisted abandoning the more radical Cultural Revolution policies. In any case, he was vehemently denounced for "ultraleftist" crimes (later changed to "ultrarightist" but most recently characterized as "leftist" and "feudalist").

The fate of Liu Shaoqi and Lin Biao demonstrated the hazardous position of those who rose to high leadership and were marked for the succession, but Zhou Enlai, as usual, was on the winning side. Zhou continued as Premier, and with Mao aging, he played a more important role now than ever. In the political arena, there was a decrease in army influence and a rebuilding of the party. More moderate economic policies were adopted, and there was a general relaxation of emphasis on revolutionary fervor. For example, when universities were first reopened in 1970, after a four-year hiatus, admission was based on a candidate's recommendations from comrades in the candidate's work unit and the approval of the appropriate revolutionary committee. In 1972, however, academic criteria for admission were reintroduced. That year, the first scientific periodicals also reappeared, but the new emphasis was on applied rather than theoretical science. Public exaltation of Mao was toned down. There were even attacks on the Little Red Book; CCP members were now urged to pursue a thorough study of Marxist writings.

In dealing with the Chinese past, the political and intellectual leadership took great pride in the antiquity of their civilization and in some of the early accomplishments of the Chinese people. There was therefore a great interest in archaeology, and many discoveries made at construction sites greatly advanced the study of the origins of Chinese civilization and the history of its material culture. This work continued during and after the Cultural Revolution, when some fine discoveries were made by amateurs. Other aspects of the Chinese past, however, were treated with less enthusiasm, in the continuing process of reinterpreting Chinese history according to the categories of Marxist theories of historical development.

One of the historical figures who fared badly in the process of reappraising the past was Confucius, who, of course, had been under attack ever since the May Fourth movement. However, Confucius was denounced with special vigor and frequency during 1973–74 in a campaign linking Lin Biao with Confucius. Both men were portrayed as "political swindlers," sinister reactionaries standing in the way of historical progress. Thus Confucius was depicted as representing a declining slave-owner class, while Lin Biao was charged with restoring capitalism. Each man exerted himself to reinstate an outdated system.

The ancient philosopher and the modern general made a strange pair, and there is some evidence suggesting that Confucius was really a surrogate for Zhou Enlai. As it was, the campaign died down without producing any contemporary political victims, but it did reflect the fact that the advocates of the Cultural Revolution still commanded some influence. These included Jiang Qing as well as the three others later denounced for forming "The Gang of Four": Zhang Chunqiao (Chang Ch'un-ch'iao), who had been appointed by Mao to lead the Shanghai Commune; Yao Wenyuan (Yao Wen-yüan), author of the attack on *Hai Rui Dismissed from Office,* which began the Cultural Revolution; and Wang Hongwen (Wang Hung-wen), a former Shanghai factory worker raised to prominence by Mao.

## The Arts

From the beginning the new regime had a direct and fundamental impact on the arts, insisting that they serve the masses. What was valued was not technique, or subtlety of expression, but revolutionary content and easy communication with the people. In keeping with this approach, major efforts were made to broaden popular participation in the arts and to put artists in closer touch with the masses, so that they might draw inspiration from them.

As far as possible, literature and the visual arts were to be not only for the people but also by the people. Thus, during the Great Leap Forward teams were sent out to collect the people's literature and to encourage peasants and workers to compose poetry and otherwise participate in the creation of art. As a result, in Shanghai alone some 200,000 people participated in producing 5 million poems. Many thousands undoubtedly were exhilarated at achieving recognition in a field previously reserved for an exclusive elite.

During the sixties and seventies, workers and peasants continued to be encouraged to participate in the creation of art. There were efforts at collective writing and painting. Another arrangement was for part-time writers to get a day off from their factory jobs in order to work on their literary projects. Professional writers were periodically "sent down" to factory or commune, so that they would not lose touch with the people. They also, as a matter of routine, invited popular criticism of their work and responded to suggestions for changes. For example, before *The Broad Road to Golden Light* (1972) was is-

Figure 13-1  Mao Zedong.

sued, 200 copies were sent to communes and factories for criticism. This novel by Hao Ran (Hao Jan, pen name of Liang Jinguang [Liang Chin-kuang], 1932–) went on to sell 4 million copies.

As earlier in the Soviet Union, the challenges and triumphs of a socialist society became the main topics of art and literature. The theme of *Broad Road*, for example, was the change from individual farming to the creation of mutual-aid teams. The same themes occurred over and over: the ideals and struggles of the revolution, the wisdom of Mao, the heroism of soldiers, the triumph of socialist virtue over selfishness, and the glories of work. Although the style is usually designated "socialist realism," it is romantic rather than realistic, intended to inspire, not to mirror life, which in practice inevitably falls short of the ideal.

A central reality in Chinese life was the importance of work. This is hardly surprising in a backward socialist state striving to feed its people, assure its national security, and otherwise catch up with the advanced industrial nations of the world. Everyone was exhorted to work hard and to contribute to the building of a new society; indeed, there was an almost puritan ethos of devotion to work. The arts both encouraged and reflected this tendency. Thus Yuan Kejia (Yüan K'o-chia, 1921–) wrote in 1958:

Labor is joy; how joyful is it?
Bathed in sweat and two hands full of mud,
Like sweet rain my sweat waters the land
And the land issues scent, better than milk.

Labor is joy; how joyful is it?
Home from a night attack, hoe in hand,
The hoe's handle is still warm,
But in bed, the warrior is already snoring.[6]

Once Yuan was an admirer of T. S. Eliot, but all that was far behind him when he wrote this poem.

Content was emphasized over form in the arts, and since that content was determined by the political authorities, the line between art and propaganda

Figure 13-2   Hang Gaoshe (Hang Kao-she), *Criticizing Lin Biao and Confucius Promotes Production.* Peasant painting from Huhsien. Exhibited in Beijing in 1973.

was often thin. To Western eyes, much that was now produced lacked appeal. Thus, none of the numerous paintings glorifying Mao Zedong matches in human appeal the sympathetic photograph shown here. (See Figure 13-1.)

Perhaps the most refreshing and enjoyable paintings came from the brushes of peasants and show scenes of people at work. Figure 13-2 shows a work of peasant art exhibited in Peking in 1973. It is filled with people at work. Most of the work is done by human muscle; children too are mobilized to help out, as in old China, although now they march in formation behind a red banner identifying them as little red soldiers. But there are other sources of power too, including a power station testifying to the electrification of irrigation, which is now general in China and has greatly helped agriculture. In accordance with the time, the painting also has an immediate political message: in front of the wall-poster stand, in the lower right, is a man making posters, "Criticize Lin, Criticize Confucius," and the theme is repeated in the painting's title. Like many peasant paintings, this one is done in bright and cheerful colors. Its tone is optimistic.

An art exhibition was held in Peking on the occasion of the twenty-fifth anniversary of the People's Republic in 1974. The works displayed suggested no new artistic departures but did offer further insights into Chinese life and art. Many of them show women at work, for it was official policy that women become fully equal with men. In *Youth Red as Fire* (see Figure 13-3) a young woman sits at the controls of a huge steel furnace, and the red of the title is echoed by the red glow of the furnace pouring out liquid white steel. This example of "socialist realism," like the peasant paintings from Huhsien, represents a break with the artistic past. However, tradition was not rejected in its entirety, for there were artists who used old techniques to render modern subjects. In Figure 13-4, the Beijing Express emerges from "Victory Tunnel," which is given depth by the use of Western perspective; but even the train on the bridge high above does not destroy the traditional flavor of the mountain setting and the overall composition.

In the performing arts, the influence of Jiang Qing, herself once an actress, was particularly strong. One of her main aims was to create revolutionary operas celebrating contemporary themes in place of the old Peking opera and its traditional plots. There were also some innovations, notably in staging opera accompanied by a piano. Some of the results are far from Western tastes. Orville Schell describes one performance as sounding "like some providentially lost Khatchaturian score," and goes on to describe an "ingeniously choreographed" harvest dance called, "We Are So Happy Because We Are Delivering Grain to the State."[7] After describing a dance featuring a father-daughter duet expressing their joy at the completion of an electric power plant, Clive Barnes, formerly the dance critic for the *New York Times*, suggested that if this seems bizarre to us, the Chinese might be just as startled by the story of a prince falling in love with a swan (Swan Lake).[8] Examples could readily be drawn from the other arts to illustrate the gulf separating Chinese and Western aesthetic perceptions.

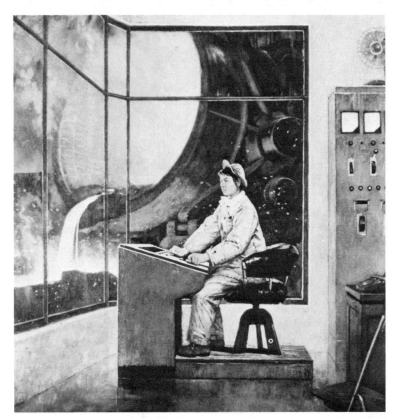

Figure 13-3
Liu Qing (Liu Ch'ing), *Youth Red as Fire.* Oil. Exhibited at the National Exhibition Commemorating the 25th Anniversary of the Founding of the People's Republic of China.

## Foreign Affairs

China's main foreign policy concern remained the Soviet Union. The concern was heightened to alarm when the U.S.S.R. invaded Czechoslovakia in 1968 and Communist Party Secretary Leonid Brezhnev announced that the U.S.S.R. had the right to intervene in socialist countries, which he accorded only "limited sovereignty." Fears of a Soviet nuclear strike, actual troop deployments along the lengthy Sino-Soviet frontier, and armed clashes in Manchuria induced China to seek broader diplomatic contacts with the United States. Previously there had been periodic exchanges of views between the ambassadors of the two countries, held first in Geneva and later in Warsaw. The fall of Lin Biao and the emergence of the knowledgeable Zhou Enlai also aided the process of improved Sino-American relations.

A contributing factor on the American side was the intention of President Nixon, elected in 1968, to withdraw the United States from the war in Vietnam. Unlike the earlier war in Korea, the Vietnam War did not bring massive Chinese intervention, but the Chinese naturally supported the Communist North Vietnamese. As long as the war raged in full force and threatened to escalate still further, a change in Sino-American relations was unlikely. But a high-level Sino-American dialogue did not have to wait for the actual end of the war—a shift in direction toward peace was enough. By 1971 both sides were ready to talk. A new approach to China was deemed a logical corollary of the Kissinger-Nixon concept of international balance-of-power politics. The Chinese were receptive. The rest of the story is familiar, including the Chinese invitation to an American ping-pong team, whose members were personally greeted by Zhou Enlai. It culminated in President Nixon's visit to Peking in February 1972 and the Shanghai Communiqué, which looked forward to the normalization of relations between China and the United States. Sino-American relations had come a long way since John Foster Dulles, then Secretary of State, had refused to shake hands with Zhou Enlai at Geneva in 1954.

The success of China's new policy was marked by the entrance of the People's Republic into the United Nations (and the expulsion of the Nationalists), the rapprochement with Japan, and recognition by almost all other countries that had not extended it earlier. One country, however, that did not establish full official relations was the United States because it was reluctant to terminate relations with the Nationalist government on Taiwan.

Figure 13-4   Ma Lizhou and Yao Lifang, *The Iron Dragon Bores Through Ten Thousand Layers of Mountains.* 1974.

# Taiwan

Both the government in Beijing and that "temporarily" housed in Taipei regarded Taiwan as an integral part of China, a view acknowledged by the United States and confirmed in the Shanghai Communiqué. But Taiwan is more than a piece of unfinished business left over from the Chinese civil war and the global Cold War. For one thing, the island has not, with the exception of the period 1945–49, been a part of mainland China since 1895. For three-quarters of a century its history has diverged from that of China proper. During the most recent thirty years it has experienced very considerable economic success along with long-term political uncertainty.

Among the approximately 2 million civilian refugees who came to Taiwan with the Nationalists, many brought to the island advanced training and skills that contributed to economic development. The same cannot be said of the 500 thousand or so military personnel who also made the trip. Still, on balance, the influx seems to have benefited Taiwan economically.

Taiwan's economic success is apparent in both agriculture and industry. In the agrarian sector there was an effective land redistribution program during the fifties, creating a peasantry that largely owned the land it worked. Here at last, with American advice, the government finally implemented a principle it had talked about for years: land to the tiller. Industrial development (stressing light industry) was advanced through the investment of great sums of money that had been brought by the Nationalists from the mainland, and was given government encouragement under a series of Four-Year Plans that began in 1953. American economic assistance and private capital investment also helped, but was terminated in 1966 as no longer necessary. Another major source of capital came from Japan, as Japanese companies invested heavily in Taiwanese plants. Thus Taiwan became a participant in Japan's economic boom and attained a level of per capita income second in Asia only to that of Japan. It acquired the characteristics of a consumer society: in 1979, over 59 percent of all households owned a color television set, over 90 percent owned a refrigerator, and although only 13 percent enjoyed air conditioning, almost 70 percent owned a motorcycle. Taiwan's modernization was not only economic: over 90 percent of the population was literate, an achievement comparable to that of any other modern land.

Although outnumbered, mainlanders retained political control. While Taiwanese—that is, people of Chinese stock who had settled earlier on the island —did win election to positions in local government, real control remained in the hands of the central government, which claimed to speak for all of China. Those who opposed the central government were watched by the secret police and were often imprisoned. Censors scrutinized the media for subversive ideas, and the people were exhorted to practice Sun Yat-sen's Three Principles of the People.

The government, as well as many of Taiwan's intellectuals, saw its mission as one of preserving old Chinese traditions. Taiwan became the home for institutes of higher learning, and a museum was built to house the priceless Palace Collection of Art, which the Nationalists had brought from the mainland. There was also a minority of artists and intellectuals who sought to draw on the old traditions in order to create new forms of expression suitable for their historical situation. As Liu Kuo-sung (1932–) has explained: "We are no longer ancient Chinese nor modern Westerners. We do not live in the Sung or Yüan society, nor in the modern European or American environment. If it is false for us to copy old Chinese paintings, isn't it the same to copy modern Western painting?"[9] Liu, who spent his formative years and received his artistic training in Taiwan but now divides his time between Hong Kong and Iowa, is deeply conversant with both traditions and has an international reputation. His *Metaphysics of Rocks* (see Figure 13-5) includes calligraphic brushwork and collage. The latter has been described by Chu-tsing Li as follows:

> In the lower middle part are two pieces of collage, one large and the other small, both suggesting rock shapes. The paper is in color, but combined with some textures printed with wrinkled paper. Thus there seem to be several kinds of rocks, done with different techniques and brushwork. Yet none of them are realistic enough to resemble real rocks. But each gives us an idea of some quality of rocks, such as jutting up, having interesting textures, or showing watery surfaces.[10]

Figure 13-5
Liu Kuo-sung,
*The Metaphysics of Rocks.*
Ink and acrylic with
collage on paper, 1968,
68.6 cm × 67.3 cm.

The political, and therefore the cultural, future of Taiwan remains in doubt. In 1972 Chiang Kai-shek died, but there was little change as the government continued under his son, Chiang Ching-kuo (1910–). Expelled from the United Nations and increasingly isolated diplomatically, Taiwan has managed to remain economically prosperous. But international politics are likely to be a major factor in settling the destiny of the more than 17 million people (well over twice the number at the end of the Second World War) who inhabit the island.

# New Directions

The year 1976 was a momentous one for the People's Republic of China. In January Zhou Enlai died. The struggle over who should succeed him as premier grew so intense that it led to rioting in Beijing before the matter was finally settled in May by Mao, who indicated his preference for Hua Guofeng (Hua Kuo-feng, 1920–). Hua, known as a capable administrator, was soon called on to demonstrate his talents, for in July China's worst earthquake in four centuries devastated Tangshan, an industrial and mining city a hundred miles from Beijing. Casualties were high, and the quake did untold damage. But the government coped effectively in organizing relief.

On September 9 Mao Zedong died. Architect of the triumph of the CCP, he had been responsible for initiating most of those features of the Chinese revolution that made it unique. He had worked mightily to have the masses of the people participate fully, not only in the labor of building a strong economy, but also in the creation of a new culture and society. He had been in failing health for some time, so his death was not unexpected. Still, it came as a shock to the people he had led for so long.

Thus 1976 marked the end of an era and the emergence of a new one. While Hua succeeded Mao as party chairman, the leadership in instituting new policies was taken by Deng Xiaoping (Teng Hsiao-p'ing, 1904–), a party veteran once castigated as second only to Liu Shaoqi in "taking the capitalist road." In July 1977 Deng became First Deputy Premier, and in the ensuing three years strengthened his position by placing like-minded men in key positions. Blamed for all the ills of recent years was the "Gang of Four," led by Jiang Qing, Mao's widow. By November 1980 the new leaders felt sufficiently secure to place the "Gang of Four" on trial, but Jiang Qing remained defiant. In January 1981 she and Zhang Chunqiao were given a suspended death sentence commutable to life imprisonment. By that time Hua Guofeng had lost the prime ministership, and in June 1981 he also lost the party chairmanship but remained in the leadership as a vice-chairman.

Deng's program was epitomized in the slogan, "The Four Modernizations." Directed at farming, industry, science, and defense, they aimed to turn China into a modern industrial state by the end of the century. The years since 1952 had seen considerable economic progress, but China remained an underdevel-

Figure 13-6 Xiao Huinang (Hsiao Hui-hsiang), *The Spring of Science*, detail. Ceramic engraving, 2,000 × 340 cm. International Airport, Peking.

oped country by international economic standards, and the Cultural Revolution had taken its toll in loss of education and technological progress. Now, under Deng, professionalism was encouraged, factory managers received greater authority, and measures were taken to improve peasants' and workers' lives. There was a spirit of pragmatism in dealing with the problems of a nation with an estimated population of close to a billion people (even with a stringent birth-control program). Specialists were sent overseas for study and training. Pacts were signed with Japanese, American, and European firms for massive importation of advanced technology. Negotiations with the United States led to the establishment of formal diplomatic relations in January 1979, which meant that henceforth the United States would have only unofficial ties with Taiwan. To commemorate the new Sino-American relationship, Deng himself visited the United States. China continued to regard the Soviet Union as its main enemy.

At home, public figures who had been disgraced during the Cultural Revolution reappeared in public—Ding Ling is only one noteworthy example. Others, notably Liu Shaoqi, were rehabilitated posthumously. A reassessment of Mao himself was undertaken, leading to the official conclusion, adopted in June 1981, that Mao had seriously erred in the Cultural Revolution but that "his merits are primary and his errors secondary."[11] In numerous ways, and within limits, there was greater tolerance for diversity. Foreign tourism was fostered and, to accommodate international travelers, contracts were signed for the construction of American tourist hotels and the bottling of Coca-Cola. Previously banned books reappeared in print, and a freer, more thoughtful, and more critical literature made its appearance. On stage and in concert, Shakespeare and Beethoven were performed once more. In the visual arts, too, there was greater variety as artists worked in a broad range of styles. Works of art catering to every level of sophistication were sent abroad to help China win friends and earn money. Reproduced here (see Figure 13-6), as an expression of the new face China is showing the world, is a detail from a ceramic engraving at Beijing's International Airport. Entitled "The Spring of Science," it celebrates not only such achievements as Einstein's theory of relativity but also love and happiness, the arts, and, in this detail, dance, sport, poetry, and music.

It is still too early to predict the outcome of the new directions China has undertaken in the last few years. As post-Mao China gradually takes shape and as the nation copes with old problems and meets new challenges, it can be expected to continue its quest for policies and styles, institutions and structures, that are consonant with its own needs and traditions and different from those of both the Soviet Union and the West.

## NOTES

1. Maurice Meisner, *Mao's China: A History of the People's Republic* (New York: The Free Press, 1977), p. 129.

2. Ch'u An-p'ing, quoted in Merle Goldman, *Literary Dissent in Communist China* (Cambridge: Harvard University Press, 1967), p. 192.

3. Yang Hsiang-k'uei, quoted in *Ibid.*, p. 193.

4. Quoted in *The Great Cultural Revolution in China,* compiled and edited by the Asia Research Center (Rutland, Vt. and Tokyo: Charles E. Tuttle, 1968), p. 114.

5. Stuart R. Schram, *The Political Thought of Mao Tse-tung* (New York: Praeger, 1969), p. 317.

6. Hsu Kai-yu, *The Chinese Literary Scene—A Writer's Visit to the People's Republic* (New York: Vintage Books, Random House, 1975), p. 227.

7. Orville Schell, *In the People's Republic: An American's Firsthand View of Living and Working in China* (New York: Random House, 1977), pp. 59–60.

8. Clive Barnes, "Shanghai Ballet and Us—Two Different Worlds," *New York Times,* June 12, 1966, sec. D, pp. 5, 6, 24.

9. Quoted in Chu-tsing Li, *Liu Kuo-sung—The Growth of a Modern Chinese Artist* (Taipei: The National Gallery of Art and Museum of History, 1969), p. 32.

10. *Ibid.,* p. 53.

11. *Resolution on CPC History (1949–81)* (Beijing: Foreign Languages Press, 1981), p. 56.

# Suggestions for
# Further Reading

# Suggestions for Further Reading

The bibliography in English on China and Japan has increased enormously during the last twenty or thirty years, making selection all the more important as well as difficult. The intent here is to give an idea of what has been published to date so that the reader may know where to look for what. No attempt has been made to be comprehensive. Rather the effort has been made to select books that are broad enough to serve as introductions to their topics, that incorporate sound and recent scholarship, and that in their totality reflect a variety of approaches. Furthermore, the selection has been made with an eye toward readability.

In keeping with the scope of the present book, only a few books on traditional China and Japan have been included. For a more extensive selection, see Conrad Schirokauer, *A Brief History of Chinese and Japanese Civilizations.* For a comprehensive list of books and articles on all periods of East Asian History, see the *Bibliography of Asian Studies* issued annually by the Association for Asian Studies.

In all cases in which only the author and title are given, the book has been published in a paperback edition. In the case of a few paperbacks that might otherwise be difficult to identify, the place and date of publication have been added, as has been done for all hardcover books. Where, as is often the case, a book falls under more than one category, it has been placed under the category that reflects its primary content. Except in special cases, books are mentioned only once. General classroom collections of readings have not been included.

## General Works

*The Cambridge History of China* under the general editorship of Dennis Twitchett and John K. Fairbank promises, when completed, to become the most extensive and authoritative treatment of Chinese history in any Western language. This multivolume project began publication in 1978, three volumes to date (Cambridge University Press, Cambridge and New York). Unfortunately, no work of that scope is planned or available for Japanese history. A standard single-volume account of East Asian history is *East Asia: Tradition and Transformation* by John K. Fairbank, Edwin O. Reischauer, and Albert M. Craig (Boston, 1973). For a solid one-volume treatment of modern Chinese history, see Immanuel C. Y. Hsü, *The Rise of Modern China,* 2nd ed. (New York, 1975). Again there is nothing quite comparable on the Japanese side, but *An Introduction to Japanese Civilization,* edited by Arthur E. Tiedemann, devotes considerable space to the modern period. Also recommended are John W. Hall, *Japan from Prehistory to Modern Times;* H. Paul Varley, *Japanese Culture: A Short History;* and Peter Duus, *The Rise of Modern Japan* (Boston, 1976). *The Chinese and the Japanese: Essays in Political and Cultural Interactions,* edited by Akira Iriye, consists of sixteen conference papers on this important topic.

Some of the most significant and influential interpretations of modern China and Japan have been advanced by social scientists. An example is *Japanese Society* by Chie Nakane. An older and famous work is Ruth Benedict, *The Chrysanthemum and the*

*Sword*, which is still worth pondering. A fascinating book, with implications for comparative psychology, is Doi Takeo, *The Anatomy of Dependence*, translated by John Bester. These books do not have counterparts in Chinese studies, but three recent compedia, all published by Stanford University Press, offer a good overview of anthropological approaches to the study of China: Maurice Freedman, ed., *Family and Kinship in Chinese Society* (1972); Arthur P. Wolf, ed., *Religion and Ritual in Chinese Society* (1974); and Margery Wolf and Roxanne Witke, eds., *Women in Chinese Society* (1975). See also C. K. Yang, *Religion in Chinese Society—A Study of Contemporary Social Functions of Religion and Some of Their Historical Factors*.

# PART I    China and Japan in the Early Modern Period

*China*

The social and economic history of China during its last dynasty has been illuminated by a number of studies, which span the Ming as well as the Ch'ing. These include two influential books by Ping-ti Ho: *Studies in the Population of China, 1368–1953* (Cambridge, Mass., 1959) and *The Ladder of Success in Imperial China: Aspects of Social Mobility, 1368–1911* (New York, 1962). For an introduction to the examination system as it operated in late traditional China, see Ichisada Miyazaki, *China's Examination Hell: The Civil Service Examinations of Imperial China*, translated by Conrad Schirokauer. An important, rather technical book is Dwight H. Perkins, *Agricultural Development in China, 1368–1963* (Chicago, 1969). A-tu Zen Sun and S. C. Sun, trans., *T'ien-kung k'ai-wu, Chinese Technology in the Seventeenth Century* (University Park, Pa., 1966) is a gold mine of information.

Hilary J. Beattie, *Land and Lineage in China: A Study of T'ung-ch'eng County, Anhwei, in the Ming and Ch'ing Dynasties* (Cambridge and New York, 1979) is a major contribution to social history. A fine collection of essays is G. William Skinner, ed., *The City in Late Imperial China* (Stanford, 1977). Two highly regarded books on economic history are W. E. Willmott, *Economic Organization in Chinese Society* (Stanford, 1972) and Evelyn Sakakida Rawski, *Agricultural Change and the Peasant Economy in South China* (Cambridge, Mass., 1972). Rawski is also the author of the important book *Education and Popular Literacy in Ch'ing China* (Ann Arbor, 1979). Chang Chung-li has contributed two books on Ch'ing social structure: *The Chinese Gentry: Studies on Their Role in Nineteenth Century Chinese Society*, and *The Income of the Chinese Gentry* (Seattle, 1962). A different approach to the analysis of social mobility is taken by Wolfram Eberhard, *Social Mobility in Traditional China* (Leiden, 1963). A good way to begin reading on Ch'ing local government is to go through T'ung-tsu Ch'ü, *Local Government in China under the Ch'ing* (Cambridge, Mass., 1962), or the more recent John Watt, *The District Magistrate in Late Imperial China* (New York, 1972). On law, see Derk Bodde and Clarence Morris, *Law in Imperial China* (Cambridge, Mass., 1967), and Sybille Van der Sprenkel, *Legal Institutions in Manchu China, A Sociological Analysis* (London, 1962). For a recent thoughtful analysis of Ch'ing government, read Thomas A. Metzger, *The Internal Organization of Ch'ing Bureaucracy: Legal, Normative, and Communication Aspects* (Cambridge, Mass., 1973). Robert B. Oxnam has devised a novel way for groups to get the feel of the Ch'ing bureaucracy; see *The Ch'ing Game: Simulation and the Study of History* (obtainable from Learning Resources in International Studies, Suite 1231, 60 East 42nd St., N.Y., N.Y. 10017).

A study of the late Ming with significant implications also for the Ch'ing is Ray Huang, *1587, A Year of No Significance: The Ming Dynasty in Decline* (New Haven, 1981). For the Ming-Ch'ing transition, see Jonathan Spence and John E. Wills, Jr., eds., *From Ming to Ch'ing: Conquest, Region, and Continuity in Seventeenth-Century*

*China.* A useful monograph on the early Ch'ing is Robert B. Oxman, *Ruling from Horse-back: Manchu Politics in the Oboi Regency, 1661–1669* (Chicago, 1975). Also see Lawrence Kessler, *K'ang-hsi and the Consolidation of Ch'ing Rule, 1661–1684* (Chicago, 1976). Jonathan Spence has written two fascinating and informative books, *Ts'ao Yin and the K'ang-hsi Emperor, Bondservant and Master* (New Haven, 1966) and *Emperor of China: Self-Portrait of K'ang-hsi.* A recent and major contribution is Silas Wu, *Passage to Power: K'ang-hsi and His Heir Apparent, 1661–1722* (Cambridge, Mass., 1979). The other great emperor of the Ch'ing is the subject of Harold L. Kahn, *Monarchy in the Emperor's Eyes: Image and Reality in the Ch'ien-lung Reign* (Cambridge, Mass., 1971). For biographical information, consult Arthur W. Hummel, ed., *Eminent Chinese of the Ch'ing Period,* 2 vols. (Washington, 1943).

The texture of ordinary life is brilliantly conveyed in *Death of Woman Wang* by Jonathan Spence. Much can also be learned from the novels of the period. *The Scholars* by Wu Ching-tzu has been translated by Yang Hsien-yi and Gladys Yang (Peking, 1957) and is analyzed by Paul S. Ropp, *Dissent in Early Modern China: Ju-lin wai-shih and Ch'ing Social Criticism* (Ann Arbor, 1981). China's most admired novel, *The Dream of the Red Chamber* by Ts'ao Hsüeh-chin, is available in partial translation by Chi-chen Wang. David Hawkes is engaged in preparing a complete translation, three volumes of which have appeared to date, published as *The Story of the Stone* by Cao Xueqin. The leading authority on the Chinese stage is A. C. Scott; see his *Introduction to the Chinese Theater* (New York, 1959). For a sensitively drawn portrait of a gentleman-poet, see Arthur Waley, *Yuan Mei: Eighteenth Century Chinese Poet.* For a man with a very different intellectual outlook, see David S. Nivison, *The Life and Thought of Chang Hsüeh-ch'eng, 1738–1801* (Stanford, 1966), a very rewarding book for advanced students. Two additional books that require some background in philosophy and Chinese thought are *The Unfolding of Neo-Confucianism* by Wm. Theodore de Bary and the Conference on Seventeenth Century Chinese Thought and *Escape from Predicament: Neo-Confucianism and China's Evolving Political Culture* by Thomas A. Metzger (New York, 1977). Both are seminal works.

*Japan*

A brilliant and well-formulated interpretation of the Tokugawa political system is provided by Harold Bolitho, *Treasures Among Men: The Fudai Daimyo in Tokugawa Japan* (New Haven, 1974). Readers would also do well to consult Conrad Totman, *Politics in the Tokugawa Bakufu, 1600–1843* (Cambridge, Mass., 1967), and Herschell Webb, *The Japanese Imperial Institution in the Tokugawa Period* (New York, 1968). Excellent studies less broad in scope are John W. Hall, *Tanuma Okitsugu, 1719–1788, Forerunner of Modern Japan,* and John W. Hall and Marious Jansen, eds., *Studies in the Institutional History of Early Modern Japan* (Princeton, 1968). A splendid study of Tokugawa economic history is Thomas C. Smith, *The Agrarian Origins of Modern Japan.* A major work on Tokugawa social history as well as on the history of values is Ronald P. Dore, *Education in Tokugawa Japan* (Berkeley, 1965). On Tokugawa values, also see Robert N. Bellah, *Tokugawa Religion: The Values of Pre-industrial Japan.*

The intellectual history of the Tokugawa period is one of the important subjects underrepresented in Western scholarship. Shigeru Matsumoto, *Motoori Norinaga, 1730–1801* (Cambridge, Mass., 1970) is worthwhile. A useful book on Tokugawa Confucianism is Joseph J. Spaeth, *Itō Jinsai* (*Monumenta Serica* monograph, Peking, 1948). A very influential interpretation by a leading twentieth-century Japanese intellectual, published in 1952 but only recently translated, is Masao Maruyama, *Studies in the Intellectual History of Tokugawa Japan,* translated by Mikiso Hane (Princeton and Tokyo, 1974). It is an important but not an easy book, suitable more for advanced students than for beginners. A more recent major contribution to the field is *Principle and Practicality: Essays in Neo-Confucianism and Practical Learning,* edited by Wm. Theodore de

Bary and Irene Bloom; it too is a book that requires some background. A thoroughly delightful book on "dutch Learning" is Donald Keene, *The Japanese Discovery of Europe, 1720–1830* (Stanford, 1969).

The lively culture of the Tokugawa townspeople is dealt with in a number of scholarly and entertaining books. A good place to begin is Howard Hibbett, *The Floating World in Japanese Fiction*. Saikaku may be read in translation in Ivan Morris, trans., *The Life of an Amorous Woman and Other Writings by Ihara Saikaku*; Wm. Theodore de Bary, trans., *Five Women Who Loved Love*; and Peter Nosco, trans., *Some Final Words of Advice*. For the theater, see two translations by Donald Keene: *Four Major Plays of Chikamatsu* and *Chūshingura—The Treasury of Loyal Retainers*. Keene's *World Within Walls: Japanese Literature of the Pre-modern Era, 1600–1867* (New York, 1976) evidences the mature scholarship of a leading student of Japanese literature who is also a gifted stylist. It is the first volume to be published of a projected four-volume history of Japanese literature. Recommended on the art of the woodcut is Richard Lane, *Masters of the Japanese Print—Their World and Their Work* (New York, 1962). For individual artists, see the volumes in the *Masterworks of Ukiyo-e* series (Kodansha International, Tokyo and New York, 1968–). There are other worthy books on Tokugawa art, popular and aristocratic. One that stands out is Elise Grilli's superb *The Art of the Japanese Screen* (New York and Tokyo, 1970), a truly beautiful book. Finally, for an introduction to the poetry appreciated by all levels of Japanese society, see Harold G. Henderson, *An Introduction to Haiku: An Anthology of Poems and Poets from Bashō to Shiki*.

*First Encounters*

An excellent introduction to the initial contacts between modern Europe and East Asia is provided by George Sansom, *The Western World and Japan*. A well-written, informative account is C. R. Boxer, *The Christian Century in Japan* (Berkeley, 1951). Also see Michael Cooper, S. J., *They Came to Japan—An Anthology of European Reports on Japan, 1543–1640* (Berkeley, 1965). Recommended for China is L. J. Gallagher, trans., *China in the Sixteenth Century: The Journals of Matteo Ricci* (New York, 1953). Also recommended is Arnold H. Rowbotham, *Missionary and Mandarin: The Jesuits at the Court of China* (Berkeley, 1942). European knowledge of Asia in early modern times and European reactions to Asian cultures and peoples is the subject of an exhaustive multi-volume work still in progress: Donald Lach, *Asia in the Making of Europe* (Chicago, 1965–). For the influence on each other of European and East Asian art from the sixteenth to the twentieth century, see Michael Sullivan, *The Meeting of Eastern and Western Art* (New York, 1973).

# PART II   China and Japan in the Modern World

Most books concentrate on either China or Japan. An exception is Ernest R. May and James C. Thomson, Jr., *American–East Asian Relations: A Survey* (Cambridge, Mass., 1972), a collection of seventeen essays that emphasize bibliography.

*China*

Volumes 10 (1800–1870) and 11 (1870–1911) of the *Cambridge History of China* contain major syntheses of scholarship on these two periods. Both are edited by John K. Fairbank. Fairbank is also the author of *Trade and Diplomacy on the China Coast: The Opening of the Treaty Ports 1841–54*, which begins with an excellent account of the Canton System and its breakdown. A good account of the Opium War is Peter Ward Fay, *The Opium War, 1840–1842*. Three other books on the war are recommended: Hsin-pao

Chang, *Commissioner Lin and the Opium War*; Arthur Waley, *The Opium War Through Chinese Eyes* (London, 1958); and Jack Beeching, *The Chinese Opium Wars*. An important book on the Opium War in terms of social history and Chinese responses to Western intrusions is Frederic Wakeman, Jr., *Strangers at the Gate: Social Disorder in South China, 1839–1861*.

For diplomatic history, see Immanuel Hsu, *China's Entrance into the Family of Nations: The Diplomatic Phase, 1858–1880* (Cambridge, Mass., 1960). A general survey helpful for those seeking to view Ch'ing foreign relations in a Chinese perspective is Morris Rossabi, *China and Inner Asia: From 1368 to the Present Day* (New York, 1975).

The best way to begin the study of China's nineteenth-century rebellions is to read Frederic Wakeman, Jr., "Rebellion and Revolution: The Study of Popular Movements in Chinese History," *Journal of Asian Studies* 36 (February 1977): 201–37. This article analyzes various approaches, discusses and lists the very substantial bibliography in this field. Although not limited to the nineteenth century, it includes many works on this period, which is more fully documented than earlier times. For the Taiping Rebellion, see Franz Michael, *The Taiping Rebellion: History and Documents*, Vol. 1. A massive and detailed study by an expert is Jen Yu-wen, *The Taiping Rebellion* (New Haven, 1973).

For the dynasty's response to the great rebellion, see Mary C. Wright, *The Last Stand of Chinese Conservatism: The T'ung-chih Restoration, 1862–1874*, a landmark of scholarship in the field. Another very influential book, although it does not make for easy reading, is Philip Kuhn, *Rebellion and Its Enemies in Late Imperial China* (Cambridge, Mass., 1970).

The following books on the attempt at Self-Strengthening are recommended: Albert Feuerwerker, *China's Early Industrialization: Sheng Hsuan-huai, 1844–1916, and Mandarin Enterprise* (Cambridge, Mass., 1958); John Rawlinson, *China's Struggle for Naval Development, 1839–95*; and Knight Biggerstaff, *The Earliest Modern Government Schools in China* (Ithaca, N.Y., 1961). Feuerwerker has also written *The Chinese Economy ca. 1870–1911* (Michigan Papers in Chinese Studies, No. 5), recommended as a starting point for the study of the period's economic history. Among Feuerwerker's additional contributions to the field is the editing of *Approaches to Modern Chinese History* (Berkeley, 1968), which includes an important article on Li Hung-chang by K. C. Liu.

Kenneth Scott Latourette, *A History of Christian Missions in China* (London, 1929) is a good historical survey of its subject. A variety of views is presented in Jessie G. Lutz, ed., *Christian Missions in China: Evangelists of What?* (Problems in Asian Civilizations series). An important, more recent publication is John K. Fairbank, ed., *The Missionary Enterprise in China and America* (Cambridge, Mass., 1974). Also recommended are Irwin T. Hyatt, Jr., *Our Ordered Lives Confess—Three Nineteenth Century Missionaries in East Shantung* (Cambridge, Mass., 1976), and K. C. Liu, *Americans and Chinese: A Historical Essay and Bibliography* (Cambridge, Mass., 1963). The anti-Christian movement is analyzed with verve and erudition in Paul Cohen, *China and Christianity: The Missionary Movement and the Growth of Chinese Antiforeignism, 1860–1870* (Cambridge, Mass., 1963).

The study of modern Chinese intellectual history has been deeply influenced by the brilliant writings of Joseph Levenson, especially his *Confucian China and Its Modern Fate*, 3 vols. He is also the author of *Liang Ch'i-ch'ao and the Mind of Modern China* (Cambridge, Mass., 1953), which should be read in tandem with the more recent Hao Chang, *Liang Ch'i-ch'ao and Intellectual Tradition in China* (Cambridge, Mass., 1971). An excellent exemplar of what can be accomplished by a master in the field of intellectual biography is Benjamin Schwartz, *In Search of Wealth and Power: Yen Fu and the West*.

The best book on the Boxers is Victor Purcell, *The Boxer Uprising: A Background Study* (Cambridge and New York, 1963). The standard study of the dynasty's last-minute reforms is Meribeth Cameron, *The Reform Movement in China, 1898–1912* (Stanford, 1931). For additional perspective on the period, emphasizing problems of regionalism, see Roger V. Des Forges, *Hsi-lang and the Chinese Revolution* (New Haven, 1973). For the revolution of 1911, an excellent collection of essays is Mary C. Wright, ed., *China in Revolution: The First Phase, 1900–1913.* Also see Ernest Young, *The Presidency of Yüan Shih-k'ai: Liberalism and Dictatorship in Early Republican China* (Ann Arbor, 1977). Recommended on the "father of the Chinese Revolution" are Harold Schiffrin, *Sun Yat-sen and the Origins of the Chinese Revolution,* and C. Martin Wilbur, *Sun Yat-sen: Frustrated Patriot* (New York, 1977). Another important and good book is Marius Jansen, *The Japanese and Sun Yat-sen* (Cambridge, Mass., 1954). Another revolutionary leader is studied in Chün-tu Hsüeh, *Huang Hsing and the Chinese Revolution* (Stanford, 1961). For Japanese influences on an earlier Chinese leader, see Philip Huang, *Liang Ch'i-ch'ao and Modern Chinese Liberalism* (Seattle, 1972).

A good survey for the years between the Revolution of 1911 and the Communist triumph of 1949 is James E. Sheridan, *China in Disintegration: The Republican Era in Chinese History, 1912–1949.* A highly regarded study of the first decade of this period is Edward Friedman, *Backward Toward Revolution: The Chinese Revolutionary Party.* On this period, also see Andrew Nathan, *Peking Politics, 1918–23: Factionalism and the Failure of Constitutionalism* (Berkeley, 1976). For the warlord period see Jerome Ch'en, *The Military-Gentry Coalition: China Under the Warlords* (Toronto, 1979) and Hsi-sheng Ch'i, *Warlord Politics in China 1916–1928* (Stanford, 1976). A number of fine books deal with individual warlords: Donald G. Gillin, *Warlord: Yen Hsi-shan in Shansi Province, 1911–1949* (Princeton, 1967); James E. Sheridan, *Chinese Warlord: The Career of Feng Yu-hsiang* (Stanford, 1966); Gavan McCormack, *Chang Tso-ling in Northeast China, 1911–1928: China, Japan, and the Manchurian Idea* (Stanford, 1977). Also see Robert A. Knapp, *Szechwan and the Chinese Republic: Provincial Militarism and Central Power 1911–1938* (New Haven, 1973).

A book filled with information on intellectual history is Chow Tse-tsung, *The May Fourth Movement: Intellectual Revolution in Modern China,* which may be read in tandem with Benjamin Schwarz, ed., *Reflections on the May Fourth Movement: A Symposium* (Cambridge, Mass., 1972). A recent, very stimulating contribution is *The Crisis of Chinese Consciousness: Radical Antitraditionalism in the May Fourth Era* by Lin Yü-sheng (Madison, Wis., 1979). For an excellent intellectual biography of a leader of the May Fourth movement, see Jerome B. Grieder, *Hu Shih and the Chinese Renaissance: Liberalism in the Chinese Revolution, 1917–1937* (Cambridge, Mass., 1970). An outstanding recent addition to the literature is Guy S. Alitto, *The Last Confucian: Liang Shu-ming and the Chinese Dilemma of Modernity* (Berkeley and Los Angeles, 1979). Also recommended are Charlotte Furth, *Ting Wen-chiang: Science and China's New Culture* (Cambridge, Mass., 1970); Laurence A. Schneider, *Ku Chieh-kang and China's New History: Nationalism and the Quest for Alternative Traditions* (Berkeley, 1971); and especially Charlotte Furth, ed., *The Limits of Change: Essays on Conservative Alternatives in Republican China* (Cambridge, Mass., 1976).

For a sensitive and perceptive account of the period's literature, see Leo Ou-fan Lee, *The Romantic Generation of Modern Chinese Writers* (Cambridge, Mass., 1973). Also see Merle Goodman, *Modern Chinese Literature in the May Fourth Era* (Cambridge, Mass., 1977). Among the novelists available in English translation are Lu Hsün, Lao Shaw, Mao Tun, and Pa Chin. On individual literary figures, see David T. Roy, *Kuo Mo-jo: The Early Years* (Cambridge, Mass., 1971), and Olga Lang, *Pa Chin and His Writings: Chinese Youth Between Two Revolutions* (Cambridge, Mass., 1967). For poetry, see Hsu Kai-yu, trans. and ed., *Twentieth Century Chinese Poetry.* For further reading consult *A Bibliography of Studies and Translations of Modern Chinese Literature (1918–1942)* by Donald A. Gibbs and Yun-cheng Li, with the assistance of Christopher C. Rand (Cambridge, Mass., 1975). Michael Sullivan, *Chinese Art in the Twentieth Century* (Berkeley, 1959) is still the best book on its subject.

The basic book on the period of KMT rule is Lloyd E. Eastman, *The Abortive Revolution: China under Nationalist Rule, 1927–1937* (Cambridge, Mass., 1974). Two other good books are James C. Thomson, *While China Faced West: American Reformers in Nationalist China, 1927–1937* (Cambridge, Mass., 1969), and John Israel, *Student Nationalism in China, 1927–1937* (Stanford, 1966). Also see Chiang Kai-shek, *China's Destiny and China's Economic Theory*, with notes and commentary by Philip Jaffe (New York, 1947). Chiang is also the author of *Soviet Russia in China: A Summing up at Seventy* (New York, 1957).

A brilliant book on the beginnings of Chinese Communism is Maurice Meisner, *Li Ta-chao and the Origins of Chinese Communism.* A long, detailed analysis of the CCP is James P. Harrison, *The Long March to Power: A History of the Chinese Communist Party 1921–72.* On the march itself, see Dick Wilson, *The Long March, 1935: The Epic of Chinese Communist Survival.* Recommended on Mao are Stuart Schram, *Mao Tse-tung;* Jerome Ch'en, *Mao and the Chinese Revolution;* and Stephen Uhally, *Mao Tse-tung, a Critical Biography.* A valuable firsthand account of the CCP in the thirties is Edgar Snow, *Red Star Over China.* On the united front, see Lyman P. Van Slyke, *Enemies and Friends: The United Front in Chinese Communist History* (Stanford, 1967).

F. F. Liu, *A Military History of Modern China, 1924–1949* (Princeton, 1956) is the best book on its subject. On Wang Ching-wei and his puppet regime, see John Hunter Boyle, *China and Japan at War 1937–1945: The Politics of Collaboration* (Stanford, 1972). For an absorbing and sensitive, sympathetic firsthand account of China in the forties, see Graham Peck, *Two Kinds of Time* (Boston, 1950). A very readable account of the American involvement is provided in Barbara W. Tuchman, *Stilwell and the American Experience in China, 1911–1945.* For a trenchant and highly informative analysis of the American role, see Michael Schaller, *The United States Crusade in China, 1938–45* (New York, 1979). For analyses of the CCP triumph of 1949, see "Part III" below.

A useful survey of the period's economic history is Albert Feuerwerker, *The Chinese Economy, 1912–1949* (Michigan Papers in Chinese Studies, No. 1, 1968). The literature on the nature of China's agrarian economy and on the economic impact of imperialism is discussed in the Wakeman article mentioned above. For the industrial sector, see John K. Chang, *Industrial Development in Pre-Communist China* (Chicago, 1969), and Jean Chesneaux, *The Chinese Labor Movement, 1919–1927* (Stanford, 1968). For anthropological perspectives, see Maurice Freedman, ed., *Family and Kinship in Chinese Society* (Stanford, 1972). Another major collection is Mark Elvin and G. William Skinner, eds., *The Chinese City Between Two Worlds* (Stanford, 1974). A good book on a fascinating topic is Ralph Croizier, *Traditional Medicine in Modern China: Science, Nationalism, and Tensions of Cultural Change* (Cambridge, Mass., 1968).

### Japan

Modernization is one of the broad themes that has stimulated scholarship on nineteenth- and twentieth-century Japanese history. This was the general theme of a series of conferences that resulted in the following collections of essays: Marius B. Jansen, ed., *Changing Japanese Attitudes Toward Modernization;* William W. Lockwood, ed., *The State and Economic Enterprise in Japan;* Ronald P. Dore, ed., *Aspects of Social Change in Modern Japan;* Robert E. Ward, ed., *Political Development in Modern Japan;* Donald H. Shively, ed., *Tradition and Modernization in Japanese Culture;* and James W. Morley, ed., *Dilemmas of Growth in Prewar Japan.* To these may be added Albert M. Craig and Donald H. Shively, eds., *Personality in Japanese History,* which also concentrates on the last two centuries. Together, these volumes provide a good review of current American scholarship and thinking about many of the key issues and developments in modern Japanese history.

Modern Japanese history begins with the Meiji Restoration, and this event, or series of events, will continue to excite scholarly curiosity and debate. A major work, built on sound scholarship and balanced judgment, written by a senior British historian, is W. G. Beasley, *The Meiji Restoration* (Stanford, 1973). Among studies that illuminate the last years of the old order is the important recent book by Conrad Totman, *The Collapse of the Tokugawa Bakufu, 1862–1868* (Honolulu, 1980). For a perceptive study of a key domain, see Albert M. Craig, *Chōshū in the Meiji Restoration* (Cambridge, Mass., 1961). Another fine study is Marius B. Jansen, *Sakamoto Ryoma and the Meiji Restoration.* For an analysis of the Restoration in terms of the history of consciousness, see H. D. Harootunian, *Toward Restoration: The Growth of Political Consciousness in Tokugawa Japan* (Berkeley, 1970), a brilliant but demanding book. A useful compilation is W. G. Beasley, trans., *Select Documents on Japanese Foreign Policy, 1853–1868* (Oxford and New York, 1955). An influential older view of the Restoration is E. H. Norman, *Japan's Emergence as a Modern State* (New York, 1940), which is included in a recent reissue of a collection of Norman's writings published under the title *Origins of the Modern Japanese State.* Norman should be read in conjunction with the critical articles of John Whitney Hall and George Akita in *Journal of Japanese Studies 3* (Summer 1977).

The most influential analysis of modern Japanese economic history is William W. Lockwood, *The Economic Development of Japan: Growth and Structural Change* (Princeton, 1954). For the economic policies and accomplishments of the crucial early years, see Thomas C. Smith, *Political Change and Industrial Development in Japan: Government Enterprise, 1868–1880.* The long-range importance of the industrial effort must not obscure the significance of agriculture, which made it possible. For background, see Smith's *Agrarian Origins,* cited in "Part I" above. For Meiji, see James I. Nakamura, *Agricultural Production and Economic Development of Japan, 1873–1922* (Princeton, 1966). For interesting discussions of the men who built Japan's modern enterprises, and of the values and ideas that went into them, see Johannes Hirschmeier, S.V.D., *The Origins of Entrepreneurship in Meiji Japan* (Cambridge, Mass., 1964), and *The Development of Japanese Business, 1600–1973* (Cambridge, Mass., 1975) by the same author, in collaboration with Tsunehiko Yui. For a more systematic analysis of the ideas that justified and inspired the effort, see Byron K. Marshall, *Capitalism and Nationalism in Prewar Japan: The Ideology of the Business Elite, 1868–1941* (Stanford, 1967).

For Meiji political history, see George Akita, *Foundations of Constitutional Government in Modern Japan, 1868–1900* (Cambridge, Mass., 1967). Also useful for the early years are Nobutaka Ike, *The Beginnings of Political Democracy in Japan* (Baltimore, 1950), and Joseph Pittau, *Political Thought in Early Meiji Japan, 1868–1889* (Cambridge, Mass., 1967). A study of a major Meiji statesman is provided in Roger F. Hackett, *Yamagata Aritomo in the Rise of Modern Japan, 1838–1922* (Cambridge, Mass., 1971). For Japanese and Western historians' evaluations of Meiji statesmen, see the survey conducted by Richard T. Chang, *Historians and Meiji Statesmen* (University of Florida Social Science Monograph, No. 41). An important institutional development is examined in Robert M. Spaulding, Jr., *Imperial Japan's Higher Civil Service Examinations* (Princeton, 1967). The schooling of the men who succeeded into positions of leadership in the world of business and letters as well as government is described and analyzed in *Schooldays in Imperial Japan: A Study in the Culture of a Student Elite* by Donald T. Roden (Berkeley, 1981).

A good way to begin studying Meiji intellectual history is by examining the life and ideas of Fukuzawa Yukichi. His *An Encouragement of Learning,* translated by David A. Dilworth and Umeyo Hirano (Tokyo, 1969), is a collection of essays written in the 1870s. Also well worth reading is his *Autobiography,* translated by Eiichi Kiyooka (New York, 1966). Important secondary studies are Carmen Blacker, *The Japanese Enlightenment: A Study of the Writings of Fukuzawa Yukichi* (Cambridge and New York, 1964), and an article by Albert Craig in the previously noted collection, *Political Development in Modern Japan,* edited by Robert E. Ward. Also see William R. Braisted, trans. and ed., *Meiroku Zasshi: Journal of the Japanese Enlightenment* (Cambridge, Mass., 1975). Two other valuable books on intellectual history are Kenneth B. Pyle, *The New Generation in Meiji Japan: Problems of Cultural Identity, 1885–1895* (Stanford, 1969), and Irwin Scheiner, *Christian Converts and Social Protest in Meiji Japan* (Berkeley, 1970).

For a variety of interpretations of Japanese expansionism, see Marlene Mayo, ed., *The Emergence of Imperial Japan: Self-Defense or Calculated Aggression?* (Problems in Asian Civilizations series). A good survey of this topic is James W. Morley, ed., *Japan's Foreign Policy, 1868–1941: A Research Guide* (New York, 1974). A detailed study is Francis Hilary Conroy, *The Japanese Seizure of Korea, 1868–1910* (Philadelphia, 1960). Indispensable for an understanding of Korea itself, and a fine starting point for anyone interested in modern Korean history, is the excellent book by James B. Palais, *Politics and Policy in Traditional Korea, 1864–1876* (Cambridge, Mass., 1975).

On the Russo-Japanese War, see Shumpei Okamoto, *The Japanese Oligarchy and the Russo-Japanese War* (New York, 1971), and John A. White, *The Diplomacy of the Russo-Japanese War* (Princeton, 1964). Also see Richard Neu, *The Uncertain Friendship: Theodore Roosevelt and Japan, 1906–1909* (Cambridge, Mass., 1967). I. H. Nish has written two books on Anglo-Japanese relations: *The Anglo-Japanese Alliance: The Diplomacy of Two Island Empires 1894–1907* (London, 1966) and *Alliance in Decline: A Study in Anglo-Japanese Relations 1908–23* (London and New York, 1972).

Late Meiji politics is analyzed by Tetsuo Najita in *Hara Kei in the Politics of Compromise, 1905–1915* (Cambridge, Mass., 1967). The best study on the political system as it evolved during the next decade is Peter Duus, *Party Rivalry and Political Change in Taishō Japan* (Cambridge, Mass., 1968). A valuable and stimulating collection of essays is Bernard S. Silberman and H. D. Harootunian, eds., *Japan in Crisis: Essays on Taishō Democracy* (Princeton, 1974). A book rich in detail is George O. Totten III, *The Social Democratic Movement in Prewar Japan* (New Haven, 1966). An indispensable book for the student of Marxism in East Asia is the fascinating study by Gail Lee Bernstein, *Japanese Marxist: A Portrait of Kawakami Hajime 1879–1946* (Cambridge, Mass., 1976). Two good books on foreign policy are James W. Morley, *The Japanese Thrust into Siberia, 1918* (New York, 1957), and Akira Iriye, *After Imperialism: The Search for a New Order in East Asia.*

Maruyama Masao, whose book on Tokugawa intellectual history was noted in "Part I" above, is also the author of a number of perceptive essays on Japanese ultranationalism published as *Thought and Behavior in Japanese Politics*, edited by Ivan Morris. Morris has also compiled and edited *Japan 1931–1945: Militarism, Fascism, Japanism?* (Problems in Asian Civilization series), which can well be used in conjunction with George O. Totten, ed., *Democracy in Prewar Japan: Groundwork or Facade?* in the same series. For a distinguished recent political analysis of the thirties, see Gordon Mark Berger, *Parties Out of Power in Japan: 1931–1941* (Princeton, 1977). A major stream of opposition to urbanization and capitalism is traced and analyzed in Thomas R. Havens, *Farm and Nation in Modern Japan: Agrarian Nationalism, 1870–1940* (Princeton, 1974). On the official ideology prevailing in the thirties, see R. K. Hall, ed., *Kokutai no Hongi. Cardinal Principles of the National Entity of Japan* (Cambridge, Mass., 1949). *Dilemmas of Growth*, edited by Morley and previously noted, also deals primarily with the thirties. A key incident is studied in Ben-Ami Shillony, *Revolt in Japan: The Young Officers and the February 26, 1936 Incident* (Princeton, 1973).

Of the quite extensive literature on Japanese expansionism and the origins of the Second World War, recommended as especially stimulating and scholarly are Robert Butow, *Tojo and the Coming of the War* (Princeton, 1961), and James B. Crowley, *Japan's Quest for Autonomy: National Security and Foreign Policy, 1930–38* (Princeton, 1966). Also recommended are the following: Sadako Ogata, *Defiance in Manchuria: The Making of Japanese Foreign Policy, 1931–32* (Berkeley, 1964); James W. Morley, ed., *Deterrent Diplomacy, Japan, Germany, and the U.S.S.R., 1935–1940* (New York, 1976); Dorothy Borg, *The United States and the Far Eastern Crisis of 1933–1938* (Cambridge, Mass., 1964); and Nobutake Ike, ed., *Japan's Decision for War: Records of the 1941 Pol-*

*icy Conferences* (Stanford, 1967). On the Japanese military, see Ernst L. Presseisen, *Before Aggression: Europeans Prepare the Japanese Army* (Tucson, 1965); Suburo Hayashi in collaboration with Alvin D. Coox, *Kōgun: The Japanese Army in the Pacific War* (Quantico, Va., 1959); and Paul S. Dull, *A Battle History of the Japanese Navy* (Annapolis, 1978). The effects of the war on the Japanese people and society are examined in *Valley of Darkness: The Japanese People and World War Two* by Thomas R. H. Havens (New York, 1978).

The Pacific War began with Pearl Harbor and ended with the atomic bomb. Both events have been written about at length and remain foci of scholarly controversies. On Pearl Harbor, see Dorothy Borg and Shumpei Okamoto, eds., *Pearl Harbor as History* (New York, 1973). For a writer, particularly an American, to deal with Hiroshima demands unusual literary sensitivity: the classic account remains *Hiroshima* by John Hersey. Also recommended is Robert Jay Lifton, *Death in Life: Survivors of Hiroshima*.

There is no general, comprehensive history of modern Japanese literature available in English, but a number of useful critical studies have been published. *Modern Japanese Fiction and Its Traditions: An Introduction* by J. Thomas Rimer (Princeton, 1978) discusses modern works in the light of persistent elements in the Japanese literary tradition as a whole. Also recommended for sensitive discussions of major novelists and their work are Masao Miyoshi, *Accomplices of Silence: The Modern Japanese Novel*, and Makoto Ueda, *Modern Japanese Writers and the Nature of Literature* (Stanford, 1976). A most enjoyable way to become acquainted with Japan's modern writers is by reading Ivan Morris's excellent collection, *Modern Japanese Stories—An Anthology* (Rutland, Vt., 1962).

For the beginning and early history of the modern Japanese novel, there are two fine books by Marleigh G. Ryan: *Japan's First Modern Novel: Ukigomo of Futabatei Shimei* (New York, 1967) and *The Development of Realism in the Fiction of Tsubouchi Shōyō* (Seattle, 1975). Studies of three novelists noted in the text are now available in the Twayne World Authors Series: *Mori Ogai* by Thomas J. Rimer (1975); *Shiga Naoya* by Francis Mathy (1974); and *Natsume Soseki* by Beongcheon Yu, author also of *Akutagawa, An Introduction* (Detroit, 1972). A study that captures atmosphere as well as insights, and is itself a literary work of art, is Edward Seidenstricker, *Kafu, The Scribbler: The Life and Writings of Nagai Kafu, 1879–1959*.

Secondary studies are no substitute for the works of the authors themselves, many of which, fortunately, are available in excellent translations. The following list is meant only to introduce the reader to this rich literature in the hope that he will then go on to explore it on his own: Mori Ogai, *The Wild Geese*, translated by Kingo Ochiai and Sanford Goldstein; the following by Natsume Sōseki: *Botchan*, translated by Umeji Sasaki, *Kokoro*, translated by Edwin McClellan, *The Wayfarer*, translated by Beongcheon Yu, *Mon*, translated by Francis Mathy; Ryunosuke Akutagawa, *Japanese Short Stories*, translated by Takashi Kojima; Kafū Nagai, *A Strange Tale from East of the River and Other Stories*, translated by Edward Seidenstricker; three novels by Tanizaki Juichirō: *Some Prefer Nettles* and *The Makioka Sisters*, translated by Edward Seidenstricker, and *Diary of a Mad Old Man*, translated by Howard Hibbett. For poetry, see Edith Marcombe Shiffert and Yūki Sawa, *Anthology of Modern Japanese Poetry*.

A useful overview of Japanese philosophy is provided by Gino K. Piovesana, *Recent Japanese Philosophical Thought: 1862–1962, A Survey* (Tokyo, revised ed., 1968); and for a statement by a major modern philosopher, see *Fundamental Problems of Philosophy* (*Nishida Kitarō's* Tetsugaku no kompon mondai), translated by David A. Dilworth (Tokyo, 1970). There is no general survey in English of the period's visual arts, but the following two books are helpful: Michiaki Kawakita, *Modern Currents in Japanese Art* (Heibonsha Survey of Japanese Art, Vol. 24, Tokyo and New York, 1974), and *Arts of Japan*, Vol. 6, *Meiji Western Painting by Minoru Harada* (New York and Tokyo, 1964). For this and other arts, including music, see also *Tradition and Modernization in Japanese Culture*, the book edited by Shively mentioned at the beginning of this subsection.

# PART III   East Asia Since the Second World War

The origins of the Cold War are one of the many issues in recent history on which interpretations have changed, both as new materials have become available and as historical perspectives have changed. It is therefore good to begin by reading a recent work, a collection of essays edited by Yōnosuke Nagai and Akira Iriye, *The Origins of the Cold War in Asia* (New York, 1977). In East Asia, of course, the Cold War did not remain cold. On Vietnam, seen not as a problem for American foreign policy but as a society with its own history and culture, there are two excellent books by Alexander B. Woodside: *Vietnam and the Chinese Model—A Comparative Study of Nguyen and Ch'ing Civil Government in the First Half of the Nineteenth Century* (Cambridge, Mass., 1971) and *Community and Revolution in Modern Vietnam* (Boston, 1976). The latter contains a list of suggested readings with critical comments. There is no book of similar intellectual scope for twentieth-century Korea, but the following are useful for political history: Chong-Sik Lee, *The Politics of Korean Nationalism* (Berkeley, 1963), and Sungjoo Han, *The Failure of Democracy in South Korea* (Berkeley, 1970). For a historical perspective on Taiwan that also has important implications for the mainland see Johanna M. Meskill, *A Chinese Pioneer Family: The Lins of Wu-feng, Taiwan 1929–1895* (Princeton, 1979). For more recent developments the following are recommended: Douglas Mendel, *The Politics of Formosan Nationalism* (Berkeley, 1970), and Walter Galenson, ed., *Economic Growth and Structural Change in Taiwan—The Postwar Experience of the Republic of China* (Ithaca, N.Y., 1979).

There is no general history of postwar Japan, but Edwin O. Reischauer, *The Japanese* (Cambridge, Mass., 1977) provides a good general introduction. On the Occupation, see the collection of papers edited by Grant K. Goodman, *The American Occupation of Japan: A Retrospective View* (Lawrence, Kansas, 1968. Distributed by Paragon Book Gallery, N.Y.); Herbert Passim, *The Legacy of the Occupation—Japan* (New York, 1968); and Kazuo Kawai, *Japan's American Interlude* (Chicago, 1960). An important Occupation accomplishment is examined by Ronald P. Dore in *Land Reform in Japan* (London, 1958).

The Japanese economy has been quite extensively studied. Good books include Hugh Patrick, ed., with the assistance of Larry Meisner, *Japanese Industrialization and Its Social Consequences*; M. Y. Yoshino, *Japan's Multinational Enterprises*; and Hugh Patrick and Henry Rosovsky, eds., *Asia's New Giant: How the Japanese Economy Works* (Washington, 1976), consisting of papers described by a reviewer as ranging in style "from semi-Galbraithian sparkle to semi-dissertation ponderosity" (see *Journal of Japanese Studies* 3 [Winter 1977]: 166). For a major study of rural life see *Village Japan* by Richard K. Beardsley, John W. Hall, and Robert E. Ward, and for a vivid account of the transformation of a Japanese village as a result of postwar prosperity see Roland P. Dore, *Shinohata: Portrait of a Japanese Village*. Dore is a social scientist who is also a gifted writer. His *City Life in Japan* is a classic. Dore is also the author of *British Factory, Japanese Factory: The Origins of National Diversity in Employment Relations* (Berkeley, 1973). Another very informative and revealing book is Robert E. Cole, *Japanese Blue Collar: Changing Traditions*.

Recommended for its analysis of Japanese politics is Nathanial Thayer, *How the Conservatives Rule Japan* (Princeton, 1969). Another aspect of the political system is discussed by Kurt Steiner, *Local Government in Japan* (Stanford, 1965). Another useful book is Nobutake Ike, *Japanese Politics: Patron-Client Democracy* (New York, 1972). See also Donald C. Hellman, *Japanese Domestic Politics and Foreign Policy: The Peace Agreement with the Soviet Union* (Berkeley, 1969), and Martin E. Weinstein, *Japan's Postwar Defense Policy, 1947–1968* (New York, 1971). There is a rich social science literature on contemporary Japanese culture and social trends. The reader will enjoy David W. Plath, ed., *Adult Episodes in Japan* (Leiden, 1975). Plath's most recent book, *Long*

*Engagements: Maturity in Modern Japan* (Stanford, 1980), offers a "consocial view of human maturity" applicable not only to the Japanese but pertinent also for the way we look at ourselves. A collection of essays by social scientists interested in the future as well as in the present and recent past is Lewis Austin, ed., *Japan: The Paradox of Progress* (New Haven, 1977). A good source for current developments in Japan is the journal *The Japan Interpreter.*

Donald Richie, *Japanese Cinema—Film Style and National Character* is a well-informed and thoughtful historical survey of the Japanese film. A good way to begin reading in contemporary Japanese literature is by using Howard Hibbett, ed., *Contemporary Japanese Literature—An Anthology of Fiction, Film, and Other Writings Since 1945,* which was published in 1977. Major postwar novelists are analyzed in the works by Miyoshi and Ueda cited above. Many novels have been translated, including some by writers not discussed in this text. The following listing of translated works by writers who are treated in the text is not complete but is representative of their best work. For Kawabata, read the following, all translated by Edward G. Seidenstricker: *Snow Country, Thousand Cranes, Japan the Beautiful and Myself,* and *The Sound of the Mountain.* For Mishima: *The Sailor Who Fell from Grace with the Sea,* translated by John Nathan, *After the Banquet,* translated by Donald Keene, and *The Temple of the Golden Pavilion,* translated by Ivan Morris. E. Dale Saunders has translated Abe Kōbō: *The Ruined Map, The Woman in the Dunes, The Box Man.* See also Abe's play "Friends," translated by Donald Keene and included in Hibbett's anthology. Two novels by Oe Kenzaburō are available in English: *A Personal Matter,* translated by John Nathan, and *The Silent Cry,* translated by John Bester (Tokyo and New York, 1974).

The literature on contemporary China is vast and very uneven. It is also growing rapidly, but few scholars have attempted a general history of the People's Republic. Fortunately, there is one distinguished book that accomplishes this: *Mao's China: A History of the People's Republic* by Maurice Meisner. The leading scholarly journal on contemporary China is *China Quarterly.* Useful reference works include G. William Skinner, ed., *Modern Chinese Society: An Analytical Bibliography, Publications in Western Languages, 1644–1972, Vol. 1.* (Stanford, 1973)—volumes 2 and 3 deal with Chinese and Japanese respectively and *Biographical Dictionary of Chinese Communism, 2* vols. (Cambridge, Mass., 1971) by Donald W. Klein and Anne B. Clark.

For analyzing the CCP triumph, the following are helpful: Lucien Bianco, *Origins of the Chinese Revolution, 1915–1949,* translated by Muriel Bell; Chalmers A. Johnson, *Peasant Nationalism and Communist Power: The Emergence of Revolutionary China, 1937–45;* Donald Gillin's critique of Johnson in *Journal of Asian Studies* 23 (February 1964): 269—89; Suzanne Pepper, *Civil War in China, 1945–1949* (Berkeley, 1978); and Pinchon P. V. Loh, *The Kuomintang Debacle of 1949: Conquest or Collapse?* (Problems in Asian Civilization series), which presents an array of views mirroring American reactions to events in China.

For an account of the revolution based on personal experience, see William Hinton, *Fanshen: A Documentary of Revolution in a Chinese Village.* Studies of cities include Ezra Vogel, *Canton Under Communism: Programs and Politics in a Provincial Capital; The City in Communist China,* edited by John Wilson Lewis (Stanford, 1971); and Kenneth G. Lieberthal, *Revolution and Tradition in Tiensin, 1949–52* (Stanford, 1980). The most ambitious and impressive attempt yet made to analyze the dynamics of the new system is Franz Schurmann, *Ideology and Organization in Communist China.* Much that has been written on the Chinese economy is quite technical and detailed. A useful overview is provided by Nai-ruen Chen and Walter Galenson, *The Chinese Economy Under Communism* (Chicago, 1969). Also see Thomas Rawski, *China's Transition to Industrialism: Producer Goods and Economic Development in the Twentieth Century* (Ann Arbor, 1980).

The leading personality of contemporary China was, of course, Mao Tse-tung. In addition to the two biographies already mentioned, the following are especially useful:

Stuart R. Schram, *The Political Thought of Mao Tse-tung,* which consists of a long introduction and selections from Mao; Dick Wilson, ed., *Mao Tse-tung in the Scales of History* (1977); and, for the philosophically minded, the difficult but rewarding *History and Will: Philosophical Perspectives of Mao Tse-tung's Thought* by Frederic Wakeman, Jr.

The origins of the Sino-Soviet split are examined in Donald S. Zagoria, *The Sino-Soviet Conflict, 1956–1961* (Princeton, 1962). On China's foreign relations, also see Jerome Cohen, ed., *The Dynamics of China's Foreign Relations* (Cambridge, Mass., 1970). For a collection of essays containing the reflections of a leading senior American student of China, see John K. Fairbank, *China Perceived: Images and Policies in Chinese-American Relations* (New York, 1974). On Sino-American relations see Michel Oksenberg and Robert B. Oxman, eds., *Dragon and Eagle: United States-China Relations, Past and Future* (New York, 1978); also *China-Watch: Sino-American Reconciliation* by Robert G. Sutter. On the Chinese army, see John Gittings, *The Role of the Chinese Army* (London and New York, 1967) and Harvey W. Nelsen, *The Chinese Military System: An Organizational Study of the Chinese People's Liberation Army* (Boulder, Colo., 1977).

*Moving a Mountain: Cultural Change in China,* edited by Goodwin C. Chu and Francis L. K. Hsu (Honolulu, 1979), is a collection of papers with a social-science approach to their subject. The Cultural Revolution continues to stimulate much interest. A valuable book that combines personal experience with analysis is David and Nancy Dall Milton, *The Wind Will Not Subside: Years in Revolutionary China, 1964–1969* (Berkeley, 1976). Also see Hong Yung Lee, *The Politics of the Chinese Cultural Revolution: A Case Study* (Berkeley, 1978). The most extensive and up-to-date literary anthology is *Literature of the People's Republic of China,* edited by Kai-yu Hsu and Ting Wang (Bloomington, 1980). For artistic developments see Arnold Chang, *Painting in the People's Republic of China: The Politics of Style* (Boulder, Colo., 1980). *The Concept of Man in Contemporary China* by Donald Munro is an analysis of Chinese ideas concerning the nature of man, with illuminating discussions on how these ideas differ from those held in the Soviet Union and the West.

Travelers' accounts generally reveal at least as much about the traveler as they do about China, and it would be an interesting exercise to systematically compare the reports of recent visitors with those of foreigners who visited China in earlier times. Among the most engaging of the contemporary books are those by professional writers (e.g., Simone de Beauvoir, Alberto Moravia), those by journalists with previous China experience (Edgar Snow, Seymour Topping), and those by specialists in Chinese studies (Ross Terrill, Orville Schell). Also noteworthy are books by journalists (e.g., David Bonavia, John Fraser) and embassy officials (Robert Garside) who have worked in Beijing.

It is a promising sign of the coming of age of Chinese and Japanese studies in the United States that they are losing their aura of exoticism, and that scholars are beginning to seriously examine East Asian experiences in various fields in order to illuminate our own Western problems. Thus in *China's Developmental Experience* (New York, 1973), edited by Michel Oksenberg, a number of scholars examine the contemporary Chinese experience for possible applicability elsewhere—including the United States. Worthy books explicitly comparative in nature include Victor H. Li, *Law Without Lawyers: A Comparative View of Law in China and the United States* and, on the Japanese side, David H. Bayley, *Forces of Order, Police Behavior in Japan and the United States,* and Robert A. Cole, *Work, Mobility and Participation: A Comparative Study of American and Japanese Industry* (Berkeley, 1979).

# Copyrights and Acknowledgments

For permission to use copyrighted material reprinted in this book, the author is grateful to the following publishers and copyright holders:

COLUMBIA UNIVERSITY PRESS   For five lines of poetry from *Sources of Japanese Tradition*, compiled by Ryusaku Tsunoda, Wm. Theodore de Bary, and Donald Keene. Reprinted by permission of Columbia University Press.

DOUBLEDAY & COMPANY, INC.   For a poem by Kobayashi Issa from *An Introduction to Haiku* by Harold G. Henderson. Copyright © 1958 by Harold G. Henderson. Reprinted by permission of Doubleday & Company, Inc.

CALVIN L. FRENCH   For a poem by Bashō from *The Poet-Painters: Buson and His Followers* by Calvin French, exhibition catalog published by the University of Michigan Museum of Art, 1974. Reprinted by permission of Calvin L. French.

GROVE PRESS, INC.   For "In Reply to a Poem from Tz'u-shan, Thanking Me for the Gift of Sung and Yüan Lyrics I Had Had Printed" by Wang P'eng-yü, from *Anthology of Chinese Literature*, vol. II, edited by Cyril Birch. Reprinted by permission of Grove Press, Inc. Copyright © 1972 by Grove Press, Inc.

HARVARD UNIVERSITY PRESS   For the Hanyu Pinyin/Wade-Giles Conversion Table from Endymion Wilkinson, *The History of Imperial China: A Research Guide* (Harvard East Asian Monographs 49). Copyright 1973 by the President and Fellows of Harvard College. Reprinted by permission of Harvard University Press.

OXFORD UNIVERSITY PRESS   For a poem by Mao Tse-tung translated from the Chinese by Michael Bullock and Jerome Ch'en, from *Mao and the Chinese Revolution* by Jerome Ch'en, © Oxford University Press 1965. Reprinted by permission of Oxford University Press.

RANDOM HOUSE, INC.   For a poem by Yüan K'o-chia from *The Chinese Literary Scene*, edited by Kai-yu Hsu. Copyright © 1975 by Kai-yu Hsu. Reprinted by permission of Random House, Inc.

STANFORD UNIVERSITY PRESS   For a figure from *Japan: A Short Cultural History* by G. B. Sansom. Reprinted with the permission of the publishers, Stanford University Press. © 1941, 1943, 1952 by G. B. Sansom.

CHARLES E. TUTTLE CO., INC.   For two lines of poetry from *The Great Cultural Revolution in China*, compiled and edited by the Asia Research Center; and for "Bamboos" by Hagiwara Sakutarō, from *Face at the Bottom of the World and Other Poems*, translated by Graeme Wilson. Both reprinted by permission of Charles E. Tuttle Co., Inc.

# Illustration Credits

# *Index*

# *Index*

Chinese entries are generally listed in Wade-Giles romanization, with *pinyin* indicated in brackets unless the two are identical. For exceptions and conversion tables, see "Note on Names and Romanization," pp. ix–xiii. Page numbers in *italics* refer to illustrations.